TAKING SIDES

Clashing Views in

State and Local
Government Issues

FIRST EDITION

TAKING SIDES

Clashing Views in

State and Local Government Issues

FIRST EDITION

Selected, Edited, and with Introductions by

John Wood
Rose State College

McGraw Hill

Connect
Learn
Succeed™

The McGraw-Hill Companies

Mc Graw Hill

Connect
Learn
Succeed™

TAKING SIDES: CLASHING VIEWS IN STATE AND LOCAL GOVERNMENT

Published by McGraw-Hill, a business unit of The McGraw-Hill Companies, Inc., 1221 Avenue of the Americas, New York, NY 10020. Copyright © 2011 by The McGraw-Hill Companies, Inc. All rights reserved. No part of this publication may be reproduced or distributed in any form or by any means, or stored in a database or retrieval system, without the prior written consent of The McGraw-Hill Companies, Inc., including, but not limited to, in any network or other electronic storage or transmission, or broadcast for distance learning.

Some ancillaries, including electronic and print components, may not be available to customers outside the United States.

Taking Sides® is a registered trademark of the McGraw-Hill Companies, Inc.
Taking Sides is published by the **Contemporary Learning Series** group within the McGraw-Hill Higher Education division.

1 2 3 4 5 6 7 8 9 0 DOC/DOC 1 0 9 8 7 6 5 4 3 2 1 0

MHID: 0-07-805005-7
ISBN: 978-0-07-805005-3
ISSN: 2152-3851

Managing Editor: *Larry Loeppke*
Director, Specialized Production: *Faye Schilling*
Senior Developmental Editor: *Jade Benedict*
Editorial Coordinator: *Mary Foust*
Production Service Assistant: *Rita Hingtgen*
Permissions Coordinator: *Shirley Lanners*
Editorial Assistant: *Cindy Hedley*
Senior Marketing Manager: *Julie Keck*
Senior Marketing Communications Specialist: *Mary Klein*
Marketing Coordinator: *Alice Link*
Project Manager: *Erin Melloy*
Design Specialist: *Brenda A. Rolwes*
Cover Graphics: *Rick D. Noel*

Compositor: MPS Limited, A Macmillan Company
Cover Image: © Ilene MacDonald/Alamy

Editors/Academic Advisory Board

Members of the Academic Advisory Board are instrumental in the final selection of articles for each edition of TAKING SIDES. Their review of articles for content, level, and appropriateness provides critical direction to the editors and staff. We think that you will find their careful consideration well reflected in this volume.

TAKING SIDES: Clashing Views in State and Local Government Issues
First Edition

EDITOR

John Wood
Rose State College

ACADEMIC ADVISORY BOARD MEMBERS

Editors/Academic Advisory Board continued

Preface

"In seeking truth you have to get both sides of a story."

—Walter Cronkite[1]

It is the mission of the *Taking Sides* series in general and that of this book more specifically to do two things: (1) provide information about opposing sides of salient issues; and (2) make both sides understandable as legitimate viewpoints, nonetheless clashing.

This first edition of *Taking Sides: Clashing Views in State and Local Government* offers 19 issues spread throughout six units that permeate state and local interest textbooks, journals, and newspapers as well as discussions on the street. These are controversial issues, many of which have been debated from the time our founding fathers fought over the content of the Constitution at the Constitutional Convention behind closed doors in the Pennsylvania State House. It is common knowledge the Convention itself was divided.

> Advocates of differing interpretations of the Constitution's drafting have taken two distinct views, some arguing that the Convention created the Constitution out of a commitment to ideas and political principles, others arguing that the participants designed the Constitution to aid and protect their social, political, and economic interests.[2]

The early Constitutional Conventional scene is partly captured in this book by the inclusion of articles from the Federalist and Anti-Federalist debates after the Constitution itself was crafted. Subsequent to the Constitution's finalization, the newly branded Federalists pushed to get their point of view out to the people through what were called the *Federalist Papers*.[3] The Anti-Federalists countered with what were later called the *Anti-Federalist Papers*.[4] Debate over representation and voice concerning the issue of states' power versus a more centralized government is covered in Issue 3 of this book. The Federalists' answer to a more centralized approach in creating both "checks and balances" and "separation of powers" is discussed in Issue 4, "Are Checks and Balances Enough to Protect Your Rights?"

Debate over the question of a predominate power structure is also examined in a more modern and hotly-contested argument over the issue of the Fifth Amendment's eminent domain, or the taking of property for private use from the formerly exclusive "private use" principle.

This book presents five units broken down as "Governorship," "Intergovernmental Relations," "Courts, Police, and Corrections," "State Legislatures," "Suburbs, Cities, and Schools," and "State and Local Policy Making."

Americans have always been skeptical of centralized power, even if paradoxically Americans like its efficiency and control. In Issue 1, we examine the Pentagon's ability to seize the governor's power over the National Guard. This issue raises the question: Will this authority give the president inordinate power and undermine our state governors? On the other hand, Issue 2 asks, Do we want governors subverting state legislators' power by cutting line items that these legislators wrestled over on behalf of their constituents? Or, should governors not have the ability to carve out unwanted pork from the budget and save taxpayers money?

In Unit 3, "Courts, Police, and Corrections," this book examines the following topics:

- Do principals have the right to strip search students? (Issue 7)
- Are mandatory minimums for drug sentencing effective? (Issue 8)
- Is it appropriate to squelch a student's freedom of speech if he or she is promoting drug use? (Issue 9)

In Unit 4, "State Legislatures," state legislative term limits (Issue 10) are debated along with whether state legislators should create their own legislative district boundaries (Issue 11). Has an independent redistricting commission composed of both parties done any better?

In Unit 5, "Suburbs, Cities and Schools," it is asked

- Is the property tax (Issue 12) legitimate at the state or local level?
- Is sprawl really a problem or overhyped? (Issue 13)
- Do we even need school boards or should the mayor just take over? (Issue 14)
- Can religious groups use public schools when the campus is closed? (Issue 15)

Finally, in the "State and Local Policy Making" unit, the book explores these debates:

- Should same-sex couples receive Constitutional protection? (Issue 16)
- Are charter schools worthwhile? (Issue 17)
- Are "concealed and carry" permits in the classroom making it safer? (Issue 18)
- Will national standards make schools more effective? (Issue 19)

In this unit, policymaking is put into action or inaction through state and public officials.

Presenting court cases makes sense in a book that examines both state and local issues; they generate and perpetuate the inevitable conflict that comes with such a vastly diverse people who come together across many locales and, in doing so, clash over values and factual misunderstandings and interests. This book covers six issues that entail court cases. The U.S. Constitution in Article 3, Section 2, states, "The judicial Power shall extend . . . to Controversies to which the United States shall be a Party." This means that a book examining the great debates in state and local government would naturally cover court cases.

Regardless of which side you find yourself on in these debates, both sides have come together to inform and create a basis for thinking beyond intractable conflict toward a consensus of mutual benefit.

A word to the instructor *An Instructor's Resource Guide with Test Questions* (multiple-choice and essay) is available through the publisher for the instructor using *Taking Sides* in the classroom. A general guidebook, *Using Taking Sides in the Classroom,* which discusses methods and techniques for integrating the pro/con approach into any classroom setting, is also available. An online version of *Using Taking Sides in the Classroom* and a correspondence service for *Taking Sides* adopters can be found at http://www.mhcls.com/usingts. *Taking Sides: Clashing Views in State and Local Government* is only one title in the *Taking Sides* series. If you are interested in seeing the table of contents for any of the other titles, please visit the *Taking Sides* Web site at http://www.mhcls.com/takingsides.

Acknowledgments This edition benefited from the research conducted by Judge Melissa Lin Klemens, who found articles on the judicial system that I included in what was eventually Issue 9, "Should State and Local Officials Reform How Justices Are Elected to the Bench?" I also want to thank the issue's Editorial Board, who, through Larry Leoppke's helpful survey of more than a hundred professors around the country, offered me feedback on issue selection for the first edition of *Taking Sides: Clashing Views in State and Local Government.* I also want to thank McGraw Hill's editors Mark Georgiev and Beth Mejia, who believed in me enough to allow me to move forward with this project after pitching the idea in the fall of 2008. Also, Jade Benedict, my editor, who always has a laid-back and approachable demeanor, all the while helping my researching and writing process.

Most of all, I want to thank my wife, Bonnie, who puts up with my late nights typing away and humors me when I often say that this is my last project . . . for a while.

Notes

1. "Both Sides of the Story," CBSNews.com (October 3, 2007). Interview of Jimmy Hoffa by Walter Cronkite. Accessed December 13, 2009, http://www.cbsnews.com/video/watch/?id=3256916n

2. Calvin Jillson, *Constitution Making: Conflict and Consensus in the Federal Convention of 1787* (New York: Agathon Press, 1988), p. xi.

3. Joseph Losco and Ralph Baker, *Am Gov* (New York: McGraw-Hill, 2009).

4. Bruce Miroff, Raymond Seidelman, and Todd Swanstorm, *The Democratic Debate: An Introduction to American Politics,* 3rd ed. (New York: Houghton Mifflin Company, 2002).

Contents In Brief

Contents

Sydney (Robert Yates) is critical of a new Constitution because he predicted an escalation of power in the federal government and an equal de-escalation of power by states. Publius (James Madison), the "Father of the Constitution," defends his new document by arguing that its new powers will be necessary, "few and defined."

Publius (James Madison) pushes for both a separation of powers and checks and balances to safeguard liberty and our rights. Aristocrotis (William Petrikin) writes a tongue-in-cheek, yet serious attempt, to counter this new constitution, which is in the Anti-Federalist's view, a serious invasion of individual liberty through a tyrannical and unlimitedly powerful government.

Justice Stevens's majority opinion supports the city of New London in condemning property for private use. Justice O'Conner's dissenting opinion supports the Kelo position in saying that eminent domain should clearly be for public use only.

Admitting that religiously based grounds for the wrongness of killing an innocent person are not convincing to many people, Doerflinger argues on mainly secular grounds having to do with inconsistencies in the arguments of supporters of physician-assisted suicide in several states. He examines the idea of autonomy, and the tendency for something like California's Humane and Dignified Death Act might spread once it becomes initially accepted in a limited way. Watts and Howell first claim that it is very important to distinguish between *assisted suicide* and *voluntary active euthanasia* has led to confusion among several states, such as Washington State, California, and New Hampshire. Basically, the first of these is suicide or killing oneself; the second involves being killed by someone else (e.g., a physician). Watts and Howell argue that most of the opposition to physician-assisted suicide turns out to be really opposition to voluntary active euthanasia; furthermore, they argue that physician-assisted suicide would not have the dire consequence that its opponents predict.

famously anti-tax nation like the U.S., it's surprising how much Americans hate property taxes." He adds that more than seven years after 2000, property taxes have shot up 26 percent per person, a much higher rate than other types of taxes.

Rob Gurwitt explains that communities annex to beat out other communities before they annex the same piece of land, but such behavior has a high cost. Thomas DiLorenzo argues that problems associated with urban sprawl are hysterically out of proportion and that market principles should prevail.

Rob Gurwitt argues that school boards, when working well, can help reform schools. Matt Miller argues that school boards are largely worthless and other reforms such as mayoral control should be pursued instead.

Supreme Court Justice Clarence Thomas affirms the right of religious groups to use school facilities after the school day ends, maintaining that restricting such use is a violation of free speech rights. Supreme Court Justice David Souter, dissenting from the Court's opinion, contends that the use of school facilities by religious groups blurs the line between public classroom instruction and private religious indoctrination and therefore violates the Establishment Clause of the Constitution.

Massachusetts Supreme Judicial Court Chief Justice Margaret Marshall rules that prohibiting same-sex couples from marrying causes hardship to a segment of the population for no rational reason. Massachusetts Supreme Judicial Court Justice Robert Cordy, in dissent, holds that a statute banning same-sex marriage is a valid exercise of the state's police power.

Journalist Joe Williams, a senior fellow with Education Sector, reviews the development of the charter school movement and finds multiple unwarranted bureaucratic impediments to its acceptance. School superintendent Marc F. Bernstein sees increasing racial and social class segregation, church-state issues, and financial harm as outgrowths of the charter school movement.

The NRA says it is a student's right to carry a gun to class to keep him or herself safe. The Brady Center says that guns just facilitate more violence and make a campus less safe.

Chester E. Finn, president; Liam Julian, associate writer and editor; and Michael J. Petrilli, vice president for national programs and policy, all of the Thomas B. Fordham Foundation, state, "National standards and tests may no longer be politically taboo." Lawrence A. Uzzell, an independent researcher and former staff member of the U.S. Department of Education and U.S. House and Senate committees on education, believes that "the key to rescuing our children from the bureaucratized government schools is radical decentralization."

Correlation Guide

The *Taking Sides* series presents current issues in a debate-style format designed to stimulate student interest and develop critical thinking skills. Each issue is thoughtfully framed with an issue summary, an issue introduction, and a postscript. The pro and con essays—selected for their liveliness and substance—represent the arguments of leading scholars and commentators in their fields.

Taking Sides: Clashing Views in State and Local Government is an easy-to-use reader that presents issues on important topics such as eminent domain laws, school boards, "concealed and carry" laws, and urban sprawl. For more information on *Taking Sides* and other *McGraw-Hill Contemporary Learning Series* titles, visit www.mhhe.com/cls.

This convenient guide matches the issues in **Taking Sides: State and Local Government** with the corresponding chapters in one of our best-selling McGraw-Hill political science textbooks by Saffell/Basehart.

Taking Sides: State and Local Government	State and Local Government: Politics and Public Policies, 9/e, by Saffell/Basehart
Issue 1: Should the Pentagon Take over the National Guard During Disasters?	**Chapter 2:** Intergovernmental Relations
Issue 2: Should Governors Have the Line-Item Veto?	**Chapter 6:** Governors, Bureaucrats, and Mayors
Issue 3: Should We Protect States Rights over the Federal Government?	**Chapter 1:** The Setting of State and Local Government
Issue 4: Are "Checks and Balances" Enough to Protect Our Rights?	**Chapter 3:** Political Parties and Interest Groups **Chapter 5:** State and Local Legislatures
Issue 5: Should We Allow Eminent Domain for Private Use?	**Chapter 3:** Political Parties and Interest Groups **Chapter 8:** Suburbs, Metropolitan Areas, and Rural Communities
Issue 6: Should a National Sense of Morality Override States Rights in the Case of Physician-Assisted Suicide?	**Chapter 10:** State and Local Policy Making
Issue 7: Is a Strip Search of Students Permissible under the Fourth Amendment?	**Chapter 7:** Courts, Police, and Corrections
Issue 8: Do Mandatory Sentencing Laws Help the Criminal Justice System?	**Chapter 7:** Courts, Police, and Corrections
Issue 9: Can a School Punish a Student for Speech That Is Reasonably Viewed as Promoting Illegal Drug Use?	**Chapter 10:** State and Local Policy Making
Issue 10: Should State Legislators Have Term Limits?	**Chapter 5:** State and Local Legislatures

(Continued)

Taking Sides: State and Local Government	State and Local Government: Politics and Public Policies, 9/e, by Saffell/Basehart
Issue 11: Should Legislators Have the Responsibility for Redistricting?	**Chapter 5:** State and Local Legislatures
Issue 12: Is Property Tax an Appropriate Revenue Source for State and Local Governments?	**Chapter 9:** Financing State and Local Government
Issue 13: Should Municipal Governments Limit Urban Sprawl?	**Chapter 8:** Suburbs, Metropolitan Areas, and Rural Communities
Issue 14: Are School Boards Necessary?	**Chapter 10:** State and Local Policy Making
Issue 15: Do Religious Groups Have a Right to Use Public School Facilities after Hours?	**Chapter 10:** State and Local Policy Making
Issue 16: Should Same-Sex Couples Receive State Constitutional Protection?	**Chapter 3:** Political Parties and Interest Groups **Chapter 10:** State and Local Policy Making
Issue 17: Do Charter Schools Merit Public Support?	**Chapter 10:** State and Local Policy Making
Issue 18: Should "Concealed and Carry" Guns Be Allowed in the Classroom?	**Chapter 2:** Intergovernmental Relations **Chapter 10:** State and Local Policy Making
Issue 19: Should Local Schools Have National Standards?	**Chapter 10:** State and Local Policy Making

Introduction

Passion Is Inversely Proportional to the Amount of Real Information Available.[1]

—Gregory Benford

Conflict and Compromise

Taking Sides: Clashing Views in State and Local Government focuses on political conflict in both America's states and cities. You may not know, but the word "conflict" in Latin is *conflictus,* meaning "striking together," or "contend."[2] In striking together, people's worldviews often clash, and they habitually move to their respective corners or passionately choose sides. The less people with varying perspectives know about the the other side of a dispute, the more often arguments escalate.

However, the Chinese word for "conflict" consists of two symbols, one for "danger" and the other "opportunity."[3] In the Chinese culture, conflict allows those on opposing sides of a dispute an opportunity to resolve their differences, but danger is also near if the conflict is not resolved. "Danger" can also mean "change"[4] and when reading these debates, you have the opportunity to be changed by them. After reading both sides of an issue in the book, you might find one of the two sides reinforced in your mind. This is because, when conflicts are not just factually controversial, but value-based, it is still important for both sides to understand where the other is coming from. At the very least, they should understand that the opposing viewpoint is legitimate, and then agree to disagree. Values signify a specific set of standards denoting both what an individual thinks is right and what is good.[5] As a result, when individuals have different value-based ideas about what is important and right, they will likely develop very different and often incongruent goals, potentially leading to conflict. However, agreeing to disagree is not always status quo, because understanding the other side and respecting it as legitimate is change in itself.

You might read both sides of any issue in this volume and find that you now agree with the other side, find both sides have great points, or disagree with both sides. Either way, understanding and respecting such conflicts reduces the insipient passion you might have for being right, reducing your potential friction with others who might disagree with you passionately. One side seldom represents the only correct or legitimate viewpoint.

Typically, the political fights we see on the street are fissures between Democrats and Republicans. Pro-lifers, for example, we typically think of as being Republican, and pro-choicers as Democrats, right? However, this country is more fractured and less black-and-white than that would suggest. A 2006

Newsweek poll found as many as 31 percent of Republicans are actually pro-choice and 25 percent of Democrats are right-to-life.[6] This poll result might be partially explained by an ideology test at "Where do you fit?" created by the Pew Charitable Trusts in 2005.[7]

The Pew Charitable Trusts study associated with the survey found major cleavages within each party, which certainly counters the prevalent notion that America intensified its division between two cohesive factions.[8] The survey actually finds nine typologies instead of the usual two. The survey finds three typologies on the Right and three on the Left. Uniquely, this Pew Charitable Trusts survey finds three typologies in the center—Upbeats (11 percent), Disaffecteds (9 percent), and Bystanders (10 percent), whereas the Right is composed of Pro-Government Conservatives (9 percent), Social Conservatives (11 percent), and Enterprisers (9 percent), and the Left is made up of Liberals (17 percent), Conservative Democrats (14 percent), and Disadvantaged Democrats (10 percent).

The nine typologies are explained below,

Center Groups[9]

(1) **Upbeats** have optimistic views of their personal finances, government capabilities, business, and of the nation.
(2) **Disaffecteds** are extremely cynical about government and unfulfilled with their personal finances. This group is also turned off by TV and newspaper news, as well as politics in general.
(3) **Bystanders** largely relegate themselves to the political margins. This is a category of mostly young people and few of them vote. Many are noncitizens.

The Right[10]

(1) **Enterprisers** are extremely patriotic and pro-business, the most likely to oppose social welfare and most apt to support an aggressive military presence.
(2) Although **Social Conservatives** agree with most Enterprisers, they are critical of business, and unlike Enterprisers, supportive of government regulation to protect the environment and the public good. Many are white evangelical Christians.
(3) **Pro-Government Conservatives** also are broadly religious and socially conservative; however, unlike Enterprisers, they fully support a conservative government but also support more government regulation and support to the poor, similar to those on the Left.

The Left[11]

(1) **Liberals** oppose aggressive foreign policy, highly support environmental protection, and firmly push government welfare.
(2) **Conservative Democrats** are very religious, like the Social Conservatives, taking more moderate stances on several foreign policy matters.

3. **Disadvantaged Democrats** are the most cynical about their chances in life and also very mistrustful of both business and government. They, however, support government programs to help those in need.

As you can see, nine different typologies break up the traditional two-party status, at least theoretically. Practically, both the Democrats and Republicans are virtually in control of the government, but each with divisions within themselves. Essentially, in these issue debates it is easy to label either side as the Democrat or Republican position, but this simple explanation falls short of reality.

A recent journal article in *Annual Review of Political Science* reinforces this idea that there is more political diversity than people realize, because the elites polarize political debates much more than the mass public is actually polarized.[12] Therefore, it is important to understand that political viewpoints are really very diverse and neither the Republican Party nor the Democratic Party is homogenous. Whether it is the Republican Party split over immigration during the Bush administration[13] or the Democrats split over health care,[14] the political divisions and gridlock are largely due to internal factions. To illustrate, the immigration issue severely divides both parties. Enterprisers and Liberals agree that immigrants strengthen America; however, the other two groups on each side tend to characterize immigrants as those who threaten America's traditional values and customs.[15] As a result, little has been accomplished constructively in terms of policy dealing with immigration reform of any kind. It is not surprising that in 2005 and 2006 two bills on immigration reform passed in Congress but failed in to become law.[16] In 2005, the U.S. House passed the Border Protection, Anti-Terrorism, and Illegal Immigration Control Act of 2005. Likewise, the Comprehensive Immigration Reform Act of 2006 passed in the U.S. Senate. However, both bills died in conference committee, where differences were too great.

In this book, there are many conflicts that on the surface seem like simple Republican/Democrat divisions. Although it is not easy to determine the ideology of any of these articles' authors, it is possible to tell how their viewpoints either differ or align with the nine aforementioned typologies. For example, In Unit 6, Issue 16, "State and Local Policy Making," regarding same-sex couples' ability to marry on the state level, Social Conservatives prioritize this issue as something they must fight; however, Enterprisers, who are typically Republicans as well, do not seem energized over this specific issue, but instead focus on the "free market."[17] Conservative Democrats also seem to find same-sex marriage a problem for them, but not quite as much as do the Social Conservatives. Liberals are the most likely to defend same-sex marriage.[18] Similarly, in this unit's Issue 18, "Should 'Concealed and Carry' Guns Be Allowed in the Classroom?" the National Rifle Association and the Brady Campaign struggle over the issue of guns. On the one hand, the Brady Campaign was inspired by James "Jim" Brady, Ronald Reagan's former White House press secretary, who was almost killed and was permanently disabled as a consequence of a 1981 assassination attempt on Reagan.[19] From this experience, Brady became a passionate supporter of gun control. Brady, who worked for Republicans all his life, was no liberal. In fact, his first campaign was the failed attempt for social conservative Phyllis Schafly's attempt at the U.S. House.[20] The Brady Campaign in this issue advocates to ban guns on university campuses for many reasons. On the other hand, the National Rifle Association is likely an Enterpriser group because of their push against regulations of any sort. Therefore, this issue is as likely to be a fight between Social Conservatives and Enterprisers as it is to be between Democrats and Republicans.

In another example, in Unit 5, "Suburbs, Cities, and Schools," Issue 13, "Should Municipal Governments Limit Urban Sprawl?" both sides are not the simple pitting of Republican and Democratic views against one another. On the "Yes" side, Journalist Rob Gurwitt writes "Not-So-Smart Growth," representing the more liberal, environmentally conscious viewpoint, whereas the "No" side, Thomas J. Dilorenzo's, "The Myth of Suburban Sprawl," is more like the Enterpriser view because it is critical of regulations by government. The Pew Charitable Trusts survey finds that government regulation to protect the environment is at a major divide among Republicans.[21] Among the three groups on the Right, only the Enterprisers fiercely fight efforts to protect the environment, and the Social Conservatives are more likely to back Liberal approaches.[22]

In a third example, Issue 15 presents the question: "Do Religious Groups Have a Right to Use Public School Facilities after Hours?" You might be surprised to find that the U.S. Supreme Court justices are not unbiased, but chosen for their ideology and political positions.[23] In this Supreme Court decision, Justice Clarence Thomas, considered the most conservative justice since the 1930s, wrote the majority decision; it was opposed by former Justice David Souter, considered by many to be moderate to liberal.[24] Souter, appointed by Bush Sr., was considered a surefire conservative appointee. However, he dismayed many conservative supporters after voting against the conservative bloc in two key cases, *Planned Parenthood v. Casey*, essentially reaffirming *Roe v. Wade*, and *Lee v. Weisman*, in which he voted down allowing prayer at a high school graduation ceremony.[25] Although conservatives call Justice Souter "liberal" for his stances, he might actually be an Enterpriser, a typology that is very conservative but not nearly as religious as Social Conservatives.

In Unit 4, "State Legislatures," two issues are discussed: Issue 10, "Should State Legislators Have Term Limits?" and Issue 11, "Should Legislators Have the Responsibility for Redistricting?" Both issues concern whether to strengthen or curb state legislative power. The former asks, should we be able to kick long-term incumbents out of office automatically? Or, do we lose expertise by pushing legislators out who are successful at re-election? The latter question concerns who should have the power to create legislative lines: the legislators themselves, or an independent, nonbiased group?

This *Taking Sides* book assumes that a diversity of perspectives can actually be a strength rather than a weakness. For example, philosopher John Rawls' difference principle says that a healthy democracy based on deliberation should maximize information from a large range and availability of perspectives, including the least well off.[26] Therefore, by entertaining clashing views, you have the opportunity to have more information at your disposal to make decisions on issues of the day.

All Politics Are Local

When former House Speaker Tip O'Neill lost his first race by 60 votes in Cambridge, Massachusetts' city council race in 1935, his father reminded him: "All politics is local. Don't forget it."[27] Politics forces state house representatives, county commissioners, and city councilmen as well as other offices to focus on what is important to the average person in their district. City councilmen often have to grapple with how to pay for faulty sewer lines, complaints of dogs barking incessantly, constituents' calls to fill numerous potholes, or the need for a neighborhood stop, and so on. Likewise, county commissioners often hear complaints about the need to grade or pave roads as well as other problems county wide. Moreover, state representatives may get phone calls on property taxes questions, putting more criminals in jail, the need for more campus security, or their stance on two gay men marrying or on abortion.

When these clashing views collide, they do so figuratively in space and time. In fact, the Latin for "local" as in, *Taking Sides: Clashing Views in State and Local Government,* is *locus,* meaning "place."[28] Cities and towns originated to take care of the needs of people who converged into one place. Some scholars argue that the origin of the city was from the Neolithic Era, approximately 10,000 years ago, with the advent of agriculture creating more food to feed an ever escalating population, and the resultant population density mandating city development and infrastructure.[29] The established benefits of agriculture pushed hunter-gatherers at the time to lay down their spears and nomadic lifestyle and pick up the sickle to harvest. In addition, protection likely brought people together.[30]

Regardless of municipal government's origin, it provides services to people, such as housing, sanitation, transportation, business locations, water, police and fire protection, and so forth. A majority of Americans identify with the place they live, specifically a city or town, giving them "a sense of community or feeling of belonging."[31] People are also involved in their place of locality. For example, more than 1 million people serve on their city or town's committees and boards, and 50 million belong to more than 250,000 home-owners' associations.[32]

States

States typically have boundaries much larger than those of cities and towns, and they are bound by the United States Constitution because of federalism.[33] Federalism is a constitutional principle that gives divided sovereignty between small political units called states and a larger centralized political unit, the national government.[34] Although the U.S. Constitution gives "supremacy" to the centralized government over the states, federalism allows states their own power to collect taxes and create laws. As you might expect, this divided sovereignty has created more than 200 years of tension between the two entities. This tension is made evident in this *Taking Sides* book with two issues from debates at the Constitutional Convention. The first, Unit 3, "Intergovernmental Relations," Issue 3 asks, the question: "Should We Protect States Rights over the Federal Government?" and is set in the opposition between the *Federalist* and the *Anti-Federalist Papers*, No. 45. The second, Issue 4, "Are 'Checks and Balances' Enough to Protect Our Rights?" brings into collision the *Federalist* and *the Anti-Federalist Papers*, No. 51.

Both questions illuminate our Founding Fathers' concerns about how to found a new nation.[35] The Federalists were rather tired and upset with what they felt were the disastrous results of the Articles of Confederation from 1781 to the time of the Constitutional Convention in the summer of 1787. The Federalists, also known as Conservative Patriots, pointed to the Article's ability to tax and thereby pay for the Revolution they had financed. Likewise, Shay's Rebellion made painfully apparent the soft underbelly of the new "league of friendship's" vulnerability.[36] However, the Anti-Federalists, or Radicals, were critical of a more centralized government that could tax and quell rebellion. Especially were they alarmed by the activities of the Sons of Liberty and most notably Lt. Daniel Shays' 800-strong revolt trying to prevent indictments against fellow farmers for back debt.[37] Moreover, the Anti-Federalists wanted to keep the Articles of Confederation as the status quo in order to maintain strong states and a weak national government weak out of fear of another King George III.

Issue 3, concerning states' rights versus the federal government, illustrates the fight over whether states or the national government should run the country. It is a struggle as to the locus, or place, for power. Should power be closer to the people, but fragmented and uncoordinated? Or should power be further from people, more centralized with coordinated action? Issue 4 again raises this tension but focuses more on how to protect our rights. Is it enough that we separate the three branches of government—president, Congress, and courts—each branch with checks and balances to offset each other's power to keep from being too centralized? Or, as Anti-Federalists contended at the time, do these checks and balances really just separate us from the "natural aristocracy," essentially the few? In other words, we might not have a king, they contended, but this "new" government does nothing in terms of keeping the elite from owning the government without the people's input.

This debate is also manifested in this book with Issue 5: "Should We Allow Eminent Domain for Public Use?" This question examines the 2005 Supreme Court case, *Kelo et al. v. City of New London*, which focused on the use of eminent domain in New London, Connecticut. In this case, the city council allowed Pfizer, a giant pharmaceutical company, to build its $300-million research facility on condemned property for "private use," traditionally not allowed by the Constitution's Fifth Amendment. Justices on the Left, led by Justice John Paul Stevens, typically a centrist, sided with New London in allowing Pfizer to take the property. The Justices on the Right lined up behind Justice Sandra Day O'Conner, who dissented, arguing that this case blurs the line between "public" and "private." It is also a case that divides up those in power, the city and Pfizer, against those, such as Susette Kelo and her neighbors, who hold less power.

The first unit, "Governors," looks at the struggle over the power of a state's chief executive. In Issue 1, we discuss governors' power opposed to the Pentagon in regard to the National Guard. In Issue 2, these two articles examine the line-item veto. Does this power give governors the legitimacy to limit the excesses of "legislative pork" by striking budget items on a bill before they sign it into law? Or is that power going too far?

In Unit 3, "Courts, Police, and Corrections," two Supreme Court cases covering the personal liberties in two schools are examined. In Issue 7, the Left wing, critical of such invasion, argues such action violates Fourth Amendment rights, whereas the Right wing of the U.S. Supreme Court, in their dissent, argued for the school's administration to possess the power to strip search a student suspected of holding drugs. Similarly, in Issue 9, the Right wing allows the school administration to punish a student who held up a "BONG HiTS 4 JESUS" banner outside his school building. Not surprisingly, the principal asked the student to put away the banner. The student refused; the principal suspended him. However, the student sued on the basis that his First Amendment rights were violated. The case became *Deborah Morse et. al. v. Joseph Frederick*, where Justice Roberts, writing for the majority, contended that it is fine to limit free speech if it "materially and substantially disrupt[s] the work and discipline of the school." In both cases, the Right side of the court wanted to give power to the school administration to keep control over its students. The Left seems to embrace more of a civil libertarian charge of protecting the student's Fourth Amendment rights in the former case and the other student's First amendment rights in the latter case.

Is seems that when state and local governments deal with people, conflict and the subsequent taking of sides naturally follow. This is because, in the places we live, we define ourselves through race, ideology, religion, economic interests, geography, and in countless other ways. We defend these definitional boundaries, and politics mobilizes us through these definitions of ourselves. Candidates rally various groups based on these definitions, to promote their own political agendas. In pursuit of idealized solutions based on these ways, we define ourselves; we conflict with others similarly in pursuit of their own interests, often crossing paths and impinging on our points of view and interests. Whether it is over our understanding of the U.S. Constitution, our definition of freedom, the proper role of regulation, or how we balance the necessity of security and our civil liberties, we struggle to defend ourselves and our way of looking at the world, even when ossified in philosophical silos. However, these readings about conflicts on the state and local level give us an opportunity to learn and deal with disputes in a more constructive way, as we are removed from the situation and examine a point of view that is not our own. Learning, especially critically, may put you outside your comfort zone.

I intend this book to move my readers to "think beyond the ink," beyond the often solidified point of view, by analyzing and evaluating both sides of an argument herein, using critical thinking skills in order to raise vital questions, come to well-reasoned conclusions and solutions, and think open-mindedly, considering alternative possibilities. I want you to effectively communicate your unique point of view to your family and friends, but most of all, to those with whom you do not necessarily agree, but with whom you may one day discover yourself in need of finding common ground.

Notes

1. Gregory Benford, *Timescape* (Spectra, 1992).

2. Dictionary.com. Accessed December 11, 2009. http://dictionary.reference
   .com/browse/conflict

3. John DeFrancis, *The Chinese Language: Fact and Fantasy* (University of
   Hawaii Press, 1984).

4. *Ibid.*

5. Otomar J. Bartos and Paul Wehr, *Using Conflict Theory* (Cambridge University Press, 2002).

6. Newsweek Poll. October 26–27, 2006. $N = 1,002$ adults nationwide.
   MoE $\pm$ 3 (for all adults). "Which side of the political debate on the abortion issue do you sympathize with more: the right-to-life movement that
   believes abortion is the taking of human life and should be outlawed; OR,
   the pro-choice movement that believes a woman has the right to choose
   what happens to her body, including deciding to have an abortion?"
   Accessed December 17, 2009, http://www.pollingreport.com/abortion.htm

7. "Where Do You Fit?" Accessed December 13, 2009, http://typology.people-press
   .org/typology/. The typology quiz was based on "two public opinion surveys
   in a nationwide poll of 2,000 interviews conducted Dec. 1–16, 2004, and a
   subsequent re-interview of 1,090 respondents."

8. "Beyond Red vs. Blue: Republicans Divided about Role of Government—
   Democrats by Social and Personal Values," The Pew Research Center for
   the People & the Press (May 10, 2005). Accessed December 13, 2009, http://
   people-press.org/report/242/beyond-red-vs-blue

9. "Survey Reports: Beyond Red vs. Blue: Profiles of the Typology Groups,"
   The Pew Research Center for the People & the Press (May 10, 2005).
   Accessed December 13, 2009, http://people-press.org/report/?pageid=949

10. *Ibid.*

11. *Ibid.*

12. Morris Fiorina and Samuel J. Abrams, "Political Polarization in the
    American Public," *Annual Review of Political Science* (June 2008).

13. Rupert Cornwell, "Republican Party Divided by Bitter Immigration Debate,
    The Independent World (May 26). Accessed December 13, 2009, http://www
    .independent.co.uk/news/world/americas/republican-party-divided-by-bitter-
    immigration-debate-479783.html

14. "Split over Health Care Bill," *The Washington Times* (November 19, 2009).
    Accessed December 13, 2009, http://www.washingtontimes.com/news/2009/nov/
    19/split-over-health-care-bill/

15. "Beyond Red vs. Blue: Republicans Divided about Role of Government—
    Democrats by Social and Personal Values."

16. Darryl Fears, "Immigration Reform Revisited," *The Washington Post* (March
    23, 2007). Accessed December 17, 2009, http://www.washingtonpost.com/
    wp-dyn/content/article/2007/03/22/AR2007032201840.html

17. "Beyond Red vs. Blue: Profiles of the Typology Groups" (May 10, 2005).
    Accessed December 13, 2009, http://people-press.org/report/?pageid=949

18. *Ibid.*

19. Victor Cohn, "James Brady and His Odyssey," *The Washington Post* (November 23, 1981), p. A1.

20. *Ibid.* Phyllis Stewart Schlafly is a conservative political activist known for her opposition to feminism and the Equal Rights Amendment.

21. "Beyond Red vs. Blue: Profiles of the Typology Groups."

22. Stephen M. Colarelli, "Conservatives Are Liberal, and Liberals Are Conservative—On the Environment," *The Independent Review* (Summer 2002). Accessed December 17, 2009, http://www.independent.org/pdf/tir/tir_07_1_colarelli.pdf

23. Justin Ewers, "Ranking the Politics of Supreme Court Justices: Four of the Five Most Conservative Justices Since 1937 Are on the Bench Today," *U.S News & World Report* (May 12, 2008). Accessed December 14, 2009, http://www.usnews.com/articles/news/national/2008/05/12/ranking-the-politics-of-supreme-court-justices.html

24. *Ibid.*

25. Ramesh Ponnuru, "Empty Souter—Supreme Court Justice David Souter," *National Review* (September 11, 1995). Accessed December 14, 2009, http://findarticles.com/p/articles/mi_m1282/is_n17_v47/ai_17374429/

26. John Rawls, *Political Liberalism* (Columbia University Press, 1996).

27. Tip O'Neill, *All Politics Is Local: And Other Rules of the Game* (Times Books, 1994), p. xv.

28. "Local," *Random House Webster's College Dictionary* (Random House, 1992).

29. Paul Bairoch, *Cities and Economic Development: From the Dawn of History to the Present* (University of Chicago Press, 1992).

30. Brendan O'Flaherty, *City Economics* (Harvard University Press, 2005).

31. Cara Wong, "Membership and Morality in American Politics: Obligation to Racial, National, and Geographic Communities," Ph.D. Dissertation at the University of California at Berkeley (2002), p. 89.

32. Community Associations Institute (CAI) Web site. Accessed December 14, 2009, http://www.caionline.org/pages/Default.aspx

33. Joseph Losco, and Ralph Baker, *Am Gov* (McGraw Hill, 2009).

34. *Ibid.*

35. *Ibid.*

36. Bruce Miroff, Raymond Seidelman, and Todd Swanstrom, *The Democratic Debate: An Introduction to American Politics,* 3rd ed. (Houghton Mifflin Company, 2002).

37. David P. Szatmary, *Shays' Rebellion: The Making of an Agrarian Insurrection* (University of Massachusetts Press, 1980).

Internet References . . .

"Military Reserves Federal Call Up Authority," by Rod Powers

About.com Guide

http://usmilitary.about.com/cs/guardandreserve/a/reservecallup.htm

Mold, Mildew, and the Military Role in Disaster Response. Jurist, Legal News and Research

http://jurist.law.pitt.edu/forumy/2005/10/
mold-mildew-and-military-role-in.php

Gubernatorial Veto Authority with Respect to Major Budget Bill(s)

See "Governors' Veto Power Regarding Appropriations Legislation"

http://www.ncsl.org/IssuesResearch/BudgetTax/
GubernatorialVetoAuthoritywithRespecttoMajor/tabid/12640/Default.aspx

Governors

*T*he trials and tribulations of the Colonial experience with England's King George III made executive power suspect. The state legislative branch dominated the colonies and later state government. Andrew Jackson's election to the presidency in 1828 represented the triumph of the "common man" over the elite, therefore raising the prestige of the executive branch; voters wanted to see the elites kicked out. Soon governors were given the veto power and longer terms of office. Ever since, debates often center on extent of the governor's power.

- Should the Pentagon Take over the National Guard During Disasters?
- Should Governors Have the Line-Item Veto?

ISSUE 1

Should the Pentagon Take over the National Guard During Disasters?

YES: **U.S. Northern Command**, from "Legislative Proposal for Activation of Federal Reserve Forces for Disasters," *Congressional Fact Sheet* (June 2009)

NO: **Philip J. Palin**, "Govs to DoD: Thanks, but No Thanks," *Homeland Security Watch* (August 13, 2009)

ISSUE SUMMARY

YES: U.S. Northern Command states that federal military personnel are necessary to safeguard the nation in times of disasters and major emergencies.

NO: Philip Palin is skeptical about governors losing control of their state guard units for only vague reasons.

$\mathbf{T}$he Pentagon approached Congress recently to grant the Secretary of Defense authority to post nearly 400,000 federal military personnel throughout the United States in case of a major disaster or emergency.

However, some governors have been suspicious of such federal power and of the prospect of the U.S. military patrolling city streets, in direct conflict with the Posse Comitatus Act of 1878.[1]

The Posse Comitatus Act is a federal law under 18 U.S.C. Section 1385, passed in June of 1878, limiting federal powers to use the military for law enforcement only.[2] This Act prohibits most National Guard, Army, Navy (Marine Corps), and Air Force personnel from exercising state law enforcement, police powers that maintain "law and order" activity in states, counties, and cities within the United States.

A "Congressional Fact Sheet," by the U.S. Northern Command in June of 2009, disseminated their "Legislative Proposal for Activation of Federal Reserve Forces for Disasters." This proposal amends current law, thereby "authorizing the Secretary of Defense to order any unit or member of the Army Reserve, Air Force Reserve, Navy Reserve, and the Marine Corps Reserve, to active duty for a major disaster or emergency," according to the fact sheet.

Palin points out that the problem is that governors were not pleased with this proposal, because they might lose control of their own National Guard and other domestically oriented military units in their states.[3]

However, Northern Command's congressional fact sheet refers not only to a "major disaster" as a focus but additionally to "emergencies," as defined in Section 5122 of Title 42 of the U.S. Code. This section basically gives the president the exclusive discretion to assign an event as either a "major disaster" or just an "emergency." Although the major disaster is well defined, the definition of "emergency" is rather vague, meaning, "any occasion or instance for which, in the determination of the President, Federal assistance is needed to supplement State and local efforts and capabilities to save lives and to protect property and public health and safety, or to lessen or avert the threat of a catastrophe in any part of the United States."

This power may expand the President's power to call up the reserves in a disaster or an emergency and would extend that power to the Secretary of Defense.

Northern Command's congressional fact sheet justifies this power by noting, "with Active Duty and National Guard forces strained by operations abroad, it is critical that the significant capabilities of the Federal Reserve forces be available to assist civil authorities in the case of major disasters or emergencies."

Notes

1. Rothchild, Matthew. (2009). "The Pentagon Wants Authority to Post Almost 400,000 Military Personnel in U.S.," *Progressive*, August 12, 2009.

2. "The Posse Comitatus Act: Setting the Record Straight on 124 Years of Mischief and Misunderstanding Before Any More Damage Is Done." (2003). *Military Law Review,* vol. 175.

3. Op cit., Rothchild.

Legislative Proposal for Activation of Federal Reserve Forces for Disasters

The Department of Defense (DOD) has submitted for consideration in the Fiscal Year 2010 National Defense Authorization Act a proposal to authorize the Secretary of Defense to order Army Reserve, Air Force Reserve, Navy Reserve, and the Marine Corps Reserve, to active duty for a major disaster or emergency. This proposal would amend chapter 1209 of title 10, United States Code, by inserting a new section authorizing the Secretary of Defense to order any unit or member of the Army Reserve, Air Force Reserve, Navy Reserve, and the Marine Corps Reserve, to active duty for a major disaster or emergency, as those terms are defined in section 5122 of title 42, U.S. Code, for a continuous period of not more than 120 days.

This legislative proposal would make the significant capabilities of the Army Reserve, Air Force Reserve, Navy Reserve, and Marine Corps Reserve available to the Secretary of Defense to assist civil authorities in responses to major disasters and emergencies, thus enabling a truly Total Force approach to disaster response. The Federal Reserve forces represent a significant capability, embedded in thousands of communities throughout our nation, which, with the exception of national emergencies, cannot be ordered to active duty to assist the primary Federal agency's response to major disasters or emergencies, even in circumstances when Reserve units may be closest to the disaster area and thus the most timely and cost-effective response.

This proposed new Title 10 section would also implement the recommendation of the Commission on the National Guard and Reserves that the "mobilization authorities for Federal Reserve forces to respond to emergencies should be expanded" to "provide the authority to involuntarily mobilize Federal Reserve components for up to 60 days in a four-month period and up to 120 days in a two-year period."

It is further important to note that certain DOD capabilities reside exclusively or in significant numbers in the Federal Reserve forces, such as aerial spray, "Hurricane Hunter" weather reconnaissance, combat surgical hospitals, search and rescue, aeromedical evacuation, mortuary affairs, engineering and logistical support. As a few examples, the President or Secretary of Defense

United States Congress, June 2009.

currently does not have the legal authority to activate the following assets in response to a natural disaster or emergency:

560th RED HORSE Squadron, Air Force Reserve Command, Charleston, South Carolina

Helicopter Anti-Submarine Squadron Seventy Five [HS 75], U.S. Navy Reserve, Jacksonville, Florida

4th Landing Support Battalion, Marine Forces Reserve, New Orleans, Louisiana

926th Engineer Group, U.S. Army Reserve, Montgomery, Alabama

With Active Duty and National Guard forces strained by operations abroad, it is critical that the significant capabilities of the Federal Reserve forces be available to assist civil authorities in the case of major disasters or emergencies. The Federal Reserve forces' capabilities are available for incidents involving the use or threat of weapons of mass destruction or a threat or attack by terrorists, under the authority of Subsection 12304(b) of Title 10, U.S. Code. The ability to activate Federal Reserve forces for major disasters or emergencies would provide the primary Federal agency the most rapid and effective military response

From an historical perspective, in two 1993 reports on the Hurricane Andrew response and then again thirteen years later in a report on the Hurricane Katrina response, the Comptroller General of the United States identified the disparity in activation authorities and recommended Congress grant the Secretary of Defense the authority to activate Federal Reserve forces for natural disasters.

The DOD proposed language, as approved by the Office of Management and Budget, states:

SEC. ___. AUTHORITY TO ORDER ARMY RESERVE, NAVY RESERVE, MARINE CORPS RESERVE, AND AIR FORCE RESERVE TO ACTIVE DUTY TO PROVIDE ASSISTANCE IN RESPONSE TO A MAJOR DISASTER OR EMERGENCY.

(a) AUTHORITY.—

(1) IN GENERAL.—Chapter 1209 of title 10, United States Code, is amended by inserting after section 12304 the following new section:

"§ 12304a. Army Reserve, Navy Reserve, Marine Corps Reserve, and Air Force Reserve: order to active duty to provide assistance in response to a major disaster or emergency

"(a) AUTHORITY.—Notwithstanding any other provision of law, to provide assistance in responding to a major disaster or emergency (as those terms are defined in section 102 of the Robert T. Stafford Disaster Relief and Emergency Assistance Act (42 U.S.C. 5122)), the Secretary of Defense may, without the consent of the member affected, order any unit, and any member not assigned to a unit organized to serve as a unit, of the Army Reserve, Navy Reserve, Marine Corps Reserve, and Air Force Reserve, under the jurisdiction of that Secretary to active duty for a continuous period of not more than 120 days.

"(b) EXCLUSION FROM STRENGTH LIMITATIONS.—Members ordered to active duty under this section shall not be counted in computing authorized strength of members on active duty or members in grade under this title or any other law.

"(c) TERMINATION OF DUTY.—Whenever any unit or member of the Reserves is ordered to active duty under this section, the service of all units or members so ordered to active duty may be terminated by order of the Secretary of Defense or law.".

(2) CLERICAL AMENDMENT.—The table of sections at the beginning of such chapter is amended by inserting after the item relating to section 12304 the following new item:

"12304a. Army Reserve, Navy Reserve, Marine Corps Reserve, Air Force Reserve: order to active duty to provide assistance in response to a major disaster or emergency.

(b) TREATMENT OF OPERATIONS AS CONTINGENCY OPERATIONS.— Section 101(a)(13)(B) of such title is amended by inserting "12304a," after "12304,".

USNORTHCOM Legislative Affairs Office:

The Pentagon, Room 2A872 Lt Col Rob Palmer, USAFR, rob.palmer@northcom.mil Washington, DC 20330 Ms. Caroline Ross, caroline.ross@js.pentagon.mil (703) 695-9188 Mr. Charles Faulkner, IV, charles.faulkner@northcom.mil U.S. Northern Command (USNORTHCOM) was established on October 1, 2002 to provide command and control of Department of Defense (DOD) homeland defense efforts and to coordinate civil support missions. The USNORTHCOM area of responsibility encompasses North America, Bermuda, the Gulf of Mexico, the Straits of Florida, the Caribbean region inclusive of the U.S. Virgin Islands, British Virgin Islands, Puerto Rico, the Bahamas, Turks and Caicos Islands, and surrounding waters out to approximately 500 nautical miles.

Philip J. Palin  **NO**

Govs to DoD: Thanks, but No Thanks

On August 7 the National Governors Association replied to a letter evidently received from Assistant Secretary of Defense Paul Stockton. The content of this letter is extracted below.

I have not yet seen a copy of the original letter from Dr. Stockton.

According to Matthew Rothschild in *The Progressive*, the letter signals an intention to seek Congressional approval to post almost 400,000 military personnel in the U.S. Rothschild continues, "This request has already occasioned a dispute with the nation's governors. And it raises the prospect of U.S. military personnel patrolling the streets of the United States, in conflict with the Posse Comitatus Act of 1878."

AP reporter Lolita Baldor offers a more expansive explanation for the governors' concern. "At the heart of the disagreement is who will exercise the muscle to command reserve troops when they are sent to a particular state to deal with a hurricane, wildfire or other disaster. The governors see the Pentagon move as a strike at state sovereignty, while the military justifies it as a natural extension of its use of federal forces."

Writing in *The Hill*, Reid Wilson, reports, "A bipartisan pair of governors is opposing a new Defense Department proposal to handle natural and terrorism-related disasters, contending that a murky chain of command could lead to more problems than solutions."

A regular reader of HLSwatch suggests there is very helpful background in a November 2008 CRS report, written by Jennifer Elsea and Chuck Mason, entitled Use of Federal Troops for Disaster Assistance: Legal Issues. The first paragraph is a great one: "Recognizing the risk that a standing army could pose to individual civil liberties and the sovereignty retained by the several states, but also cognizant of the need to provide for the defense of the nation against foreign and domestic threats, the framers of the Constitution incorporated a system of checks and balances to divide the control of the military between the President and Congress and to share the control of the militia with the states. This report summarizes the constitutional and statutory authorities and limitations relevant to the employment of the armed forces to provide disaster relief and law enforcement assistance."

At this point, I don't have anything to add that you can't find in what these reporters and researchers have produced. Please access the original stories. If anyone has a copy of Paul's letter, please let me know.

Text of NGA Response to DoD Letter

The Honorable Paul Stockton
Assistant Secretary of Defense for Homeland Defense
and Americas' Security Affairs
The Pentagon
Washington, D.C. 20301

Dear Assistant Secretary Stockton:

On behalf of the nation's governors, we would like to thank you for your letter regarding the legislative proposal to provide the Secretary of Defense with expanded authorities to assist in the response to domestic disasters. While we appreciate the outreach, governors remain cautious about changes to the military's authority to engage independently in domestic emergency response situations. The proposal you suggest may have merit, but its consideration must be preceded by a discussion regarding the tactical control of forces serving inside a state in response to a disaster or emergency.

It is our position that to carry out our homeland defense and homeland security responsibilities, governors must retain command and control over the domestic use of their own National Guard forces (Title 32 or State Active Duty status), supporting National Guard forces from other states, and Title 10 forces operating within the supported governor's state or territory. Consequently, when a dual status command has not been established under 32 United States Code 325, governors, acting through their Adjutants General and Joint Force Headquarters—State, must have tactical control over all Title 10 active duty and reserve military forces engaged in domestic operations within the governor's state or territory.

We are concerned that the legislative proposal you discuss in your letter would invite confusion on critical command and control issues, complicate interagency planning, establish stove-piped response efforts, and interfere with governors' constitutional responsibilities to ensure the safety and security of their citizens. One of the key lessons learned from the response to the terrorist attacks on September 11, 2001, and to Hurricanes Katrina and Rita in 2005 was the need for clear chains of command to avoid duplication of effort and to ensure the most effective use of response resources. Without assigning a governor tactical control of Title 10 forces assisting in a response, and without the use of a dual-hatted National Guard commander to ensure coordination between Title 32 and Title 10 forces, strong potential exists for confusion in mission execution and the dilution of governors' control over situations with which they are more familiar and better capable of handling than a federal military commander.

We look forward to discussing potential tactical control solutions. For example, current military doctrine explicitly allows members of the United

States armed forces to serve under the operational direction of foreign commanders, with the President retaining ultimate command over U.S. forces. If the command relationship with the President can be maintained while American active duty personnel are operating under the control of foreign commanders, we see no convincing reason why it cannot be maintained while active duty personnel are under the control of a state governor acting through the Adjutant General. The Commission on the National Guard and Reserves' Second Report to Congress dated March 1, 2007, specifically recommends governor direction of state and federal military assets to synchronize the military response to disasters:

"Recommendation 8. As part of Department of Defense efforts to develop plans for consequence management and support to civil authorities that account for state-level activities and incorporate the use of National Guard and Reserve forces as first military responders (see Recommendation 19), the Department of Defense should develop protocols that allow governors to direct the efforts of federal military assets responding to an emergency such as a natural disaster."

We do not yet understand how the legislative proposal would increase the number of DoD personnel available to assist disaster victims. Under existing legislation, DoD has the authority to order members of the Army Reserve, Navy Reserve, Marine Corps Reserve, and Air Force Reserve to active duty to assist in responses to major disasters and emergencies in the United States. Further, we are not yet convinced the proposed legislative changes would increase the responsiveness of DoD personnel. Under existing legislation, when emergency conditions dictate, local military commanders and responsible DoD component officials are authorized to respond to requests from local authorities and to initiate immediate response actions to save lives, prevent human suffering, or mitigate great property damage under imminently serious conditions.

As you know, a similar proposal was contained in the House of Representatives' version of the National Defense Authorization Act for Fiscal Year 2009, but was removed during conference because of governors' concerns. In the Joint Explanatory Statement that accompanied the bill, Congress made clear that DoD should engage governors to address their concerns before moving the proposal forward:

"The Department of Defense should engage with the community of governors to work out an understanding of unity of effort during domestic terrorist events and public emergencies. This key underlying issue must be addressed to allow this and other promising proposals to be enacted."

Governors and their Adjutants General would welcome the opportunity to work with you and others at DoD and the National Guard Bureau to discuss tactical control during disasters and to identify legislative and operational opportunities to improve our response to such events. The best way to facilitate such consultation and communication is for DoD to quickly establish the Council of Governors as required by the National Defense Authorization Act for Fiscal Year 2008. Doing so will provide an appropriate forum to address these issues and other aspects of defense support to civilian authorities.

Sincerely,
Governor James H. Douglas
Governor Joe Manchin III
cc:
The Honorable Robert M. Gates, Secretary of Defense
The Honorable William J. Lynn, III, Deputy Secretary of Defense
Admiral Michael Mullen, Chairman, Joint Chiefs of Staff
The Honorable Michèle Flournoy, Under Secretary of Defense for Policy
General Victor E. Renuart, Commander, U.S. Northern Command and North American Aerospace Defense Command
General Craig R. McKinley, Chief, National Guard Bureau

POSTSCRIPT

Should the Pentagon Take over the National Guard During Disasters?

Under Reconstruction, 10 Southern state governments were reconstituted under U.S. Army oversight. During this time, from 1863–1877, civil combat had subsided and martial law reigned over the South. At this time, the military supervised elections, watched over local government, and were tasked to protect freedmen and public officials from violence.[1] Although Blacks were enrolled as voters, Confederates, especially leaders, were prohibited from voting for a period of time.[2] The Posse Comitatus Act passed in 1878 was a prohibition of military occupation of the United States of America by its own army.

The 1956 amended version of the Posse Comitatus Act reads in 18 U.S.C. § 1385:

> Use of Army and Air Force as posse comitatus: Whoever, except in cases and under circumstances expressly authorized by the Constitution or Act of Congress, willfully uses any part of the Army or the Air Force as a posse comitatus or otherwise to execute the laws shall be fined under this title or imprisoned not more than two years, or both.

However, because of the aftermath of Hurricane Katrina, President G. W. Bush on September 26, 2006, advocated for Congress to create a new federal law to deem U.S. armed forces appropriate to enforce laws on American soil after more than 100 years of prohibition. G. W. Bush's push to change the law was realized with additions to the John Warner National Defense Authorization Act for Fiscal Year 2007, subsequently made legal in October of 2006.[3] Section 1076 of this new law modified Sec. 333 of the "Insurrection Act," basically broadening the president's power to deploy soldiers within the United States to implement the laws, that is, to deploy armed forces to quell public unrest and or disorder after a national disaster, serious health emergency, or terrorist attack. The previous law was limited only to domestic violence, conspiracy, insurrection, or a combination thereof.

Nevertheless, H.R. 4986: National Defense Authorization Act for Fiscal Year 2008 repealed the previous Act signed only a year before.[4] Behind the charge against the president's expanded powers were two senators, Vermont Senator Patrick Leahy and Missouri Senator Kit Bond (R-MO). Senator Leahy contends that these new changes make it too easy for the president to use this new broadened power to push his authority over the National Guard without the governor's consent.[5] Senator's Leahy and Bond's bid to repeal worked with the passage of H.R. 4986.

A year later, the Pentagon is calling for this expanded power back, but with mixed results.

Web Links

"Military Reserves Federal Call Up Authority," by Rod Powers, About.com: US Military. Available at Guidehttp://usmilitary.about.com/cs/guardandreserve/a/reservecallup.htm

"Mold, Mildew, and the Military Role in Disaster Response," *Jurist, Legal News and Research*. Accessed December 6, 2009, from http://jurist.law.pitt.edu/forumy/2005/10/mold-mildew-and-military-role-in.php

Notes

1. Foner, Eric. 2002. *Reconstruction: America's Unfinished Revolution, 1863–1877*. Harper Perennial Modern Classics.

2. *Ibid.*

3. H.R. 5122: John Warner National Defense Authorization Act for Fiscal Year 2007. Accessed November 30, 2009, from http://www.govtrack.us/congress/bill.xpd?bill=h109-5122

4. H.R. 4986: National Defense Authorization Act for Fiscal Year 2008. Accessed November 30, 2009, from http://www.govtrack.us/congress/bill.xpd?bill=h110-4986

5. "Statement of Sen. Patrick Leahy on Legislation to Repeal Changes to the Insurrection Act" (S. 513) February 7, 2007. Accessed November 30, 2009, from http://leahy.senate.gov/press/200702/020707.html

ISSUE 2

Should Governors Have the Line-Item Veto?

YES: The California Chamber of Commerce, the California Taxpayers' Association, and the California Business Roundtable, from Brief of Amicus Curiae of the *St. John's Well Child and Family Center et al. v. Arnold Schwarzenegger, California Governor, and John Chiang, California Controller* (October 7, 2009)

NO: Los Angeles County Democratic Central Committee, from Brief of Amicus Curiae of the *St. John's Well Child and Family Center et al. v. Arnold Schwarzenegger, California Governor, and John Chiang, California Controller* (September 20, 2009)

ISSUE SUMMARY

YES: Three former California governors argue that there cannot be fiscal integrity in state government without checks and balances; the line-item veto does that.

NO: California Democrats claim that Governor Arnold Schwarzenegger goes beyond what the state constitution allows and this overreach has had devastating consequences to the welfare of many Californians.

On July 29th, Republican California Governor Arnold Schwarzenegger cut $500 million from the budget with a few strokes of a pen.[1] The governor more specifically cut funding to elderly, children's health care programs, and AIDS prevention and treatment. Democrats were outraged and within months filed legal claims against the governor for his use of the line-item veto.

In an amicus brief, George Deukmejian, Pete Wilson, and Gray Davis, former California governors, teamed up to say that in their 21 years of collective service, the line-item veto was necessary and supported by California's Constitution, specifically Article IV, section 10(e). These former governors along with CalChamber, a voice for California businesses and the California Business Roundtable a nonpartisan, nonprofit organization of CEOs from leading corporations, agree.

These former governors' amicus brief reiterates that the California state constitution gives the governor the ability, through veto power, to control spending by either eliminating or reducing the dollar amount in line items of a bill that he or she finds wasteful in the state budget, even after the budget has been passed by both of the state legislature's chambers.

Conversely, the Los Angeles Democratic Party (LACDP) and the Riverside County Democratic Central Committee (RCDCC) claim that the state constitution does not give Governor Arnold Schwarzenegger line-item veto authority, especially for such severe budget cuts. In the brief, the Democratic groups argue that when the governor is acting with veto authority, he is acting as a "special agent with limited powers," and those powers are outlined as enumerated powers; any actions outside these powers are null and void. These Democratic groups argue further that Governor Schwarzenegger crossed the line into unconstitutional territory with his overreach of power in severely cutting the budget and harming California's "most vulnerable residents" through his line-item veto.

The Democratic brief brings up the example of "Gloria" (a pseudonym to protect her identity). Women such as Gloria, they argue, are not able to access services important to themselves and their children's health and well-being. Gloria is described in this brief as having three children and being HIV-positive and hospital bound because of medical difficulties from her "complicated medical regime."

In addition, the governor's cuts will devastate Culver City's Women at Risk, an organization which does not receive state funding and which has already found itself organizationally strained because the group's referrals have tripled from a high of 12 percent to upward of 35 percent after the line-item veto.

However, the governor is in charge of administering the state government to benefit Californian citizens, according to the governors' brief. It says further that the Democrats and others, in their opposing brief, "Under the guise of a fiscal crisis, petitioners, intervenors and amici have invented a theory out of whole cloth to deprive governors of the authority that has been conferred on them by the California Constitution since 1922. Neutering a governor during a fiscal crisis is irresponsible, particularly when such action is not supported by logic, reason or law."

Whether or not governors have the right to cut line items from a budget (as opposed to having veto power only over the entire budget), cutting a line item has real-life implications that can result in detrimental consequences to people who depend on its aid, according to Democrats.

Note

1. Michael Rothfeld and Shane Goldmacher, "Schwarzenegger Cuts $500 Million More as He Signs Budget," *New York Times* (July 29, 2009), http://www.latimes.com/news/local/la-me-california-budget29-2009jul29,0,7361988.story

YES ⤶

Brief of Amicus Curiae of the *St. John's Well Child and Family Center et al. v. Arnold Schwarzenegger, California Governor, and John Chiang*

I. Introduction

The constitutional powers of the Governor with respect to the state budgetary process are fully and accurately set forth in the Governor's Opposition to this petition for writ of mandate. The Constitution sets forth distinct powers to the legislative and executive branches. Those powers are at the heart of the checks and balances system underlying the government of this state. The directive of the Constitution is to give a governor the ability to control spending by reducing or eliminating appropriations through the veto power. It is this power that the petitioners, intervenors, and amici are attempting to erode.

As more fully articulated below, reduced to their essentials, the arguments advanced by the petitioners, intervenors, and amici are that a governor loses control of the Budget Act upon approval, and that subsequent measures that reduce appropriations are beyond a governor's authority to selectively eliminate or reduce because they are not "items of appropriation." In short, what petitioners, intervenors and amici argue is, after the budget bill is enacted, the Legislature may, through a single bill, make selective and multiple reductions in the prior appropriations, leaving a governor only the power to veto the entire bill.

The mischief such a scheme could generate is manifest. It renders the original budget process irrelevant in that spending levels agreed to by two-thirds vote of the Legislature in the Budget Act could be overturned by a majority vote of the Legislature in a single bill on the theory that spending reductions are not items of appropriation subject to two-thirds vote of the Legislature. Moreover, such a scheme flies in the face of Article IV, section 10(e) of the California Constitution, which empowers a governor as chief executive officer of the State to "reduce or eliminate one or more items of appropriations." For the reasons stated herein and in the Governor's Opposition, there is no legal support for such an illogical, novel and destructive theory.

U.S. Senate, October 7, 2009.

A. An Item of Appropriation Includes Increases or Decreases in Spending Authority.

All parties to this litigation appear to be in agreement that the narrow issue to be resolved is whether a reduction in a Budget Act is, itself, an item of appropriation subject to a governor's power to reduce or eliminate items of appropriation. All parties to this litigation also appear in agreement that an "appropriation" confers spending authority on a particular entity of government. However, petitioners, intervenors and amici contend that only an *increase* in spending authority amounts to an "appropriation" and that a provision that reduces spending authority is not an appropriation. Apart from the lack of any case law to support that position, it is illogical. Whether spending authority is increased or decreased, it is still spending authority. No one can seriously disagree that when the Governor reduces spending authority in the budget bill that reduction is part of the appropriation process. There can be no dispute that this multi-itemed bill is an amendment to the Budget Act, otherwise it could not contain multiple appropriations. California Constitution, Article IV, section 12(d) provides "No bill except the budget bill may contain more than one item of appropriation." There is no substantive difference between reducing an item of appropriation in the original Budget Act and in a subsequent amendment to the Budget Act. Both involve changes in spending authority.

Further, the Legislative Digest prepared by the Legislative Counsel for AB 1, expressly states that AB 1 is an amendment to the appropriations in the Budget Act of 2009. The Digest provides:

> Legislative Counsel's Digest
>
> AB 1, Evans, Budget Act of 2009: revisions
>
> The Budget Act of 2009 (Chapter 1 of 2009–10 Third Extraordinary Session) made appropriations for the support of state government for the 2009–10 fiscal year.
>
> This bill would make revisions to those appropriations for the 2009–10 fiscal year. This bill would make specified reductions in certain appropriations.

Any reasonable person reading the Digest would assume the multiple budget items identified in AB 1 are, as they must be under Article IV, section 12(d), items of appropriation. However, in an opinion issued by Legislative Counsel after the Governor exercised his line item veto power, cited by intervenors in support of their position, Counsel inexplicably concludes:

> Thus the fact that provisions of A.B. 1 are related to existing appropriations previously authorized by the Budget Act of 2009 does not mean that those provisions are items of appropriation subject to the Governor's line-item veto.

Counsel's conclusion cannot be reconciled with Article IV, section 12(d) or the Legislative Counsel's Digest. Counsel's opinion would suggest that there was a deliberate attempt, not disclosed in the Digest, to place multiple non-appropriation items in a bill containing multiple items of appropriations that did, in fact, authorize increases[1] in spending in order to give the appearance of compliance with Article IV, section 12(d). Once the bill was passed and signed by the Governor, Counsel now contends these non-appropriation items cannot be vetoed, citing *Harbor v. Deukmejian* (1987) 43 Cal.3d 1078. This "gotcha" tactic must fail for lack of any credible legal support.

Outside the arcane area of state budgetary practices, no one can reasonably disagree that when a bank sets a limit on its customer's credit card, it has conferred spending authority up to that limit. When it reduces that credit limit, it still confers spending authority, but at a lower limit. The contention that the Governor is not engaged in the establishment of spending authority when he reduced the items of appropriation at issue in this matter flies in the face of common sense.

B. Application of *Harbor v. Deukmejian* Would Invalidate the Entire Bill.

Petitioners, intervenors, and amici argue, in effect, that because a reduction in an appropriation is not, itself, an appropriation, the Governor's constitutional authority only extends to vetoing the entire bill, citing *Harbor v. Deukmejian*. *Harbor* involved a trailer bill containing multiple statutory amendments intended to implement the appropriations set forth in the Budget Act. None of those amendments purported to decrease or increase the appropriations in the Budget Act. The court concluded that those amendments were not items of appropriation and could not be selectively vetoed by the Governor pursuant to his line-item veto authority under Article IV, section 10(e). Thus, *Harbor* never addressed the narrow issue before this court.

More relevant to this litigation, however, the Court in *Harbor* held the trailer bill was invalid on the basis that it violated the single subject prohibition in Article IV, section 9. If petitioners, intervenors and amici are correct that the multiple reductions at issue do not constitute an appropriation and for this reason cannot be selectively reduced by the Governor, then because each item involves a different statutory program, like the trailer bill in *Harbor,* the entire bill would be invalid. It is a well recognized maxim that legislation should be construed, if reasonably possible, to preserve its constitutionality. . . .

C. The Legislature Is Attempting the Same Ploy That Failed in *Wood v. Riley*.

Legislative attempts to circumvent the Governor's veto authority are not new. In the early and frequently cited case of *Wood v. Riley* (1923) 192 Cal. 293, the Legislature sought to insulate an appropriation from the Governor's line-item veto by casting it as a "transfer." The court rejected the ploy, stating (Id. at 305): "To sustain the contention of the petitioner that the proviso in question did not amount to an item of appropriation and was therefore removed from the effect of the executive veto would be to hold that the Legislature might, by indirection, defeat the purpose of the constitutional amendment giving the Governor power to control the expenditures of the state, when it could not accomplish that purpose directly or by an express provision in appropriation bills."

That the Legislature is engaged in the same ploy attempted in *Wood* is evident from the manner in which it worded the language of items in dispute in this action. Rather than merely amending these items, as it did some others, to simply reflect the reduced amount, the Legislature *added* an item that expressly stated it reduced the prior appropriation. . . .

Even Petitioner Saint John's Well Child and Family Center apparently concedes that the amendment language that makes no reference to a "reduction" would probably be subject to the Governor's line-item veto, but contends that the express reduction language should be treated as substantively different. The distinction between the two forms is the classic distinction without a difference. What is revealing about the two formats, however, is that the Legislature was intentionally trying to insulate the items addressed in this litigation from the Governor's line-item veto authority.

D. The Governor's Vetoes Are Not Affected By the Defeat of Proposition 76.

Intervenors attempt to characterize the Governor's vetoes as a midyear budget correction, asserting that the voters denied the Governor such authority when they rejected Proposition 76 on the November 2005 General Election ballot.

Intervenors assert: "Thus, the voters have made clear that the question of how to deal with a fiscal emergency should be decided by the Legislature." Proposition 76 would have allowed the Governor to unilaterally make reductions in spending if the Legislature failed to enact legislation to deal with a fiscal emergency. The failure of Proposition 76 did not deprive the Governor of his right to exercise the line-item veto.

II. Conclusion

The supreme executive power of the state is vested in the Governor. (Cal. Const, art. V, sec. 1.) The Governor is responsible for the administration of state government for the benefit of its citizens. One of the most important functions of a governor is to control state spending. The line-item veto is an essential tool in carrying out that function. Under the guise of a fiscal crisis, petitioners, intervenors and amici have invented a theory out of whole cloth to deprive governors of the authority that has been conferred on them by the California Constitution since 1922. Neutering a governor during a fiscal crisis is irresponsible, particularly when such action is not supported by logic, reason or law. Checks and balances are what keep democratic governments functioning through the good times and bad times. Petitioners, intervenors and amici, seek to upset that balance. We respectfully request this Court to reject their petition for writ of mandate.

Note

1. Sections 6 and 10 of AB 1 add a total of $64,682,000 and $16,973,000, respectively, to judicial branch appropriations.

Brief of Amicus Curiae of the *St. John's Well Child and Family Center et al. v. Arnold Schwarzenegger, California Governor, and John Chiang*

I. Introduction

The Los Angeles County Democratic Central Committee, also known as the Los Angeles Democratic Party (LACDP) is the official governing body of the Democratic Party in the County of Los Angeles. It is the largest local Democratic Party entity in the United States, representing over 2.2 million registered Democrats in the 88 cities and the unincorporated areas of Los Angeles County. As the local Democratic Party organization representing these 2.2 million Californians, the LACDP has long fought to vindicate the values and principles described in the Platform of the California Democratic Party. Among these is the aspiration to "[l]ift at-risk families and working poor families out of poverty so they can become independent and lead self-sufficient lives," establish health care as "a right not a privilege," and uphold the democratic principles embodied in our State Constitution.

The Riverside County Democratic Central Committee (RCDCC) is the official governing body of the Democratic Party in the County of Riverside. It represents and serves all registered Democrats in a 2,000 square mile County with over 2,100,000 residents; 74 incorporated and unincorporated communities; 9 colleges; 2 military installations and 9 Native American Indian Reservations. The RCDCC is actively working to protect and promote the rights of residents of Riverside County, including those who are disabled; gay, bisexual, lesbian and transgender; undocumented immigrants, workers, seniors, the medically indigent, prisoners, veterans, students, the homeless, hungry, the disenfranchised and victims of domestic violence. When Governor Schwarzenegger purportedly used the "line-item-veto" to eliminate $489 million of funding for programs and persons who the Democratic Party in California serves, it acted in contravention of the purposes of the RCDDC.[1]

As described in the Petition, this case involves the attempted exercise by Governor Arnold Schwarzenegger of authority not granted to him under the Constitution of the State of California. This fact alone would be sufficient to

U.S. Senate, September 20, 2009.

establish the public importance of this case. Yet, it is the devastating nature of the cuts imposed by Governor Schwarzenegger, and the immediate irreparable harm which these cuts will inflict on some of California's most vulnerable residents, which are the most compelling reasons for this Court to hear and resolve—in Petitioners' favor—the matters at issue in this writ.

II. Argument

A. This Case Arises Out of a Purported Exercise by Governor Schwarzenegger of Authority Not Granted to the Governor by Our State Constitution

This Court has original jurisdiction "in proceedings for extraordinary relief in the nature of mandamus, certiorari, and prohibition." Jurisdiction is only exercised where the case presents issues of great public importance that must be resolved promptly. *San Francisco Unified School Dist. v. Johnson* (1971) 3 Cal.3d 937, 944. Here, both of these factors are satisfied. This case is of the utmost public importance for two reasons: (1) this case arises out of the Governor's exercise of authority not granted to him by our state constitution; and (2) the consequences of this constitutionally unwarranted action are devastating to the welfare of the many Californians dependent on essential state services.

When a governor is acting in his legislative capacity, as he is when exercising his line item veto authority, the governor is acting as a "special agent with limited powers." *Lukens v. Nye* (1909) 156 Cal. 498. 501–02. These powers are solely those "specifically enumerated" in the State Constitution and any acts outside the scope of those powers are "wholly ineffectual and void for any and every purpose." *Id*. For the reasons articulated by Intervenors Karen Bass and Darrell Steinberg [Intervenors' Memorandum of Points and Authorities, Part I, pp. 15–21, and Part II.A., pp. 21–25], it is manifest that, here, by purporting to further reduce an already enacted appropriation, Governor Schwarzenegger traveled outside the ambit of his "limited powers." Such an ultra vires act by our State's chief executive is, in and of itself, a sufficient basis for this Court to find the issues in this case to be of great public importance.

B. The Catastrophic Consequences to the Well-Being of Many of California's Most Vulnerable Residents of the Governor's Constitutionally Unwarranted Exercise of Line Item Veto Authority Vividly Demonstrate the Public Importance of This Case and the Urgent Need for Prompt Extraordinary Relief

Important as the legal issues in this case are, it is the great human cost of leaving intact the Governor's constitutionally unwarranted cuts in vital services which most vividly demonstrates the public importance of this case and the urgent need for prompt extraordinary relief.

Press reports make manifest the scope and severity of the elimination of (or drastic reduction in) public services effectuated by the Governor's purported line item veto:

- In total, the Governor's veto encompasses $316 million in cuts from health and social service programs. . . .
- Domestic violence programs will be devastated by the Governor's cuts. $16.3 million has been eliminated from the California Department of Public Health's domestic violence programs, a program that supports domestic violence shelters throughout the state. Press Release, Stop Family Violence, CA Governor Eliminates State Funding to Domestic Violence Programs (July 28, 2009). . . . As a result, many domestic violence agencies will be unable to provide emergency shelter, transitional housing, legal advocacy, restraining order assistance, counseling, and other vital services to those in need.
- HIV and AIDS services will also be greatly curtailed due to $85 million in cuts included in the Governor's line-item vetoes. Press Release, AIDS Project Los Angeles, APLA Condemns Destructive $85 million cut to state HIV/AIDS Programs (July 28,2009) ("APLA Press Release").
- One program that will be eliminated as a result of these cuts to HIV and AIDS programming is the Therapeutic Monitoring Program, which tracks the effectiveness of HIV/AIDS drugs. Rex Wockner, Schwarzenegger decimates AIDS services (July 29, 2009).

As compelling as the above numbers are, they only tell part of the story of the harms inflicted by the Governor's cuts. The Governor's cuts have forced organizations that provide vital services to the most vulnerable members of our society to scale back those services resulting in real people being denied the help that they desperately need. For instance, as described in the Declaration of Carol Broadus, Women Alive, a bilingual counseling and education program for and by women living with HIV/AIDS, will, as a result of the line item veto at issue in this case, terminate its HIV treatment education program on October 15, 2009. This will have a catastrophic impact on women like "Gloria" (a pseudonym to protect her identity) and those women like her who will now be unable to access services vital to their health and the well-being of their children. As described in the declaration, Gloria is an HIV-positive woman with three dependent children who was admitted to the hospital due to medical complications arising from her inability to "stick to her complicated medication regimen." With assistance from a treatment coordinator—whose services will now be terminated as a result of the veto-imposed cuts—Gloria was able to modify her regimen and stay out of the hospital.

It will also have a devastating impact on the women and men in Women Alive's peer support and treatment programs. As one participant said, without this program she will be left without help in coping with her medical needs while simultaneously fighting to put food on the table and obtain child care for her children so she can go to work. Another participant noted that the services lost through the termination of Women Alive's heterosexual HIV men's support services will leave him with no appropriate alternative to which to go to obtain assistance with housing and other needs his physician cannot provide.

The Governor's line item veto will bring about this same kind of devastation to the beneficiaries of the programs of Culver City's Women at Risk, an organization that does not receive government funding. Women at Risk will not suffer a loss of funding, but it is already experiencing an unprecedented increase in demand for its services as government-funded programs cut back or eliminate services. According to Carmen Johnson, Executive Director of Women at Risk, the number of referrals to the organization have tripled from 10 to 12 per month before the line item veto to 30 to 35 per month at present. Johnson describes an HIV-positive 27-year-old mother of two who was able to access antiretroviral medication for one month because of Women at Risk's financial help, but notes that in the wake of the line item veto, there are—and will be—many more women who are similarly situated and, as a result, will be "forced to choose between either paying for food or paying for medication."

These severe and possibly life-threatening consequences of the line item veto are not limited to agencies providing services to those with HIV/AIDS. Clients and potential clients of agencies providing assistance to victims of domestic violence also find themselves in dire straights. According to Judy Vaughan, Executive Director of Los Angeles' Alexandria House, as a direct result of the line item veto, domestic violence assistance organizations across the state are cutting back on services. As a result, the calls to her agency for assistance with the consequences of domestic violence incidents has also tripled, from 100 calls per month before the line item veto to 300 calls per month at present. As a result of this and the fact that in the current economic climate "families have to stay at Alexandria House longer than ever," it has become increasingly difficult to accommodate new families, "forcing [many women and their children] to stay in [homes beset by] violent relationships." Johnson cites the example of a woman to whom Alexandria House had to deny housing because of a lack of space. Although Alexandria House was able to house her for a month in a motel, if it cannot obtain additional voucher money on this woman's behalf, the woman will "be forced to either live in the street with her children or return to the violent relationship that she is trying to escape."

As the examples above illustrate, the consequences of the cuts effectuated by the line item veto—especially on those impacted by HIV/AIDS and domestic violence—is grave and urgent. This urgency would not exist if not for the Governor's purported line item vetoes, which will take effect immediately if they are allowed to stand.

Due to the great public importance of this litigation and the urgency with which the dispute must be resolved, this Court should find it has jurisdiction and should grant Petitioners immediate extraordinary relief. See *San Francisco Unified School Dist. v. Johnson* (1971) 3 Cal.3d 937, 944.

III. Conclusion

For the foregoing reasons, the LACDP and RCDCC, as amici curiae, respectfully urge this Court to grant the writ petition and prevent the devastating cuts imposed by Governor Schwarzenegger's legally unjustifiable exercise of the line item veto.

Note

1. Declaration references are to the declarations appended to LACDP's and RCDCC's concurrently filed Application for Leave to File Declarations.

POSTSCRIPT

Should Governors Have the Line-Item Veto?

In 2008, Governor Tim Pawlenty approved $717 million for projects for Minnesota. Before he did so, though, he used his veto pen to trim $208 million from the bonding package.[1] And most of the projects he vetoed were based in St. Paul, Minnesota. For example, with a stroke of his pen, he cut the Central Corridor Light Rail line, an $11 million expansion for the Como Zoo, plus $24 million to transfer the University of Minnesota's Bell Museum of Natural History to St. Paul from the Minneapolis campus. Governor Pawlenty said that "the state had 'misplaced priorities' that would fund a sheet music museum but not a new nursing facility for veterans."[2] Pawlenty charged he could have vetoed the whole budget bill; as an alternative, he deducted only 13 percent from it by means of 52 line-item vetoes. Democrats challenged his cuts, saying that he had focused mainly on their districts, predominantly St. Paul. The open question here is, was the governor playing politics as the Democrats charge, or was he cutting the legislative fat and ridding the state of "misplaced priorities," as he asserts?

Most state governors in the United States have the line-item veto, except for in seven states.[3] State constitutions tend to make legislators the most powerful branch on the state level.[4] Yet many states have bolstered governor's powers through the line-item veto. A line-item veto is not the same across states. Former Wisconsin Governor Tommy Thompson would strike passages and individual letters from bills, creating new legislative meanings in what was popularly called "the Vanna White veto."[5] He gained this notoriety after he rather upset the Democratic state legislature in reaction to the former governor altering a piece of legislation from a bill that set the maximum 48-hour detention period for juvenile offenders to one that is 10 days long. This particular power was prohibited by the legislature thereafter, but none of his 1,900 budget vetoes were ever successfully overturned.[6] In only 12 states does the governor have the power to reduce state spending by striking a number from the legislative appropriation.

The power in a governor's veto lies partly with the fact that state legislators can bypass a veto, but only with a supermajority, such as two-thirds, of their legislative body.[7] Because this kind of agreement is often incredibly hard to obtain, it remains a potent gubernatorial threat. The state legislature can check the governor by overriding a veto, but this is an unusual occurrence. Governors only veto 5 percent of legislation, and only 10 percent of these vetoes are overridden. So, although a veto, especially a line-item veto, is powerful, it is still only a threat that more often than not promotes compromise between the two branches. When governors call the specific line items they take out "turkeys." Are governors cutting out these "turkeys" appropriately? Should they have this power?

For more information on this subject, see "Gubernatorial Veto Authority with Respect to Major Budget Bill(s)" (http://www.ncsl.org/IssuesResearch/BudgetTax/GubernatorialVetoAuthoritywithRespecttoMajor/tabid/12640/Default.aspx).

Notes

1. "St. Paul Mayor Coleman on Governor's Line Item Veto Cuts," Minnesota Public Radio (April 7, 2008). Accessed December 6, 2009, http://minnesota.publicradio.org/display/web/2008/04/07/stpaulmayor/

2. "Pawlenty Slashes $200 Million from Bonding Bill."Accessed December 6, 2009, http://www.startribune.com/politics/state/17360219.html

3. "Gubernatorial Veto Authority with Respect to Major Budget Bill(s). Legislative Budget Procedures: Enactment of the Budget Table 6-3: Governors' Veto Power Regarding Appropriations Legislation." Accessed December 4, 2009, http://www.ncsl.org/IssuesResearch/BudgetTax/GubernatorialVetoAuthoritywithRespecttoMajor/tabid/12640/Default.aspx

4. Kevin Smith, Alan Greenblatt, and Michele Mariani, *Governing States & Localities*, 2nd ed. (Congressional Quarterly, 2008).

5. *Ibid.*, p. 90.

6. *Ibid.*, p. 90.

7. Thomas Dye and Susan MacManus, *Politics in the States and Communities*, 11th ed. (Prentice Hall, 2003).

Internet References . . .

Tenth Amendment Center

http://www.tenthamendmentcenter.com/nullification/10th-amendment-resolutions/

Exploring Constitutional Conflicts

http://www.law.umkc.edu/faculty/projects/ftrials/conlaw/tenth&elev.htm

Find Law.com. Reserved Powers

http://caselaw.lp.findlaw.com/data/constitution/amendment10/01.html

UNIT 2

Intergovernmental Relations

*F*ederalism, or the relationship between the state and national governments, can be thought of statically as legal principle or a structure or just a matter of politics. In the former view of federalism, power is fixed in the long term. In the latter view, power is shared in an ever-changing and interdependent way.

- Should We Protect States' Rights over the Federal Government?
- Are "Checks and Balances" Enough to Protect Our Rights?
- Should We Allow Eminent Domain for Private Use?
- Should a National Sense of Morality Override States Rights in the Case of Physician-Assisted Suicide?

ISSUE 3

Should We Protect States' Rights over the Federal Government?

YES: Sydney (a.k.a. Robert Yates), from "Powers of National Government Dangerous to State Governments; New York as an Example," *Anti-Federalist* No. 45 (June 13 and 14, 1788)

NO: Publius (a.k.a. James Madison), from "The Alleged Danger from the Powers of the Union to the State Governments Considered for the Independent Journal," *The Federalist,* No. 45 (January 26, 1788)

ISSUE SUMMARY

YES: Sydney (Robert Yates) is critical of a new Constitution because he predicted an escalation of power in the federal government and an equal de-escalation of power by states.

NO: Publius (James Madison), the "Father of the Constitution," defends his new document by arguing that its new powers will be necessary, "few and defined."

James Madison never would have guessed the immense power of the national or federalized government today as evidenced by what he argues in the 45th *Federalist Paper*: "The powers delegated by the proposed Constitution to the federal government are few and defined. Those which are to remain in the State governments are numerous and indefinite."

However, Robert Yates, also known under the pen name "Sydney," seemed to anticipate this enormous power, as found in the "necessary and proper clause" today. Nearly 150 years later, federal power expanded, especially under the New Deal era.[1] Although *Anti-Federalist* No. 45 counters Madison's arguments, the *Anti-Federalist Papers* were not a strictly organized project as were the *Federalist Papers*. These *Anti-Federalist Papers* were cobbled together years later by Morton Borden, arranging them to parallel the *Federalist Papers*.[2] Yates counters Madison's argument that the powers of the federal government are "few and defined."

> The state governments are considered in . . . [the new constitution] as mere dependencies, existing solely by its toleration, and possessing powers of which they may be deprived whenever the general government is disposed to do so.

Yates refers to his own state constitution of New York in further arguing that the "powers vested in the legislature of this state by these paragraphs will be weakened." Yates logically surmises this usurpation of power from the state legislature because the Constitution states in Article II that "all legislative powers therein granted shall be vested in the Congress of the United States, which shall consist of a Senate and House of Representatives."

Conversely, Madison, in this *Federalist Paper,* argues further that this new Constitution does not really increase the federal government's powers, but only in effect causes the federal government to be more effective in carrying out its current duties.

> If the new Constitution be examined with accuracy, it will be found that the change which it proposes consists much less in the addition of NEW POWERS to the Union, than in the invigoration of its ORIGINAL POWERS. The regulation of commerce, it is true, is a new power; but that seems to be an addition which few oppose, and from which no apprehensions are entertained. The powers relating to war and peace, armies and fleets, treaties and finance, with the other more considerable powers, are all vested in the existing Congress by the articles of Confederation. The proposed change does not enlarge these powers; it only substitutes a more effectual mode of administering them.

According to Madison, central to these powers is the power to tax, already existing in the Articles of Confederation, which was the current form of government at the time.

> The change relating to taxation may be regarded as the most mportant; and yet the present Congress have as complete authority to REQUIRE of the States indefinite supplies of money for the common defense and general welfare, as the future Congress will have to require them of individual citizens.

In addition, Madison states that this new nationalized government will actually be subservient to the states. For example, he notes that the new nationalized government relies on states to pass amendments and furthermore these states actually propose and pass amendments when they so choose.

This debate manifests today in the fight between Madison's Article I, Section 8 "Necessary and Proper Clause," giving power to the federal government to do as those in power see fit, versus the Bill of Rights' Tenth Amendment, pushed by the Anti-Federalists, which states, "The powers not delegated to the United States by the Constitution, nor prohibited by it to the States, are reserved to the States respectively, or to the people."

Notes

1. David M. Kennedy, *Freedom from Fear: The American People in Depression and War, 1929–1945* (Oxford University Press, 1999). pp. 364.

2. See *Anti-Federalist Papers* (Michigan State University Press, 1965), pp. 143–149.

Anti-Federalist No. 45: Powers of National Government Dangerous to State Governments; New York as an Example

Although a variety of objections to the proposed new constitution for the government of the United States have been laid before the public by men of the best abilities, I am led to believe that representing it in a point of view which has escaped their observation may be of use, that is, by comparing it with the constitution of the State of New York.

The following contrast is therefore submitted to the public, to show in what instances the powers of the state government will be either totally or partially absorbed, and enable us to determine whether the remaining powers will, from those kind of pillars, be capable of supporting the mutilated fabric of a government which even the advocates for the new constitution admit excels "the boasted models of Greece or Rome, and those of all other nations, in having precisely marked out the power of the government and the rights of the people."

It may be proper to premise that the pressure of necessity and distress (and not corruption) had a principal tendency to induce the adoption of the state constitutions and the existing confederation; that power was even then vested in the rulers with the greatest caution; and that, as from every circumstance we have reason to infer that the Dew constitution does not originate from a pure source, we ought deliberately to trace the extent and tendency of the trust we are about to repose, under the conviction that a reassumption of that trust will at least be difficult, if not impracticable. If we take a retrospective view of the measures of Congress . . . we can scarcely entertain a doubt but that a plan has long since been framed to subvert the confederation; that that plan has been matured with the most persevering industry and unremitted attention; and that the objects expressed in the preamble to the constitution, that is "to promote the general welfare and secure the blessings of liberty to ourselves and our posterity," were merely the ostensible, and not the real reasons of its framers. . . .

The state governments are considered in . . . [the new constitution] as mere dependencies, existing solely by its toleration, and possessing powers of

From *Antifederalist Papers*, No. 45, June 13–14, 1788.

which they may be deprived whenever the general government is disposed so to do. If then the powers of the state governments are to be totally absorbed, in which all agree, and only differ as to the mode—whether it will be effected by a rapid progression, or by as certain, but slower, operations—what is to limit the oppression of the general government? Where are the rights, which are declared to be incapable of violation? And what security have people against the wanton oppression of unprincipled governors? No constitutional redress is pointed out, and no express declaration is contained in it, to limit the boundaries of their rulers. Beside which the mode and period of their being elected tends to take away their responsibility to the people over whom they may, by the power of the purse and the sword, domineer at discretion. Nor is there a power on earth to tell them, What dost thou? or, Why dost thou so? I shall now proceed to compare the constitution of the state of New York with the proposed federal government, distinguishing the paragraphs in the former, which are rendered nugatory by the latter; those which are in a great measure enervated, and such as are in the discretion of the general government to permit or not. . . .

1 & 37

The 1st "Ordains, determines, and declares that no authority shall on any pretence whatever be exercised over the people or the members of this State, but such as shall be derived from and granted by them."

The 37th, "That no purchases or contracts for the sale of lands with or of the Indians within the limits of this state, shall be binding on the Indians, or deemed valid, unless made under the authority and with the consent of the legislature of this state."

. . . What have we reasonably to expect will be their conduct [i.e., the new national government] when possessed of the powers "to regulate commerce with foreign nations, and among the several states, and with the Indian tribes," when they are armed with legislative, executive, and judicial powers, and their laws the supreme laws of the land. And when the states are prohibited, without the consent of Congress, to lay any "imposts or duties on imports," and if they do they shall be for the use of the Treasury of the United States—and all such laws subject to the revision and control of Congress.

It is . . . evident that this state, by adopting the new government, will enervate their legislative rights, and totally surrender into the hands of Congress the management and regulation of the Indian trade to an improper government, and the traders to be fleeced by iniquitous impositions, operating at one and the same time as a monopoly and a poll-tax. . . .

The 2nd provides "that the supreme legislative power within this state shall be vested in two separate and distinct bodies of men, the one to be called the assembly, and the other to be called the senate of the state of New York, who together shall form the legislature."

The 3rd provides against laws that may be hastily and inadvertently passed, inconsistent with the spirit of the constitution and the public good, and that "the governor, the chancellor and judges of the supreme court, shall revise all bills about to be passed into laws, by the legislature."

The 9th provides "that the Assembly shall be the judge of their own members, and enjoy the same privileges, and proceed in doing business in like manner as the assembly of the colony of New York of right formerly did."

The 12th provides "that the senate shall, in like manner, be judges of their own members," etc.

The 31st describes even the style of laws—that the style of all laws shall be as follows: "Be it enacted by the people of the state of New York represented in senate and assembly," and that all writs and proceedings shall run in the name of the people of the state of New York, and [be] tested in the name of the chancellor or the chief judge from whence they shall issue.

The powers vested in the legislature of this state by these paragraphs will be weakened, for the proposed new government declares that "all legislative powers therein granted shall be vested in a congress of the United States, which shall consist of a senate and a house of representatives," and it further prescribes, that "this constitution and the laws of the United States, which shall be made in pursuance thereof; and all treaties made, or which shalt be made under the authority of the United States, shall be the supreme law of the land, and the judges in every state shall be bound thereby, anything in the constitution or laws of any state to the contrary notwithstanding; and the members of the several state legislatures, and all executive and judicial officers, both of the United States and of the several states, shall be bound by oath or affirmation to support this constitution."

Those who are full of faith, suppose that the words "in pursuance thereof" are restrictive, but if they reflect a moment and take into consideration the comprehensive expressions of the instrument, they will find that their restrictive construction is unavailing, and this is evidenced by 1st art., 8th sect., where this government has a power "to lay and collect all taxes, duties, imposts and excises, to pay the debts, and provide for the common defense and general welfare of the United States," and also "to make all laws which shall be necessary and proper for carrying into execution the foregoing powers vested by this constitution in the government of the United States, or in any department or office thereof."

. . . To conclude my observation on this head, it appears to me as impossible that these powers in the state constitution and those in the general government can exist and operate together, as it would be for a man to serve two masters whose interests clash, and secure the approbation of both. Can there at the same time and place be and operate two supreme legislatures, executives, and judicials? Will a "guarantee of a republican form of government to every state in the union" be of any avail, or secure the establishment and retention of state rights?

If this guarantee had remained, as it was first reported by the committee of the whole house, to wit, "that a republican constitution, and its existing laws, ought to be guaranteed to each state by the United States," it would have been substantial; but the changing the word constitution into the word form bears no favorable appearance. . . .

13, 35, 41

By the 13th paragraph "no member of this State shall be disfranchised, or deprived of any of the rights or privileges secured to the subjects of the State by the constitution, unless by the law of the land, or judgment of its peers."

The 35th adopts, under certain exceptions and modifications, the common law of England, the statute law of England and Great Britain, and the acts of the legislature of the colony, which together formed the law on the 19th of April, 1775.

The 41st provides "that the trial by jury remain inviolate forever; that no acts of attainder shall be passed by the legislature of this State for crimes other than those committed before the termination of the present war. And that the legislature shall at no time hereafter institute any new courts but such as shall proceed according to the course of the common law.

There can be no doubt that if the new government be adopted in all its latitude, every one of these paragraphs will become a dead letter. Nor will it solve any difficulties, if the United States guarantee "to every state in the union a republican form of government;" we may be allowed the form and not the substance, and that it was so intended will appear from the changing the word constitution to the word form and the omission of the words, and its existing laws. And I do not even think it uncharitable to suppose that it was designedly done; but whether it was so or not, by leaving out these words the jurisprudence of each state is left to the mercy of the new government. . . .

17, 18, 19, 20, 21, 27, 40

The 17th orders "That the supreme executive power and authority of this State shall be vested in a governor."

By the 18th he is commander-in-chief of the militia and admiral of the navy of the State; may grant pardons to all persons convicted of crimes; he may suspend the execution of the sentence in treason or murder.

By the 19th paragraph he is to see that the laws and resolutions of the legislature be faithfully executed.

The 20th and 21st paragraphs give the lieutenant-governor, on the death, resignation, removal from office, or impeachment of the governor, all the powers of a governor.

By the 27th he [the Governor] is president of the council of appointment, and has a casting vote and the commissioning of all officers.

The 40th paragraph orders that the militia at all times, both in peace and war, shall be armed and disciplined, and kept in readiness; in what manner the Quakers shall be excused; and that a magazine of warlike stores be forever kept at the expense of the State, and by act of the legislature, established, maintained, and continued in every county in the State.

Whoever considers the following powers vested in the [national] government, and compares them with the above, must readily perceive they are either all enervated or annihilated.

By the 1st art., 8th sec., 15th, 16th and 17th clauses, Congress will be empowered to call forth the militia to execute the laws of the union, suppress insurrections and repel invasions; to provide for organizing, arming and disciplining the militia, for the governing such part of them as may be employed in the service of the United States, and for the erection of forts, magazines, etc.

And by the 2nd art., 2nd sec., "The president shall be commander-in-chief of the army and navy of the United States, and of the militia of the several States when called into actual service of the United States . . . except in cases of impeachment."

And by the 6th art., "The members of the several state legislatures, and all the executive and judicial officers; both of the United States, and of the several states, shall be bound by oath or affirmation to support the constitution."

Can this oath be taken by those who have already taken one under the constitution of this state? . . . From these powers lodged in Congress and the powers vested in the states, it is clear that there must be a government within a government; two legislative, executive, and judicial powers. The power of raising an army in time of peace, and to command the militia, will give the president ample means to enforce the supreme laws of the land. . . .

42

This paragraph provides "that it shalt be in the discretion of the legislature to naturalize all such persons and in such manner as they shall think proper."

The 1st art., 8th sec., 4th clause, give to the new government power to establish a uniform rule of naturalization. And by the 4th art., 2nd sec., "the citizens of each state shall be entitled to all the privileges and immunities of citizens in the several states," whereby the clause is rendered entirely nugatory.

From this contrast it appears that the general government, when completely organized, will absorb all those powers of the state which the framers of its constitution had declared should be only exercised by the representatives of the people of the state; that the burdens and expense of supporting a state establishment will be perpetuated; but its operations to ensure or contribute to any essential measures promotive of the happiness of the people may be totally prostrated, the general government arrogating to itself the right of interfering in the most minute objects of internal police, and the most trifling domestic concerns of every state, by possessing a power of passing laws "to provide for the general welfare of the United States," which may affect life, liberty and property in every modification they may think expedient, unchecked by cautionary reservations, and unrestrained by a declaration of any of those rights which the wisdom and prudence of America in the year 1776 held ought to be at all events protected from violation.

In a word, the new constitution will prove finally to dissolve all the power of the several state legislatures, and destroy the rights and liberties of the people; for the power of the first will be all in all, and of the latter a mere shadow and form without substance, and if adopted we may (in imitation of the Carthagenians) say, *Delenda vit America*.

James Madison  **NO**

Federalist Paper No. 45: The Alleged Danger from the Powers of the Union to the State Governments Considered for the Independent Journal

To the People of the State of New York:

Having shown that no one of the powers transferred to the federal government is unnecessary or improper, the next question to be considered is, whether the whole mass of them will be dangerous to the portion of authority left in the several States.

The adversaries to the plan of the convention, instead of considering in the first place what degree of power was absolutely necessary for the purposes of the federal government, have exhausted themselves in a secondary inquiry into the possible consequences of the proposed degree of power to the governments of the particular States. But if the Union, as has been shown, be essential to the security of the people of America against foreign danger; if it be essential to their security against contentions and wars among the different States; if it be essential to guard them against those violent and oppressive factions which embitter the blessings of liberty, and against those military establishments which must gradually poison its very fountain; if, in a word, the Union be essential to the happiness of the people of America, is it not preposterous, to urge as an objection to a government, without which the objects of the Union cannot be attained, that such a government may derogate from the importance of the governments of the individual States? Was, then, the American Revolution effected, was the American Confederacy formed, was the precious blood of thousands spilt, and the hard-earned substance of millions lavished, not that the people of America should enjoy peace, liberty, and safety, but that the government of the individual States, that particular municipal establishments, might enjoy a certain extent of power, and be arrayed with certain dignities and attributes of sovereignty? We have heard of the impious doctrine in the Old World, that the people were made for kings, not kings for the people.

From *The Federalist No. 45*, 1788.

Is the same doctrine to be revived in the New, in another shape that the solid happiness of the people is to be sacrificed to the views of political institutions of a different form? It is too early for politicians to presume on our forgetting that the public good, the real welfare of the great body of the people, is the supreme object to be pursued; and that no form of government whatever has any other value than as it may be fitted for the attainment of this object. Were the plan of the convention adverse to the public happiness, my voice would be, Reject the plan. Were the Union itself inconsistent with the public happiness, it would be, Abolish the Union. In like manner, as far as the sovereignty of the States cannot be reconciled to the happiness of the people, the voice of every good citizen must be, Let the former be sacrificed to the latter. How far the sacrifice is necessary, has been shown. How far the unsacrificed residue will be endangered, is the question before us.

Several important considerations have been touched in the course of these papers, which discountenance the supposition that the operation of the federal government will by degrees prove fatal to the State governments. The more I revolve the subject, the more fully I am persuaded that the balance is much more likely to be disturbed by the preponderancy of the last than of the first scale.

We have seen, in all the examples of ancient and modern confederacies, the strongest tendency continually betraying itself in the members, to despoil the general government of its authorities, with a very ineffectual capacity in the latter to defend itself against the encroachments. Although, in most of these examples, the system has been so dissimilar from that under consideration as greatly to weaken any inference concerning the latter from the fate of the former, yet, as the States will retain, under the proposed Constitution, a very extensive portion of active sovereignty, the inference ought not to be wholly disregarded. In the Achaean league it is probable that the federal head had a degree and species of power, which gave it a considerable likeness to the government framed by the convention. The Lycian Confederacy, as far as its principles and form are transmitted, must have borne a still greater analogy to it. Yet history does not inform us that either of them ever degenerated, or tended to degenerate, into one consolidated government. On the contrary, we know that the ruin of one of them proceeded from the incapacity of the federal authority to prevent the dissensions, and finally the disunion, of the subordinate authorities. These cases are the more worthy of our attention, as the external causes by which the component parts were pressed together were much more numerous and powerful than in our case; and consequently less powerful ligaments within would be sufficient to bind the members to the head, and to each other.

In the feudal system, we have seen a similar propensity exemplified. Notwithstanding the want of proper sympathy in every instance between the local sovereigns and the people, and the sympathy in some instances between the general sovereign and the latter, it usually happened that the local sovereigns prevailed in the rivalship for encroachments. Had no external dangers enforced internal harmony and subordination, and particularly, had the local sovereigns possessed the affections of the people, the great kingdoms in

Europe would at this time consist of as many independent princes as there were formerly feudatory barons.

The State government will have the advantage of the Federal government, whether we compare them in respect to the immediate dependence of the one on the other; to the weight of personal influence which each side will possess; to the powers respectively vested in them; to the predilection and probable support of the people; to the disposition and faculty of resisting and frustrating the measures of each other.

The State governments may be regarded as constituent and essential parts of the federal government; whilst the latter is nowise essential to the operation or organization of the former. Without the intervention of the State legislatures, the President of the United States cannot be elected at all. They must in all cases have a great share in his appointment, and will, perhaps, in most cases, of themselves determine it. The Senate will be elected absolutely and exclusively by the State legislatures. Even the House of Representatives, though drawn immediately from the people, will be chosen very much under the influence of that class of men, whose influence over the people obtains for themselves an election into the State legislatures. Thus, each of the principal branches of the federal government will owe its existence more or less to the favor of the State governments, and must consequently feel a dependence, which is much more likely to beget a disposition too obsequious than too overbearing towards them. On the other side, the component parts of the State governments will in no instance be indebted for their appointment to the direct agency of the federal government, and very little, if at all, to the local influence of its members.

The number of individuals employed under the Constitution of the United States will be much smaller than the number employed under the particular States. There will consequently be less of personal influence on the side of the former than of the latter. The members of the legislative, executive, and judiciary departments of thirteen and more States, the justices of peace, officers of militia, ministerial officers of justice, with all the county, corporation, and town officers, for three millions and more of people, intermixed, and having particular acquaintance with every class and circle of people, must exceed, beyond all proportion, both in number and influence, those of every description who will be employed in the administration of the federal system. Compare the members of the three great departments of the thirteen States, excluding from the judiciary department the justices of peace, with the members of the corresponding departments of the single government of the Union; compare the militia officers of three millions of people with the military and marine officers of any establishment which is within the compass of probability, or, I may add, of possibility, and in this view alone, we may pronounce the advantage of the States to be decisive. If the federal government is to have collectors of revenue, the State governments will have theirs also. And as those of the former will be principally on the seacoast, and not very numerous, whilst those of the latter will be spread over the face of the country, and will be very numerous, the advantage in this view also lies on the same side. It is true, that the Confederacy is to possess, and may exercise, the power of collecting internal as well as external taxes throughout the States; but it is probable that this power will not be resorted to, except for supplemental purposes of revenue; that an option will then be given to the States to supply their quotas by previous collections of their own; and that the eventual collection, under the immediate authority of the Union, will generally be made by the officers, and according to the rules, appointed by the several States. Indeed it is extremely probable, that in other instances, particularly in the organization of the judicial power, the officers of the States will be clothed with the correspondent authority of the Union. Should it happen, however, that separate collectors of internal revenue should be appointed under the federal government, the influence of the whole number would not bear a comparison with that of the multitude of State officers in the opposite scale. Within every district to which a federal collector would be allotted, there would not be less than thirty or forty, or even more, officers of different descriptions, and many of them persons of character and weight, whose influence would lie on the side of the State.

The powers delegated by the proposed Constitution to the federal government are few and defined. Those which are to remain in the State governments are numerous and indefinite. The former will be exercised principally on external objects, as war, peace, negotiation, and foreign commerce; with which last the power of taxation will, for the most part, be connected. The powers reserved to the several States will extend to all the objects which, in the ordinary course of affairs, concern the lives, liberties, and properties of the people, and the internal order, improvement, and prosperity of the State.

The operations of the federal government will be most extensive and important in times of war and danger; those of the State governments, in times of peace and security. As the former periods will probably bear a small proportion to the latter, the State governments will here enjoy another advantage over the federal government. The more adequate, indeed, the federal powers may be rendered to the national defense, the less frequent will be those scenes of danger which might favor their ascendancy over the governments of the particular States.

If the new Constitution be examined with accuracy and candor, it will be found that the change which it proposes consists much less in the addition of NEW POWERS to the Union, than in the invigoration of its ORIGINAL POWERS. The regulation of commerce, it is true, is a new power; but that seems to be an addition which few oppose, and from which no apprehensions are entertained. The powers relating to war and peace, armies and fleets, treaties and finance, with the other more considerable powers, are all vested in the existing Congress by the articles of Confederation. The proposed change does not enlarge these powers; it only substitutes a more effectual mode of administering them. The change relating to taxation may be regarded as the most important; and yet the present Congress have as complete authority to REQUIRE of the States indefinite supplies of money for the common defense and general welfare, as the future Congress will have to require them of individual citizens; and the latter will be no more bound than the States themselves have been, to pay the quotas respectively taxed on them. Had the States complied punctually with the articles of Confederation, or could their compliance have been enforced by as peaceable means as may be used with success towards single persons, our past experience is very far from countenancing an opinion, that the State governments would have lost their constitutional powers, and have gradually undergone an entire consolidation. To maintain that such an event would have ensued, would be to say at once, that the existence of the State governments is incompatible with any system whatever that accomplishes the essential purposes of the Union.

PUBLIUS.

POSTSCRIPT

Should We Protect States' Rights over the Federal Government?

Just a few years after the Federalist/Anti-Federalist debate over states' rights, the dispute flickered again briefly in the Supreme Court; it still tempers today. For example, 37 "State Sovereignty Resolutions," also called "Tenth Amendment Resolutions," in as many states, have been introduced in their respective state legislatures, seven of which passed—Oklahoma, Alaska, Tennessee, Idaho, Louisiana, North Dakota, and South Dakota.[1] This legislation symbolically gives "notice and demand" to the federal government to "cease and desist any and all activities outside the scope of their constitutionally delegated powers."[2]

The balance of powers between the federal government and the states is defined in the U.S. Constitution's Supremacy Clause, Article VI, paragraph 2. The Supremacy Clause established the U.S. Constitution, federal statutes, as well as U.S. treaties to be treated as "the supreme law of the land." Justices are expected to uphold these sources of American law. State judges are mandated to uphold them, even if state law interpretations conflict.

The Supremacy Clause was upheld in *McCulloch v. Maryland* in 1819.[3] In this case, Chief Justice John Marshall asserted the Supremacy Clause as paramount over state laws. Maryland attempted to stop the Second Bank of the United States's operation through the imposition of a tax on all notes that did not have Maryland charters. At this point in history, this U.S. bank was the only "out-of-state" bank in Maryland's borders. For the first time, the Constitution's Article I, Section 8 "Necessary and Proper Clause" was invoked because the implied powers failed to deal with this issue.

The head of the Baltimore Bank Branch, James McCulloch, refused to pay the tax imposed on "out-of-state" banks.[4] Maryland said that because the U.S. Constitution did not specifically note with its expressed powers that the federal government could charter a bank, the Second Bank was unconstitutionally organized and had no authority to deny the tax. The Supreme Court, headed by Justice John Marshall, reversed the appellate win of Maryland to side with McCulloch, because the expressed powers are actually too numerous to list and therefore, sometimes, the "necessary and proper clause" is appropriate, as long as the power is rationally applied and not already prohibited by the U.S. Constitution.

More recently, in a 2001 Supreme Court case, the *Board of Trustees of the University of Alabama v. Garrett*, 531 U.S. 356, explored the enforcement powers Congress has under the Constitution's Fourteenth Amendment.[5] The court found that the Americans with Disabilities Act (ADA), a federal law, was unconstitutional in that it allowed private citizens to sue states for civil damages. In this case, the U.S. Supreme Court bucked the Supremacy Clause in siding with the states over a federal government law, showing chinks in the armor of the Supremacy Clause.

Historically, states' rights also have been used as code words.[6] The States' Rights Democratic Party broke away from the Democratic Party in 1948. In their party platform, they vigorously opposed racial integration, pushing to keep Jim Crow laws as well as white supremacy alive. Often known as "Dixiecrats," the States' Rights Party embraced the slogan "Segregation Forever!" Strom Thurmond ran on the States' Rights Democratic Party presidential ticket in 1948. Later, George Wallace claimed that segregation was a symbol of the larger states' rights struggle.

Notes

1. Tenth Amendment Center. Accessed December 7, 2009, http://www .tenthamendmentcenter.com/nullification/10th-amendment-resolutions/

2. *Ibid.*

3. *McCulloch v. State,* 17 U.S. 316, 1819. 17 U.S. 316 (Wheat.) *McCulloch v. State of Maryland et al.,* February Term, 1819. *FindLaw.* Accessed December 1, 2009, http://caselaw.lp.findlaw.com/scripts/getcase.pl?court= US&vol=17&invol=316

4. *Ibid.*

5. *Board of Trustees of the University of Alabama v. Garrett,* 531 U.S. 356. Cornell School of Law. Accessed December 1, 2009, http://www.law.cornell.edu/ supct/html/99-1240.ZS.html

6. Allen Lichtman, *White Protestant Nation: The Rise of the American Conservative Movement* (Atlantic Monthly Press, 2008).

ISSUE 4

Are "Checks and Balances" Enough to Protect Our Rights?

YES: Publius (a.k.a. James Madison), "The Structure of the Government Must Furnish the Proper Checks and Balances Between the Different Departments," *The Federalist,* No. 51 (February 6, 1788)

NO: Aristocrotis (a.k.a. William Petrikin), from "Do Checks and Balances Really Secure the Rights of the People?" *Anti-Federalist* No. 51, from *Government of Nature Delineated; Or An Exact Picture of the New Federal Constitution* (Carlisle, PA, 1788)

ISSUE SUMMARY

YES: Publius (James Madison) pushes for both a separation of powers and checks and balances to safeguard liberty and our rights.

NO: Aristocrotis (William Petrikin) writes a tongue-in-cheek, yet serious attempt, to counter this new constitution, which is in the Anti-Federalist's view, a serious invasion of individual liberty through a tyrannical and unlimitedly powerful government.

Publius, also known as James Madison, wrote the 51st *Federalist Paper* on February 6, 1788. This paper was one of the more famous of the 85 articles that appeared in both the *New York Packet* and the *Independent Journal* between October 1787 and 1788.

The 51st *Federalist Paper* discusses the both checks and balances and the separation of powers for a new constitution (our current U.S. Constitution). Most notably is Madison's justification for a separation of powers where he argues that "Ambition must be made to counteract ambition." This sentiment can also be found in Madison's concern with the ever present problem of factions—interest groups—by countering them with other numerous factions.

In opposition to Madison's tome is William Petrikin's satire. Petrikin was a Pennsylvania tailor and Scottish Immigrant, who likely penned this issue's *Anti-Federalist* No. 51, under the alias "Aristocrotis." Unlike the *Federalist Papers,* which systematically defended the Constitution, the *Anti-Federalist Papers* were later collected by Morton Borden, arranging them to mirror the *Federalist Papers.* A main focus of this *Anti-Federalist* No. 51 is that this new concept of checks and balances by Madison was not highly regarded by the Anti-Federalists. Their focus was instead on the unlimited taxing power of the Constitution through Congress. He also finds that the Anti-Federalists saw the Constitution's ability to raise and maintain a standing army during peacetime as ominous, leading eventually to empire both at home and abroad.

Petrikin found the whole argument of a separation of powers an invasion of individual liberty through a tyrannical and unlimitedly powerful government. He sarcastically exclaims:

Happy thy servants! happy thy vassals! and happy thy slaves, which fit under the shade of thy omnipotent authority, and behold the glory of thy majesty! For such a state who would not part with ideal blessings of liberty? Who would not cheerfully resign the nominal advantages of freedom?

Furthermore, in this Federalist paper, Madison argues this new Constitution, crafted in the Constitutional Convention, creates a "more correct judgment of the principles and structure of the government. He explains that the convention created safeguards to protect people's rights. One of the safeguards is to keep separate branches from appointing others and if this principle is "rigorously adhered to," each branch would be more directly elected by the people.

However, Petrikin argues that our freedoms are actually uninterruptable and their meaning fuzzy in this new document. He says, "for the convention has so happily worded themselves, that every part of this constitution either bears double meaning, or no meaning at all; and if any concessions are made to the people in one place, it is effectually canceled in another. . . . "

Additionally, Madison argues, judicial members should be insulated from political pressure, which could lead to biased judgments by people who are positioned to be nonpartisan and impartial. Likewise, since the legislative branch is so powerful, it should be divided into two different chambers with different election cycles. In contrast, Petrikin expressed concerns about the separate branches, fearing they would become powerful and uncontrollable tyrannies. Later, the Anti-Federalists would counter the Federalists by pushing and passing a Bill of Rights, something the Federalists only reluctantly agreed to, passing a couple years after the Constitution itself in 1791.

Furthermore, the government, he says, would be divided both through three branches and federalism—federal from the state. He notes that because of this division of power, a "double security arises to the rights of the people. The governments will control each other, at the same time that each will be controlled by itself."

On the other hand, Paul Ellenbogen argues along with other Anti-Federalists that the upper chamber, the Senate, was created as a way to maintain a balance between the "natural aristocracy" (the few) and the people (the many), not as a compromise between large and small states.

These arguments, more than 200 years old, continue between those who trust a stronger national government with checks and balances among branches and those who want a more decentralized government without a standing army or the ability to tax.

Federalist Paper No. 51: The Structure of the Government Must Furnish the Proper Checks and Balances Between the Different Departments

To the People of the State of New York:

To what expedient, then, shall we finally resort, for maintaining in practice the necessary partition of power among the several departments, as laid down in the Constitution? The only answer that can be given is, that as all these exterior provisions are found to be inadequate, the defect must be supplied, by so contriving the interior structure of the government as that its several constituent parts may, by their mutual relations, be the means of keeping each other in their proper places. Without presuming to undertake a full development of this important idea, I will hazard a few general observations, which may perhaps place it in a clearer light, and enable us to form a more correct judgment of the principles and structure of the government planned by the convention.

In order to lay a due foundation for that separate and distinct exercise of the different powers of government, which to a certain extent is admitted on all hands to be essential to the preservation of liberty, it is evident that each department should have a will of its own; and consequently should be so constituted that the members of each should have as little agency as possible in the appointment of the members of the others. Were this principle rigorously adhered to, it would require that all the appointments for the supreme executive, legislative, and judiciary magistracies should be drawn from the same fountain of authority, the people, through channels having no communication whatever with one another. Perhaps such a plan of constructing the several departments would be less difficult in practice than it may in contemplation appear. Some difficulties, however, and some additional expense would attend the execution of it. Some deviations, therefore, from the principle must be admitted. In the constitution of the judiciary department in particular, it might be inexpedient to insist rigorously on the principle: first, because peculiar qualifications being essential in the members, the primary consideration ought to be to select that mode of choice which best secures

From *The Federalist* No. 51, 1787.

these qualifications; secondly, because the permanent tenure by which the appointments are held in that department, must soon destroy all sense of dependence on the authority conferring them.

It is equally evident, that the members of each department should be as little dependent as possible on those of the others, for the emoluments annexed to their offices. Were the executive magistrate, or the judges, not independent of the legislature in this particular, their independence in every other would be merely nominal.

But the great security against a gradual concentration of the several powers in the same department, consists in giving to those who administer each department the necessary constitutional means and personal motives to resist encroachments of the others. The provision for defense must in this, as in all other cases, be made commensurate to the danger of attack. Ambition must be made to counteract ambition. The interest of the man must be connected with the constitutional rights of the place. It may be a reflection on human nature, that such devices should be necessary to control the abuses of government. But what is government itself, but the greatest of all reflections on human nature? If men were angels, no government would be necessary. If angels were to govern men, neither external nor internal controls on government would be necessary. In framing a government which is to be administered by men over men, the great difficulty lies in this: you must first enable the government to control the governed; and in the next place oblige it to control itself. A dependence on the people is, no doubt, the primary control on the government; but experience has taught mankind the necessity of auxiliary precautions.

This policy of supplying, by opposite and rival interests, the defect of better motives, might be traced through the whole system of human affairs, private as well as public. We see it particularly displayed in all the subordinate distributions of power, where the constant aim is to divide and arrange the several offices in such a manner as that each may be a check on the other—that the private interest of every individual may be a sentinel over the public rights. These inventions of prudence cannot be less requisite in the distribution of the supreme powers of the State.

But it is not possible to give to each department an equal power of self-defense. In republican government, the legislative authority necessarily predominates. The remedy for this inconveniency is to divide the legislature into different branches; and to render them, by different modes of election and different principles of action, as little connected with each other as the nature of their common functions and their common dependence on the society will admit. It may even be necessary to guard against dangerous encroachments by still further precautions. As the weight of the legislative authority requires that it should be thus divided, the weakness of the executive may require, on the other hand, that it should be fortified. An absolute negative on the legislature appears, at first view, to be the natural defense with which the executive magistrate should be armed. But perhaps it would be neither altogether safe nor alone sufficient. On ordinary occasions it might not be exerted with the requisite firmness, and on extraordinary occasions it might be perfidiously abused. May not this defect of an absolute negative be supplied by some qualified connection between this weaker department and the weaker branch of the stronger department, by which the latter may be led to support the constitutional rights of the former, without being too much detached from the rights of its own department?

If the principles on which these observations are founded be just, as I persuade myself they are, and they be applied as a criterion to the several State constitutions, and to the federal Constitution it will be found that if the latter does not perfectly correspond with them, the former are infinitely less able to bear such a test.

There are, moreover, two considerations particularly applicable to the federal system of America, which place that system in a very interesting point of view.

First. In a single republic, all the power surrendered by the people is submitted to the administration of a single government; and the usurpations are guarded against by a division of the government into distinct and separate departments. In the compound republic of America, the power surrendered by the people is first divided between two distinct governments, and then the portion allotted to each subdivided among distinct and separate departments. Hence a double security arises to the rights of the people. The different governments will control each other, at the same time that each will be controlled by itself.

Second. It is of great importance in a republic not only to guard the society against the oppression of its rulers, but to guard one part of the society against the injustice of the other part. Different interests necessarily exist in different classes of citizens. If a majority be united by a common interest, the rights of the minority will be insecure. There are but two methods of providing against this evil: the one by creating a will in the community independent of the majority—that is, of the society itself; the other, by comprehending in the society so many separate descriptions of citizens as will render an unjust combination of a majority of the whole very improbable, if not impracticable. The first method prevails in all governments possessing an hereditary or self-appointed authority. This, at best, is but a precarious security; because a power independent of the society may as well espouse the unjust views of the major, as the rightful interests of the minor party, and may possibly be turned against both parties. The second method will be exemplified in the federal republic of the United States. Whilst all authority in it will be derived from and dependent on the society, the society itself will be broken into so many parts, interests, and classes of citizens, that the rights of individuals, or of the minority, will be in little danger from interested combinations of the majority. In a free government the security for civil rights must be the same as that for religious rights. It consists in the one case in the multiplicity of interests, and in the other in the multiplicity of sects. The degree of security in both cases will depend on the number of interests and sects; and this may be presumed to depend on the extent of country and number of people comprehended under the same government. This view of the subject must particularly recommend a proper federal system to all the sincere and considerate friends of republican government, since it shows that in exact proportion as the territory of the Union may be formed into more circumscribed Confederacies, or States oppressive combinations of a majority will be facilitated: the best security, under the republican forms, for the rights of every class of citizens, will be diminished: and consequently the stability and independence of some member of the government, the only other security, must be proportionately increased. Justice is the end of government. It is the end of civil society. It ever has been and ever will be pursued until it be obtained, or until liberty be lost in the pursuit. In a society under the forms of which the stronger faction can readily unite and oppress the weaker, anarchy may as truly be said to reign as in a state of nature, where the weaker individual is not secured against the violence of the stronger; and as, in the latter state, even the stronger individuals are prompted, by the uncertainty of their condition, to submit to a government which may protect the weak as well as themselves; so, in the former state, will the more powerful factions or parties be gradnally induced, by a like motive, to wish for a government which will protect all parties, the weaker as well as the more powerful. It can be little doubted that if the State of Rhode Island was separated from the Confederacy and left to itself, the insecurity of rights under the popular form of government within such narrow limits would be displayed by such reiterated oppressions of factious majorities that some power altogether independent of the people would soon be called for by the voice of the very factions whose misrule had proved the necessity of it. In the extended republic of the United States, and among the great variety of interests, parties, and sects which it embraces, a coalition of a majority of the whole society could seldom take place on any other principles than those of justice and the general good; whilst there being thus less danger to a minor from the will of a major party, there must be less pretext, also, to provide for the security of the former, by introducing into the government a will not dependent on the latter, or, in other words, a will independent of the society itself. It is no less certain than it is important, notwithstanding the contrary opinions which have been entertained, that the larger the society, provided it lie within a practical sphere, the more duly capable it will be of self-government. And happily for the *republican cause*, the practicable sphere may be carried to a very great extent, by a judicious modification and mixture of the *federal principle*.

PUBLIUS

William Petrikin

 **NO**

Anti-Federalist No. 51: Do Checks and Balances Really Secure the Rights of the People?

The present is an active period. Europe is in a ferment breaking their constitutions; America is in a similar state, making a constitution. For this valuable purpose a convention was appointed, consisting of such as excelled in wisdom and knowledge, who met in Philadelphia last May. For my own part, I was so smitten with the character of the members, that I had assented to their production, while it was yet in embryo. And I make no doubt but every good republican did so too. But how great was my surprise, when it appeared with such a venerable train of names annexed to its tail, to find some of the people under different signatures—such as Centinel, Old Whig, Brutus, etc.—daring to oppose it, and that too with barefaced arguments, obstinate reason and stubborn truth. This is certainly a piece of the most extravagant impudence to presume to contradict the collected wisdom of the United States; or to suppose a body, who engrossed the whole wisdom of the continent, was capable of erring. I expected the superior character of the convention would have secured it from profane sallies of a plebeian's pen; and its inherent infallibility debarred the interference of impertinent reason or truth. It was too great an act of condescension to permit the people, by their state conventions, "to assent and ratify," what the grand convention prescribed to them; but to inquire into its principles, or investigate its properties, was a presumption too daring to escape resentment. Such licentious conduct practiced by the people, is a striking proof of our feeble governments, and calls aloud for the pruning knife, i.e., the establishment of some proper plan of discipline. This the convention, in the depth of their united wisdom hath prescribed, which when established, will certainly put a stop to the growing evil. A consciousness of this, is, no doubt, the cause which stimulates the people to oppose it with so much vehemence. They deprecate the idea of being confined within their proper sphere; they cannot endure the thought of being obliged to mind their own business, and leave the affairs of government to those whom nature hath destined to rule. I say nature, for it is a fundamental principle, as clear as an axiom, that nature hath placed proper degrees and subordinations amongst mankind and ordained a few[1] to rule, and many to obey. I am not obliged to prove this principle because it would be madness in the extreme to attempt to prove a self-evident truth.

From *Antifederalist Papers*, No. 51, 1788.

But with all due submission to the infallible wisdom of the grand convention, let me presume to examine whether they have not, in the new plan of government, inviolably adhered to this supreme principle. . . .

In article first, section first, of the new plan, it is declared that "all legislative powers herein granted shall be vested in a Congress of the United States which shall consist of a Senate"—very right, quite agreeable to nature "and House of Representatives"—not quite so right. This is a palpable compliance with the humors and corrupt practices of the times. But what follows in section 2 is still worse: "The House of Representatives shall be composed of members chosen every second year by the people of the several states." This is a most dangerous power, and must soon produce fatal and pernicious consequences, were it not circumscribed and poised by proper checks and balances. But in this is displayed the unparalleled sagacity of the August convention: that when such bulwarks of prejudice surrounded the evil, so as to render it both difficult and dangerous to attack it by assault and storm, they have invested and barricaded it so closely as will certainly deprive it of its baneful influence and prevent its usual encroachments. They have likewise stationed their miners and sappers so judiciously, that they will certainly, in process of time, entirely reduce and demolish this obnoxious practice of popular election. There is a small thrust given to it in the body of the conveyance itself. The term of holding elections is every two years; this is much better than the detestable mode of annual elections, so fatal to energy. However, if nothing more than this were done, it would still remain an insupportable inconvenience. But in section 4 it is provided that congress by law may alter and make such regulations with respect to the times, places, and manner of holding elections, as to them seemeth fit and proper. This is certainly a very salutary provision, most excellently adapted to counterbalance the great and apparently dangerous concessions made to the plebeians in the first and second sections. With such a prudent restriction as this they are quite harmless: no evil can arise from them if congress have only the sagacity and fortitude to avail themselves of the power they possess by this section. For when the stated term (for which the primary members was elected) is nigh expired, congress may appoint [the] next election to be held in one place in each state; and so as not to give the rabble needless disgust, they may appoint the most central place for that purpose. They can never be at a loss for an ostensible reason to vary and shift from place to place until they may fix it at any extremity of the state it suits. This will be the business of the senate, to observe the particular places in each state, where their influence is most extensive, and where the inhabitants are most obsequious to the will of their superiors, and there appoint the elections to be held. By this means, such members will be returned to the house of representatives (as it is called) as the president and senate shall be pleased to recommend; and they no doubt will recommend such gentlemen only as are distinguished by some peculiar federal feature—so that unanimity and concord will shine conspicuous through every branch of government. This section is ingeniously calculated, and must have been intended by the convention, to exterminate electioneering entirely. For by putting the time of election in the hands of congress they have thereby given them a power to perpetuate themselves when they shall find it safe and convenient to make the experiment. For though a preceding clause says, "that representatives shall be chosen for two years, and senators for six years," yet this clause being subsequent annuls the former, and puts it in the power of congress, (when some favorable juncture intervenes) to alter the time to four and twelve years. This cannot be deemed an unconstitutional stretch of power, for the constitution in express terms puts the time of holding elections in their power, and certainly they are the proper judges when to exert that power. Thus by doubling the period from time to time, its extent will soon be rendered coeval with the life of man. And it is but a very short and easy transition from this to hereditary succession, which is most agreeable to the institutions of nature, who in all her works, hath ordained the descendant of every species of beings to succeed its immediate progenitor, in the same actions, ends and order.

The indefatigable laborious ass never aspires to the honors, nor assumes the employment of the sprightly warlike steed, nor does he ever pretend that it is his right to succeed him in all his offices and dignities, because he bears some resemblance to the defunct in his figure and nature. The llama, though useful enough for the purposes for which he was intended by nature, is every way incompetent to perform the offices of the elephant; nor does he ever pretend to usurp his elevated station. Every species of beings, animate and inanimate, seem fully satisfied with the station assigned them by nature. But perverse, obstinate man, he alone spurns at her institutions, and inverts her order.[2] He alone repines at his situation, and endeavors to usurp the station of his superiors. But this digression has led me from the subject in hand. . . .

The next object that presents itself is the power which the new constitution gives to congress to regulate the manner of elections. The common practice of voting at present is by ballot. By this mode it is impossible for a gentleman to know how he is served by his dependent, who may be possessed of a vote. Therefore this mode must be speedily altered for that viva voce, which will secure to a rich man all the votes of his numerous dependents and friends and their dependents. By this means he may command any office in the gift of the people, which he pleases to set up for. This will answer a good end while electioneering exists; and will likewise contribute something towards its destruction. A government founded agreeable to nature must be entirely independent; that is, it must be beyond the reach of annoyance or control from every power on earth, Now in order to render it thus, several things are necessary.

1st. The means of their own support must be within the immediate reach of the rulers. For this purpose they must possess the sole power of taxation. As this is a principal article, it ought, in all things to have preeminence; and therefore the convention has placed it in front. "The congress shall have power to lay and collect taxes, duties, imposts and excises," so that they shall never be at a loss for money while there is a shilling on the continent, for their power to procure it is as extensive as their desires; and so it ought, because they can never desire any thing but is good and salutary. For there is no doubt but the convention will transfer their infallibility to the new congress, and so secure them from doing evil. This power of taxation will answer many valuable purposes, besides the support of government. In the first place, in the course of its operation, it will annihilate the relics of the several state legislators. For every tax which they may lay, will be deemed by congress an infringement upon the federal constitution, which constitution and the laws of congress being paramount to all other authority, will of consequence nullify every inferior law which the several states may think proper to enact, particularly such as relate to taxes; so that they being deprived of the means of existence, their pretended sovereignties will gradually wither away.

2dly. It will create and diffuse a spirit of industry among the people. They will then be obliged to labor for money to pay their taxes. There will be no trifling from time to time, as is done now. The new government will have energy sufficient to compel immediate payment.

3dly. This will make the people attend to their own business, and not be dabbling in politics—things they are entirely ignorant of; nor is it proper they should understand. But it is very probable that the exercise of this power may be opposed by the refractory plebeians, who (such is the perverseness of their natures) often refuse to comply with what is manifestly for their advantage. But to prevent all inconvenience from this quarter the congress have power to raise and support armies. This is the second thing necessary to render government independent. The creatures who compose these armies are a species of animals, wholly at the disposal of government; what others call their natural rights they resign into the hands of their superiors—even the right of self-preservation (so precious to all other beings) they entirely surrender, and put their very lives in the power of their masters. Having no rights of their own to care for, they become naturally jealous and envious of those possessed by others. They are therefore proper instruments in the hands of government to divest the people of their usurped rights. But the capital business of these armies will be to assist the collectors of taxes, imposts, and excise, in raising the revenue; and this they will perform with the greatest alacrity, as it is by this they are supported; but for this they would be in a great measure useless; and without this they could not exist. . . .

From these remarks, I think it is evident, that the grand convention hath dexterously provided for the removal of every thing that hath ever operated as a restraint upon government in any place or age of the world. But perhaps some weak heads may think that the constitution itself will be a check upon the new congress. But this I deny, for the convention has so happily worded themselves, that every part of this constitution either bears double meaning, or no meaning at all; and if any concessions are made to the people in one place, it is effectually canceled in another—so that in fact this constitution is much better and gives more scope to the rulers than they durst safely take if there was no constitution at all. For then the people might contend that the power was inherent in them, and that they had made some implied reserves in the original grant. But now they cannot, for every thing is expressly given away to government in this plan. Perhaps some people may think that power which the house of representatives possesses, of impeaching the officers of government, will be a restraint upon them. But this entirely vanishes, when it is considered that the senate hath the principal say in appointing these officers, and that they are the sole judges of all impeachments. Now it would be absurd to suppose that they would remove their own servants for performing their secret orders. . . . For the interest of rulers and the ruled will then be two distinct things. The mode of electing the president is another excellent regulation, most wisely calculated to render him the obsequious machine of congress. He is to be chosen by electors appointed in such manner as the state legislators shall direct. But then the highest in votes cannot be president, without he has the majority of all the electors; and if none have this majority, then the congress is to choose the president out of the five highest on the return. By this means the congress will always have the making of the president after the first election. So that if the reigning president pleases his masters, he need be under no apprehensions of being turned out for any severities used to the people, for though the congress may not have influence enough to procure him the majority of the votes of the electoral college, yet they will always be able to prevent any other from having such a majority; and to have him returned among the five highest, so that they may have the appointing of him themselves. All these wise regulations, prove to a demonstration, that the grand convention was infallible. The congress having thus disentangled themselves from all popular checks and choices, and being supported by a well disciplined army and active militia, will certainly command dread and respect abroad, obedience and submission at home. They will then look down with awful dignity and tremendous majesty from the pinnacle of glory to which fortune has raised them upon the insignificant creatures, their subjects, whom they have reduced to that state of vassalage and servile submission, for which they were primarily destined by nature. America will then be great amongst the nations[3] and princess amongst the provinces. Her fleets will cover the deserts of the ocean and convert it into a popular city; and her invincible armies overturn the thrones of princes. The glory of Britain[4] shall fall like lightning before her puissant arm; when she ariseth to shake the nations, and take vengeance on all who dare oppose her. O! thou most venerable and August congress! with what astonishing ideas my mind is ravished! when I contemplate thy rising grandeur, and anticipate thy future glory! Happy thy servants! happy thy vassals! and happy thy slaves, which fit under the shade of thy omnipotent authority, and behold the glory of thy majesty! for such a state who would not part with ideal blessings of liberty? who would not cheerfully resign the nominal advantages of freedom? the dazzling splendor of Assyrian, Persian, Macedonian and Roman greatness will then be totally eclipsed by the radiant blaze of this glorious western luminary! These beautiful expressions, aristocracy, and oligarchy, upon which the popular odium hath fixed derision and contempt, will then resume their natural emphasis; their genuine signification will be perfectly understood, and no more perverted or abused.

ARISTOCROTIS

1. If any person is so stupidly dull as not to discern who these few are, I would refer such to nature herself for information. Let them observe her ways and be wise. Let them mark those men whom she hath endued with the necessary qualifications of authority; such as the dictatorial air, the magisterial voice, the imperious tone, the haughty

countenance, the lofty look, the majestic mien. Let them consider those whom she hath taught to command with authority, but comply with disgust; to be fond of sway, but impatient of control; to consider themselves as Gods, and all the rest of mankind as two-legged brutes. Now it is evident that the possessors of these divine qualities must have been ordained by nature to dominion and empire; for it would be blasphemy against her supreme highness to suppose that she confers her gifts in vain. Fortune hath also distinguished those upon whom nature hath imprinted the lineaments of authority. She hath heaped her favors and lavished her gifts upon those very persons whom nature delighteth to honor. Indeed, instinct hath taught those men that authority is their natural right, and therefore they grasp at it with an eagerness bordering on rapacity.

2. This is only to be understood of the inferior class of mankind. The superior order have aspiring feelings given them by nature, such as ambition, emulation, etc., which makes it their duty to persevere in the pursuit of gratifying these refined passions.

3. That is, if we may credit the prognostications with which our federal news-papers and pamphlets daily teem.

4. Britain once the supreme ruler of this country, but her authority was rejected. Not, as a great many believe, because her claims were tyrannical and oppressive, but because her dominion excluded those from monopolizing the government into their own hands, whom nature had qualified to rule. It is certainly no more than the natural right of rulers "to bind their subjects, in all cases whatsoever." This power is perfectly synonymous with that clause in the constitution which invests congress with power to make all laws which shall be "necessary and proper for carrying into execution the foregoing powers and all other powers," etc., and that which says "the constitution, laws, and treaties of congress shall be the supreme law of the land; any thing in the constitutions or laws of any of the states to the contrary notwithstanding." But nothing less would satisfy Britain, than a power to bind the natural rulers as well as subjects.

POSTSCRIPT

Are "Checks and Balances" Enough to Protect Our Rights?

The word *federalism* derives from *foedus* in Latin, meaning "formal agreement or covenant."[1] Federalism itself is a covenant between the states and national government. Former Supreme Court Justice Salmon Chase, in *Texas v. White*, said that there is a need for U.S. constitutional limits to avert a concentration of power whether it is at the state or national level.[2]

> [T]he preservation of the States, and the maintenance of their governments, are as much within the design and care of the Constitution, as the preservation of the Union. . . . The Constitution, in all its provisions, looks to an indestructible Union, composed of indestructible States.[3]

Checks and balances is a concept in which separate branches of government are legally able to prevent actions by other branches, whether on the state or the national level, and are forced to share power, especially in constitutional governments.[4] The separation of powers in the United States, into legislative, executive, and judicial branches, is important to ensure that no branch becomes too powerful.

The Greek historian Polybius influenced future scholars on the importance of the separation of powers, through his study of the ancient Roman mixed constitution. This Roman government encompassed three main areas: (1) monarchy, represented by the consul; (2) aristocracy, through the Senate; and (3) democracy, with the people.[5]

In addition, both the separation of powers and the theory of checks and balances ensures no branch is more powerful than the others. Dr. Donald Grinde Jr., history professor at the University of Vermont, found that few people know that at the Constitutional Convention, John Adams gave his colleagues an example of separation of powers by citing the Iroquois Confederacy with its three distinct branches.[6]

Although neither separation of powers nor checks and balances is explicitly written anywhere in the Constitution, there are several places in the text where different branches limit each other. Below are five examples of checks and balances in the Constitution, explicitly in Article I and II. Article III, the judicial branch, later incorporated judicial review through *Marbury v. Madison* (1803).[7]

- **Article I, Section 7—Revenue Bills, Legislative Process, Presidential Veto,** "Every Bill which shall have passed the House of Representatives and the Senate, shall, before it become a Law, be presented to the President of the United States."

- **Article I, Section 3—The Senate**, "The Vice President of the United States shall be President of the Senate, but shall have no Vote, unless they be equally divided."
- **Article I, Section 3—The Senate**, "The Senate shall have the sole Power to try all Impeachments. When sitting for that Purpose, they shall be on Oath or Affirmation. When the President of the United States is tried, the Chief Justice shall preside: And no Person shall be convicted without the Concurrence of two-thirds of the Members present."
- **Article II, Section 3—State of the Union, Convening Congress**, "He shall from time to time give to the Congress Information of the State of the Union,"
- **Article II, Section 1—The President**, "The Congress may determine the Time of chusing the Electors, and the Day on which they shall give their Votes."

Notes

1. Dictionary. Accessed December 7, 2009, http://www.babylon.com/definition/foedus/English

2. *Texas v. White,* 74 U.S. (7 Wall.) 700, 19L. Ed. 227 (1868), http://www.law.cornell.edu/supct/html/historics/USSC_CR_0074_0700_ZO.html

3. Ibid.

4. Joseph Losco and Ralph Baker, *Am Gov 2009* (McGraw-Hill, 2009).

5. Polybius, son of Lycortas, Achaean statesman, wrote a biography of Philopoemen that reflected his admiration for that great Achaean leader; and an interest in military matters found expression in his lost book, *Tactics. Encyclopeadia Britannica*. Accessed December 1, 2009, http://www.britannica.com/EBchecked/topic/468317/Polybius

6. Carol Hiltner, "The Iroquois Confederacy: Our Forgotten National Heritage," *The Spirit of the Ma'at*. vol 2., 2002. Accessed December 1, 2009, http://www.spiritofmaat.com/archive/may2/iroquois.htm

7. H. L. Pohlman, *Constitutional Debate in Action: Governmental Powers* (Lanham: Rowman & Littlefield, 2005).

ISSUE 5

Should We Allow Eminent Domain for Private Use?

YES: John Paul Stevens, from Majority Opinion, *Susette Kelo et al., Petitioners v. City of New London, Connecticut et al.* (June 23, 2005)

NO: Sandra Day O'Conner, from Dissenting Opinion, *Susette Kelo et al., Petitioners v. City of New London, Connecticut et al.* (June 23, 2005)

ISSUE SUMMARY

YES: Justice Stevens's majority opinion supports the city of New London in condemning property for private use.

NO: Justice O'Conner's dissenting opinion supports the Kelo position in saying that eminent domain should clearly be for public use only.

The *Kelo v. City of New London* case was appealed from a decision by the Connecticut Supreme Court in which New London, Connecticut, won.[1] Eminent domain for economic development did not violate the Fifth Amendment's public use section of the U.S. Constitution, according to the state supreme court. Therefore, if an economic development project generates increased taxes and new jobs, and additionally rejuvenates rundown urban areas, then the project is considered a public use even if the project was initiated by a private party.

Even though the City of New London won, the decision was criticized extensively.[2] Several commentators and public opinion charged that this broad view of eminent domain was a violation of the Fifth Amendment, in which private corporations rights trumped private individual homeowner's rights.

Justice John Paul Stevens wrote the majority opinion with four other Justices in a 5-4 decision, favoring the City of New London. Stevens's decision was followed by Justices Steven Breyer, Ruth Bader Ginsburg, David Souter, and Anthony Kennedy. Although Kennedy's vote was counted with the majority, he actually wrote a concurring opinion. His opinion specified in more detail a judicial review on the correct standard for the economic development of property, or what some call "takings," than in Stevens's majority opinion.[3] Basically, Kennedy, while agreeing with the majority, pushed for more evidence to take away someone's property if it is considered dilapidated. Stevens argues that Pfizer's facility would actually create jobs in the area.

Justice Sandra Day O'Conner carved out a dissent, joined by Justices Antonin Scalia, Clarence Thomas, and former Chief Justice William Rehnquist.

Justice O'Connor rejected the idea that unelected and unaccountable private corporations should benefit from eminent domain; in this case Pfizer and its $300 million research facility on a site immediately adjacent to Fort Trumbull, would be the primary beneficiary of this specific taking of property. Therefore, this takings power is not unlike a "reverse Robin Hood," taking from the poor and giving to the rich, which would become the norm, not the exception anymore.

> Any property may now be taken for the benefit of another private party, but the fallout from this decision will not be random. The beneficiaries are likely to be those citizens with disproportionate influence and power in the political process, including large corporations and development firms.

O'Conner argues that the majority decision eradicates "any distinction between private and public use of property—and thereby effectively delete[s] the words 'for public use' from the Takings Clause of the Fifth Amendment."

Stevens's opinion is that the new development would bring a revitalized New London with a new waterfront conference hotel in the middle of a "small urban village," including shopping and restaurants, and a "riverwalk." This includes around 80 houses in a modern urban neighborhood, interlinked by public walkway, including a state park. Stevens says further, "the court long ago rejected any literal requirement that condemned property be put into use for the general public" (p. 4). Stevens cites *Fallbrook Irrigation Dist. v. Bradley*, 164 U.S. 112, 158–164 (1896); *Strickley v. Highland Boy Gold Mining Co.*, 200 U.S. 527, 531 (1906); and *Berman v. Parker*, 348 U.S. 26 (1954), as precedents that have broadly defined "public purpose."

Conversely, the dissenting opinion personifies their position in describing the case as one beyond complicated legalize to one in which it was personally brought to the court by nine home owners, representing the Fort Trumbull neighborhood of New London, Connecticut. O'Conner uses Wilhelmina Dery as an example. Dery's family lived in a house on Walbach Street for more than 100 years. Ms. Dery will unwillingly be kicked out of her family homestead because of a broadly defined "private purpose" cleverly cloaked as a "public purpose."

On the one side, new development will potentially bring new jobs and taxes to revitalize New London city hall, but on the other side, citizens in Fort Trumbull, the affected neighborhood, will likely be reluctantly pushed out of their family homes by private corporations turning a quick buck.

Notes

1. Adam Liptak, "The Nation; Case Won on Appeal (to Public)," *New York Times* (July 30, 2006).
2. *Ibid.*
3. Kennedy's concurring opinion. Cornell University Law School, Supreme Court file, accessed November 19, 2009, http://www4.law.cornell.edu/supct/html/04-108.ZC.html

YES

John Paul Stevens

Majority Opinion, *Susette Kelo et al., Petitioners v. City of New London, Connecticut, et al.*: On Writ of Certiorari to the Supreme Court of Connecticut

Justice Stevens delivered the opinion of the Court.

In 2000, the city of New London approved a development plan that, in the words of the Supreme Court of Connecticut, was "projected to create in excess of 1,000 jobs, to increase tax and other revenues, and to revitalize an economically distressed city, including its downtown and waterfront areas." 268 Conn. 1, 5, 843 A. 2d 500, 507 (2004). In assembling the land needed for this project, the city's development agent has purchased property from willing sellers and proposes to use the power of eminent domain to acquire the remainder of the property from unwilling owners in exchange for just compensation. The question presented is whether the city's proposed disposition of this property qualifies as a "public use" within the meaning of the Takings Clause of the Fifth Amendment to the Constitution.[1]

I

The city of New London (hereinafter City) sits at the junction of the Thames River and the Long Island Sound in southeastern Connecticut. Decades of economic decline led a state agency in 1990 to designate the City a "distressed municipality." In 1996, the Federal Government closed the Naval Undersea Warfare Center, which had been located in the Fort Trumbull area of the City and had employed over 1,500 people. In 1998, the City's unemployment rate was nearly double that of the State, and its population of just under 24,000 residents was at its lowest since 1920.

These conditions prompted state and local officials to target New London, and particularly its Fort Trumbull area, for economic revitalization. To this end, respondent New London Development Corporation (NLDC), a private nonprofit entity established some years earlier to assist the City in planning economic development, was reactivated. In January 1998, the

From Supreme Court of the United States, June 23, 2005.

State authorized a $5.35 million bond issue to support the NLDC's planning activities and a $10 million bond issue toward the creation of a Fort Trumbull State Park. In February, the pharmaceutical company Pfizer Inc. announced that it would build a $300 million research facility on a site immediately adjacent to Fort Trumbull; local planners hoped that Pfizer would draw new business to the area, thereby serving as a catalyst to the area's rejuvenation. After receiving initial approval from the city council, the NLDC continued its planning activities and held a series of neighborhood meetings to educate the public about the process. In May, the city council authorized the NLDC to formally submit its plans to the relevant state agencies for review.[2] Upon obtaining state-level approval, the NLDC finalized an integrated development plan focused on 90 acres of the Fort Trumbull area.

The Fort Trumbull area is situated on a peninsula that juts into the Thames River. The area comprises approximately 115 privately owned properties, as well as the 32 acres of land formerly occupied by the naval facility (Trumbull State Park now occupies 18 of those 32 acres). The development plan encompasses seven parcels. Parcel 1 is designated for a waterfront conference hotel at the center of a "small urban village" that will include restaurants and shopping. This parcel will also have marinas for both recreational and commercial uses. A pedestrian "riverwalk" will originate here and continue down the coast, connecting the waterfront areas of the development. Parcel 2 will be the site of approximately 80 new residences organized into an urban neighborhood and linked by public walkway to the remainder of the development, including the state park. This parcel also includes space reserved for a new U.S. Coast Guard Museum. Parcel 3, which is located immediately north of the Pfizer facility, will contain at least 90,000 square feet of research and development office space. Parcel 4A is a 2.4-acre site that will be used either to support the adjacent state park, by providing parking or retail services for visitors, or to support the nearby marina. Parcel 4B will include a renovated marina, as well as the final stretch of the riverwalk. Parcels 5, 6, and 7 will provide land for office and retail space, parking, and water-dependent commercial uses. 1 App. 109–113.

The NLDC intended the development plan to capitalize on the arrival of the Pfizer facility and the new commerce it was expected to attract. In addition to creating jobs, generating tax revenue, and helping to "build momentum for the revitalization of downtown New London," *id.*, at 92, the plan was also designed to make the City more attractive and to create leisure and recreational opportunities on the waterfront and in the park.

The city council approved the plan in January 2000, and designated the NLDC as its development agent in charge of implementation. See Conn. Gen. Stat. §8–188 (2005). The city council also authorized the NLDC to purchase property or to acquire property by exercising eminent domain in the City's name. §8–193. The NLDC successfully negotiated the purchase of most of the real estate in the 90-acre area, but its negotiations with petitioners failed. As a consequence, in November 2000, the NLDC initiated the condemnation proceedings that gave rise to this case.[3]

II

Petitioner Susette Kelo has lived in the Fort Trumbull area since 1997. She has made extensive improvements to her house, which she prizes for its water view. Petitioner Wilhelmina Dery was born in her Fort Trumbull house in 1918 and has lived there her entire life. Her husband Charles (also a petitioner) has lived in the house since they married some 60 years ago. In all, the nine petitioners own 15 properties in Fort Trumbull—4 in parcel 3 of the development plan and 11 in parcel 4A. Ten of the parcels are occupied by the owner or a family member; the other five are held as investment properties. There is no allegation that any of these properties is blighted or otherwise in poor condition; rather, they were condemned only because they happen to be located in the development area.

In December 2000, petitioners brought this action in the New London Superior Court. They claimed, among other things, that the taking of their properties would violate the "public use" restriction in the Fifth Amendment. After a 7-day bench trial, the Superior Court granted a permanent restraining order prohibiting the taking of the properties located in parcel 4A (park or marina support). It, however, denied petitioners relief as to the properties located in parcel 3 (office space). 2 App. to Pet. for Cert. 343–350.[4]

After the Superior Court ruled, both sides took appeals to the Supreme Court of Connecticut. That court held, over a dissent, that all of the City's proposed takings were valid. It began by upholding the lower court's determination that the takings were authorized by chapter 132, the State's municipal development statute. See Conn. Gen. Stat. §8–186 *et seq.* (2005). That statute expresses a legislative determination that the taking of land, even developed land, as part of an economic development project is a "public use" and in the "public interest." 268 Conn., at 18–28, 843 A. 2d, at 515–521. Next, relying on cases such as *Hawaii Housing Authority v. Midkiff*, 467 U.S. 229 (1984), and *Berman v. Parker*, 348 U.S. 26 (1954), the court held that such economic development qualified as a valid public use under both the Federal and State Constitutions. 268 Conn., at 40, 843 A. 2d, at 527.

Finally, adhering to its precedents, the court went on to determine, first, whether the takings of the particular properties at issue were "reasonably necessary" to achieving the City's intended public use, *id.*, at 82, 843 A. 2d, at 552–553, and, second, whether the takings were for "reasonably foreseeable needs," *id.*, at 93, 843 A. 2d, at 558–559. The court upheld the trial court's factual findings as to parcel 3, but reversed the trial court as to parcel 4A, agreeing with the City that the intended use of this land was sufficiently definite and had been given "reasonable attention" during the planning process. *Id.*, at 120–121, 843 A. 2d, at 574.

The three dissenting justices would have imposed a "heightened" standard of judicial review for takings justified by economic development. Although they agreed that the plan was intended to serve a valid public use, they would have found all the takings unconstitutional because the City had failed to adduce "clear and convincing evidence" that the economic benefits of the plan would in fact come to pass. *Id.*, at 144, 146, 843 A. 2d, at 587, 588

(Zarella, J., joined by Sullivan, C. J., and Katz, J., concurring in part and dissenting in part).

We granted certiorari to determine whether a city's decision to take property for the purpose of economic development satisfies the "public use" requirement of the Fifth Amendment. 542 U.S. ___ (2004).

III

Two polar propositions are perfectly clear. On the one hand, it has long been accepted that the sovereign may not take the property of *A* for the sole purpose of transferring it to another private party *B*, even though *A* is paid just compensation. On the other hand, it is equally clear that a State may transfer property from one private party to another if future "use by the public" is the purpose of the taking; the condemnation of land for a railroad with common-carrier duties is a familiar example. Neither of these propositions, however, determines the disposition of this case.

As for the first proposition, the City would no doubt be forbidden from taking petitioners' land for the purpose of conferring a private benefit on a particular private party. See *Midkiff*, 467 U.S., at 245 ("A purely private taking could not withstand the scrutiny of the public use requirement; it would serve no legitimate purpose of government and would thus be void"); *Missouri Pacific R. Co. v. Nebraska*, 164 U.S. 403 (1896).[5] Nor would the City be allowed to take property under the mere pretext of a public purpose, when its actual purpose was to bestow a private benefit. The takings before us, however, would be executed pursuant to a "carefully considered" development plan. 268 Conn., at 54, 843 A. 2d, at 536. The trial judge and all the members of the Supreme Court of Connecticut agreed that there was no evidence of an illegitimate purpose in this case.[6] Therefore, as was true of the statute challenged in *Midkiff*, 467 U.S., at 245, the City's development plan was not adopted "to benefit a particular class of identifiable individuals."

On the other hand, this is not a case in which the City is planning to open the condemned land—at least not in its entirety—to use by the general public. Nor will the private lessees of the land in any sense be required to operate like common carriers, making their services available to all comers. But although such a projected use would be sufficient to satisfy the public use requirement, this "Court long ago rejected any literal requirement that condemned property be put into use for the general public." *Id.*, at 244. Indeed, while many state courts in the mid-19th century endorsed "use by the public" as the proper definition of public use, that narrow view steadily eroded over time. Not only was the "use by the public" test difficult to administer (e.g., what proportion of the public need have access to the property? at what price?),[7] but it proved to be impractical given the diverse and always evolving needs of society.[8] Accordingly, when this Court began applying the Fifth Amendment to the States at the close of the 19th century, it embraced the broader and more natural interpretation of public use as "public purpose." See, e.g., *Fallbrook Irrigation Dist. v. Bradley*, 164 U.S. 112, 158–164 (1896). Thus, in a case upholding a mining company's use of an aerial bucket line to transport ore over property it did not own, Justice Holmes' opinion for the Court stressed "the inadequacy of use by the general public as a universal test." *Strickley v. Highland Boy Gold Mining Co.,* 200 U.S. 527, 531 (1906).[9] We have repeatedly and consistently rejected that narrow test ever since.[10]

The disposition of this case therefore turns on the question whether the City's development plan serves a "public purpose." Without exception, our cases have defined that concept broadly, reflecting our longstanding policy of deference to legislative judgments in this field.

In *Berman v. Parker,* 348 U.S. 26 (1954), this Court upheld a redevelopment plan targeting a blighted area of Washington, D.C., in which most of the housing for the area's 5,000 inhabitants was beyond repair. Under the plan, the area would be condemned and part of it utilized for the construction of streets, schools, and other public facilities. The remainder of the land would be leased or sold to private parties for the purpose of redevelopment, including the construction of low-cost housing.

The owner of a department store located in the area challenged the condemnation, pointing out that his store was not itself blighted and arguing that the creation of a "better balanced, more attractive community" was not a valid public use. *Id.,* at 31. Writing for a unanimous Court, Justice Douglas refused to evaluate this claim in isolation, deferring instead to the legislative and agency judgment that the area "must be planned as a whole" for the plan to be successful. *Id.,* at 34. The Court explained that "community redevelopment programs need not, by force of the Constitution, be on a piecemeal basis—lot by lot, building by building." *Id.,* at 35. The public use underlying the taking was unequivocally affirmed:

"We do not sit to determine whether a particular housing project is or is not desirable. The concept of the public welfare is broad and inclusive. . . . The values it represents are spiritual as well as physical, aesthetic as well as monetary. It is within the power of the legislature to determine that the community should be beautiful as well as healthy, spacious as well as clean, well-balanced as well as carefully patrolled. In the present case, the Congress and its authorized agencies have made determinations that take into account a wide variety of values. It is not for us to reappraise them. If those who govern the District of Columbia decide that the Nation's Capital should be beautiful as well as sanitary, there is nothing in the Fifth Amendment that stands in the way." *Id.,* at 33.

In *Hawaii Housing Authority v. Midkiff,* 467 U.S. 229 (1984), the Court considered a Hawaii statute whereby fee title was taken from lessors and transferred to lessees (for just compensation) in order to reduce the concentration of land ownership. We unanimously upheld the statute and rejected the Ninth Circuit's view that it was "a naked attempt on the part of the state of Hawaii to take the property of A and transfer it to B solely for B's private use and benefit." *Id.,* at 235 (internal quotation marks omitted). Reaffirming *Berman's* deferential approach to legislative judgments in this field, we concluded that the State's purpose of eliminating the "social and economic evils of a land oligopoly" qualified as a valid public use. 467 U.S., at 241–242. Our opinion also rejected the contention that the mere fact that the State immediately transferred the properties to private individuals upon condemnation somehow diminished the public character of the taking. "[I]t is only the taking's purpose, and not its mechanics," we explained, that matters in determining public use. *Id.*, at 244.

In that same Term we decided another public use case that arose in a purely economic context. In *Ruckelshaus v. Monsanto, Co.*, 467 U.S. 986 (1984), the Court dealt with provisions of the Federal Insecticide, Fungicide, and Rodenticide Act under which the Environmental Protection Agency could consider the data (including trade secrets) submitted by a prior pesticide applicant in evaluating a subsequent application, so long as the second applicant paid just compensation for the data. We acknowledged that the "most direct beneficiaries" of these provisions were the subsequent applicants, *id.*, at 1014, but we nevertheless upheld the statute under *Berman* and *Midkiff*. We found sufficient Congress' belief that sparing applicants the cost of time-consuming research eliminated a significant barrier to entry in the pesticide market and thereby enhanced competition. 467 U.S., at 1015.

Viewed as a whole, our jurisprudence has recognized that the needs of society have varied between different parts of the Nation, just as they have evolved over time in response to changed circumstances. Our earliest cases in particular embodied a strong theme of federalism, emphasizing the "great respect" that we owe to state legislatures and state courts in discerning local public needs. See *Hairston v. Danville & Western R. Co.*, 208 U.S. 598, 606–607 (1908) (noting that these needs were likely to vary depending on a State's "resources, the capacity of the soil, the relative importance of industries to the general public welfare, and the long-established methods and habits of the people").[11] For more than a century, our public use jurisprudence has wisely eschewed rigid formulas and intrusive scrutiny in favor of affording legislatures broad latitude in determining what public needs justify the use of the takings power.

IV

Those who govern the City were not confronted with the need to remove blight in the Fort Trumbull area, but their determination that the area was sufficiently distressed to justify a program of economic rejuvenation is entitled to our deference. The City has carefully formulated an economic development plan that it believes will provide appreciable benefits to the community, including—but by no means limited to—new jobs and increased tax revenue. As with other exercises in urban planning and development,[12] the City is endeavoring to coordinate a variety of commercial, residential, and recreational uses of land, with the hope that they will form a whole greater than the sum of its parts. To effectuate this plan, the City has invoked a state statute that specifically authorizes the use of eminent domain to promote economic development. Given the comprehensive character of the plan, the thorough deliberation that preceded its adoption, and the limited scope of our review, it is appropriate for us, as it was in *Berman*, to resolve the challenges of the individual owners, not on a piecemeal basis, but rather in light of the entire plan. Because that plan unquestionably serves a public purpose, the takings challenged here satisfy the public use requirement of the Fifth Amendment.

To avoid this result, petitioners urge us to adopt a new bright-line rule that economic development does not qualify as a public use. Putting aside the unpersuasive suggestion that the City's plan will provide only purely economic benefits, neither precedent nor logic supports petitioners' proposal. Promoting economic development is a traditional and long accepted function of government. There is, moreover, no principled way of distinguishing economic development from the other public purposes that we have recognized. In our cases upholding takings that facilitated agriculture and mining, for example, we emphasized the importance of those industries to the welfare of the States in question, see, e.g., *Strickley*, 200 U.S. 527; in *Berman,* we endorsed the purpose of transforming a blighted area into a "well-balanced" community through redevelopment, 348 U.S., at 33;[13] in *Midkiff*, we upheld the interest in breaking up a land oligopoly that "created artificial deterrents to the normal functioning of the State's residential land market," 467 U.S., at 242; and in *Monsanto*, we accepted Congress' purpose of eliminating a "significant barrier to entry in the pesticide market," 467 U.S., at 1014–1015. It would be incongruous to hold that the City's interest in the economic benefits to be derived from the development of the Fort Trumbull area has less of a public character than any of those other interests. Clearly, there is no basis for exempting economic development from our traditionally broad understanding of public purpose.

Petitioners contend that using eminent domain for economic development impermissibly blurs the boundary between public and private takings. Again, our cases foreclose this objection. Quite simply, the government's pursuit of a public purpose will often benefit individual private parties. For example, in *Midkiff*, the forced transfer of property conferred a direct and significant benefit on those lessees who were previously unable to purchase their homes. In *Monsanto*, we recognized that the "most direct beneficiaries" of the data-sharing provisions were the subsequent pesticide applicants, but benefiting them in this way was necessary to promoting competition in the pesticide market. 467 U.S., at 1014.[14] The owner of the department store in *Berman* objected to "taking from one businessman for the benefit of another businessman," 348 U.S., at 33, referring to the fact that under the redevelopment plan land would be leased or sold to private developers for redevelopment.[15] Our rejection of that contention has particular relevance to the instant case: "The public end may be as well or better served through an agency of private enterprise than through a department of government—or so the Congress might conclude. We cannot say that public ownership is the sole method of promoting the public purposes of community redevelopment projects." *Id.*, at 34.[16]

It is further argued that without a bright-line rule nothing would stop a city from transferring citizen *A*'s property to citizen *B* for the sole reason that citizen *B* will put the property to a more productive use and thus pay more taxes. Such a one-to-one transfer of property, executed outside the confines of an integrated development plan, is not presented in this case. While such an unusual exercise of government power would certainly raise a suspicion that a private purpose was afoot,[17] the hypothetical cases posited by petitioners can be confronted if and when they arise.[18] They do not warrant the crafting of an artificial restriction on the concept of public use.[19]

Alternatively, petitioners maintain that for takings of this kind we should require a "reasonable certainty" that the expected public benefits will actually accrue. Such a rule, however, would represent an even greater departure from our precedent. "When the legislature's purpose is legitimate and its means are not irrational, our cases make clear that empirical debates over the wisdom of takings—no less than debates over the wisdom of other kinds of socioeconomic legislation—are not to be carried out in the federal courts." *Midkiff*, 467 U.S., at 242.[20] Indeed, earlier this Term we explained why similar practical concerns (among others) undermined the use of the "substantially advances" formula in our regulatory takings doctrine. See *Lingle v. Chevron U.S.A., Inc.*, 544 U.S. ___, ___ (2005) (slip op., at 14–15) (noting that this formula "would empower—and might often require—courts to substitute their predictive judgments for those of elected legislatures and expert agencies"). The disadvantages of a heightened form of review are especially pronounced in this type of case. Orderly implementation of a comprehensive redevelopment plan obviously requires that the legal rights of all interested parties be established before new construction can be commenced. A constitutional rule that required postponement of the judicial approval of every condemnation until the likelihood of success of the plan had been assured would unquestionably impose a significant impediment to the successful consummation of many such plans.

Just as we decline to second-guess the City's considered judgments about the efficacy of its development plan, we also decline to second-guess the City's determinations as to what lands it needs to acquire in order to effectuate the project. "It is not for the courts to oversee the choice of the boundary line nor to sit in review on the size of a particular project area. Once the question of the public purpose has been decided, the amount and character of land to be taken for the project and the need for a particular tract to complete the integrated plan rests in the discretion of the legislative branch." *Berman*, 348 U.S., at 35–36.

In affirming the City's authority to take petitioners' properties, we do not minimize the hardship that condemnations may entail, notwithstanding the payment of just compensation.[21] We emphasize that nothing in our opinion precludes any State from placing further restrictions on its exercise of the takings power. Indeed, many States already impose "public use" requirements that are stricter than the federal baseline. Some of these requirements have been established as a matter of state constitutional law,[22] while others are expressed in state eminent domain statutes that carefully limit the grounds upon which takings may be exercised.[23] As the submissions of the parties and their *amici* make clear, the necessity and wisdom of using eminent domain to promote economic development are certainly matters of legitimate public debate.[24] This Court's authority, however, extends only to determining whether the City's proposed condemnations are for a "public use" within the meaning of the Fifth Amendment to the Federal Constitution. Because over a century of our case law interpreting that provision dictates an affirmative answer to that question, we may not grant petitioners the relief that they seek.

The judgment of the Supreme Court of Connecticut is affirmed.

It is so ordered.

Notes

1. "[N]or shall private property be taken for public use, without just compensation." U.S. Const., Amdt. 5. That Clause is made applicable to the States by the Fourteenth Amendment. See *Chicago, B. & Q. R. Co. v. Chicago,* 166 U.S. 226 (1897).

2. Various state agencies studied the project's economic, environmental, and social ramifications. As part of this process, a team of consultants evaluated six alternative development proposals for the area, which varied in extensiveness and emphasis. The Office of Planning and Management, one of the primary state agencies undertaking the review, made findings that the project was consistent with relevant state and municipal development policies. See 1 App. 89–95.

3. In the remainder of the opinion we will differentiate between the City and the NLDC only where necessary.

4. While this litigation was pending before the Superior Court, the NLDC announced that it would lease some of the parcels to private developers in exchange for their agreement to develop the land according to the terms of the development plan. Specifically, the NLDC was negotiating a 99-year ground lease with Corcoran Jennison, a developer selected from a group of applicants. The negotiations contemplated a nominal rent of $1 per year, but no agreement had yet been signed. See 268 Conn. 1, 9, 61, 843 A. 2d 500, 509–510, 540 (2004).

5. See also *Calder v. Bull,* 3 Dall. 386, 388 (1798) ("An act of the Legislature (for I cannot call it a law) contrary to the great first principles of the social compact, cannot be considered a rightful exercise of legislative authority. . . . A few instances will suffice to explain what I mean. . . . [A] law that takes property from A. and gives it to B: It is against all reason and justice, for a people to entrust a Legislature with such powers; and, therefore, it cannot be presumed that they have done it. The genius, the nature, and the spirit, of our State Governments, amount to a prohibition of such acts of legislation; and the general principles of law and reason forbid them" (emphasis deleted)).

6. See 268 Conn., at 159, 843 A. 2d, at 595 (Zarella, J., concurring in part and dissenting in part) ("The record clearly demonstrates that the development plan was not intended to serve the interests of Pfizer, Inc., or any other private entity, but rather, to revitalize the local economy by creating temporary and permanent jobs, generating a significant increase in tax revenue, encouraging spin-off economic activities and maximizing public access to the waterfront"). And while the City intends to transfer certain of the parcels to a private developer in a long-term lease—which developer, in turn, is expected to lease the office space and so forth to other private tenants—the identities of those private parties were not known when the plan was adopted. It is, of course, difficult to accuse the government of having taken *A*'s property to benefit the private interests of *B* when the identity of *B* was unknown.

7. See, e.g., *Dayton Gold & Silver Mining Co. v. Seawell,* 11 Nev. 394, 410, 1876 WL 4573, *11 (1876) ("If public occupation and enjoyment of the object for which land is to be condemned furnishes the only and true test for

the right of eminent domain, then the legislature would certainly have the constitutional authority to condemn the lands of any private citizen for the purpose of building hotels and theaters. Why not? A hotel is used by the public as much as a railroad. The public have the same right, upon payment of a fixed compensation, to seek rest and refreshment at a public inn as they have to travel upon a railroad").

8. From upholding the Mill Acts (which authorized manufacturers dependent on power-producing dams to flood upstream lands in exchange for just compensation), to approving takings necessary for the economic development of the West through mining and irrigation, many state courts either circumvented the "use by the public" test when necessary or abandoned it completely. See Nichols, The Meaning of Public Use in the Law of Eminent Domain, 20 B.U. L. Rev. 615, 619–624 (1940) (tracing this development and collecting cases). For example, in rejecting the "use by the public" test as overly restrictive, the Nevada Supreme Court stressed that "[m]ining is the greatest of the industrial pursuits in this state. All other interests are subservient to it. Our mountains are almost barren of timber, and our valleys could never be made profitable for agricultural purposes except for the fact of a home market having been created by the mining developments in different sections of the state. The mining and milling interests give employment to many men, and the benefits derived from this business are distributed as much, and sometimes more, among the laboring classes than with the owners of the mines and mills. . . . The present prosperity of the state is entirely due to the mining developments already made, and the entire people of the state are directly interested in having the future developments unobstructed by the obstinate action of any individual or individuals." *Dayton Gold & Silver Mining Co.,* 11 Nev., at 409–410, 1876 WL, at *11.

9. See also *Clark v. Nash,* 198 U.S. 361 (1905) (upholding a statute that authorized the owner of arid land to widen a ditch on his neighbor's property so as to permit a nearby stream to irrigate his land).

10. See, e.g., *Mt. Vernon-Woodberry Cotton Duck Co. v. Alabama Interstate Power Co.,* 240 U.S. 30, 32 (1916) ("The inadequacy of use by the general public as a universal test is established"); *Ruckelshaus v. Monsanto Co.,* 467 U.S. 986, 1014–1015 (1984) ("This Court, however, has rejected the notion that a use is a public use only if the property taken is put to use for the general public").

11. See also *Clark,* 198 U.S., at 367–368; *Strickley v. Highland Boy Gold Mining Co.,* 200 U.S. 527, 531 (1906) ("In the opinion of the legislature and the Supreme Court of Utah the public welfare of that State demands that aerial lines between the mines upon its mountain sides and railways in the valleys below should not be made impossible by the refusal of a private owner to sell the right to cross his land. The Constitution of the United States does not require us to say that they are wrong"); *O'Neill v. Leamer,* 239 U.S. 244, 253 (1915) ("States may take account of their special exigencies, and when the extent of their arid or wet lands is such that a plan for irrigation or reclamation according to districts may fairly be regarded as one which promotes the public interest, there is nothing in the Federal Constitution which denies to them the right to formulate this policy or to exercise the power of eminent domain in carrying it into effect. With

the local situation the state court is peculiarly familiar and its judgment is entitled to the highest respect").

12. Cf. *Village of Euclid v. Ambler Realty Co.*, 272 U.S. 365 (1926).

13. It is a misreading of *Berman* to suggest that the only public use upheld in that case was the initial removal of blight. See Reply Brief for Petitioners 8. The public use described in *Berman* extended beyond that to encompass the purpose of *developing* that area to create conditions that would prevent a reversion to blight in the future. See 348 U.S., at 34–35 ("It was not enough, [the experts] believed, to remove existing buildings that were insanitary or unsightly. It was important to redesign the whole area so as to eliminate the conditions that cause slums. . . . The entire area needed redesigning so that a balanced, integrated plan could be developed for the region, including not only new homes, but also schools, churches, parks, streets, and shopping centers. In this way it was hoped that the cycle of decay of the area could be controlled and the birth of future slums prevented"). Had the public use in *Berman* been defined more narrowly, it would have been difficult to justify the taking of the plaintiff's non-blighted department store.

14. Any number of cases illustrate that the achievement of a public good often coincides with the immediate benefiting of private parties. See, e.g., *National Railroad Passenger Corporation v. Boston & Maine Corp.*, 503 U.S. 407, 422 (1992) (public purpose of "facilitating Amtrak's rail service" served by taking rail track from one private company and transferring it to another private company); *Brown v. Legal Foundation of Wash.*, 538 U.S. 216 (2003) (provision of legal services to the poor is a valid public purpose). It is worth noting that in *Hawaii Housing Authority v. Midkiff*, 467 U.S. 229 (1984), *Monsanto*, and *Boston & Maine Corp.*, the property in question retained the same use even after the change of ownership.

15. Notably, as in the instant case, the private developers in *Berman* were required by contract to use the property to carry out the redevelopment plan. See 348 U.S., at 30.

16. Nor do our cases support Justice O'Connor's novel theory that the government may only take property and transfer it to private parties when the initial taking eliminates some "harmful property use." *Post*, at 8 (dissenting opinion). There was nothing "harmful" about the nonblighted department store at issue in *Berman*, 348 U.S. 26; see also n. 13, *supra;* nothing "harmful" about the lands at issue in the mining and agriculture cases, see, e.g., *Strickley*, 200 U.S. 527; see also nn. 9, 11, *supra;* and certainly nothing "harmful" about the trade secrets owned by the pesticide manufacturers in *Monsanto*, 467 U.S. 986. In each case, the public purpose we upheld depended on a private party's *future* use of the concededly nonharmful property that was taken. By focusing on a property's future use, as opposed to its past use, our cases are faithful to the text of the Takings Clause. See U.S. Const., Amdt. 5. ("[N]or shall private property be taken for public use, without just compensation"). Justice O'Connor's intimation that a "public purpose" may not be achieved by the action of private parties, see *post*, at 8, confuses the *purpose* of a taking with its *mechanics*, a mistake we warned of in *Midkiff*, 467 U.S., at 244. See also *Berman*, 348 U.S., at 33–34 ("The public end may be as well or better served through an agency of private enterprise than through a department of government").

17. Courts have viewed such aberrations with a skeptical eye. See, e.g., *99 Cents Only Stores v. Lancaster Redevelopment Agency*, 237 F. Supp. 2d 1123 (CD Cal. 2001); cf. *Cincinnati v. Vester*, 281 U.S. 439, 448 (1930) (taking invalid under state eminent domain statute for lack of a reasoned explanation). These types of takings may also implicate other constitutional guarantees. See *Village of Willowbrook v. Olech*, 528 U.S. 562 (2000) (per curiam).

18. Cf. *Panhandle Oil Co. v. Mississippi ex rel. Knox*, 277 U.S. 218, 223 (1928) (Holmes, J., dissenting) ("The power to tax is not the power to destroy while this Court sits").

19. A parade of horribles is especially unpersuasive in this context, since the Takings Clause largely "operates as a conditional limitation, permitting the government to do what it wants so long as it pays the charge." *Eastern Enterprises v. Apfel*, 524 U.S. 498, 545 (1998) (Kennedy, J., concurring in judgment and dissenting in part). Speaking of the takings power, Justice Iredell observed that "[i]t is not sufficient to urge, that the power may be abused, for, such is the nature of all power—such is the tendency of every human institution: and, it might as fairly be said, that the power of taxation, which is only circumscribed by the discretion of the Body, in which it is vested, ought not to be granted, because the Legislature, disregarding its true objects, might, for visionary and useless projects, impose a tax to the amount of nineteen shillings in the pound. We must be content to limit power where we can, and where we cannot, consistently with its use, we must be content to repose a salutory confidence." *Calder*, 3 Dall., at 400 (opinion concurring in result).

20. See also *Boston & Maine Corp.*, 503 U.S., at 422–423 ("[W]e need not make a specific factual determination whether the condemnation will accomplish its objectives"); *Monsanto*, 467 U.S., at 1015, n. 18 ("Monsanto argues that EPA and, by implication, Congress, misapprehended the true 'barriers to entry' in the pesticide industry and that the challenged provisions of the law create, rather than reduce, barriers to entry. . . . Such economic arguments are better directed to Congress. The proper inquiry before this Court is not whether the provisions in fact will accomplish their stated objectives. Our review is limited to determining that the purpose is legitimate and that Congress rationally could have believed that the provisions would promote that objective").

21. The *amici* raise questions about the fairness of the measure of just compensation. See, e.g., Brief for American Planning Association et al. as *Amici Curiae* 26–30. While important, these questions are not before us in this litigation.

22. See, e.g., *County of Wayne v. Hathcock*, 471 Mich. 445, 684 N. W. 2d 765 (2004).

23. Under California law, for instance, a city may only take land for economic development purposes in blighted areas. Cal. Health & Safety Code Ann. §§33030–33037 (West 1997). See, e.g., *Redevelopment Agency of Chula Vista v. Rados Bros.*, 95 Cal. App. 4th 309 (2002).

24. For example, some argue that the need for eminent domain has been greatly exaggerated because private developers can use numerous techniques, including secret negotiations or precommitment strategies, to

overcome holdout problems and assemble lands for genuinely profitable projects. See Brief for Jane Jacobs as *Amicus Curiae* 13–15; see also Brief for John Norquist as *Amicus Curiae*. Others argue to the contrary, urging that the need for eminent domain is especially great with regard to older, small cities like New London, where centuries of development have created an extreme overdivision of land and thus a real market impediment to land assembly. See Brief for Connecticut Conference for Municipalities et al. as *Amici Curiae* 13, 21; see also Brief for National League of Cities et al. as *Amici Curiae*.

Dissenting Opinion, *Susette Kelo et al., Petitioners v. City of New London, Connecticut, et al.*: On Writ of Certiorari to the Supreme Court of Connecticut

Justice O'Connor, with whom The Chief Justice, Justice Scalia, and Justice Thomas join, dissenting.

Over two centuries ago, just after the Bill of Rights was ratified, Justice Chase wrote:

"An act of the Legislature (for I cannot call it a law) contrary to the great first principles of the social compact, cannot be considered a rightful exercise of legislative authority. . . . A few instances will suffice to explain what I mean. . . . [A] law that takes property from A. and gives it to B: It is against all reason and justice, for a people to entrust a Legislature with such powers; and, therefore, it cannot be presumed that they have done it." *Calder v. Bull*, 3 Dall. 386, 388 (1798) (emphasis deleted).

Today the Court abandons this long-held, basic limitation on government power. Under the banner of economic development, all private property is now vulnerable to being taken and transferred to another private owner, so long as it might be upgraded—i.e., given to an owner who will use it in a way that the legislature deems more beneficial to the public—in the process. To reason, as the Court does, that the incidental public benefits resulting from the subsequent ordinary use of private property render economic development takings "for public use" is to wash out any distinction between private and public use of property—and thereby effectively to delete the words "for public use" from the Takings Clause of the Fifth Amendment. Accordingly I respectfully dissent.

I

Petitioners are nine resident or investment owners of 15 homes in the Fort Trumbull neighborhood of New London, Connecticut. Petitioner Wilhelmina Dery, for example, lives in a house on Walbach Street that has been in her

From Supreme Court of the United States, June 23, 2005.

family for over 100 years. She was born in the house in 1918; her husband, petitioner Charles Dery, moved into the house when they married in 1946. Their son lives next door with his family in the house he received as a wedding gift, and joins his parents in this suit. Two petitioners keep rental properties in the neighborhood.

In February 1998, Pfizer Inc., the pharmaceuticals manufacturer, announced that it would build a global research facility near the Fort Trumbull neighborhood. Two months later, New London's city council gave initial approval for the New London Development Corporation (NLDC) to prepare the development plan at issue here. The NLDC is a private, nonprofit corporation whose mission is to assist the city council in economic development planning. It is not elected by popular vote, and its directors and employees are privately appointed. Consistent with its mandate, the NLDC generated an ambitious plan for redeveloping 90 acres of Fort Trumbull in order to "complement the facility that Pfizer was planning to build, create jobs, increase tax and other revenues, encourage public access to and use of the city's waterfront, and eventually 'build momentum' for the revitalization of the rest of the city." App. to Pet. for Cert. 5.

Petitioners own properties in two of the plan's seven parcels—Parcel 3 and Parcel 4A. Under the plan, Parcel 3 is slated for the construction of research and office space as a market develops for such space. It will also retain the existing Italian Dramatic Club (a private cultural organization) though the homes of three plaintiffs in that parcel are to be demolished. Parcel 4A is slated, mysteriously, for " 'park support.' " *Id.*, at 345–346. At oral argument, counsel for respondents conceded the vagueness of this proposed use, and offered that the parcel might eventually be used for parking. Tr. of Oral Arg. 36.

To save their homes, petitioners sued New London and the NLDC, to whom New London has delegated eminent domain power. Petitioners maintain that the Fifth Amendment prohibits the NLDC from condemning their properties for the sake of an economic development plan. Petitioners are not hold-outs; they do not seek increased compensation, and none is opposed to new development in the area. Theirs is an objection in principle: They claim that the NLDC's proposed use for their confiscated property is not a "public" one for purposes of the Fifth Amendment. While the government may take their homes to build a road or a railroad or to eliminate a property use that harms the public, say petitioners, it cannot take their property for the private use of other owners simply because the new owners may make more productive use of the property.

II

The Fifth Amendment to the Constitution, made applicable to the States by the Fourteenth Amendment, provides that "private property [shall not] be taken for public use, without just compensation." When interpreting the Constitution, we begin with the unremarkable presumption that every word in the document has independent meaning, "that no word was unnecessarily used, or needlessly added." *Wright v. United States*, 302 U.S. 583, 588 (1938).

In keeping with that presumption, we have read the Fifth Amendment's language to impose two distinct conditions on the exercise of eminent domain: "the taking must be for a 'public use' and 'just compensation' must be paid to the owner." *Brown v. Legal Foundation of Wash.*, 538 U.S. 216, 231–232 (2003).

These two limitations serve to protect "the security of Property," which Alexander Hamilton described to the Philadelphia Convention as one of the "great obj[ects] of Gov[ernment]." 1 Records of the Federal Convention of 1787, p. 302 (M. Farrand ed. 1934). Together they ensure stable property ownership by providing safeguards against excessive, unpredictable, or unfair use of the government's eminent domain power—particularly against those owners who, for whatever reasons, may be unable to protect themselves in the political process against the majority's will.

While the Takings Clause presupposes that government can take private property without the owner's consent, the just compensation requirement spreads the cost of condemnations and thus "prevents the public from loading upon one individual more than his just share of the burdens of government." *Monongahela Nav. Co. v. United States*, 148 U.S. 312, 325 (1893); see also *Armstrong v. United States*, 364 U.S. 40, 49 (1960). The public use requirement, in turn, imposes a more basic limitation, circumscribing the very scope of the eminent domain power: Government may compel an individual to forfeit her property for the *public's* use, but not for the benefit of another private person. This requirement promotes fairness as well as security. Cf. *Tahoe-Sierra Preservation Council, Inc. v. Tahoe Regional Planning Agency*, 535 U.S. 302, 336 (2002) ("The concepts of 'fairness and justice' . . . underlie the Takings Clause").

Where is the line between "public" and "private" property use? We give considerable deference to legislatures' determinations about what governmental activities will advantage the public. But were the political branches the sole arbiters of the public–private distinction, the Public Use Clause would amount to little more than hortatory fluff. An external, judicial check on how the public use requirement is interpreted, however limited, is necessary if this constraint on government power is to retain any meaning. See *Cincinnati v. Vester*, 281 U.S. 439, 446 (1930) ("It is well established that . . . the question [of] what is a public use is a judicial one").

Our cases have generally identified three categories of takings that comply with the public use requirement, though it is in the nature of things that the boundaries between these categories are not always firm. Two are relatively straightforward and uncontroversial. First, the sovereign may transfer private property to public ownership—such as for a road, a hospital, or a military base. See, e.g., *Old Dominion Land Co. v. United States*, 269 U.S. 55 (1925); *Rindge Co. v. County of Los Angeles*, 262 U.S. 700 (1923). Second, the sovereign may transfer private property to private parties, often common carriers, who make the property available for the public's use–such as with a railroad, a public utility, or a stadium. See, e.g., *National Railroad Passenger Corporation v. Boston & Maine Corp.*, 503 U.S. 407 (1992); *Mt. Vernon-Woodberry Cotton Duck Co. v. Alabama Interstate Power Co.*, 240 U.S. 30 (1916). But "public ownership" and "use-by-the-public" are sometimes too constricting and impractical ways to define the scope of the Public Use Clause. Thus we have allowed that, in certain circumstances and to meet certain exigencies, takings that serve a public purpose also satisfy the Constitution even if the property is destined for subsequent private use. See, e.g., *Berman v. Parker*, 348 U.S. 26 (1954); *Hawaii Housing Authority v. Midkiff*, 467 U.S. 229 (1984).

This case returns us for the first time in over 20 years to the hard question of when a purportedly "public purpose" taking meets the public use requirement. It presents an issue of first impression: Are economic development takings constitutional? I would hold that they are not. We are guided by two precedents about the taking of real property by eminent domain. In *Berman*, we upheld takings within a blighted neighborhood of Washington, D.C. The neighborhood had so deteriorated that, for example, 64.3% of its dwellings were beyond repair. 348 U.S., at 30. It had become burdened with "overcrowding of dwellings," "lack of adequate streets and alleys," and "lack of light and air." *Id.*, at 34. Congress had determined that the neighborhood had become "injurious to the public health, safety, morals, and welfare" and that it was necessary to "eliminat[e] all such injurious conditions by employing all means necessary and appropriate for the purpose," including eminent domain. *Id.*, at 28. Mr. Berman's department store was not itself blighted. Having approved of Congress' decision to eliminate the harm to the public emanating from the blighted neighborhood, however, we did not second-guess its decision to treat the neighborhood as a whole rather than lot by lot. *Id.*, at 34–35; see also *Midkiff*, 467 U.S., at 244 ("it is only the taking's purpose, and not its mechanics, that must pass scrutiny").

In *Midkiff*, we upheld a land condemnation scheme in Hawaii whereby title in real property was taken from lessors and transferred to lessees. At that time, the State and Federal Governments owned nearly 49% of the State's land, and another 47% was in the hands of only 72 private landowners. Concentration of land ownership was so dramatic that on the State's most urbanized island, Oahu, 22 landowners owned 72.5% of the fee simple titles. *Id.*, at 232. The Hawaii Legislature had concluded that the oligopoly in land ownership was "skewing the State's residential fee simple market, inflating land prices, and injuring the public tranquility and welfare," and therefore enacted a condemnation scheme for redistributing title. *Ibid*.

In those decisions, we emphasized the importance of deferring to legislative judgments about public purpose. Because courts are ill-equipped to evaluate the efficacy of proposed legislative initiatives, we rejected as unworkable the idea of courts' " 'deciding on what is and is not a governmental function and . . . invalidating legislation on the basis of their view on that question at the moment of decision, a practice which has proved impracticable in other fields.' " *Id.*, at 240–241 (quoting *United States ex rel. TVA v. Welch*, 327 U.S. 546, 552 (1946)); see *Berman, supra*, at 32 ("[T]he legislature, not the judiciary, is the main guardian of the public needs to be served by social legislation"); see also *Lingle v. Chevron U.S.A., Inc.*, 544 U.S. __ (2005). Likewise, we recognized our inability to evaluate whether, in a given case, eminent domain is a necessary means by which to pursue the legislature's ends. *Midkiff, supra*, at 242; *Berman, supra*, at 103.

Yet for all the emphasis on deference, *Berman* and *Midkiff* hewed to a bedrock principle without which our public use jurisprudence would collapse: "A purely private taking could not withstand the scrutiny of the public use requirement; it would serve no legitimate purpose of government and would thus be void." *Midkiff*, 467 U.S., at 245; *id.*, at 241 ("[T]he Court's cases have repeatedly stated that 'one person's property may not be taken for the benefit of another private person without a justifying public purpose, even though compensation be paid'" (quoting *Thompson v. Consolidated Gas Util. Corp.*, 300 U.S. 55, 80 (1937))); see also *Missouri Pacific R. Co. v. Nebraska*, 164 U.S. 403, 417 (1896). To protect that principle, those decisions reserved "a role for courts to play in reviewing a legislature's judgment of what constitutes a public use . . . [though] the Court in *Berman* made clear that it is 'an extremely narrow' one." *Midkiff, supra*, at 240 (quoting *Berman, supra*, at 32).

The Court's holdings in *Berman* and *Midkiff* were true to the principle underlying the Public Use Clause. In both those cases, the extraordinary, precondemnation use of the targeted property inflicted affirmative harm on society—in *Berman* through blight resulting from extreme poverty and in *Midkiff* through oligopoly resulting from extreme wealth. And in both cases, the relevant legislative body had found that eliminating the existing property use was necessary to remedy the harm. *Berman, supra*, at 28–29; *Midkiff, supra*, at 232. Thus a public purpose was realized when the harmful use was eliminated. Because each taking *directly* achieved a public benefit, it did not matter that the property was turned over to private use. Here, in contrast, New London does not claim that Susette Kelo's and Wilhelmina Dery's well-maintained homes are the source of any social harm. Indeed, it could not so claim without adopting the absurd argument that any single-family home that might be razed to make way for an apartment building, or any church that might be replaced with a retail store, or any small business that might be more lucrative if it were instead part of a national franchise, is inherently harmful to society and thus within the government's power to condemn.

In moving away from our decisions sanctioning the condemnation of harmful property use, the Court today significantly expands the meaning of public use. It holds that the sovereign may take private property currently put to ordinary private use, and give it over for new, ordinary private use, so long as the new use is predicted to generate some secondary benefit for the public—such as increased tax revenue, more jobs, maybe even aesthetic pleasure. But nearly any lawful use of real private property can be said to generate some incidental benefit to the public. Thus, if predicted (or even guaranteed) positive side-effects are enough to render transfer from one private party to another constitutional, then the words "for public use" do not realistically exclude *any* takings, and thus do not exert any constraint on the eminent domain power.

There is a sense in which this troubling result follows from errant language in *Berman* and *Midkiff*. In discussing whether takings within a blighted neighborhood were for a public use, *Berman* began by observing: "We deal, in other words, with what traditionally has been known as the police power." 348 U.S., at 32. From there it declared that "[o]nce the object is within the authority of Congress, the right to realize it through the exercise of eminent domain is clear." *Id.*, at 33. Following up, we said in *Midkiff* that "[t]he 'public use' requirement is coterminous with the scope of a sovereign's police powers." 467 U.S., at 240. This language was unnecessary to the specific holdings of those decisions. *Berman* and *Midkiff* simply did not put such language to the constitutional test, because the takings in those cases were within the police power but also for "public use" for the reasons I have described. The case before us now demonstrates why, when deciding if a taking's purpose is constitutional, the police power and "public use" cannot always be equated. The Court protests that it does not sanction the bare transfer from A to B for B's benefit. It suggests two limitations on what can be taken after today's decision. First, it maintains a role for courts in ferreting out takings whose sole purpose is to bestow a benefit on the private transferee—without detailing how courts are to conduct that complicated inquiry. *Ante*, at 7. For his part, Justice Kennedy suggests that courts may divine illicit purpose by a careful review of the record and the process by which a legislature arrived at the decision to take—without specifying what courts should look for in a case with different facts, how they will know if they have found it, and what to do if they do not. *Ante*, at 2–3 (concurring opinion). Whatever the details of Justice Kennedy's as-yet-undisclosed test, it is difficult to envision anyone but the "stupid staff[er]" failing it. See *Lucas v. South Carolina Coastal Council*, 505 U.S. 1003, 1025–1026, n. 12 (1992). The trouble with economic development takings is that private benefit and incidental public benefit are, by definition, merged and mutually reinforcing. In this case, for example, any boon for Pfizer or the plan's developer is difficult to disaggregate from the promised public gains in taxes and jobs. See App. to Pet. for Cert. 275–277.

Even if there were a practical way to isolate the motives behind a given taking, the gesture toward a purpose test is theoretically flawed. If it is true that incidental public benefits from new private use are enough to ensure the "public purpose" in a taking, why should it matter, as far as the Fifth Amendment is concerned, what inspired the taking in the first place? How much the government does or does not desire to benefit a favored private party has no bearing on whether an economic development taking will or will not generate secondary benefit for the public. And whatever the reason for a given condemnation, the effect is the same from the constitutional perspective—private property is forcibly relinquished to new private ownership.

A second proposed limitation is implicit in the Court's opinion. The logic of today's decision is that eminent domain may only be used to upgrade—not downgrade—property. At best this makes the Public Use Clause redundant with the Due Process Clause, which already prohibits irrational government action. See *Lingle*, 544 U.S. __. The Court rightfully admits, however, that the judiciary cannot get bogged down in predictive judgments about whether the public will actually be better off after a property transfer. In any event, this constraint has no realistic import. For who among us can say she already makes the most productive or attractive possible use of her property? The specter of condemnation hangs over all property. Nothing is to prevent the State from replacing any Motel 6 with a Ritz-Carlton, any home with a shopping mall, or any farm with a factory. Cf. *Bugryn v. Bristol*, 63 Conn. App. 98, 774 A. 2d 1042 (2001) (taking the homes and farm of four owners in their 70's and 80's and giving it to an "industrial park"); *99 Cents Only Stores v. Lancaster Redevelopment Authority*, 237 F. Supp. 2d 1123 (CD Cal. 2001) (attempted taking of 99 Cents store to replace with a Costco); *Poletown Neighborhood Council v. Detroit*, 410 Mich. 616, 304 N. W. 2d 455 (1981) (taking a working-class, immigrant community in Detroit and giving it to a General Motors assembly plant), overruled by *County of Wayne v. Hathcock*, 471 Mich. 415, 684 N. W. 2d 765 (2004); Brief for the Becket Fund for Religious Liberty as *Amicus Curiae* 4–11 (describing takings of religious institutions' properties); Institute for Justice, D. Berliner, Public Power, Private Gain: A Five-Year, State-by-State Report Examining the Abuse of Eminent Domain (2003) (collecting accounts of economic development takings).

The Court also puts special emphasis on facts peculiar to this case: The NLDC's plan is the product of a relatively careful deliberative process; it proposes to use eminent domain for a multipart, integrated plan rather than for isolated property transfer; it promises an array of incidental benefits (even aesthetic ones), not just increased tax revenue; it comes on the heels of a legislative determination that New London is a depressed municipality. See, e.g., *ante*, at 16 ("[A] one-to-one transfer of property, executed outside the confines of an integrated development plan, is not presented in this case"). Justice Kennedy, too, takes great comfort in these facts. *Ante*, at 4 (concurring opinion). But none has legal significance to blunt the force of today's holding. If legislative prognostications about the secondary public benefits of a new use can legitimate a taking, there is nothing in the Court's rule or in Justice Kennedy's gloss on that rule to prohibit property transfers generated with less care, that are less comprehensive, that happen to result from less elaborate process, whose only projected advantage is the incidence of higher taxes, or that hope to transform an already prosperous city into an even more prosperous one.

Finally, in a coda, the Court suggests that property owners should turn to the States, who may or may not choose to impose appropriate limits on economic development takings. *Ante*, at 19. This is an abdication of our responsibility. States play many important functions in our system of dual sovereignty, but compensating for our refusal to enforce properly the Federal Constitution (and a provision meant to curtail state action, no less) is not among them.

◦⟨◇⟩◦

It was possible after *Berman* and *Midkiff* to imagine unconstitutional transfers from A to B. Those decisions endorsed government intervention when private property use had veered to such an extreme that the public was suffering as a consequence. Today nearly all real property is susceptible to condemnation on the Court's theory. In the prescient words of a dissenter from the infamous decision in *Poletown*, "[n]ow that we have authorized local legislative bodies to decide that a different commercial or industrial use of property will produce greater public benefits than its present use, no homeowner's, merchant's or manufacturer's property, however productive or valuable to its owner, is immune from condemnation for the benefit of other private interests that will put it to a 'higher' use." 410 Mich., at 644–645, 304 N. W. 2d, at 464 (opinion of Fitzgerald, J.). This is why economic development takings "seriously jeopardiz[e] the security of all private property ownership." *Id.*, at 645, 304 N. W. 2d, at 465 (Ryan, J., dissenting).

Any property may now be taken for the benefit of another private party, but the fallout from this decision will not be random. The beneficiaries are likely to be those citizens with disproportionate influence and power in the political process, including large corporations and development firms. As for the victims, the government now has license to transfer property from those with fewer resources to those with more. The Founders cannot have intended this perverse result. "[T]hat alone is a *just* government," wrote James Madison, "which *impartially* secures to every man, whatever is his *own*." For the National Gazette, Property, (Mar. 29, 1792), reprinted in 14 Papers of James Madison 266 (R. Rutland et al. eds. 1983).

I would hold that the takings in both Parcel 3 and Parcel 4A are unconstitutional, reverse the judgment of the Supreme Court of Connecticut, and remand for further proceedings.

POSTSCRIPT

Should We Allow Eminent Domain for Public Use?

The public reaction to the *Kelo v. New London* case was not overly positive.[1] The public often seemed to view the outcome of the *Kelo* case as a huge potential violation of their property rights. More specifically, many felt the Fifth Amendment was misinterpreted, helping corporations over homeowners.[2]

The Fifth Amendment, as it relates to eminent domain, basically the "taking" of private property for "public use," reads:

> . . . nor be deprived of life, liberty, or property, without due process of law; nor shall private property be taken for public use, without just compensation.

Before the *Kelo* decision, eight states outlawed eminent domain for economic development except to eliminate blight. In the last few years after the decision, 43 states amended their laws involving eminent domain.[3] The Castle Coalition, which advocates against broad eminent domain powers, proclaims on its Web site:

> The floodgates to eminent domain abuse have busted open. However, there is a silver lining. The court said, "Nothing in our opinion precludes any State from placing further restrictions on its exercise of the takings power." Heeding public outcry in the wake of *Kelo*, legislators at every level of government are taking a closer look at eminent domain laws.

Groups such as the American Conservative Union "sharply condemned" the *Kelo* ruling as well.[4] However, the *Washington Post*'s editorial board sided with New London.[5] The editorial board argued that the plan has flaws, but with the good intention to turn around years of an economically declining climate. "However unfortunate New London's plans may prove, stopping the city based on a standardless judicial inquiry into how 'public' its purpose really is would be far worse."

Congress reacted to the "public use" of eminent domain with Texas Senator John Cornyn's introduction of the "Protection of Homes, Small Businesses and Private Property Act of 2005,"[6] with the intent to limit eminent domain use for economic development. This bill forbids utilizing the powers of eminent domain if "public use" is primarily for economic development. However, the bill never passed.

G. W. Bush, a year after the decision, issued an executive order limiting the federal government's use of eminent domain.[7] Bush contended his executive order intended "to strengthen the rights of the American people against the taking of their private property."

In the *Kelo* case, the Supreme Court has butted heads with Congress, the executive branch, and many citizens, exercising its independence and check-and-balance powers.

Notes

1. Castle Coalition: Citizens Fighting Eminent Domain Abuse Web site. Accessed December 1, 2009, http://www.castlecoalition.org/index.php?option=com_content&task=view&id=34&Itemid=119

2. Nicole Stelle Garnett, "The Neglected Political Economy of Eminent Domain," 105 *Mich. L. Rev.* 101, 136.

3. Edward J. Lopez, "Pass a Law, Any Law, Fast! State Legislative Responses to the Kelo Backlash," *Review of Law & Economics* (Berkeley Electronic Press April 1, 2009) 5(1).

4. Bill Lauderback, "Judicial Activism Strikes Again: Supreme Court Rules Government Can Seize Your Home," American Conservative Union. Accessed December 1, 2009, http://www.conservative.org/pressroom/06232005_un.asp

5. "Eminent Latitude," *Washington Post* (June 24, 2005). Accessed December 1, 2009, http://www.washingtonpost.com/wp-dyn/content/article/2005/06/23/AR2005062301698.html

6. Thomas.loc.gov. "Protection of Homes, Small Businesses, and Private Property Act of 2005." Introduced in Senate, S 1313 IS 109th Congress, 1st Session, June 27, 2005. Accessed December 1, 2009, http://thomas.loc.gov/cgi-bin/query/z?c109:S.1313:

7. Executive Order, "Protecting the Property Rights of the American People." White House Press Release (June 23, 2006). Accessed December 1, 2009, http://georgewbush-whitehouse.archives.gov/news/releases/2006/06/20060623-10.html

ISSUE 6

Should a National Sense of Morality Override States Rights in the Case of Physician-Assisted Suicide?

YES: Richard Doerflinger, from "Assisted Suicide: Pro-Choice or Anti-Life?" *Hastings Center Report* (January/February 1989)

NO: David T. Watts and Timothy Howell, from "Assisted Suicide Is Not Voluntary Active Euthanasia," *Journal of the American Geriatrics Society* (October 1992)

ISSUE SUMMARY

YES: Admitting that religiously based grounds for the wrongness of killing an innocent person are not convincing to many people, Doerflinger argues on mainly secular grounds having to do with inconsistencies in the arguments of supporters of physician-assisted suicide in several states. He examines the idea of autonomy, and the tendency for something like California's Humane and Dignified Death Act might spread once it becomes initially accepted in a limited way.

NO: Watts and Howell first claim that it is very important to distinguish between *assisted suicide* and *voluntary active euthanasia* has led to confusion among several states, such as Washington State, California, and New Hampshire. Basically, the first of these is suicide or killing oneself; the second involves being killed by someone else (e.g., a physician). Watts and Howell argue that most of the opposition to physician-assisted suicide turns out to be really opposition to voluntary active euthanasia; furthermore, they argue that physician-assisted suicide would not have the dire consequence that its opponents predict.

The initial situation here is that someone—usually a terminally ill patient—wishes to die and requests physician assistance. (After all, the doctor knows what drugs will do the job, and there have been cases of laypeople botching a suicide attempt and ending up alive but paralyzed.) But a physician who agrees to this request seems to be going against all his or her training and experience (including the Hippocratic Oath and a career devoted to the preservation of life and health). Furthermore, according to the ordinary understanding of murder (as well according to the legal definition and most religious views), to participate in purposely bringing about the death of an innocent person would be murder. (It is no defense to a charge of murder that the victim asked to be killed—contrast the case of killing in self-defense, where such killing is indeed a defense against the charge of murder and is generally considered not to be wrong anyway.)

Consider one particular case that was reported a few years ago. A physicist who had long been exposed to X-rays in his scientific practice had cancer. The disease was at an advanced stage. During the course of the cancer, the physicist had lost his left hand and two of the fingers on the right hand; he had lost other body parts as well; and he had lost his sight. Hospitalized, and in great pain, he was given about a year to live. He was not able to kill himself and begged his brothers to kill him. The first two brothers refused. But the third brother agreed, brought a gun to the hospital, and shot his dying brother.

Many people would be quite sympathetic in a case like this, but nevertheless warn us of a "slippery slope." If we allow physician-assisted suicide, it might be said, the policy would expand. Even if we grant that in fact a case like the physicist's is the most appropriate case for physician-assisted suicide, most cases would not be like that. What about a physicist who lapses into a coma and can't express his wishes? Or a person who is still at the early stages of some fatal disease and is not in great pain at the moment, but has nothing to look forward to but death? What about a great athlete who wants to die because he now finds himself confined to a wheelchair? What about elderly people who request that they be killed through physician-assisted suicide because they are not well and do not wish to be "a burden" on their offspring? How about family members who wish to inherit something (rather than see it go to fruitless medical expenses) and will subtly get the message across to their aged relatives that "it's time to go"? The list goes on. The problem, opponents to physician-assisted suicide might say, is that once you begin to allow this in some cases, it's easy to begin sliding down a slippery slope and ending up with results that are not at all what was desired in the first place.

In the following essays, Richard Doerflinger first argues that physician-assisted suicide is wrong and that the whole idea of there being such a thing as "rational suicide" is flawed. Then David Watts and Timothy Howell distinguish between various categories of euthanasia and suicide, and conclude that there really are cases of rational suicide and that physician-assisted suicide is not necessarily wrong.

YES

Assisted Suicide: Pro-Choice or Anti-Life?

The intrinsic wrongness of directly killing the innocent, even with the victim's consent, is all but axiomatic in the Jewish and Christian worldviews that have shaped the laws and mores of Western civilization and the self-concept of its medical practitioners. This norm grew out of the conviction that human life is sacred because it is created in the image and likeness of God, and called to fulfillment in love of God and neighbor.

With the pervasive secularization of Western culture, norms against euthanasia and suicide have to a great extent been cut loose from their religious roots to fend for themselves. Because these norms seem abstract and unconvincing to many, debate tends to dwell not on the wrongness of the act as such but on what may follow from its acceptance. Such arguments are often described as claims about a "slippery slope," and debate shifts to the validity of slippery slope arguments in general.

Since it is sometimes argued that acceptance of assisted suicide is an outgrowth of respect for personal autonomy, and not lack of respect for the inherent worth of human life. I will outline how autonomy-based arguments in favor of assisting suicide do entail a statement about the value of life. I will also distinguish two kinds of slippery slope argument often confused with each other, and argue that those who favor social and legal acceptance of assisted suicide have not adequately responded to the slippery slope claims of their opponents.

Assisted Suicide versus Respect for Life

Some advocates of socially sanctioned assisted suicide admit (and a few boast) that their proposal is incompatible with the conviction that human life is of intrinsic worth. Attorney Robert Risley has said that he and his allies in the Hemlock Society are "so bold" as to seek to "overturn the sanctity of life principle" in American society. A life of suffering, "racked with pain," is "not the kind of life we cherish."[1]

Others eschew Risley's approach, perhaps recognizing that it creates a slippery slope toward practices almost universally condemned. If society is to help terminally ill patients to commit suicide because it agrees that death is

From *Hastings Center Report*, Special Supplement, vol. 19, no. 1, January/February 1989, pp. 16–19. Copyright © 1989 by The Hastings Center. Reprinted by permission of the publisher and author.

objectively preferable to a life of hardship, it will be difficult to draw the line at the seriously ill or even at circumstances where the victim requests death.

Some advocates of assisted suicide therefore take a different course, arguing that it is precisely respect for the dignity of the human person that demands respect for individual freedom as the noblest feature of that person. On this rationale a decision as to when and how to die deserves the respect and even the assistance of others because it is the ultimate exercise of self-determination—"ultimate" both in the sense that it is the last decision one will ever make and in the sense that through it one takes control of one's entire self. What makes such decisions worthy of respect is not the fact that death is chosen over life but that it is the individual's own free decision about his or her future.

Thus Derek Humphry, director of the Hemlock Society, describes his organization as "pro-choice" on this issue. Such groups favor establishment of a constitutional "right to die" modeled on the right to abortion delineated by the U.S. Supreme Court in 1973. This would be a right to choose *whether or not* to end one's own life, free of outside government interference. In theory, recognition of such a right would betray no bias toward choosing death.

Life versus Freedom

This autonomy-based approach is more appealing than the straight-forward claim that some lives are not worth living, especially to Americans accustomed to valuing individual liberty above virtually all else. But the argument departs from American traditions on liberty in one fundamental respect.

When the Declaration of Independence proclaimed the inalienable human rights to be "life, liberty, and the pursuit of happiness," this order-ing reflected a long-standing judgment about their relative priorities. Life, a human being's very earthly existence, is the most fundamental right because it is the necessary condition for all other worldly goods including freedom; free-dom in turn makes it possible to pursue (without guaranteeing that one will attain) happiness. Safeguards against the deliberate destruction of life are thus seen as necessary to protect freedom and all other human goods. This line of thought is not explicitly religious but is endorsed by some modern religious groups:

> The first right of the human person is his life. He has other goods and
> some are more precious, but this one is fundamental—the condition of
> all the others. Hence it must be protected above all others.[2]

On this view suicide is not the ultimate exercise of freedom but its ultimate self-contradiction: A free act that by destroying life, destroys all the individual's future earthly freedom. If life is more basic than freedom, soci-ety best serves freedom by discouraging rather than assisting self-destruction. Sometimes one must limit particular choices to safeguard freedom itself, as when American society chose over a century ago to prevent people from sell-ing themselves into slavery even of their own volition.

It may be argued in objection that the person who ends his life has not truly suffered loss of freedom, because unlike the slave he need not continue to exist under the constraints of a loss of freedom. But the slave does have some freedom, including the freedom to seek various means of liberation or at least the freedom to choose what attitude to take regarding his plight. To claim that a slave is worse off than a corpse is to value a situation of limited freedom less than one of no freedom whatsoever, which seems inconsistent with the premise of the "pro-choice" position. Such a claim also seems tantamount to saying that some lives (such as those with less than absolute freedom) are objectively not worth living, a position that "pro-choice" advocates claim not to hold.

It may further be argued in objection that assistance in suicide is only being offered to those who can no longer meaningfully exercise other freedoms due to increased suffering and reduced capabilities and lifespan. To be sure, the suffering of terminally ill patients who can no longer pursue the simplest everyday tasks should call for sympathy and support from everyone in contact with them. But even these hardships do not constitute total loss of freedom of choice. If they did, one could hardly claim that the patient is in a position to make the ultimate free choice about suicide. A dying person capable of making a choice of that kind is also capable of making less monumental free choices about coping with his or her condition. This person generally faces a bewildering array of choices regarding the assessment of his or her past life and the resolution of relationships with family and friends. He or she must finally choose at this time what stance to take regarding the eternal questions about God, personal responsibility, and the prospects of a destiny after death.

In short, those who seek to maximize free choice may with consistency reject the idea of assisted suicide, instead facilitating all choices *except* that one which cuts short all choices.

In fact proponents of assisted suicide do *not* consistently place freedom of choice as their highest priority. They often defend the moderate nature of their project by stating, with Derek Humphry, that "we do not encourage suicide for any reason except to relieve unremitting suffering." It seems their highest priority is the "pursuit of happiness" (or avoidance of suffering) and not "liberty" as such. Liberty or freedom of choice loses its value if one's choices cannot relieve suffering and lead to happiness; life is of instrumental value, insofar as it makes possible choices that can bring happiness.

In this value system, choice as such does not warrant unqualified respect. In difficult circumstances, as when care of a suffering and dying patient is a great burden on family and society, the individual who chooses life despite suffering will not easily be seen as rational, thus will not easily receive understanding and assistance for this choice.

In short, an unqualified "pro-choice" defense of assisted suicide lacks coherence because corpses have no choices. A particular choice, that of death, is given priority over all the other choices it makes impossible, so the value of choice as such is not central to the argument.

A restriction of this rationale to cases of terminal illness also lacks logical force. For if ending a brief life of suffering can be good, it would seem that ending a long life of suffering may be better. Surely the approach of the California "Humane and Dignified Death Act"—where consensual killing of a patient expected to die in six months is presumably good medical practice, but killing the same patient a month or two earlier is still punishable as homicide—is completely arbitrary.

Slippery Slopes, Loose Cannons

Many arguments against sanctioning assisted suicide concern a different kind of "slippery slope": Contingent factors in the contemporary situation may make it virtually inevitable in practice, if not compelling at the level of abstract theory, that removal of the taboo against assisted suicide will lead to destructive expansions of the right to kill the innocent. Such factors may not be part of euthanasia advocates' own agenda; but if they exist and are beyond the control of these advocates, they must be taken into account in judging the moral and social wisdom of opening what may be a Pandora's box of social evils.

To distinguish this sociological argument from our dissection of the conceptual *logic* of the rationale for assisted suicide, we might call it a "loose cannon" argument. The basic claim is that socially accepted killing of innocent persons will interact with other social factors to threaten lives that advocates of assisted suicide would agree should be protected. These factors at present include the following:

The psychological vulnerability of elderly and dying patients. Theorists may present voluntary and involuntary euthanasia as polar opposites; in practice there are many steps on the road from dispassionate, autonomous choice to subtle coercion. Elderly and disabled patients are often invited by our achievement-oriented society to see themselves as useless burdens on younger, more vital generations. In this climate, simply offering the *option* of "self-deliverance" shifts a burden of proof, so that helpless patients must ask themselves why they are *not* availing themselves of it. Society's offer of death communicates the message to certain patients that they *may* continue to live if they wish but the rest of us have no strong interest in their survival. Indeed, once the choice of a quick and painless death is officially accepted as rational, resistance to this choice may be seen as eccentric or even selfish.[3]

The crisis in health care costs. The growing incentives for physicians, hospitals, families, and insurance companies to control the cost of health care will bring additional pressures to bear on patients. Curt Garbesi, the Hemlock Society's legal consultant, argues that autonomy-based groups like Hemlock must "control the public debate" so assisted suicide will not be seized upon by public officials as a cost-cutting device. But simply basing one's own defense of assisted suicide on individual autonomy does not solve the problem. For in the economic sphere also, offering the option of suicide would subtly shift burdens of proof.

Adequate health care is now seen by at least some policymakers as a human right, as something a society owes to all its members. Acceptance of assisted suicide as an option for those requiring expensive care would not only offer health care providers an incentive to make that option seem attractive—it would also demote all other options to the status of strictly private choices by the individual. As such they may lose their moral and legal claim to public support—in much the same way that the U.S. Supreme Court, having protected abortion under a constitutional "right of privacy," has quite logically denied any government obligation to provide public funds for this strictly private choice. As life-extending care of the terminally ill is increasingly seen as strictly elective, society may become less willing to appropriate funds for such care, and economic pressures to choose death will grow accordingly.

Legal doctrines on "substituted judgment." American courts recognizing a fundamental right to refuse life-sustaining treatment have concluded that it is unjust to deny this right to the mentally incompetent. In such cases the right is exercised on the patient's behalf by others, who seek either to interpret what the patient's own wishes might have been or to serve his or her best interests. Once assisted suicide is established as a fundamental right, courts will almost certainly find that it is unjust not to extend this right to those unable to express their wishes. Hemlock's political arm, Americans Against Human Suffering, has underscored continuity between "passive" and "active" euthanasia by offering the Humane and Dignified Death Act as an amendment to California's "living will" law, and by including a provision for appointment of a proxy to choose the time and manner of the patient's death. By such extensions our legal system would accommodate nonvoluntary, if not involuntary, active euthanasia.

Expanded definitions of terminal illness. The Hemlock Society wishes to offer assisted suicide only to those suffering from terminal illnesses. But some Hemlock officials have in mind a rather broad definition of "terminal illness." Derek Humphry says "two and a half million people alone are dying of Alzheimer's disease."[4] At Hemlock's 1986 convention, Dutch physician Pieter Admiraal boasted that he had recently broadened the meaning of terminal illness in his country by giving a lethal injection to a young quadriplegic woman—a Dutch court found that he acted within judicial guidelines allowing euthanasia for the terminally ill, because paralyzed patients have difficulty swallowing and could die from aspirating their food at any time.

The medical and legal meaning of terminal illness has already been expanded in the United States by professional societies, legislatures, and courts in the context of so-called passive euthanasia. A Uniform Rights of the Terminally Ill Act proposed by the National Conference of Commissioners on Uniform State Laws in 1986 defines a terminal illness as one that would cause the patient's death in a relatively short time if life-preserving treatment is *not* provided—prompting critics to ask if all diabetics, for example, are "terminal" by definition. Some courts already see comatose and vegetative states as "terminal" because they involve an inability to swallow that will lead to death unless artificial feeding is instituted. In the *Hilda Peter* case, the New Jersey Supreme Court declared that the traditional state interest in "preserving life" referred only to "cognitive and sapient life" and not to mere "biological" existence, implying that unconscious patients are terminal, or perhaps as good as dead, so far as state interests are concerned. Is there any reason to think that American law would suddenly resurrect the older, narrower meaning of "terminal illness" in the context of *active* euthanasia?

Prejudice against citizens with disabilities. If definitions of terminal illness expand to encompass states of severe physical or mental disability, another social reality will increase the pressure on patients to choose death: long-standing prejudice, sometimes bordering on revulsion, against people with disabilities. While it is seldom baldly claimed that disabled people have "lives not worth living," able-bodied people often say they could not live in a severely disabled state or would prefer death. In granting Elizabeth Bouvia a right to refuse a feeding tube that preserved her life, the California Appeals Court bluntly stated that her physical handicaps led her to "consider her existence meaningless" and that "she cannot be faulted for so concluding." According to disability rights expert Paul Longmore, in a society with such attitudes toward the disabled, "talk of their 'rational' or 'voluntary' suicide is simply Orwellian newspeak."[5]

Character of the medical profession. Advocates of assisted suicide realize that most physicians will resist giving lethal injections because they are trained, in Garbesi's words, to be "enemies of death." The California Medical Association firmly opposed the Humane and Dignified Death Act, seeing it as an attack on the ethical foundation of the medical profession.

Yet California appeals judge Lynn Compton was surely correct in his concurring opinion in the *Bouvia* case, when he said that a sufficient number of willing physicians can be found once legal sanctions against assisted suicide are dropped. Judge Compton said this had clearly been the case with abortion, despite the fact that the Hippocratic Oath condemns abortion as strongly as it condemns euthanasia. Opinion polls of physicians bear out the judgment that a significant number would perform lethal injections if they were legal.

Some might think this division or ambivalence about assisted suicide in the medical profession will restrain broad expansions of the practice. But if anything, Judge Compton's analogy to our experience with abortion suggests the opposite. Most physicians still have qualms about abortion, and those who perform abortions on a full-time basis are not readily accepted by their colleagues as paragons of the healing art. Consequently they tend to form their own professional societies, bolstering each other's positive self-image and developing euphemisms to blunt the moral edge of their work.

Once physicians abandon the traditional medical self-image, which rejects direct killing of patients in all circumstances, their new substitute self-image may require ever more aggressive efforts to make this killing more widely practiced and favorably received. To allow killing by physicians in certain circumstances may create a new lobby of physicians in favor of expanding medical killing.

The human will to power. The most deeply buried yet most powerful driving force toward widespread medical killing is a fact of human nature: Human beings are tempted to enjoy exercising power over others; ending another person's life is the ultimate exercise of that power. Once the taboo against killing has been set aside, it becomes progressively easier to channel one's aggressive instincts into the destruction of life in other contexts. Or as James Burtchaell has said: "There is a sort of virginity about murder; once one has violated it, it is awkward to refuse other invitations by saying, 'But that would be murder!'"[6]

Some will say assisted suicide for the terminally ill is morally distinguishable from murder and does not logically require termination of life in other circumstances. But my point is that the skill and the instinct to kill are more easily turned to other lethal tasks once they have an opportunity to exercise themselves. Thus Robert Jay Lifton has perceived differences between the German "mercy killings" of the 1930s and the later campaign to annihilate the Jews of Europe, yet still says that "at the heart of the Nazi enterprise . . . is the destruction of the boundary between healing and killing."[7] No other boundary separating these two situations was as fundamental as this one, and thus none was effective once it was crossed. As a matter of historical fact, personnel who had conducted the "mercy killing" program were quickly and readily recruited to operate the killing chambers of the death camps.[8] While the contemporary United States fortunately lacks the anti-Semitic and totalitarian attitudes that made the Holocaust possible, it has its own trends and pressures that may combine with acceptance of medical killing to produce a distinctively American catastrophe in the name of individual freedom.

These "loose cannon" arguments are not conclusive. All such arguments by their nature rest upon a reading and extrapolation of certain contingent factors in society. But their combined force provides a serious case against taking the irreversible step of sanctioning assisted suicide for any class of persons, so long as those who advocate this step fail to demonstrate why these predictions are wrong. If the strict philosophical case on behalf of "rational suicide" lacks coherence, the pragmatic claim that its acceptance would be a social benefit lacks grounding in history or common sense.

References

1. Presentation at the Hemlock Society's Third National Voluntary Euthanasia Conference, "A Humane and Dignified Death," September 25–27, 1986, Washington, DC. All quotations from Hemlock Society officials are from the proceedings of this conference unless otherwise noted.

2. Vatican Congregation for the Doctrine of the Faith, *Declaration on Procured Abortion* (1974), para. 11.

3. I am indebted for this line of argument to Dr. Eric Chevlen.

4. Denis Herbstein, "Campaigning for the Right to Die," *International Herald Tribune,* 11 September 1986.

5. Paul K. Longmore, "Elizabeth Bouvia, Assisted Suicide and Social Prejudice," *Issues in Law & Medicine* 3:2 (1987), 168.

6. James T. Burtchaell, *Rachel Weeping and Other Essays on Abortion* (Kansas City: Andrews & McMeel, 1982), 188.

7. Robert Jay Lifton, *The Nazi Doctors: Medical Killing and the Psychology of Genocide* (New York: Basic Books, 1986), 14.

8. Yitzhak Rad, *Belzec, Sobibor, Treblinka* (Bloomington, IN: Indiana University Press, 1987), 11, 16–17.

David T. Watts
and Timothy Howell

 **NO**

Assisted Suicide Is Not Voluntary Active Euthanasia

Ongoing developments continue to spotlight the controversial issues of voluntary active euthanasia and assisted suicide. In November 1991, Washington State's Initiative 119, which would have allowed physicians, in certain circumstances, to aid terminally ill patients' dying, was defeated by 56% to 44%.[1] Dr. Jack Kevorkian assisted in the suicides of two non-terminally ill women in October 1991, leading to the suspension of his Michigan medical license.[2] Murder charges were later brought against Kevorkian by a grand jury. In New Hampshire, a bill has been introduced which would allow physicians to assist patients' suicides but not perform active euthanasia.[3, 4]

Such developments highlight some of the confusion emerging from discussions of voluntary active euthanasia (V.A.E.) and assisted suicide. A significant source of confusion has been the tendency to join these concepts or even to consider them synonymous. For example, the AGS Position Statement on V.A.E. and a recent article by Teno and Lynn in the *Journal of the American Geriatrics Society* both reject easing restrictions on V.A.E. and assisted suicide while making arguments *only* against euthanasia.[5, 6] The National Hospice Organization also opposes euthanasia and assisted suicide, but it, too, appears to blur the distinction between them in stating that "euthanasia encompasses . . . in some settings, physician-assisted suicide."[7] Others appear to use the terms euthanasia and assisted suicide synonymously in arguing against both.[8]

In contrast, the AMA Ethics and Health Policy Counsel argues against physician-assisted suicide and distinguishes this from euthanasia.[9] The AMA Council on Ethical and Judicial Affairs also acknowledges there is "an ethically relevant distinction between euthanasia and assisted suicide that makes assisted suicide a more attractive option." Yet it then goes on to assert that "the ethical concerns about physician-assisted suicide are similar to those of euthanasia since both are essentially interventions intended to cause death."[10]

In order to weigh and appreciate the merits of the different arguments for and against V.A.E. and physician-assisted suicide, it is critical that appropriate distinctions be made. For example, we believe the arguments made in the references cited above and by others[11, 12] against euthanasia are telling. However, we find that these same arguments are substantially weaker when used against assisted suicide. And while we agree with the AMA Council on Ethical and Judicial Affairs that an ethically relevant distinction exists between euthanasia and

From *Journal of the American Geriatrics Society*, vol. 40, no. 10, October 1992, pp. 1043–1046.
Copyright © 1992 by American Geriatrics Society. Reprinted by permission of Wiley-Blackwell.

assisted suicide, we think it is important to distinguish further between different forms of assisted suicide. Only by doing so can we begin to sort out some of the apparent confusion in attitudes toward these issues. We caution our readers that the literature on this topic, while growing, remains preliminary, with little empirical research yet completed.[13] Our arguments, however, are philosophical in nature and do not ultimately stand or fall on empirical data.

Definitions

Voluntary active euthanasia: Administration of medications or other interventions intended to cause death at a patient's request.

Assisted suicide: Provision of information, means, or direct assistance by which a patient may take his or her own life. Assisted suicide involves several possible levels of assistance: *providing information,* for example, may mean providing toxicological information or describing techniques by which someone may commit suicide; *providing the means* can involve written prescriptions for lethal amounts of medication; supervising or *directly aiding* includes inserting an intravenous line and instructing on starting a lethal infusion.

These levels of assistance have very different implications. Providing only information or means allows individuals to retain the greatest degree of control in choosing the time and mode of their deaths. Physician participation is only indirect. This type of limited assistance is exemplified by the widely reported case of Dr. Timothy Quill, who prescribed a lethal quantity of barbiturates at the request of one of his patients who had leukemia.[14] By contrast, supervising or directly aiding is the type of physician involvement characterizing the case of Dr. Jack Kevorkian and Janet Adkins. Adkins was a 54-year-old woman with a diagnosis of Alzheimer-type dementia who sought Kevorkian's assistance in ending her life. Dr. Kevorkian inserted an intravenous catheter and instructed Mrs. Adkins on activating a lethal infusion of potassium following barbiturate sedation, a process personally monitored by Kevorkian.[15] This form of assisted suicide carries significant potential for physician influence or control of the process, and from it there is only a relatively short step to physician initiation (i.e., active euthanasia). We therefore reject physician-supervised suicide for the arguments commonly made against V.A.E., namely, that legalization would have serious adverse consequences, including potential abuse of vulnerable persons, mistrust of physicians, and diminished availability of supportive services for the dying.[6, 7, 10–12] We find each of these arguments, however, insufficient when applied to more limited forms of physician-assisted suicide (i.e., providing information or means).

Will Assisted Suicide Lead to Abuse of Vulnerable Persons?

A major concern is that some patients will request euthanasia or assisted suicide out of convenience to others.[6, 9] It is certainly possible that a patient's desire to avoid being a burden could lead to such a request. With euthanasia, there is danger that a patient's request might find too ready acceptance. With assisted suicide, however, the ultimate decision, and the ultimate action, are the patient's, not the physician's. This places an important check and balance on physician initiation or patient acquiescence in euthanasia. As the AMA Council on Ethical and Judicial Affairs acknowledges, a greater level of patient autonomy is afforded by physician-assisted suicide than by euthanasia.[10]

Culturally or socially mediated requests for assisted suicide would remain a significant concern. Patients might also request aid in suicide out of fear, pain, ambivalence, or depression.[16] The requirement that patients commit the ultimate act themselves cannot alone provide a sufficient safeguard. It would be incumbent on physicians to determine, insofar as possible, that requests for assisted suicide were not unduly influenced and that reversible conditions were optimally treated. As to how physicians might respond to such requests, data from the Netherlands indicate that about 75% of euthanasia requests in that country are refused.[17] It is our impression that most requests for assisted suicide, therefore, appear to represent opportunities for improved symptom control. We believe most serious requests would likely come from patients experiencing distressing symptoms of terminal illness.[18] By opening the door for counseling or treatment of reversible conditions, requests for assisted suicide might actually lead to averting some suicides which would have otherwise occurred.

Another concern regarding euthanasia is that it could come to be accepted without valid consent and that such a practice would more likely affect the frail and impoverished. The Remmelink Commission's investigation of euthanasia in the Netherlands appeared to justify such concerns in estimating that Dutch physicians may have performed 1,000 acts of involuntary euthanasia involving incompetent individuals.[19] But while euthanasia opens up the possibility of invalid consent, with assisted suicide consent is integral to the process. Because the choice of action clearly rests with the individual, there is substantially less likelihood for the abuse of assisted suicide as a societal vehicle for cost containment. And there is little basis for assuming that requests for assisted suicide would come primarily from frail and impoverished persons. Prolonged debilitation inherent in many illnesses is familiar to an increasing number of patients, family members, and health professionals. Such illnesses represent a greater financial threat to the middle- and upper-middle class, since the poor and disenfranchised have less to spend down to indigency. Thus, we suspect requests to assisted suicide might actually be more common from the educated, affluent, and outspoken.

Patients diagnosed with terminal or debilitating conditions are often vulnerable. We agree that such patients might request assisted suicide out of fear of pain, suffering, or isolation, and that too ready acceptance of such requests could be disastrous. Yet, we believe that patients' interests can be safeguarded by requirements for persistent, competent requests as well as thorough assessments for conditions, such as clinical depression, which could be reversed, treated, or ameliorated. Foley recently outlined an approach to the suicidal cancer patient.[20] We share her view that many such patients' requests to terminate life are altered by the availability of expert, continuing hospice services. We concur with Foley and others in calling for the wider availability of such services,[5, 6] so that requests for assisted suicide arising from pain, depression, or other distressing symptoms can be reduced to a minimum.

Would Assisted Suicide Undermine Trust Between Patients and Physicians?

The cardinal distinction between V.A.E. and assisted suicide is that V.A.E. is killing by physicians, while suicide is self-killing. Prohibiting both euthanasia and physician-supervised suicide (i.e., with direct physician involvement) should diminish worries that patients might have about physicians wrongly administering lethal medicine. At present, physician-patient trust is compromised by widespread concern that physicians try too hard to keep dying patients alive. The very strength of the physician-patient relationship has been cited as a justification for physician involvement in assisted suicide.[21]

A number of ethicists have expressed concern that both euthanasia and assisted suicide, if legalized, would have a negative impact on the way society perceives the role of physicians.[6, 9, 11, 12] Limited forms of assisted suicide, however, have been viewed more positively.[22] Public and professional attitudes appear to be evolving on this issue. A 1990 Gallup poll found that 66% of respondents believed someone in great pain, with "no hope of improvement," had the moral right to commit suicide; in 1975 the figure was 41%.[23] A panel of distinguished physicians has stated that it is not immoral for a physician to assist in the rational suicide of a terminally ill person.[24] The recent publication of a book on techniques of committing or assisting suicide evoked wide interest and significant support for the right of people to take control of their dying.[25] For a significant segment of society, physician involvement in assisted suicide may be welcomed, not feared. Furthermore, while relatively few might be likely to seek assistance with suicide if stricken with a debilitating illness, a substantial number might take solace knowing they could request such assistance.

There is another argument raised against V.A.E. that we believe also falters when used to object to assisted suicide. It has been maintained that prohibiting euthanasia forces physicians to focus on the humane care of dying patients, including meticulous attention to their symptoms.[6, 18] This argument implies that physicians find it easier to relieve the suffering of dying patients by ending their lives rather than attempting the difficult task of palliating their symptoms. But for some patients, the suffering may not be amenable to even the most expert palliation. Even in such instances, some argue that limited forms of assisted suicide should be prohibited on the grounds that not to forbid them would open the door for more generalized, less stringent applications of assisted suicide.

To us, this "slippery slope" argument seems to imply that the moral integrity of the medical profession must be maintained, even if at the cost of prolonged, unnecessary suffering by at least some dying patients. We believe such a posture is itself inhumane and not acceptable. It contradicts a fundamental principle that is an essential ingredient of physician-patient trust: that patient comfort should be a primary goal of the physician in the face of incurable illness. Furthermore, by allowing limited physician involvement in assisted suicide, physicians can respect both the principle of caring that guides them and the patients for whom caring alone is insufficient. We concede that there is another alternative: terminally ill patients who cannot avoid pain while awake may be given continuous anesthetic levels of medication.[6] But this is exactly the sort of dying process we believe many in our society want to avoid.

Will Assisted Suicide and Euthanasia Weaken Societal Resolve to Increase Resources Allocated to Care of the Dying?

This argument assumes that V.A.E. and assisted suicide would both be widely practiced, and that their very availability would decrease tangible concern for those not choosing euthanasia or suicide. However, euthanasia is rarely requested even by terminal cancer patients.[6] In the Netherlands, euthanasia accounts for less than 2% of all deaths.[17] These data suggest that even if assisted suicide were available to those with intractable pain or distressing terminal conditions, it would likely be an option chosen by relatively few. With assisted suicide limited to relatively few cases, this argument collapses. For with only a few requesting assisted suicide, the vast number of patients with debilitating illnesses would be undiminished, and their numbers should remain sufficient to motivate societal concern for their needs. Furthermore, to withhold assisted suicide from the few making serious, valid requests would be to subordinate needlessly the interests of these few to those of the many. Compounding their tragedy would be the fact that these individuals could not even benefit from any increase in therapeutic resources prompted by their suffering, insofar as their conditions are, by definition, not able to be ameliorated.

Conclusion

We have argued that assisted suicide and voluntary active euthanasia are different and that each has differing implications for medical practice and society. Further discussion should consider the merits and disadvantages of each, a process enhanced by contrasting them. We have further argued that different forms of assisted suicide can be distinguished both clinically and philosophically. Although some may argue that all forms of assisted suicide are fundamentally the same, we believe the differences can be contrasted as starkly as a written prescription and a suicide machine.

We do not advocate ready acceptance of requests for suicide, nor do we wish to romanticize the concept of rational suicide.[26] In some situations, however, where severe debilitating illness cannot be reversed, suicide may represent a rational choice. If this is the case, then physician assistance could make the process more humane. Along with other geriatricians, we often face dilemmas involving the management of chronic illnesses in late life. We believe we can best serve our patients, and preserve their trust, by respecting their desire for autonomy, dignity, and quality, not only of life, but of dying.

References

1. Caplan A. Patient rights measure needs push from Bush. Wis State J November 13, 1991, p 11A.

2. Holyfield J. Doctor who helped suicides has his license suspended. Wis State J November 21, 1991, p 5A.

3. Beresford L., ed. Euthanasia movement may be helping spur new additional attention to pain relief. Hospice News Serv 1992;3:1–3.

4. Anonymous. New Hampshire: Lawmakers file suicide bill. Wis State J November 13, 1991, p 3A.

5. AGS Public Policy Committee. Voluntary active euthanasia. J Am Geriatr Soc 1991;39:826.

6. Teno J. Lynn J. Voluntary active euthanasia: The individual case and public policy. J Am Geriatr Soc 1991;39:827–830.

7. National Hospice Organization. Statement of the National Hospice Organization Opposing the Legalization of Euthanasia and Assisted Suicide. Arlington, VA: National Hospice Organization, 1991.

8. Travis R. Two arguments against euthanasia (letter). Gerontologist 1991; 31:561–562.

9. Orentlicher D. Physician participation in assisted suicide. JAMA 1989; 262:1844–1845.

10. AMA. Report of the Council on Ethical and Judicial Affairs: Decisions Near the End of Life. Chicago, IL: American Medical Association. 1991.

11. Singer PA. Should doctors kill patients? Can Med Assoc J 1988; 138:1001–1001.

12. Singer PA, Siegler M. Euthanasia—a critique. N Engl J Med 1990; 322:1881–1883.

13. Watts DT, Howell T, Priefer BA. Geriatricians' attitudes toward assisting suicide of dementia patients. J Am Geriatr Soc 1992, September 40:878–885.

14. Quill TE. Death and dignity: A case of individualized decision making. N Engl J Med 1991;324:691–694.

15. Cassel CK, Meier DE. Morals and moralism in the debate over euthanasia and assisted suicide. N Engl J Med 1990;323:750–752.

16. Jackson DL, Youngner S. Patient autonomy and "death with dignity": Some clinical caveats. N Engl J Med 1979;301:404–408.

17. Van der Maas PJ, Van Delden JJM, Pijnenborg L. Looman CWN. Euthanasia and other medical decisions concerning the end of life. Lancet 1991; 338:669–74.

18. Palmore EB. Arguments for assisted suicide (letter). Gerontologist 1991; 31:854.

19. Karel R. Undertreatment of pain, depression needs to be addressed before euthanasia made legal in U.S. Psychiatric News. December 20, 1991, pp 5, 13, 23.

20. Foley KM. The relationship of pain and symptom management to patient requests for physician-assisted suicide. J Pain Symptom Manag 1991; 6:289–297.

21. Jecker NS. Giving death a hand. When the dying and the doctor stand in a special relationship. J Am Geriatr Soc 1991;39:831–835.

22. American College of Physicians ACP to DA, Grand Jury: Dr. Quill acted "humanely." ACP Observer, September, 1991, p 5.

23. Ames K, Wilson L, Sawhill R et al. Last rights. Newsweek August 26, 1991, pp 40–41.

24. Wanzer SH, Federman DD, Adelstein SJ et al. The physician's responsibility toward hopelessly ill patients: A second look. N Engl J Med 1989;320:844–849.

25. Humphry D. Final Exit: The Practicalities of Self-Deliverance and Assisted Suicide for the Dying. Eugene, OR: The Hemlock Society (distributed by Carol Publishing, Secaucus, NJ). 1991.

26. Conwell Y, Caine ED. Rational suicide and the right to die: Reality and myth. N Engl J Med 1991;325:1100–1103.

POSTSCRIPT

Should a National Sense of Morality Override States Rights in the Case of Physician-Assisted Suicide?

We normally understand that physician-assisted suicide, if adopted as a matter of policy, will bring with it certain regulations and safeguards. Clearly, just asking a physician for assistance is not going to be sufficient. Even ordinary people are sometimes depressed, and it is understandable that people with a serious illness are even more likely to be depressed. So, at a minimum, people who request physician-assisted suicide would have to be screened for depression.

Moreover, as Watts and Howell, explain, levels of physician assistance can vary from merely providing information, writing prescriptions, and so on, all the way up to the methods practiced by Dr. Kevorkian, including the use of his "suicide machines." In fact, although much of the public gets its ideas about what physician-assisted suicide is from Dr. Kevorkian, most proponents of physician-assisted suicide regard what he does as an example of what can happen if we *don't* have regulations and safeguards in place.

It is sometimes difficult for young and healthy people to imagine themselves at the end of life. But some people will have lived through their own relatives' deaths. And the very fact that we are all going to die—although no one knows the exact circumstances and whether we will go peacefully or in pain—makes this a real issue for all of us. The uncertainty that exists might make some people lean toward the side of the issue that provides the greater scope for leeway, allowing some provision for physician-assisted suicide, perhaps as a sort of "insurance" that may not even be needed.

Some of the opposition to the idea of physician-assisted suicide might come from a general repulsion against taking life. This is a good reaction to have. But it doesn't mean that the reaction is a substitute for judgment. Likewise, some of the opposition might come from a negative association of this with the Nazis. Again, the negative reaction is good one. What is required here, though, is an ability to get past purely emotional responses and mental associations. What we need are reasoning and careful thinking.

Further resources on this issue can be found in James H. Ondrey, *Physician-Assisted Suicide* (Greenhaven Press, 2006); Gerald Dworkin, R. G. Frey, and Sissela Bok, *Euthanasia and Physician-Assisted Suicide (For and Against)* (Cambridge University Press, 2005); and Ian Dowbiggin, *A Merciful End: The Euthanasia Movement in Modern America* (Oxford University Press, 2007).

Perhaps of unique interest is Derek Humphry's *Final Exit: The Practicalities of Self-Deliverance and Assisted Suicide for the Dying,* 3rd ed. (Delta, 2003). This book was written by a founder of the Hemlock Society (now merged into the Compassion & Choices organization); the book contains useful information and is also a practical "how-to" guide so that "self-deliverance" (suicide) can be successfully achieved.

Internet References . . .

Drug War Facts.org

Mandatory Minimum Sentencing

http://www.drugwarfacts.org/cms/node/52

Families Against Mandatory Minimums

http://www.famm.org/

Criminal Resource Manual

Discussion of Selected Section 844 Offenses, U.S. Attorneys

**http://www.justice.gov/usao/eousa/foia_reading_room/
usam/title9/crm01445.htm**

Brennan Center For Justice

State Judicial Elections

**http://www.brennancenter.org/content/section/category/
state_judicial_elections**

CQResearcher Blog

Judicial Elections: Overview from the April 24, 2009 CQ Researcher Report

**http://cqresearcherblog.blogspot.com/2009/04/
judicial-elections-overview-from-april.html**

UNIT 3

Courts, Police, and Corrections

*I*t *is the legal system that most directly affects people in their daily lives. Although there tends to be a focus in the U.S. Supreme Court, most cases are dealt with at the state level. Courts deal with a plethora of areas from constitutional rights to sentencing to who presides on the bench.*

- Is a Strip Search of Students Permissible under the Fourth Amendment?
- Do Mandatory Sentencing Laws Help the Criminal Justice System?
- Can a School Punish a Student for Speech That Is Reasonably Viewed as Promoting Illegal Drug Use?

ISSUE 7

Is a Strip Search of Students Permissible under the Fourth Amendment?

YES: Clarence Thomas, from Dissenting Opinion, *Safford Unified School District #1 et al. v. April Redding*, U.S. Supreme Court (June 25, 2009)

NO: David Souter, from Majority Opinion, *Safford Unified School District #1 et al. v. April Redding*, U.S. Supreme Court (June 25, 2009)

ISSUE SUMMARY

YES: Supreme Court Justice Clarence Thomas argues that the Fourth Amendment is not violated when there is reasonable suspicion that the student is in possession of drugs banned by school policy and the search is in an area where small pills could be concealed.

NO: Supreme Court Justice David Souter holds that a search in school requires a reasonable belief that evidence of wrongdoing will be found and that the search is not excessively intrusive in light of the age and sex of the student.

T he Fourth Amendment to the Constitution requires authorities to obtain a search warrant before conducting a search. In order to do this, they must persuade a judge that probable cause exists that a crime has been committed and that the evidence sought will be found in the place to be searched. The warrant requirement is the key constitutional element restricting the power of the police to decide unilaterally to invade the privacy of someone's home.

There are exceptions to this requirement. For example, warrants are not required when a person is searched after an arrest or when the object seized is in plain view. Nor is a warrant needed if the invasion of privacy is less intrusive than a full-scale search. Patting down the outside of someone's clothing when the police believe the person might have a weapon only requires "reasonable suspicion." In such situations, the police do not need to meet the standard of probable cause but also may not extensively search the person.

Public schools are another context in which searches have been allowed even when probable cause was not present. For example, the Court has held that search warrants are not required for school officials to search school lockers if there are reasonable grounds for believing that the search will reveal evidence of criminal behavior (*New Jersey v. T. L. O.*, a juvenile, 105 S. Ct. 733, [1985]). In the case here, the Supreme Court was asked to rule on a search that was extremely intrusive and where the grounds for believing that the search would turn up drugs were questionable.

The Supreme Court is not required to accept a case for review, and in recent decades, it has been deciding fewer and fewer cases. When it does decide to hear a case, it requires the parties to prepare and submit their legal arguments in writing and then to appear at an oral argument to answer questions that the justices might have. Often, observers at the oral argument make predictions about how the justices will vote based on the questions they ask and the comments they make at the oral argument.

The oral argument in the *Redding* case had many of the male members of the Court asking questions that appeared to be insensitive to the feelings of a 13-year-old girl subjected to a strip search. Justice Breyer, for example, asked, "Why is this a major thing to say strip down to your underclothes, which children do when they change for gym?" Justice Souter commented that if he were the principal in a school, he "would rather have the kid embarrassed by a strip search . . . than have some other kids dead because the stuff is distributed at lunchtime and things go awry." One correspondent at the Court wrote after the oral argument "after today's argument, it's plain the court will overturn a Ninth Circuit Court of Appeals' opinion finding a school's decision to strip search a 13-year-old girl unconstitutional. That the school in question was looking for a prescription pill with the mind-altering force of a pair of Advil—and couldn't be bothered to call the child's mother first—hardly matters."

As it turned out, the case was decided 8-1 in favor of Ms. Redding, and the majority opinion was written by Justice Souter. For some, this was an example of the justices, and the law, being influenced by public opinion. For others, who have seen many decisions that would not have been predicted given the questioning at the oral argument, the outcome in this case was much less of a surprise.

YES

Clarence Thomas

Dissenting Opinion, *Safford Unified School District et al. v. April Redding*

JUSTICE THOMAS, concurring in the judgment in part and dissenting in part.

I agree with the Court that the judgment against the school officials with respect to qualified immunity should be reversed. . . . Unlike the majority, however, I would hold that the search of Savana Redding did not violate the Fourth Amendment. The majority imposes a vague and amorphous standard on school administrators. It also grants judges sweeping authority to second-guess the measures that these officials take to maintain discipline in their schools and ensure the health and safety of the students in their charge. This deep intrusion into the administration of public schools exemplifies why the Court should return to the common-law doctrine of *in loco parentis* under which "the judiciary was reluctant to interfere in the routine business of school administration, allowing schools and teachers to set and enforce rules and to maintain order." *Morse* v. *Frederick,* 551 U.S. 393, 414 (2007) (THOMAS, J., concurring). But even under the prevailing Fourth Amendment test established by *New Jersey* v. *T. L. O.,* 469 U.S. 325 (1985), all petitioners, including the school district, are entitled to judgment as a matter of law in their favor.

I

"Although the underlying command of the Fourth Amendment is always that searches and seizures be reasonable, what is reasonable depends on the context within which a search takes place." *Id.,* at 337. Thus, although public school students retain Fourth Amendment rights under this Court's precedent, see *id.,* at 333–337, those rights "are different . . . than elsewhere; the 'reasonableness' inquiry cannot disregard the schools' custodial and tutelary responsibility for children," *Vernonia School Dist. 47J* v. *Acton,* 515 U.S. 646, 656 (1995); see also *T. L. O.,* 469 U.S., at 339 (identifying "the substantial interest of teachers and administrators in maintaining discipline in the classroom and on school grounds"). For nearly 25 years this Court has understood that "[m]aintaining order in the classroom has never been easy, but in more recent years, school disorder has often taken particularly ugly forms: drug use and violent crime in the schools have become major social problems." . . . In schools, "[e]vents

From Supreme Court of the United States, June 25, 2009.

calling for discipline are frequent occurrences and sometimes require immediate, effective action." *Goss* v. *Lopez,* 419 U.S. 565, 580 (1975); see also *T. L. O.,* 469 U.S., at 340 (explaining that schools have a "legitimate need to maintain an environment in which learning can take place").

For this reason, school officials retain broad authority to protect students and preserve "order and a proper educational environment" under the Fourth Amendment. . . . This authority requires that school officials be able to engage in the "close supervision of schoolchildren, as well as . . . enforc[e] rules against conduct that would be perfectly permissible if undertaken by an adult." . . . Seeking to reconcile the Fourth Amendment with this unique public school setting, the Court in *T. L. O.* held that a school search is "reasonable" if it is "justified at its inception" and '"reasonably related in scope to the circumstances which justified the interference in the first place.'" . . . The search under review easily meets this standard.

A

A "search of a student by a teacher or other school official will be 'justified at its inception' when there are reasonable grounds for suspecting that the search will turn up evidence that the student has violated or is violating either the law or the rules of the school." *T. L. O., supra,* at 341–342 (footnote omitted). As the majority rightly concedes, this search was justified at its inception because there were reasonable grounds to suspect that Redding possessed medication that violated school rules. . . . A finding of reasonable suspicion "does not deal with hard certainties, but with probabilities." *United States* v. *Cortez,* 449 U.S. 411, 418 (1981); see also *T. L. O., supra,* at 346 ("[T]he requirement of reasonable suspicion is not a requirement of absolute certainty"). To satisfy this standard, more than a mere "hunch" of wrongdoing is required, but "considerably" less suspicion is needed than would be required to "satisf[y] a preponderance of the evidence standard." *United States* v. *Arvizu,* 534 U.S. 266, 274 (2002) (internal quotation marks omitted).

Furthermore, in evaluating whether there is a reasonable "particularized and objective" basis for conducting a search based on suspected wrongdoing, government officials must consider the "totality of the circumstances." . . . School officials have a specialized understanding of the school environment, the habits of the students, and the concerns of the community, which enables them to "'formulat[e] certain common-sense conclusions about human behavior.'" *United States* v. *Sokolow,* 490 U.S. 1, 8 (1989) (quoting *Cortez, supra,* at 418). And like police officers, school officials are "entitled to make an assessment of the situation in light of [this] specialized training and familiarity with the customs of the [school]." See *Arvizu, supra,* at 276.

Here, petitioners had reasonable grounds to suspect that Redding was in possession of prescription and nonprescription drugs in violation of the school's prohibition of the "non-medical use, possession, or sale of a drug" on school property or at school events. 531 F. 3d 1071, 1076 (CA9 2008) (en banc); see also *id.,* at 1107 (Hawkins, J., dissenting) (explaining that the school policy defined "drugs" to include "'[a]ny prescription or over-the-counter drug, except those for which permission to use in school has been granted'"). As an initial matter, school officials were aware that a few years earlier, a student had become "seriously ill" and "spent several days in intensive care" after ingesting prescription medication obtained from a classmate. . . . Fourth Amendment searches do not occur in a vacuum; rather, context must inform the judicial inquiry. . . . In this instance, the suspicion of drug possession arose at a middle school that had "a history of problems with students using and distributing prohibited and illegal substances on campus." . . .

The school's substance-abuse problems had not abated by the 2003–2004 school year, which is when the challenged search of Redding took place. School officials had found alcohol and cigarettes in the girls' bathroom during the first school dance of the year and noticed that a group of students including Redding and Marissa Glines smelled of alcohol. . . . Several weeks later, another student, Jordan Romero, reported that Redding had hosted a party before the dance where she served whiskey, vodka, and tequila. . . . Romero had provided this report to school officials as a result of a meeting his mother scheduled with the officials after Romero "bec[a]me violent" and "sick to his stomach" one night and admitted that "he had taken some pills that he had got[ten] from a classmate." . . . At that meeting, Romero admitted that "certain students were bringing drugs and weapons on campus." . . . One week later, Romero handed the assistant principal a white pill that he said he had received from Glines. . . . He reported "that a group of students [were] planning on taking the pills at lunch." . . .

School officials justifiably took quick action in light of the lunchtime deadline. The assistant principal took the pill to the school nurse who identified it as prescription-strength 400-mg Ibuprofen. . . . A subsequent search of Glines and her belongings produced a razor blade, a Naproxen 200-mg pill, and several Ibuprofen 400-mg pills. . . . When asked, Glines claimed that she had received the pills from Redding. . . . A search of Redding's planner, which Glines had borrowed, then uncovered "several knives, several lighters, a cigarette, and a permanent marker." . . . Thus, as the majority acknowledges, . . . the totality of relevant circumstances justified a search of Redding for pills.

B

The remaining question is whether the search was reasonable in scope. Under *T. L. O.,* "a search will be permissible in its scope when the measures adopted are reasonably related to the objectives of the search and not excessively intrusive in light of the age and sex of the student and the nature of the infraction." 469 U.S., at 342. The majority concludes that the school officials' search of Redding's underwear was not "'reasonably related in scope to the circumstances which justified the interference in the first place,'" . . . notwithstanding the officials' reasonable suspicion that Redding "was involved in pill distribution." . . . According to the majority, to be reasonable, this school search required a showing of "danger to the students from the power of the drugs or their quantity" or a "reason to suppose that [Redding] was carrying pills in her underwear." . . . Each of these additional requirements is an unjustifiable departure from bedrock Fourth Amendment law in the school setting, where this Court has heretofore read the Fourth Amendment to grant considerable leeway to school officials. Because the school officials searched in a location where the pills could have been hidden, the search was reasonable in scope under *T. L. O.*

1

The majority finds that "subjective and reasonable societal expectations of personal privacy support . . . treat[ing]" this type of search, which it labels a "strip search," as "categorically distinct, requiring distinct elements of justification on the part of school authorities for going beyond a search of clothing and belongings." . . . Thus, in the majority's view, although the school officials had reasonable suspicion to believe that Redding had the pills on her person, . . . they needed some greater level of particularized suspicion to conduct this "strip search." There is no support for this contortion of the Fourth Amendment.

The Court has generally held that the reasonableness of a search's scope depends only on whether it is limited to the area that is capable of concealing the object of the search. See, *e.g.*, *Wyoming* v. *Houghton,* 526 U.S. 295, 307 (1999) (Police officers "may inspect passengers' belongings found in the car that are capable of concealing the object of the search"); *Florida* v. *Jimeno,* 500 U.S. 248, 251 (1991) ("The scope of a search is generally defined by its expressed object"); *United States* v. *Johns,* 469 U.S. 478, 487 (1985) (search reasonable because "there is no plausible argument that the object of the search could not have been concealed in the packages"); *United States* v. *Ross,* 456 U.S. 798, 820 (1982) ("A lawful search . . . generally extends to the entire area in which the object of the search may be found").[1]

In keeping with this longstanding rule, the "nature of the infraction" referenced in *T. L. O.* delineates the proper scope of a search of students in a way that is identical to that permitted for searches outside the school—*i.e.*, the search must be limited to the areas where the object of that infraction could be concealed. See *Horton* v. *California,* 496 U.S. 128, 141 (1990) ("Police with a warrant for a rifle may search only places where rifles might be" (internal quotation marks omitted)); *Ross, supra,* at 824 ("[P]robable cause to believe that undocumented aliens are being transported in a van will not justify a warrantless search of a suitcase"). A search of a student therefore is permissible in scope under *T. L. O.* so long as it is objectively reasonable to believe that the area searched could conceal the contraband. The dissenting opinion below correctly captured this Fourth Amendment standard, noting that "if a student brought a baseball bat on campus in violation of school policy, a search of that student's shirt pocket would be patently unjustified." 531 F. 3d, at 1104 (opinion of Hawkins, J.).

The analysis of whether the scope of the search here was permissible under that standard is straightforward. Indeed, the majority does not dispute that "general background possibilities" establish that students conceal "contraband in their underwear." . . . It acknowledges that school officials had reasonable suspicion to look in Redding's backpack and outer clothing because if "Wilson's reasonable suspicion of pill distribution were not understood to support searches of outer clothes and backpack, it would not justify any search worth making." . . . The majority nevertheless concludes that proceeding any further with the search was unreasonable. See *ante*, at 8–10; see also *ante*, at 1 (Ginsburg, J., concurring in part and dissenting in part) ("Any reasonable search for the pills would have ended when inspection of Redding's backpack and jacket pockets yielded nothing"). But there is no support for this conclusion. The reasonable suspicion that Redding possessed the pills for distribution purposes did not dissipate simply because the search of her backpack turned up nothing. It was eminently reasonable to conclude that the backpack was empty because Redding was secreting the pills in a place she thought no one would look. See *Ross, supra,* at 820 ("Contraband goods rarely are strewn" about in plain view; "by their very nature such goods must be withheld from public view").

Redding would not have been the first person to conceal pills in her undergarments. See Hicks, "Man Gets 17-Year Drug Sentence," [Corbin, KY] *Times-Tribune,* Oct. 7, 2008, p. 1 (Drug courier "told officials she had the [Oxycontin] pills concealed in her crotch"); Conley, Whitehaven: Traffic Stop Yields Hydrocodone Pills, [Memphis] *Commercial Appeal,* Aug. 3, 2007, p. B3 ("An additional 40 hydrocodone pills were found in her pants"); Caywood, Police Vehicle Chase Leads to Drug Arrests, [Worcester] *Telegram & Gazette,* June 7, 2008, p. A7 (25-year-old "allegedly had a cigar tube stuffed with pills tucked into the waistband of his pants"); Hubartt, 23-Year-Old Charged With Dealing Ecstasy, The [Fort Wayne] *Journal Gazette,* Aug. 8, 2007, p. C2 ("[W]hile he was being put into a squad car, his pants fell down and a plastic bag containing pink and orange pills fell on the ground"); Sebastian Residents Arrested in Drug Sting, *Vero Beach Press Journal,* Sept. 16, 2006, p. B2 (Arrestee "told them he had more pills 'down my pants'"). Nor will she be the last after today's decision, which announces the safest place to secrete contraband in school.

2

The majority compounds its error by reading the "nature of the infraction" aspect of the *T. L. O.* test as a license to limit searches based on a judge's assessment of a particular school policy. According to the majority, the scope of the search was impermissible because the school official "must have been aware of the nature and limited threat of the specific drugs he was searching for" and because he "had no reason to suspect that large amounts of the drugs were being passed around, or that individual students were receiving great numbers of pills." . . . Thus, in order to locate a rationale for finding a Fourth Amendment violation in this case, the majority retreats from its observation that the school's firm no-drug policy "makes sense, and there is no basis to claim that the search was unreasonable owing to some defect or shortcoming of the rule it was aimed at enforcing." . . .

Even accepting the majority's assurances that it is not attacking the rule's reasonableness, it certainly is attacking the rule's importance. This approach directly conflicts with *T. L. O.* in which the Court was "unwilling to adopt a standard under which the legality of a search is dependent upon a judge's evaluation of the relative importance of school rules." 469 U.S., at 342, n. 9. Indeed, the Court in *T. L. O.* expressly rejected the proposition that the majority seemingly endorses—that "some rules regarding student conduct are by nature too 'trivial' to justify a search based upon reasonable suspicion." *Ibid.;* see also *id.,* at 343, n. 9 ("The promulgation of a rule forbidding specified conduct persumably reflects a judgment on the part of school officials that such conduct is destructive of school order or of a proper educational environment. Absent any suggestion that the rule violates some substantive constitutional guarantee, the courts should as a general matter, defer to that judgment").

The majority's decision in this regard also departs from another basic principle of the Fourth Amendment: that law enforcement officials can enforce with the same vigor all rules and regulations irrespective of the perceived importance of any of those rules. "In a long line of cases, we have said that when an officer has probable cause to believe a person committed even a minor crime in his presence, the balancing of private and public interests is not in doubt. The arrest is constitutionally reasonable." *Virginia* v. *Moore,* 553 U.S. _, _ (2008) (slip op., at 6). The Fourth Amendment rule for searches is the same: Police officers are entitled to search regardless of the perceived triviality of the underlying law. As we have explained, requiring police to make "sensitive, case-by-case determinations of government need," *Atwater* v. *Lago Vista,* 532 U.S. 318, 347 (2001), for a particular prohibition before conducting a search would "place police in an almost impossible spot," *id.,* at 350.

The majority has placed school officials in this "impossible spot" by questioning whether possession of Ibuprofen and Naproxen causes a severe enough threat to warrant investigation. Had the suspected infraction involved a street drug, the majority implies that it would have approved the scope of the search. . . . In effect, then, the majority has replaced a school rule that draws no distinction among drugs with a new one that does. As a result, a full search of a student's person for prohibited drugs will be permitted only if the Court agrees that the drug in question was sufficiently dangerous. Such a test is unworkable and unsound. School officials cannot be expected to halt searches based on the possibility that a court might later find that the particular infraction at issue is not severe enough to warrant an intrusive investigation.[2]

A rule promulgated by a school board represents the judgment of school officials that the rule is needed to maintain "school order" and "a proper educational environment." *T. L. O.,* 469 U.S., at 343, n. 9. Teachers, administrators, and the local school board are called upon both to "protect the . . . safety of students and school personnel" and "maintain an environment conducive to learning." *Id.,* at 353 (Blackmun, J., concurring in judgment). They are tasked with "watch[ing] over a large number of students" who "are inclined to test the outer boundaries of acceptable conduct and to imitate the misbehavior of a peer if that misbehavior is not dealt with quickly." *Id.,* at 352. In such an environment, something as simple as a "water pistol or peashooter can wreak [havoc] until it is taken away." *Ibid.* The danger posed by unchecked distribution and consumption of prescription pills by students certainly needs no elaboration.

Judges are not qualified to second-guess the best manner for maintaining quiet and order in the school environment. . . . It is a mistake for judges to assume the responsibility for deciding which school rules are important enough to allow for invasive searches and which rules are not.

3

Even if this Court were authorized to second-guess the importance of school rules, the Court's assessment of the importance of this district's policy is flawed. It is a crime to possess or use prescription-strength Ibuprofen without a prescription. See Ariz. Rev. Stat. Ann. §13-3406(A)(1) (West Supp. 2008) ("A person shall not knowingly . . . [p]ossess or use a prescription-only drug unless the person obtains the prescription-only drug pursuant to a valid prescription of a prescriber who is licensed pursuant to [state law]"). By prohibiting unauthorized prescription drugs on school grounds—and conducting a search to ensure students abide by that prohibition—the school rule here was consistent with a routine provision of the state criminal code. It hardly seems unreasonable for school officials to enforce a rule that, in effect, proscribes conduct that amounts to a crime. . . .

Admittedly, the Ibuprofen and Naproxen at issue in this case are not the prescription painkillers at the forefront of the prescription-drug-abuse problem. See Prescription for Danger 3 ("Pain relievers like Vicodin and OxyContin are the prescription drugs most commonly abused by teens"). But they are not without their own dangers. As nonsteroidal anti-inflammatory drugs (NSAIDs), they pose a risk of death from overdose. The Pill Book 821, 827 (H. Silverman, ed., 13th ed. 2008) (observing that Ibuprofen and Naproxen are NSAIDs and "[p]eople have died from NSAID overdoses"). Moreover, the side-effects caused by the use of NSAIDs can be magnified if they are taken in combination with other drugs. See, *e.g.*, Reactions Weekly, p. 18 (Issue no. 1235, Jan. 17, 2009) ("A 17-year-old girl developed allergic interstitial nephritis and renal failure while receiving escitalopram and ibuprofen"); *id.*, at 26 (Issue no. 1232, Dec. 13, 2008) ("A 16-month-old boy developed iron deficiency anaemia and hypoalbuminaemia during treatment with naproxen"); *id.*, at 15 (Issue no. 1220, Sept. 20, 2008) (18-year-old "was diagnosed with pill-induced oesophageal perforation" after taking ibuprofen "and was admitted to the [intensive care unit]"); *id.*, at 20 (Issue no. 1170, Sept. 22, 2007) ("A 12-year-old boy developed anaphylaxis following ingestion of ibuprofen").

If a student with a previously unknown intolerance to Ibuprofen or Naproxen were to take either drug and become ill, the public outrage would likely be directed toward the school for failing to take steps to prevent the unmonitored use of the drug. In light of the risks involved, a school's decision to establish and enforce a school prohibition on the possession of any unauthorized drug is thus a reasonable judgment.

✦

In determining whether the search's scope was reasonable under the Fourth Amendment, it is therefore irrelevant whether officials suspected Redding of possessing prescription-strength Ibuprofen, nonprescription-strength Naproxen, or some harder street drug. Safford prohibited its possession on school property. Reasonable suspicion that Redding was in possession of drugs in violation of these policies, therefore, justified a search extending to any area where small pills could be concealed. The search did not violate the Fourth Amendment. . . .

Notes

[1.] The Court has adopted a different standard for searches involving an "intrusio[n] into the human body." *Schmerber* v. *California,* 384 U.S. 757, 770 (1966). The search here does not implicate the Court's cases governing bodily intrusions, however, because it did not involve a "physical intrusion, penetrating beneath the skin," *Skinner* v. *Railway Labor Executives' Assn.,* 489 U.S. 602, 616 (1989).

[2.] JUSTICE GINSBURG suggests that requiring Redding to "sit on a chair outside [the assistant principal's] office for over two hours" and failing to call her parents before conducting the search constitutes an "[a]buse of authority" that "should not be shielded by official immunity." See *ante,* at 1–2. But the school was under no constitutional obligation to call Redding's parents before conducting the search: "[R]easonableness under the Fourth Amendment does not require employing the least intrusive means, because the logic of such elaborate less-restrictive-alternative arguments could raise insuperable barriers to the exercise of virtually all search-and-seizure powers." *Board of Ed. of Independent School Dist. No. 92 of Pottawatomie Cty.* v. *Earls,* 536 U.S. 822, 837 (2002) (internal quotation marks and brackets omitted). For the same reason, the Constitution did not require school officials to ask "followup questions" after they had already developed reasonable suspicion that Redding possessed drugs. See *ante,* at 6, 10 (majority opinion); *ante,* at 1 (opinion of GINSBURG, J.). In any event, the suggestion that requiring Redding to sit in a chair for two hours amounted to a deprivation of her constitutional rights, or that school officials are required to engage in detailed interrogations before conducting searches for drugs, only reinforces the conclusion that the Judiciary is ill-equipped to second-guess the daily decisions made by public administrators. Cf. *Beard* v. *Banks,* 548 U.S. 521, 536–537 (2006) (THOMAS, J., concurring in judgment).

David Souter  **NO**

Majority Opinion, *Safford Unified School District et al. v. April Redding*

J USTICE SOUTER delivered the opinion of the Court.

The issue here is whether a 13-year-old student's Fourth Amendment right was violated when she was subjected to a search of her bra and underpants by school officials acting on reasonable suspicion that she had brought forbidden prescription and over-the-counter drugs to school. Because there were no reasons to suspect the drugs presented a danger or were concealed in her underwear, we hold that the search did violate the Constitution, but because there is reason to question the clarity with which the right was established, the official who ordered the unconstitutional search is entitled to qualified immunity from liability.

I

The events immediately prior to the search in question began in 13-year-old Savana Redding's math class at Safford Middle School one October day in 2003. The assistant principal of the school, Kerry Wilson, came into the room and asked Savana to go to his office. There, he showed her a day planner, unzipped and open flat on his desk, in which there were several knives, lighters, a permanent marker, and a cigarette. Wilson asked Savana whether the planner was hers; she said it was, but that a few days before she had lent it to her friend, Marissa Glines. Savana stated that none of the items in the planner belonged to her.

Wilson then showed Savana four white prescription-strength ibuprofen 400-mg pills, and one over-the-counter blue naproxen 200-mg pill, all used for pain and inflammation but banned under school rules without advance permission. He asked Savana if she knew anything about the pills. Savana answered that she did not. Wilson then told Savana that he had received a report that she was giving these pills to fellow students; Savana denied it and agreed to let Wilson search her belongings. Helen Romero, an administrative assistant, came into the office, and together with Wilson they searched Savana's backpack, finding nothing.

At that point, Wilson instructed Romero to take Savana to the school nurse's office to search her clothes for pills. Romero and the nurse, Peggy

From Supreme Court of the United States, June 25, 2009.

Schwallier, asked Savana to remove her jacket, socks, and shoes, leaving her in stretch pants and a T-shirt (both without pockets), which she was then asked to remove. Finally, Savana was told to pull her bra out and to the side and shake it, and to pull out the elastic on her underpants, thus exposing her breasts and pelvic area to some degree. No pills were found.

Savana's mother filed suit against Safford Unified School District #1, Wilson, Romero, and Schwallier for conducting a strip search in violation of Savana's Fourth Amendment rights. The individuals (hereinafter petitioners) moved for summary judgment, raising a defense of qualified immunity. The District Court for the District of Arizona granted the motion on the ground that there was no Fourth Amendment violation, and a panel of the Ninth Circuit affirmed. 504 F. 3d 828 (2007).

A closely divided Circuit sitting en banc, however, reversed. Following the two-step protocol for evaluating claims of qualified immunity, see *Saucier* v. *Katz*, 533 U.S. 194, 200 (2001), the Ninth Circuit held that the strip search was unjustified under the Fourth Amendment test for searches of children by school officials set out in *New Jersey* v. *T. L. O.*, 469 U.S. 325 (1985). 531 F. 3d 1071, 1081–1087 (2008). The Circuit then applied the test for qualified immunity, and found that Savana's right was clearly established at the time of the search: "'[t]hese notions of personal privacy are "clearly established" in that they inhere in all of us, particularly middle school teenagers, and are inherent in the privacy component of the Fourth Amendment's proscription against unreasonable searches.'" *Id.*, at 1088–1089 (quoting *Brannum* v. *Overton Cty. School Bd.*, 516 F. 3d 489, 499 (CA6 2008)). The upshot was reversal of summary judgment as to Wilson, while affirming the judgments in favor of Schwallier, the school nurse, and Romero, the administrative assistant, since they had not acted as independent decisionmakers. 531 F. 3d, at 1089.

We granted certiorari, 555 U.S. ___ (2009), and now affirm in part, reverse in part, and remand.

II

The Fourth Amendment "right of the people to be secure in their persons . . . against unreasonable searches and seizures" generally requires a law enforcement officer to have probable cause for conducting a search. "Probable cause exists where 'the facts and circumstances within [an officer's] knowledge and of which [he] had reasonably trustworthy information [are] sufficient in themselves to warrant a man of reasonable caution in the belief that' an offense has been or is being committed," *Brinegar* v. *United States*, 338 U.S. 160, 175–176 (1949) (quoting *Carroll* v. *United States*, 267 U.S. 132, 162 (1925)), and that evidence bearing on that offense will be found in the place to be searched.

In *T. L. O.*, we recognized that the school setting "requires some modification of the level of suspicion of illicit activity needed to justify a search," 469 U.S., at 340, and held that for searches by school officials "a careful balancing of governmental and private interests suggests that the public interest is best served by a Fourth Amendment standard of reasonableness that stops short of probable cause.". . . We have thus applied a standard of reasonable suspicion to determine the legality of a school administrator's search of a student, . . . and have held that a school search "will be permissible in its scope when the measures adopted are reasonably related to the objectives of the search and not excessively intrusive in light of the age and sex of the student and the nature of the infraction." . . .

A number of our cases on probable cause have an implicit bearing on the reliable knowledge element of reasonable suspicion, as we have attempted to flesh out the knowledge component by looking to the degree to which known facts imply prohibited conduct, see, *e.g., Adams* v. *Williams,* 407 U.S. 143, 148 (1972); *id.,* at 160, n. 9 (Marshall, J., dissenting), the specificity of the information received, see, *e.g., Spinelli* v. *United States,* 393 U.S. 410, 416–417 (1969), and the reliability of its source, see, *e.g., Aguilar* v. *Texas, 378* U.S. 108, 114 (1964). At the end of the day, however, we have realized that these factors cannot rigidly control, *Illinois* v. *Gates,* 462 U.S. 213, 230 (1983), and we have come back to saying that the standards are "fluid concepts that take their substantive content from the particular contexts" in which they are being assessed. *Ornelas* v. *United States,* 517 U.S. 690, 696 (1996).

Perhaps the best that can be said generally about the required knowledge component of probable cause for a law enforcement officer's evidence search is that it raise a "fair probability," *Gates,* 462 U.S., at 238, or a "substantial chance," *id.,* at 244, n. 13, of discovering evidence of criminal activity. The lesser standard for school searches could as readily be described as a moderate chance of finding evidence of wrongdoing.

III

A

In this case, the school's policies strictly prohibit the nonmedical use, possession, or sale of any drug on school grounds, including "'[a]ny prescription or over-the-counter drug, except those for which permission to use in school has been granted pursuant to Board policy.'" . . .[1] A week before Savana was searched, another student, Jordan Romero (no relation of the school's administrative assistant), told the principal and Assistant Principal Wilson that "certain students were bringing drugs and weapons on campus," and that he had been sick after taking some pills that "he got from a classmate." . . . On the morning of October 8, the same boy handed Wilson a white pill that he said Marissa Glines had given him. He told Wilson that students were planning to take the pills at lunch.

Wilson learned from Peggy Schwallier, the school nurse, that the pill was Ibuprofen 400 mg, available only by prescription. Wilson then called Marissa out of class. Outside the classroom, Marissa's teacher handed Wilson the day planner, found within Marissa's reach, containing various contraband items. Wilson escorted Marissa back to his office.

In the presence of Helen Romero, Wilson requested Marissa to turn out her pockets and open her wallet. Marissa produced a blue pill, several white ones, and a razor blade. Wilson asked where the blue pill came from, and Marissa answered, "'I guess it slipped in when *she* gave me the IBU 400s.'" . . . When Wilson asked whom she meant, Marissa replied, "'Savana Redding.'" . . . Wilson then enquired about the day planner and its contents; Marissa denied knowing anything about them. Wilson did not ask Marissa any followup questions to determine whether there was any likelihood that Savana presently had pills: neither asking when Marissa received the pills from Savana nor where Savana might be hiding them.

Schwallier did not immediately recognize the blue pill, but information provided through a poison control hotline . . . indicated that the pill was a 200-mg dose of an anti-inflammatory drug, generically called naproxen, available over the counter. At Wilson's direction, Marissa was then subjected to a search of her bra and underpants by Romero and Schwallier, as Savana was later on. The search revealed no additional pills.

It was at this juncture that Wilson called Savana into his office and showed her the day planner. Their conversation established that Savana and Marissa were on friendly terms: while she denied knowledge of the contraband, Savana admitted that the day planner was hers and that she had lent it to Marissa. Wilson had other reports of their friendship from staff members, who had identified Savana and Marissa as part of an unusually rowdy group at the school's opening dance in August, during which alcohol and cigarettes were found in the girls' bathroom. Wilson had reason to connect the girls with this contraband, for Wilson knew that Jordan Romero had told the principal that before the dance, he had been at a party at Savana's house where alcohol was served. Marissa's statement that the pills came from Savana was thus sufficiently plausible to warrant suspicion that Savana was involved in pill distribution.

This suspicion of Wilson's was enough to justify a search of Savana's backpack and outer clothing.[2] If a student is reasonably suspected of giving out contraband pills, she is reasonably suspected of carrying them on her person and in the carryall that has become an item of student uniform in most places today. If Wilson's reasonable suspicion of pill distribution were not understood to support searches of outer clothes and backpack, it would not justify any search worth making. And the look into Savana's bag, in her presence and in the relative privacy of Wilson's office, was not excessively intrusive, any more than Romero's subsequent search of her outer clothing.

B

Here it is that the parties part company, with Savana's claim that extending the search at Wilson's behest to the point of making her pull out her underwear was constitutionally unreasonable. The exact label for this final step in the intrusion is not important, though strip search is a fair way to speak of it. Romero and Schwallier directed Savana to remove her clothes down to her underwear, and then "pull out" her bra and the elastic band on her underpants. . . . Although Romero and Schwallier stated that they did not see anything when Savana followed their instructions, . . . we would not define strip search and its Fourth Amendment consequences in a way that would guarantee litigation about who was looking and how much was seen. The very fact of Savana's pulling her underwear away from her body in the presence of the two officials who were able to see her necessarily exposed her breasts and pelvic area to some degree, and both subjective and reasonable societal expectations of personal privacy support the treatment of such a search as categorically distinct, requiring distinct elements of justification on the part of school authorities for going beyond a search of outer clothing and belongings.

Savana's subjective expectation of privacy against such a search is inherent in her account of it as embarrassing, frightening, and humiliating. The reasonableness of her expectation (required by the Fourth Amendment standard) is indicated by the consistent experiences of other young people similarly searched, whose adolescent vulnerability intensifies the patent intrusiveness of the exposure. See Brief for National Association of Social Workers et al. as *Amici Curiae* 6–14; Hyman & Perone, The Other Side of School Violence: Educator Policies and Practices that may Contribute to Student Misbehavior, 36 J. School Psychology 7, 13 (1998) (strip search can "result in serious emotional damage"). The common reaction of these adolescents simply registers the obviously different meaning of a search exposing the body from the experience of nakedness or near undress in other school circumstances. Changing for gym is getting ready for play; exposing for a search is responding to an accusation reserved for suspected wrongdoers and fairly understood as so degrading that a number of communities have decided that strip searches in schools are never reasonable and have banned them no matter what the facts may be, see, *e.g.*, New York City Dept. of Education, Reg. No. A-432, p. 2 (2005), . . . ("Under no circumstances shall a strip-search of a student be conducted").

The indignity of the search does not, of course, outlaw it, but it does implicate the rule of reasonableness as stated in *T. L. O.*, that "the search as actually conducted [be] reasonably related in scope to the circumstances which justified the interference in the first place." 469 U.S., at 341 (internal quotation marks omitted). The scope will be permissible, that is, when it is "not excessively intrusive in light of the age and sex of the student and the nature of the infraction." *Id.*, at 342.

Here, the content of the suspicion failed to match the degree of intrusion. Wilson knew beforehand that the pills were prescription-strength ibuprofen and over-the-counter naproxen, common pain relievers equivalent to two Advil, or one Aleve. . . . He must have been aware of the nature and limited threat of the specific drugs he was searching for, and while just about anything can be taken in quantities that will do real harm, Wilson had no reason to suspect that large amounts of the drugs were being passed around, or that individual students were receiving great numbers of pills.

Nor could Wilson have suspected that Savana was hiding common painkillers in her underwear. Petitioners suggest, as a truth universally acknowledged, that "students . . . hid[e] contraband in or under their clothing," Reply Brief for Petitioners 8, and cite a smattering of cases of students with contraband in their underwear, *id.*, at 8–9. But when the categorically extreme intrusiveness of a search down to the body of an adolescent requires some justification in suspected facts, general background possibilities fall short; a reasonable search that extensive calls for suspicion that it will pay off. But nondangerous school contraband does not raise the specter of stashes in intimate places, and there is no evidence in the record of any general practice among Safford Middle School students of hiding that sort of thing in underwear; neither Jordan nor Marissa suggested to Wilson that Savana was doing that, and the preceding search of Marissa that Wilson ordered yielded nothing. Wilson never even determined when Marissa had received the pills from Savana; if it had been a few days before, that would weigh heavily against any reasonable conclusion that Savana presently had the pills on her person, much less in her underwear.

In sum, what was missing from the suspected facts that pointed to Savana was any indication of danger to the students from the power of the drugs or their quantity, and any reason to suppose that Savana was carrying pills in her underwear. We think that the combination of these deficiencies was fatal to finding the search reasonable.

In so holding, we mean to cast no ill reflection on the assistant principal, for the record raises no doubt that his motive throughout was to eliminate drugs from his school and protect students from what Jordan Romero had gone through. Parents are known to overreact to protect their children from danger, and a school official with responsibility for safety may tend to do the same. The difference is that the Fourth Amendment places limits on the official, even with the high degree of deference that courts must pay to the educator's professional judgment.

We do mean, though, to make it clear that the *T. L. O.* concern to limit a school search to reasonable scope requires the support of reasonable suspicion of danger or of resort to underwear for hiding evidence of wrongdoing before a search can reasonably make the quantum leap from outer clothes and backpacks to exposure of intimate parts. The meaning of such a search, and the degradation its subject may reasonably feel, place a search that intrusive in a category of its own demanding its own specific suspicions.

IV

A school official searching a student is "entitled to qualified immunity where clearly established law does not show that the search violated the Fourth Amendment." *Pearson* v. *Callahan,* 555 U.S. _, _ (2009) (slip op., at 18). To be established clearly, however, there is no need that "the very action in question [have] previously been held unlawful." *Wilson* v. *Layne,* 526 U.S. 603, 615 (1999). The unconstitutionality of outrageous conduct obviously will be unconstitutional, this being the reason, as Judge Posner has said, that "[t]he easiest cases don't even arise." *K. H.* v. *Morgan,* 914 F. 2d 846, 851 (CA7 1990). But even as to action less than an outrage, "officials can still be on notice that their conduct violates established law . . . in novel factual circumstances." *Hope* v. *Pelzer,* 536 U.S. 730, 741 (2002).

T. L. O. directed school officials to limit the intrusiveness of a search, "in light of the age and sex of the student and the nature of the infraction," 469 U.S., at 342, and as we have just said at some length, the intrusiveness of the strip search here cannot be seen as justifiably related to the circumstances. But we realize that the lower courts have reached divergent conclusions regarding how the *T. L. O.* standard applies to such searches.

A number of judges have read *T. L. O.* as the en banc minority of the Ninth Circuit did here. The Sixth Circuit upheld a strip search of a high school student for a drug, without any suspicion that drugs were hidden next to her body. *Williams* v. *Ellington,* 936 F. 2d 881, 882–883, 887 (1991). And other courts considering qualified immunity for strip searches have read *T. L. O.* as "a series of abstractions, on the one hand, and a declaration of seeming deference to the judgments of school officials, on the other," *Jenkins* v. *Talladega City Bd. of Ed.,* 115 F. 3d 821, 828 (CA11 1997) (en banc), which made it impossible "to establish clearly the contours of a Fourth Amendment right . . . [in] the wide variety of possible school settings different from those involved in *T. L. O.*" itself. *Ibid.* See also *Thomas* v. *Roberts,* 323 F. 3d 950 (CA11 2003) (granting qualified immunity to a teacher and police officer who conducted a group strip search of a fifth grade class when looking for a missing $26).

We think these differences of opinion from our own are substantial enough to require immunity for the school officials in this case. We would not suggest that entitlement to qualified immunity is the guaranteed product of disuniform views of the law in the other federal, or state, courts, and the fact that a single judge, or even a group of judges, disagrees about the contours of a right does not automatically render the law unclear if we have been clear. That said, however, the cases viewing school strip searches differently from the way we see them are numerous enough, with well-reasoned majority and dissenting opinions, to counsel doubt that we were sufficiently clear in the prior statement of law. We conclude that qualified immunity is warranted.

V

The strip search of Savana Redding was unreasonable and a violation of the Fourth Amendment, but petitioners Wilson, Romero, and Schwallier are nevertheless protected from liability through qualified immunity. Our conclusions here do not resolve, however, the question of the liability of petitioner Safford Unified School District #1 under *Monell* v. *New York City Dept. of Social Servs.,* 436 U.S. 658, 694 (1978), a claim the Ninth Circuit did not address. The judgment of the Ninth Circuit is therefore affirmed in part and reversed in part, and this case is remanded for consideration of the *Monell* claim.

It is so ordered.

Notes

[1.] When the object of a school search is the enforcement of a school rule, a valid search assumes, of course, the rule's legitimacy. But the legitimacy of the rule usually goes without saying as it does here. The Court said plainly in *New Jersey* v. *T. L. O.,* 469 U.S. 325, 342, n. 9 (1985), that standards of conduct for schools are for school administrators to determine without second-guessing by courts lacking the experience to appreciate what may be needed. Except in patently arbitrary instances, Fourth Amendment analysis takes the rule as a given, as it obviously should do in this case. There is no need here either to explain the imperative of keeping drugs out of schools, or to explain the reasons for the school's rule banning all drugs, no matter how benign, without advance permission. Teachers are not pharmacologists trained to identify pills and powders, and an effective drug ban has to be enforceable fast. The plenary ban makes sense, and there is no basis to claim that the search was unreasonable owing to some defect or shortcoming of the rule it was aimed at enforcing.

[2.] 'There is no question here that justification for the school officials' search was required in accordance with the *T. L. O.* standard of reasonable suspicion, for it is common ground that Savana had a reasonable expectation of privacy covering the personal things she chose to carry in her backpack, cf. 469 U.S., at 339, and that Wilson's decision to look through it was a "search" within the meaning of the Fourth Amendment.

POSTSCRIPT

Is a Strip Search of Students Permissible under the Fourth Amendment?

The *Redding* case is an example of a physical intrusion using physical means. Technological advances, however, are posing new challenges. We are developing technological capabilities to do things at a distance and to obtain information that previously would have required entering a physical location. Law enforcement's ability to invade privacy at a distance is increasing, and the Supreme Court is likely to be faced with cases in which data is collected without the student or citizen being aware of it. The Court has already upheld some novel search techniques outside of school, and most searches permitted outside of school are likely to be permitted in school. Consider the following:

- *Dow Chemical v. United States,* 476 U.S. 227 (1986)—The Court allowed aerial pictures taken by the Environmental Protection Agency (EPA) even though the company had refused to allow inspectors to enter.
- *Florida v. Riley,* 488 U.S. 445, 450 (1989)—The Court allowed a search in which a police officer in a helicopter looked into a greenhouse from a height of 400 feet and observed through openings in the roof what he thought was marijuana.
- *California v. Ciraolo,* 476 U.S. 207, 213–214 (1986)—The Court held that police officers were not "searching" when they flew over the defendant's property and observed marijuana growing.
- *Smith v. Maryland,* 442 U.S. 735, 742–744 (1979)—The Court allowed the authorities to look at "pen registers," or records of telephone numbers dialed, without a warrant.

One exception to the trend is *Danny Lee Kyllo v. United States,* 533 U.S. 27 (2001), where the Court held that the use without a warrant of thermal imaging devices that reveal information "that would previously have been unknowable without physical intrusion" violates the Fourth Amendment. The police had used the thermal imaging technology on the assumption that to grow marijuana indoors, one needs to provide a lot of light so plants can photosynthesize.

In *United States v. Place,* 462 U.S. 696 (1983), the Court allowed the use of dogs when the sniff "discloses only the presence or absence of narcotics." We are in an era in which there are many electronic substitutes for such dogs. We are also in an era in which we can be tracked via cameras in many locations and GPS systems in cell phones. We are, in other words, in an era in which the meaning of the Fourth Amendment is likely to be an issue in increasing numbers of cases.

Background information on law enforcement and the drug problem can be found on the Web site of the Drug Enforcement Administration of the U.S. Department of Justice at http://www.usdoj.gov/dea. The thermal imaging issue is discussed in Kathleen A. Lomas, "Bad Physics and Bad Law: A Review of the Constitutionality of Thermal Imagery Surveillance after *United States v. Elkins*," 34 *U.S.F. L. Rev.* 799 (2000). Other articles about new technologies and the Fourth Amendment are Tobias W. Mock, "The TSA's New X-Ray Vision: The Fourth Amendment Implications of 'Body-Scan' Searches at Domestic Airport Security Checkpoints," 49 *Santa Clara Law Review* 213 (2009) and Ian James Samuel, "Warrantless Location Tracking," 83 *N.Y.U. L. Rev.* 1324 (2008). A report on the oral argument in the *Redding* case is Dahlia Lithwick, "Search Me: The Supreme Court Is Neither Hot nor Bothered by Strip Searches," *Slate* (http://www.slate.com/id/2216608).

ISSUE 8

Do Mandatory Sentencing Laws Help the Criminal Justice System?

YES: David Risley, Assistant U.S. Attorney, Illinois, from "Mandatory Minimum Sentences: An Overview," *Drug Watch International* (May 2000)

NO: Lois Forer, from "Justice by Numbers," *The Washington Monthly* (April 1992)

ISSUE SUMMARY

YES: David Risley argues that mandatory minimum sentences sends a message that serious drug crimes should not be trivialized.

NO: Lois Forer, who is a judge, finds that mandatory sentencing is often too inflexible to give guidance in cases where the case is complicated and other circumstances tell the judge that the person will not repeat.

David Risley begins his article by saying that the purpose of mandatory minimum sentences is to counter any perceptions on the part of the public or criminals themselves that serious drug crimes are trivial matters. Drug dealers, he argues, seldom view the risks as too high and hope for a light sentence. Therefore, Congress stepped in through the establishment of mandatory minimum sentences for serious drug offenses. Risley further notes that "Congress sent a clear message to drug dealers: No matter who the judge is, serious crime will get you serious time."

Lois Forer counters that Americans push for mandatory minimums because of their unfettered belief "in the sanctity of punishment." She claims that if society viewed crime more practically, we would create more rational alternatives to prison in many cases.

Before the creation of mandatory minimum sentences in the 1970s and before the rise in serious drug offenses, Risley argues, federal judges had too much discretion to impose whatever sentences they deemed appropriate, even up to the maximum allowed by statute. Therefore, sentences judges imposed for similar offenses by similar defendants varied widely. Risley argues further that strangely enough, lenient sentences became predominant in high-crime areas, that is, large metropolitan and drug importation centers where there is a large degree of desensitization.

Forer argues alternatively: "Why not permit judges more freedom in making their decisions, provided that they give legitimate reasons?" When every case is unique, it is hard to place a cookie-cutter approach on sentencing. Forer also says that these inflexible cookie-cutter sentences are often too harsh, without the possibility to take into consideration other facts about the case, such as the five-year prison sentence eventually imposed on Micheal S. for wielding a toy gun to hold up a taxi cab and take $50 from the driver and the passenger, though harming neither one. Forer says she takes this approach on the bench because of her experience in sentencing one-time offender Michael S. to only 11 months in prison; the Supreme Court later upheld an appeal, requiring the author to sentence Michael S. to a mandatory five years in prison. Forer soon resigned over this case.

However, Risley says, on the contrary, these sentences are flexible. He also makes the point that it takes a lot for mandatory sentencing to kick in. He explains that in the federal system there are two levels of mandatory minimum sentences. The first level requires a minimum sentence of five years in prison, doubled if there was a prior felony. The second level carries a minimum sentence of 10 years, doubled for a prior felony; with two prior convictions, there is a mandatory life sentence.

Forer contends, however, that mandatory minimums are unconstitutional because (1) they violate the Constitution's separation of powers as a mandatory minimum bypasses the judge with the prosecutor's choice of sentencing; (2) they are "arbitrary and capricious" because even purse snatching, in her example, has mandatory minimums, but not incest or child molestation; and (3) a person's mental state is not considered, so a retarded man receives the same sentence as a repeat offender.

Mandatory sentencing is an open question. Is Risley right in thinking that mandatory sentences create a fairer and clearer judicial system and give the public a sense that the court system is taking sentencing seriously? Or is Forer correct in believing that sentencing is not flexible enough for judicial discretion, violates the separation of powers, and is too harsh in cases where the offender is unlikely to repeat the crime?

YES

David Risley

Mandatory Minimum Sentences: An Overview

The purpose of mandatory minimum sentences is to prevent the judicial trivialization of serious drug crimes. They do that well, to which some protest. Because the federal sentencing system is the model most often cited, it will be used for illustration throughout the following discussion.

Before the advent of mandatory minimum sentences in serious drug cases, federal judges had unbridled discretion to impose whatever sentences they deemed appropriate, in their personal view, up to the statutory maximum. Because individual judges differ widely in their personal views about crime and sentencing, the sentences they imposed for similar offenses by similar defendants varied widely. What some judges treated as serious offenses, and punished accordingly, others minimized with much more lenient sentences.

Ironically, more lenient sentences became particularly prevalent in areas with high volumes of major drug crime, such as large metropolitan and drug importation centers. Perhaps the sheer volume of cases in such areas led to a certain degree of desensitization. When serious crime becomes routine, there is human tendency to treat it routinely, and sentences often drop accordingly. In some areas across the country, that phenomenon can even be seen with crimes such as murder.

While the ideal is that sentences be perfectly personalized by wise, prudent, and consistent judges to fit every individual defendant and crime, the reality is that judges are human, and their wide human differences and perspectives lead to widely different sentences, if given completely unbridled discretion.

Such wide disparity in sentencing is inherently unfair, at least to those who receive stiff sentences for crimes for which others are punished only lightly. But such inconsistency was welcomed by drug dealers, since it meant they could hope for a light sentence for serious drug crimes. That, of course, created a much bigger problem.

Drug dealers are risk takers by nature. Lack of certainty of serious sentences for serious crimes encourages, rather than deters, such risk takers to elevate their level of criminal activity in the hope that, if caught, they will be lucky enough to draw a lenient judge and receive a lenient sentence. The only possible deterrence for people who are willing to take extreme risks is to take away their cause for such hope.

Some counter that drug dealers are undeterrable by criminal sanctions because they sell drugs to support their own addictions, and so should be treated for their addictions rather than imprisoned. While there may be some merit to that argument for many low-level street dealers, it is generally untrue of their suppliers, and even many other street dealers. Most dealers and distributors at any substantial level do not use drugs themselves, or do so only infrequently. They are exploiters and predators, and users are their captive prey. Drug dealing is a business. As in any other business, drug addicts are unreliable and untrustworthy, especially around drugs, and so make poor business partners. Because drug dealers usually run their operations as high-risk businesses, they necessarily weigh those risks carefully, and so are deterrable when the risks become too high. Many dealers who used to carry firearms, for example, now avoid doing so when they are selling drugs due to the high mandatory federal penalties when guns and drugs are mixed.

However, drug dealers seldom view the risks as too high when they see reason to hope for a light sentence. Congress, however, can, and did, step in to take away that hope. By establishing mandatory minimum sentences for serious drug offenses, Congress sent a clear message to drug dealers: no matter who the judge is, serious crime will get you serious time.

To those who do not view crimes subject to mandatory minimum sentences as serious, including drug dealers and their support systems, that message is objectionable. To most, it is welcome. Mandatory minimum sentences put steel in the spine of our criminal justice system.

The natural question which follows is, what level of dealing must defendants reach before being subject to mandatory minimum sentences, and what are those sentences? The answer varies with the type of drug and whether the defendant is a repeat offender.

In the federal system, there are two levels of mandatory minimums, with each level doubling for defendants with prior convictions. The first tier requires a minimum sentence of imprisonment for five years (10 with a prior felony drug conviction), and the second tier requires a minimum of 10 years (20 with one prior felony drug conviction, and mandatory life with two such prior convictions). Of that, defendants can receive a reduction in the time they serve in prison of only 54 days per year as a reward for "good behavior," which means they must actually serve about 85% of their sentences.

For a prior drug offense to be considered a felony, it must be punishable by more than one year. In the federal system and most states, a drug offense is rarely classified as a felony unless it involves distribution of the drugs involved, or an intent to do so. For most practical purposes, therefore, a prior felony conviction for a drug such as marijuana can be read to mean a prior conviction for distribution. And, since most small distribution cases are reduced to misdemeanor simple possession (personal use) charges as part of plea bargains, especially for first-time offenders, a prior felony drug conviction for a drug such as marijuana usually means the prior conviction either involved a substantial amount of the drug or a repeat offender undeserving of another such break.

In the case of marijuana, those who oppose mandatory minimum sentencing on so-called "humanitarian" grounds seldom mention that, to be eligible for even a five-year minimum sentence, a defendant must be convicted of an offense involving at least 100 kilograms (220 pounds) of marijuana, or, in the case of a marijuana growing operation, at least 100 plants. Such defendants are not low-level offenders.

With marijuana available at the Mexican border in Texas for wholesale prices between $600 to $1100 per pound, and selling in most areas at a retail price of between $1200 to $2000 per pound, and with any reasonably healthy cultivated marijuana plant producing at least one and sometimes two pounds of finished product, eligibility for even the lowest mandatory minimum sentence requires conviction of an offense involving between $132,000 to $440,000 worth of marijuana, or plants capable of producing marijuana worth a bulk retail price of between $120,000 to $450,000.

To be eligible for the next, 10-year tier of minimum sentence, a defendant must be convicted of an offense involving 1000 kilograms (1.1 tons) of marijuana or 1000 marijuana plants. Even at a low wholesale price of $600 per pound, such offenses involve marijuana worth at least $1.3 million. One kilogram equals 2.2 pounds. Conversely, one pound equals 453.6 grams, and one ounce equals 28.35 grams.

It would be difficult to describe any offense involving between $120,000 to $450,000 worth of drugs as undeserving of even a five-year prison sentence. Yet, those who oppose mandatory minimum sentences for marijuana and other drug offenses do just that, usually by attempting to convey the false impression [that] the criminals they are attempting to protect are only low-level offenders.

In examining the deterrent potential of such mandatory minimum sentences, one must consider that the profit potential for marijuana offenses is relatively high, and the penalties relatively low, which makes marijuana an attractive drug in which to deal, as evidenced by its widespread availability. To illustrate, if a dealer bought 200 pounds of marijuana in Texas for $900 per pound, for a total of $180,000, transported it to the Midwest and sold it for as low as $1400 per pound, for a total of $280,000 with minimal overhead, the profit for just one such trip would be $100,000. When the street-level price of between $125 to $300 per ounce is considered, or the lower acquisition costs if the marijuana is grown by the dealer himself, the profit potential for such a venture can be huge, and yet still not involve enough drugs to trigger even the lowest mandatory minimum penalty. Since the chance of getting caught for any single trip of that sort is relatively low, the prospect of a quick $100,000 profit lures plenty of eager dealers, even with the risk of spending close to five years in prison.

Of course, if drug dealers are undeterrable, as the actions of many demonstrate they are, the only realistic options left are to either give up and allow them to ply their predatory trade unhindered (the legalization "solution"), or incapacitate them with even longer sentences.

The debate, it would seem, should be about whether the mandatory minimum penalties for marijuana offenses are currently too lenient, not too harsh.

Mandatory Minimums as a Check on Sentencing Guidelines

The next question is whether the more recent advent of the federal sentencing guidelines, which also limit judicial sentencing discretion, made mandatory minimum penalties obsolete. The answer is definitely no. As a practical matter, only through mandatory minimum sentences can Congress maintain sentencing benchmarks for serious drug crimes which cannot be completely circumvented by the commission which establishes, and sometimes quietly alters, those guidelines. One of the best illustrations is that of the sentencing guidelines for marijuana growers, who have achieved favorable treatment under the sentencing guidelines, but fortunately not under Congress' statutory mandatory minimum sentences.

To appreciate the significance of that illustration, one must understand a little about the sentencing guideline system, and its relationship to mandatory minimum sentences. As part of the Sentencing Reform Act of 1984, Congress mandated the formation of the United States Sentencing Commission as an independent agency in the judicial branch composed of seven voting members, appointed by the President with the advice and consent of the Senate, at least three of whom must be federal judges, not more than four of whom may be from the same political party, serving staggered six-year terms. That Commission was charged with the formidable task of establishing binding sentencing guidelines to dramatically narrow judges' sentencing discretion, in order to provide reasonable uniformity in sentencing throughout the country, while at the same time taking into reasonable account the myriad of differences between the hundreds of federal crimes and limitless array of individual defendants.

The result of that enormous undertaking was the adoption, effective November 1987, of the United States Sentencing Guidelines. Using its provisions, contained in a book one inch thick, courts determine the seriousness of the offense and the extent of the defendant's past criminal history, and use that information to determine on a chart the relatively narrow sentencing range within which they have sentencing discretion. In drug cases, the seriousness of the offense (offense level) is determined mostly on the basis of the amount of drugs for which a defendant is accountable, with adjustments for factors such as role in the offense, whether a firearm was involved, and whether the defendant accepted responsibility for his or her actions through a candid guilty plea.

As part of its broad delegation of authority, Congress provided that changes promulgated by the Commission to the Sentencing Guidelines automatically become law unless Congress, within a 180-day waiting period, affirmatively acts to reject them. By that means Congress avoided a great deal of detailed work, but also created the possibility that changes to the Sentencing Guidelines to which they would object if carefully considered would become law if no one raises a sufficient alarm.

Because the Commission has only seven voting members, a change of only one member can result in the reversal of a previous 4-3 vote, sometimes with great consequences. Congress is ill-equipped to deal with the intricacies of the impact of many amendments to the Sentencing Guidelines, and is sometimes preoccupied with other, more pressing or "hot button" issues. Therefore, the only realistic check on the delegation of authority to the Commission to make changes in drug sentences is the trump card of mandatory minimums.

That is true because defendants receive the higher of whatever sentence is called for by the statutory mandatory minimums or the Sentencing Guidelines. If the Commission promulgates a change to the Sentencing Guidelines that calls for lower sentences than required by the statutory mandatory minimums, the mandatory minimums trump the Sentencing Guidelines. In other words, the mandatory minimums are mandatory, and are beyond the control of the Commission.

With that background, the vital importance of mandatory minimum sentences as at least a partial check over the Commission in drug sentences is dramatically illustrated by the changes the Commission made regarding sentences for marijuana growers. The mandatory minimum sentences for marijuana growers imposed by Congress, which kick in at 100 plants, equate one marijuana plant with one kilogram (2.2 pounds) of marijuana. Until November 1995, the Sentencing Guidelines used that same equivalency in calculating the offense level in cases involving 50 or more plants, but for cases involving less than 50 plants considered one plant as the equivalent of only 100 grams (3.5 ounces). That 10:1 ratio between the amount of marijuana to which plants were considered to represent was a major logical inconsistency, since marijuana plants do not produce significantly more or less marijuana just because they happen to be in the company of more or less than 49 other marijuana plants.

The Commission solved that inconsistency in early 1995 by promulgating an amendment to the Sentencing Guidelines which, instead of eliminating the unrealistically low 100-gram equivalency for smaller cases, eliminated the one-kilogram equivalency for larger cases. Congress did nothing, so, as of November 1995, the Sentencing Guidelines treat all marijuana plants as if they were only capable of producing 3.5 ounces of marijuana.

In explanation, the Commission stated:

> In actuality, a marihuana plant does not produce a yield of one kilogram of marihuana. The one plant = 100 grams of marihuana equivalency used by the Commission for offenses involving fewer than 50 marihuana plants was selected as a reasonable approximation of the actual average yield of marihuana plants taking into account (1) studies reporting the actual yield of marihuana plants (37.5 to 412 grams depending on growing conditions); (2) that all plants regardless of size are counted for guideline purposes while, in actuality, not all plants will produce useable marihuana (e.g., some plants may die of disease before maturity, and when plants are grown outdoors some plants may be consumed by animals); and (3) that male plants, which are counted for guideline purposes, are frequently culled because they do not produce the same quality marihuana as do female plants. To enhance fairness and consistency, this amendment adopts the equivalency of 100 grams per marihuana plant for all guideline determinations.

Contrary to those claims, no self-respecting commercial marijuana grower would ever admit his plants produce no more than 412 grams (14.5 ounces) of marijuana, much less that they average only 100 grams. Based upon long experience with actual marijuana growing operations, it is widely accepted in law enforcement circles that cultivated marijuana plants typically produce about one pound of marijuana (453 grams), and sometimes two pounds (907 grams). While it is true that some growers cull out the male plants in order to produce the potent form of marijuana known as sinsemilla, derived from the unpollinated female plant, not all growers do so. And, the observations of the Commission completely ignore the fact that a marijuana plant is a renewable resource—the seeds from one plant can be used to grow several more plants. It is unrealistic, therefore, to treat one plant as representing only that amount of marijuana it can produce itself, and to require courts to assume all marijuana growers standing before them are incapable of producing more than 100 grams of marijuana per plant.

Fortunately, Congress was more realistic in establishing its mandatory minimum sentences. And, for cases involving 100 or more plants, those mandatory minimums trump the Sentencing Guidelines. The result, however, is still a boon to commercial marijuana growers who are informed enough to keep the number of plants in their operations under 100, or under 1000. That is because the interaction between the lenient Sentencing Guidelines and the stricter mandatory minimums produces a stair step effect on sentences at the 100 and 1000 plant marks.

If a marijuana grower is caught raising 99 marijuana plants, no mandatory minimum sentence is triggered. Under the Sentencing Guidelines, those plants would be treated as the equivalent of 9.9 kilograms of marijuana ($26,135 worth, using a conservative price of $1200 per pound), which, for an offender caught for the first time, would result in an unadjusted sentencing guideline range of only 15 to 21 months. With the normal adjustment to reward a candid guilty plea, that guideline range would drop to 10 to 16 months.

In contrast, if that same grower raised just one more plant, for a total of 100, the first tier of mandatory minimum sentences would be triggered, and the court would be required to impose a sentence of five years. The jump from a maximum sentence of 20 months for 99 plants up to five years for 100 plants is due solely to the overriding effect of the mandatory minimum sentence.

Not until that same grower was caught with 800 to 999 plants, treated as the equivalent of 80 to 99.9 kilograms of marijuana (at least $211,200 worth), would his unadjusted sentencing guideline range reach the 51- to 63-month mark, and even then a candid guilty plea would drop it to 37 to 46 months. Consequently, the five-year mandatory minimum would probably still control the sentence. But, if the grower were caught with just one more plant, raising the total to 1000, the second tier of mandatory minimum sentences would be triggered, requiring a sentence of 10 years. Again, the jump from a maximum sentence of 63 months for 999 plants up to 10 years for 1000 plants is due solely to Congress' mandatory minimum sentence scheme.

Without those mandatory minimum sentences, the commission's view that marijuana plants should only be treated as the equivalent of 100 grams of marijuana would be controlling, which marijuana growers would doubtless applaud. Only because of the mandatory minimums does the more sensible view of Congress that each marijuana plant should be treated as the equivalent of one kilogram of marijuana impact growing operations involving 100 or more plants.

Ultimately, whether the effect of those mandatory minimum sentences is good or bad depends upon how seriously one views marijuana use. If a person believes a sentence of five years is too harsh for growing 100 marijuana plants conservatively capable of producing between $26,400 to $120,000 worth of marijuana, or distributing 220 pounds of marijuana worth at least $264,000, the mandatory minimum sentences for marijuana should be abolished. If, however, a five year sentence for such crimes seems reasonable, or even lenient, the mandatory minimums should be retained, and perhaps toughened.

There is no doubt about on which side of that question the marijuana growers, dealers, users, and their supporters stand. There is also little room to doubt on which side those who take marijuana crimes seriously should stand.

Lois G. Forer

 **NO**

Justice by Numbers

Michael S. would have been one of the more than 600,000 incarcerated persons in the United States. He would have been a statistic, yet another addition to a clogged criminal justice system. But he's not—in part because to me Michael was a human being: a slight 24-year-old with a young wife and small daughter. Not that I freed him; I tried him and found him guilty. He is free now only because he is a fugitive. I have not seen him since the day of his sentencing in 1984, yet since that day our lives have been inextricably connected. Because of his case I retired from the bench.

Michael's case appeared routine. He was a typical offender: young, black, and male, a high-school dropout without a job. The charge was an insignificant holdup that occasioned no comment in the press. And the trial itself was, in the busy life of a judge, a run-of-the-mill event.

The year before, Michael, brandishing a toy gun, held up a taxi and took $50 from the driver and the passenger, harming neither. This was Michael's first offense. Although he had dropped out of school to marry his pregnant girlfriend, Michael later obtained a high school equivalency diploma. He had been steadily employed, earning enough to send his daughter to parochial school—a considerable sacrifice for him and his wife. Shortly before the holdup, Michael had lost his job. Despondent because he could not support his family, he went out on a Saturday night, had more than a few drinks, and then robbed the taxi.

There was no doubt that Michael was guilty. But the penalty posed problems. To me, a robbery in a taxi is not an intrinsically graver offense than a robbery in an alley, but to the Pennsylvania legislature, it is. Because the holdup occurred on public transportation, it fell within the ambit of the state's mandatory sentencing law—which required a minimum sentence of five years in the state penitentiary. In Pennsylvania, a prosecutor may decide not to demand imposition of that law, but Michael's prosecuting attorney wanted the five-year sentence.

One might argue that a five-year sentence for a $50 robbery is excessive or even immoral, but to a judge, those arguments are necessarily irrelevant. He or she has agreed to enforce the law, no matter how ill-advised, unless the law is unconstitutional.

I believed the mandatory sentencing law was, and like many of my colleagues I had held it unconstitutional in several other cases for several reasons.

From *Washington Monthly*, April 1992, pp. 12–14, 16–18. Copyright © 1992 by Washington Monthly. Reprinted by permission.

We agreed that it violates the constitutional principle of separation of powers because it can be invoked by the prosecutor, and not by the judge. In addition, the act is arbitrary and capricious in its application. Robbery, which is often a simple purse snatching, is covered, but not child molestation or incest, two of society's most damaging offenses. Nor can a defendant's previous record or mental state be considered. A hardened repeat offender receives the same sentence as a retarded man who steals out of hunger. Those facts violate the fundamental Anglo-American legal principles of individualized sentencing and proportionality of the penalty to the crime.

Thus in Michael's case, I again held the statute to be unconstitutional and turned to the sentencing guidelines—a state statute designed to give uniform sentences to offenders who commit similar crimes. The minimum sentence prescribed by the guidelines was 24 months.

A judge can deviate from the prescribed sentence if he or she writes an opinion explaining the reasons for the deviation. While this sounds reasonable in theory, "downwardly departing" from the guidelines is extremely difficult. The mitigating circumstances that influence most judges are not included in the limited list of factors on which "presumptive" sentence is based—that an offender is a caretaker of small children; that the offender is mentally retarded; or that the offender, like Michael, is emotionally distraught.

So I decided to deviate from the guidelines, sentencing Michael to 11-and-a-half months in the county jail and permitting him to work outside the prison during the day to support his family. I also imposed a sentence of two years' probation following his imprisonment conditioned upon repayment of the $50. My rationale for the lesser penalty, outlined in my lengthy opinion, was that this was a first offense, no one was harmed, Michael acted under the pressures of unemployment and need, and he seemed truly contrite. He had never committed a violent act and posed no danger to the public. A sentence of close to a year seemed adequate to convince Michael of the seriousness of his crime. Nevertheless, the prosecutor appealed.

Michael returned to his family, obtained steady employment, and repaid the victims of his crime. I thought no more about Michael until 1986, when the state supreme court upheld the appeal and ordered me to resentence him to a minimum of five years in the state penitentiary. By this time Michael had successfully completed his term of imprisonment and probation, including payment of restitution. I checked Michael's record. He had not been rearrested.

I was faced with a legal and moral dilemma. As a judge I had sworn to uphold the law, and I could find no legal grounds for violating an order of the supreme court. Yet five years' imprisonment was grossly disproportionate to the offense. The usual grounds for imprisonment are retribution, deterrence, and rehabilitation. Michael had paid his retribution by a short term of imprisonment and by making restitution to the victims. He had been effectively deterred from committing future crimes. And by any measurable standard he had been rehabilitated. There was no social or criminological justification for sending him back to prison. Given the choice between defying a court order or my conscience, I decided to leave the bench where I had sat for 16 years.

That didn't help Michael, of course; he was resentenced by another judge to serve the balance of the five years: four years and 15 days. Faced with this prospect, he disappeared. A bench warrant was issued, but given the hundreds of fugitives—including dangerous ones—loose in Philadelphia, I doubt that anyone is seriously looking for him.

But any day he may be stopped for a routine traffic violation; he may apply for a job or a license; he may even be the victim of a crime—and if so, the ubiquitous computer will be alerted and he will be returned to prison to serve the balance of his sentence, plus additional time for being a fugitive. It is not a happy prospect for him and his family—nor for America, which is saddled with a punishment system that operates like a computer—crime in, points tallied, sentence out—utterly disregarding the differences among the human beings involved.

The mandatory sentencing laws and guidelines that exist today in every state were designed to smooth out the inequities in the American judiciary, and were couched in terms of fairness to criminals—they would stop the racist judge from sentencing black robbers to be hanged, or the crusading judge from imprisoning pot smokers for life. Guidelines make sense, for that very reason. But they have had an ugly and unintended result—an increase in the number of American prisoners and an increase in the length of the sentences they serve. Meanwhile, the laws have effectively neutralized judges who prefer sentencing the nonviolent to alternative programs or attempt to keep mothers with young children out of jail.

Have the laws made justice fairer—the central objective of the law? I say no, and a recent report by the Federal Sentencing Commission concurs. It found that, even under mandatory sentencing laws, black males served 83.4 months to white males' 53.7 months for the same offenses. (Prosecutors are more likely to demand imposition of the mandatory laws for blacks than for whites.)

Most important, however, as mandatory sentencing packs our prisons and busts our budgets, it doesn't prevent crime very effectively. For certain kinds of criminals, alternative sentencing is the most effective type of punishment. That, by the way, is a cold, hard statistic—rather like Michael will be when they find him.

Sentenced to Death

In the past two decades, all 50 state legislatures have enacted mandatory sentencing laws, sentencing guideline statutes, or both. The result: In 1975 there were 263,291 inmates in federal and state prisons. Today there are over 600,000—more than in any other nation—the bill for which comes to $20.3 billion a year. Yet incarceration has not reduced the crime rate or made our streets and communities safer. The number of known crimes committed in the U.S. has increased 10 percent in the last five years.

How did we get into this no-win situation? Like most legislative reforms, it started with good intentions. In 1970, after the turmoil of the sixties, legislators were bombarded with pleas for "law and order." A young, eager, newly appointed federal judge, Marvin Frankel, had an idea.

Before his appointment, Frankel had experienced little personal contact with the criminal justice system. Yet his slim book, *Fair and Certain Punishment,* offered a system of guidelines to determine the length of various sentences. Each crime was given a certain number of points. The offender was also given a number of points depending upon his or her prior record, use of a weapon, and a few other variables. The judge merely needed to add up the points to calculate the length of imprisonment.

The book was widely read and lauded for two main reasons. First, it got tough on criminals and made justice "certain." A potential offender would know in advance the penalty he would face and thus be deterred. (Of course, a large proportion of street crimes are not premeditated, but that fact was ignored.) And second, it got tough on the "bleeding heart" judges. All offenders similarly situated would be treated the same.

The plan sounded so fair and politically promising that many states rushed to implement it in the seventies. In Pennsylvania, members of the legislature admonished judges not to oppose the guidelines because the alternative would be even worse: mandatory sentences. In fact, within a few years almost every jurisdiction had both sentencing guidelines and mandatory sentencing laws. Since then, Congress has enacted some 60 mandatory sentencing laws on the federal level.

As for unfairnesses in sentencing—for instance, the fact that the robber with his finger in his jacket gets the same sentence as the guy with a semiautomatic— these could have been rectified by giving appellate courts jurisdiction to review sentences, as is the law in Canada. This was not done on either the state or federal level. Thus what influential criminologist James Q. Wilson had argued during the height of the battle had become the law of the land: The legal system should "most definitely stop pretending that the judges know any better than the rest of us how to provide 'individualized justice.'"

Hardening Time

I'm not sure I knew better than the rest of you, but I knew a few things about Michael and the correctional system I would be throwing him into. At the time of Michael's sentencing, both the city of Philadelphia and the commonwealth of Pennsylvania were, like many cities and states, in such poor fiscal shape that they did not have money for schools and health care, let alone new prisons, and the ones they did have were overflowing. The city was under a federal order to reduce the prison population; untried persons accused of dangerous crimes were being released, as were offenders who had not completed their sentences.

As for Michael, his problems and those of his family were very real to me. Unlike appellate judges who never see the individuals whose lives and property they dispose of, a trial judge sees living men and women. I had seen Michael and his wife and daughter. I had heard him express remorse. I had favorable reports about him from the prison and his parole officer. Moreover, Michael, like many offenders who appeared before me, had written to me several times. I felt I knew him.

Of course, I could have been wrong. As Wilson says, judges are not infallible—and most of them know that. But they have heard the evidence, seen the offender, and been furnished with presentence reports and psychiatric evaluations. They are in a better position to evaluate the individual and devise an appropriate sentence than anyone else in the criminal justice system.

Yet under mandatory sentencing laws, the complexities of each crime and criminal are ignored. And seldom do we ask what was once a legitimate question in criminal justice: What are the benefits of incarceration? The offenders are off the streets for the period of the sentence, but once released, most will soon be rearrested. (Many crimes are committed in prison, including murder, rape, robbery, and drug dealing.) They have not been "incapacitated," another of the theoretical justifications for imprisonment. More likely, they have simply been hardened.

Sentence Structure

Is there another way to sentence criminals without endangering the public? I believe there is. During my tenure on the bench, I treated imprisonment as the penalty of last resort, not the penalty of choice. And my examination of 16 years' worth of cases suggests my inclination was well founded. While a recent Justice Department study found that two thirds of all prisoners are arrested for other offenses within three years of release, more than two thirds of the 1,000-plus offenders I sentenced to probation conditioned upon payment of reparations to victims successfully completed their sentences and were not re-arrested. I am not a statistician, so I had my records analyzed and verified by Elmer Weitekamp, then a doctoral candidate in criminology at the Wharton School of the University of Pennsylvania. He confirmed my findings.

The offenders who appeared before me were mostly poor people, poor enough to qualify for representation by a public defender. I did not see any Ivan Boeskys or Leona Helmsleys, and although there was a powerful mafia in Philadelphia, I did not see any dons, either. Approximately three fourths of these defendants were nonwhite. Almost 80 percent were high school dropouts. Many were functionally illiterate. Almost a third had some history of mental problems, were retarded, or had been in special schools. One dreary day my court reporter said plaintively, "Judge, why can't we get a better class of criminal?"

Not all of these offenders were sentenced to probation, obviously. But I had my own criteria or guidelines—very different from those established by most states and the federal government—for deciding on a punishment. My primary concern was public safety. The most important question I asked myself was whether the offender could be deterred from committing other crimes. No one can predict with certainty who will or will not commit a crime, but there are indicators most sensible people recognize as danger signals.

First, was this an irrational crime? If an arsonist sets a fire to collect insurance, that is a crime but also a rational act. Such a person can be deterred by being made to pay for the harm done and the costs to the fire department.

However, if the arsonist sets fires just because he likes to see them, it is highly unlikely that he can be stopped from setting others, no matter how high the fine. Imprisonment is advisable even though it may be a first offense.

Second, was there wanton cruelty? If a robber maims or slashes the victim, there is little likelihood that he can safely be left in the community. If a robber simply displays a gun but does not fire it or harm the victim, then one should consider his life history, provocation, and other circumstances in deciding whether probation is appropriate.

Third, is this a hostile person? Was his crime one of hatred, and does he show any genuine remorse? Most rapes are acts of hostility, and the vast majority of rapists have a record of numerous sexual assaults. I remember one man who raped his mother. I gave him the maximum sentence under the law—20 years—but with good behavior, he got out fairly quickly. He immediately raped another elderly woman. Clearly, few rapists can safely be left in the community, and in my tenure, I incarcerated every one.

Yet gang rape, although a brutal and horrifying crime, is more complicated. The leader is clearly hostile and should be punished severely. Yet the followers can't be so neatly categorized. Some may act largely out of cowardice and peer pressure.

Fourth, is this a person who knows he is doing wrong but cannot control himself? Typical of such offenders are pedophiles. One child abuser who appeared before me had already been convicted of abusing his first wife's child. I got him on the second wife's child and sentenced him to the maximum. Still, he'll get out with good behavior, and I shudder to think about the children around him when he does. This is one case in which justice is not tough enough.

By contrast, some people who have committed homicide present very little danger of further violence—although many more do. Once a young man came before me because he had taken aim at a person half a block away and then shot him in the back, killing him. Why did he do it? "I wanted to get me a body." He should never get out. But the mandatory codes don't make great distinctions between him and another murderer who came before me, a woman who shot and killed a boy after he and his friends brutally gang-raped her teenage daughter.

I found this woman guilty of first-degree murder, but I found no reason to incarcerate her. She had four young children to support who would have become wards of the welfare department and probably would have spent their childhoods in a series of foster homes. I placed her on probation—a decision few judges now have the discretion to impose. She had not been arrested before. She has not been arrested since.

Of course, the vast majority of men, women, and children in custody in the United States are not killers, rapists, or arsonists. They're in prison for some type of theft—a purse snatching, burglary, or embezzlement. Many of these criminals can be punished without incarceration. If you force a first-time white-collar criminal to pay heavily for his crimes—perhaps three times the value of the money or property taken—he'll get the message that crime does not pay. As for poor people, stealing is not always a sign that the individual is an unreasonable risk to the community. It's often a sign that they want something—a car, Air Jordans—that they are too poor to buy themselves. Many of them, if they are not violent, can also be made to make some restitution and learn that crime doesn't pay.

Of course, to most of us, the idea of a nonprison sentence is tantamount to exoneration; a criminal sentenced to probation has effectively "gotten off." And there's a reason for that impression: Unless the probationer is required by the sentencing judge to perform specific tasks, probation is a charade. The probationer meets with the probation officer, briefly, perhaps once a month— making the procedure a waste of time for both. The officer duly records the meeting and the two go their separate ways until the probationer is arrested for another offense.

When I made the decision not to send a criminal to prison, I wanted to make sure that the probation system I sent them into had teeth. So I set firm conditions. If the offender was functionally illiterate, he was unemployable and would probably steal or engage in some other illegal activity once released. Thus in my sentencing, I sent him to school and ordered the probation officer to see that he went. (I use the masculine pronoun deliberately for I have never seen an illiterate female offender under the age of 60.) I ordered school dropouts to get their high school equivalency certificates and find jobs. All offenders were ordered to pay restitution or reparations within their means or earning capacity to their victims. Sometimes it was as little as $5 a week. Offenders simply could not return to their old, feckless lifestyles without paying some financial penalty for their wrongdoing.

Monitoring probation wasn't easy for me, or the probation officers with whom I worked. Every day I'd come into my office, look at my calendar, and notice that, say, 30 days had passed since Elliott was let out. So I'd call the probation office. Has Elliott made his payment? Is he going to his GED class? And so on. If the answer was no, I'd hold a violation hearing with the threat of incarceration if the conditions were not met within 30 days. After I returned a few people to jail for noncompliance, both my offenders and their probation officers knew I meant business. (Few probation officers protested my demands; their jobs were more meaningful and satisfying, they said.)

Of course, probation that required education and work and payment plans meant real work for criminals, too. But there was a payoff both the probation officers and I could see: As offenders worked and learned and made restitution, their attitudes often changed dramatically.

Time and Punishment

My rules of sentencing don't make judgeship easier; relying on mandatory sentencing is a far better way to guarantee a leisurely, controversy-free career on the bench. But my rules are, I believe, both effective and transferable: an application of common sense that any reasonable person could follow to similar ends. What prevents Americans from adopting practical measures like these is an atavistic belief in the sanctity of punishment. Even persons who have never heard of Immanuel Kant or the categorical imperative to punish believe that violation of law must be followed by the infliction of pain.

If we Americans treated crime more practically—as socially unacceptable behavior that should be curbed for the good of the community—we might begin to take a rational approach to the development of alternatives to prison. We might start thinking in terms not of punishment but of public safety, deterrence, and rehabilitation. Penalties like fines, work, and payment of restitution protect the public better and more cheaply than imprisonment in many cases.

Mind you, sentencing guidelines are not inherently evil. Intelligent guidelines would keep some judges from returning repeat offenders to the streets and others from putting the occasional cocaine user away for 10 years. Yet those guidelines must allow more latitude for the judge and the person who comes before him. While some states' sentencing laws include provisions that allow judges to override the mandatory sentences in some cases, the laws are for the most part inflexible—they deny judges the freedom to discriminate between the hardened criminal and the Michael. Richard H. Girgenti, the criminal justice director of New York state, has long proposed that the legislature give judges more discretion to impose shorter sentences for nonviolent and noncoercive felonies. This common-sense proposal has not been acted on in New York or any other state with mandatory sentencing laws.

Current laws are predicated on the belief that there must be punishment for every offense in terms of prison time rather than alternative sentences. But when it comes to determining the fate of a human being, there must be room for judgment. To make that room, we must stop acting as if mathematic calculations are superior to human thought. We must abolish mandatory sentencing laws and change the criteria on which sentencing guidelines are based.

Why not permit judges more freedom in making their decisions, provided that they give legitimate reasons? (If a judge doesn't have a good reason for deviating—if he's a reactionary or a fool—his sentencing decision will be overturned.) And why not revise the guidelines to consider dangerousness rather than the nomenclature of the offense? If we made simple reforms like these, thousands of non-threatening, nonhabitual offenders would be allowed to recompense their victims and society in a far less expensive and far more productive way.

You may be wondering, after all this, if I have a Willie Horton in my closet—a criminal whose actions after release privately haunt me. I do. I sentenced him to 10 to 20 years in prison—the maximum the law allowed—for forcible rape. He was released after eight years and promptly raped another woman. I could foresee what would happen but was powerless to impose a longer sentence.

And then there are the other cases that keep me up nights: those of men and women I might have let out, but didn't. And those of people like Michael, for whom justice shouldn't have been a mathematical equation.

POSTSCRIPT

Do Mandatory Sentencing Laws Help the Criminal Justice System?

Recently, mandatory minimum sentencing has become more controversial. For example, in New York, reform of the Rockefeller Drug Laws, which passed in the early 1970s, stalled because prosecutors and legislators said the reform could create loopholes, releasing drug kingpins from jail early.[1] In addition, even though 20-something youth counselor Veronica Rodriguez's six-year conviction, for pulling a 13-year-old boy's head against her covered breasts, was upheld by the Oregon Supreme Court in 2009, the court concluded that such a disproportionate sentence "shock[s] the moral sense."[2]

Mandatory sentencing limits a judge's discretion in ruling for criminal cases. Simply stated, mandatory sentencing requires a minimum number of years a convicted person must serve in prison. Nationwide, federal courts follow the federal Sentencing Guidelines.[3] To illustrate, if a person is arrested for possessing 5 to 49 grams of pure, or 50 to 499 grams of a mixture, of methamphetamine on a first offense, according to this sentencing guideline, he or she will automatically receive a penalty of no "less than 5 years, and not more than 40 years." If there is a death or serious injury involved in the drug-related arrest, "the penalty is not less than 20 or more than life" and a "fine of not more than $2 million if an individual."[4] For a second offense, the sentence ranges from 10 years to life.

On the one hand, those in favor of mandatory sentencing have faith that adherence to guidelines lowers crime rates as well as guarantees sentencing uniformity. Mandatory sentencing promotes a deterrence to prospective criminals and those who might repeat criminal activity, avoiding criminal activity because a binding sentence is a result if he or she is caught.

On the other hand, mandatory sentencing opponents found studies reveal criminals avoid crime not because of the length of sentence, but the likelihood they will be caught and convicted.[5] Familes Against Mandatory Minimums (FAMM)—like former Judge Lois Forer, from the issue presented—argued that justices lose control over sentencing because they lose discretion even when facts warrant another possible sentencing.[6] FAMM's Web site stated there are two ways defendants can get out of a mandatory sentence: (1) If the defendant can provide "substantial assistance" through turning in others to the government; and (2) if the sentence is excessive because the defendant is a drug offender for the first time, then the defendant is eligible for a "safety valve." However, FAMM, which advocated for the "safety value" option, argued that the criteria are still too narrow and as a result many defendants are still needlessly sentenced to decades behind bars.[7]

Through FAMM, Representative Maxine Waters introduced House Resolution 1466: "Major Drug Trafficking Prosecution Act of 2009."[8] This bill disconnected mandatory minimum prison sentences from drug trafficking. As of press time, legislation was still in committee.

Notes

1. Madison Gray, "Mandatory Sentencing: Stalled Reform," *Time* (August 17). Accessed December 3, 2009, http://www.time.com/time/nation/article/0,8599,1653862,00.html#ixzz0YeypyoUl

2. "Oregon Supreme Court Rejects Mandatory Sentencing," *Associated Press* (September 24, 2009).

3. U.S. Drug Enforcement Agency. Accessed December 3, 2009, http://www.justice.gov/dea/agency/penalties.htm

4. *Ibid.*

5. Steven Landsburg, "Does Crime Pay? Yes, for Those Who Don't Wince at the Small Chance of a Big Punishment," *Slate* (December 9). Accessed December 3, 2009.

6. Families Against Mandatory Minimums Website, "Understanding Federal Sentencing." Accessed December 3, 2009, http://www.famm.org/FederalSentencing/UnderstandingFederalSentencing.aspx

7. *Ibid.*

8. Govtrack.us: A Civic Project to Track Congress. Accessed December 3, 2009, http://www.govtrack.us/congress/bill.xpd?bill=h111-1466

ISSUE 9

Can a School Punish a Student for Speech That Is Reasonably Viewed as Promoting Illegal Drug Use?

YES: John Roberts, from Majority Opinion, *Deborah Morse et. al. v. Joseph Frederick,* U.S. Supreme Court (June 25, 2007)

NO: John Paul Stevens, from Dissenting Opinion, *Deborah Morse et al. v. Joseph Frederick,* U.S. Supreme Court (June 25, 2007)

ISSUE SUMMARY

YES: Supreme Court Chief Justice John Roberts rules that a student's First Amendment rights are not violated by restrictions on speech that can reasonably be regarded as encouraging illegal drug use.

NO: Supreme Court Justice John Paul Stevens argues that an ambiguous reference to drugs does not justify limiting a student's speech.

There are several selections in this book that involve student rights, and some link to drug use. In two of the issues, the legal question concerns privacy. In one of them, the Court had to consider whether a strip search of a student thought to be in possession of a drug violated the Fourth Amendment. In another, the Court focused on the issue of drug testing and under what circumstances drug testing could be required even when actual drug use by the student is not suspected. The issue under consideration here is different in that the primary legal issue is the First Amendment and freedom of expression.

In this case, some students at a school-supervised event occurring outside the school building held up a banner stating, "BONG HiTS 4 JESUS." The principal requested that the students fold up the banner, but one student refused and was suspended. The student sued, claiming that his First Amendment rights of free speech had been violated. The school claimed that the sign could reasonably be interpreted to be encouraging drug use and that this justified a restriction on the student's speech.

This is a case that not only was decided by a 5-4 vote at the Supreme Court but that involved a significant disagreement in the lower courts. The District Court, the first court to hear the case, had found no violation of free speech rights. The Court of Appeals reversed, finding that although the banner may have expressed approval of marijuana use, there was no threat of the speech causing any disruption and, therefore, the suspension was unwarranted.

The only points of agreement in these lower-court opinions seem to have been that although students in public schools do have First Amendment rights, they also do not enjoy all the rights of someone who is speaking outside the school context. The challenge for the Supreme Court was to clarify when and in what circumstances the rights of a student might be limited. As you read the case, consider whether the Court is successful in achieving this goal.

Relatively few cases are cited in the opinions, largely because there have been relatively few cases involving free speech in schools. This was the first Supreme Court decision in more than 20 years and only the fourth case in 40 years that focused on the First Amendment rights of students. In the first of these, *Tinker v. Des Moines Independent Community School District* (1969), the Court ruled in favor of students who were protesting the Vietnam War by wearing armbands to school. In the two cases from the 1980s, *Bethel School District v. Fraser* (1986) and *Hazelwood School District v. Kuhlmeier* (1988), the Court ruled against the students. The first of these involved a speech that contained many sexual innuendos by a student. The second involved censorship of the school newspaper.

YES

John Roberts

Majority Opinion, *Deborah Morse et al. v. Joseph Frederick*

CHIEF JUSTICE ROBERTS delivered the opinion of the Court.

At a school-sanctioned and school-supervised event, a high school principal saw some of her students unfurl a large banner conveying a message she reasonably regarded as promoting illegal drug use. Consistent with established school policy prohibiting such messages at school events, the principal directed the students to take down the banner. One student—among those who had brought the banner to the event—refused to do so. The principal confiscated the banner and later suspended the student. The Ninth Circuit held that the principal's actions violated the First Amendment, and that the student could sue the principal for damages.

Our cases make clear that students do not "shed their constitutional rights to freedom of speech or expression at the schoolhouse gate." *Tinker v. Des Moines Independent Community School Dist.*, 393 U.S. 503, 506 (1969). At the same time, we have held that "the constitutional rights of students in public school are not automatically coextensive with the rights of adults in other settings," *Bethel School Dist. No. 403 v. Fraser*, 478 U.S. 675, 682 (1986), and that the rights of students "must be 'applied in light of the special characteristics of the school environment.'" *Hazelwood School Dist. v. Kuhlmeier*, 484 U.S. 260, 266 (1988) (quoting *Tinker, supra*, at 506). Consistent with these principles, we hold that schools may take steps to safeguard those entrusted to their care from speech that can reasonably be regarded as encouraging illegal drug use. We conclude that the school officials in this case did not violate the First Amendment by confiscating the pro-drug banner and suspending the student responsible for it.

I

On January 24, 2002, the Olympic Torch Relay passed through Juneau, Alaska, on its way to the winter games in Salt Lake City, Utah. The torchbearers were to proceed along a street in front of Juneau-Douglas High School (JDHS) while school was in session. Petitioner Deborah Morse, the school principal, decided to permit staff and students to participate in the Torch Relay as an approved social event or class trip. . . . Students were allowed to leave class to observe

From Supreme Court of the United States, June 25, 2007.

the relay from either side of the street. Teachers and administrative officials monitored the students' actions.

Respondent Joseph Frederick, a JDHS senior, was late to school that day. When he arrived, he joined his friends (all but one of whom were JDHS students) across the street from the school to watch the event. Not all the students waited patiently. Some became rambunctious, throwing plastic cola bottles and snowballs and scuffling with their classmates. As the torchbearers and camera crews passed by, Frederick and his friends unfurled a 14-foot banner bearing the phrase: "BONG HiTS 4 JESUS." . . . The large banner was easily readable by the students on the other side of the street.

Principal Morse immediately crossed the street and demanded that the banner be taken down. Everyone but Frederick complied. Morse confiscated the banner and told Frederick to report to her office, where she suspended him for 10 days. Morse later explained that she told Frederick to take the banner down because she thought it encouraged illegal drug use, in violation of established school policy. Juneau School Board Policy No. 5520 states: "The Board specifically prohibits any assembly or public expression that . . . advocates the use of substances that are illegal to minors. . . ." *Id.*, at 53a. In addition, Juneau School Board Policy No. 5850 subjects "[p]upils who participate in approved social events and class trips" to the same student conduct rules that apply during the regular school program. *Id.*, at 58a.

Frederick administratively appealed his suspension, but the Juneau School District Superintendent upheld it, limiting it to time served (8 days). In a memorandum setting forth his reasons, the superintendent determined that Frederick had displayed his banner "in the midst of his fellow students, during school hours, at a school-sanctioned activity." *Id.*, at 63a. He further explained that Frederick "was not disciplined because the principal of the school 'disagreed' with his message, but because his speech appeared to advocate the use of illegal drugs." *Id.*, at 61a.

The superintendent continued:

> "The common-sense understanding of the phrase 'bong hits' is that it is a reference to a means of smoking marijuana. Given [Frederick's] inability or unwillingness to express any other credible meaning for the phrase, I can only agree with the principal and countless others who saw the banner as advocating the use of illegal drugs. [Frederick's] speech was not political. He was not advocating the legalization of marijuana or promoting a religious belief. He was displaying a fairly silly message promoting illegal drug usage in the midst of a school activity, for the benefit of television cameras covering the Torch Relay. [Frederick's] speech was potentially disruptive to the event and clearly disruptive of and inconsistent with the school's educational mission to educate students about the dangers of illegal drugs and to discourage their use." *Id.*, at 61a–62a.

Relying on our decision in *Fraser,* . . . the superintendent concluded that the principal's actions were permissible because Frederick's banner was "speech or action that intrudes upon the work of the schools." . . . The Juneau School District Board of Education upheld the suspension.

Frederick then filed suit under 42 U.S.C. §1983, alleging that the school board and Morse had violated his First Amendment rights. He sought declaratory and injunctive relief, unspecified compensatory damages, punitive damages, and attorney's fees. The District Court granted summary judgment for the school board and Morse, ruling that they were entitled to qualified immunity and that they had not infringed Frederick's First Amendment rights. The court found that Morse reasonably interpreted the banner as promoting illegal drug use—a message that "directly contravened the Board's policies relating to drug abuse prevention." . . . Under the circumstances, the court held that "Morse had the authority, if not the obligation, to stop such messages at a school-sanctioned activity." . . .

The Ninth Circuit reversed. Deciding that Frederick acted during a "school-authorized activit[y]," and "proceed[ing] on the basis that the banner expressed a positive sentiment about marijuana use," the court nonetheless found a violation of Frederick's First Amendment rights because the school punished Frederick without demonstrating that his speech gave rise to a "risk of substantial disruption." 439 F. 3d 1114, 1118, 1121–1123 (2006). The court further concluded that Frederick's right to display his banner was so "clearly established" that a reasonable principal in Morse's position would have understood that her actions were unconstitutional, and that Morse was therefore not entitled to qualified immunity. . . .

We granted certiorari on two questions: whether Frederick had a First Amendment right to wield his banner, and, if so, whether that right was so clearly established that the principal may be held liable for damages. . . . We resolve the first question against Frederick, and therefore have no occasion to reach the second.

II

At the outset, we reject Frederick's argument that this is not a school speech case—as has every other authority to address the question. . . . The event occurred during normal school hours. It was sanctioned by Principal Morse "as an approved social event or class trip," . . . and the school district's rules expressly provide that pupils in "approved social events and class trips are subject to district rules for student conduct." . . . Teachers and administrators were interspersed among the students and charged with supervising them. The high school band and cheerleaders performed. Frederick, standing among other JDHS students across the street from the school, directed his banner toward the school, making it plainly visible to most students. Under these circumstances, we agree with the superintendent that Frederick cannot "stand in the midst of his fellow students, during school hours, at a school-sanctioned activity and claim he is not at school." . . . There is some uncertainty at the outer boundaries as to when courts should apply school-speech precedents, see *Porter v. Ascension Parish School Bd.*, 393 F. 3d 608, 615, n. 22 (CA5 2004), but not on these facts.

III

The message on Frederick's banner is cryptic. It is no doubt offensive to some, perhaps amusing to others. To still others, it probably means nothing at all. Frederick himself claimed "that the words were just nonsense meant to attract television cameras." 439 F. 3d, at 1117–1118. But Principal Morse thought the banner would be interpreted by those viewing it as promoting illegal drug use, and that interpretation is plainly a reasonable one.

As Morse later explained in a declaration, when she saw the sign, she thought that "the reference to a 'bong hit' would be widely understood by high school students and others as referring to smoking marijuana." . . . She further believed that "display of the banner would be construed by students, District personnel, parents and others witnessing the display of the banner, as advocating or promoting illegal drug use"—in violation of school policy . . . ("I told Frederick and the other members of his group to put the banner down because I felt that it violated the [school] policy against displaying . . . material that advertises or promotes use of illegal drugs").

We agree with Morse. At least two interpretations of the words on the banner demonstrate that the sign advocated the use of illegal drugs. First, the phrase could be interpreted as an imperative: "[Take] bong hits . . ."—a message equivalent, as Morse explained in her declaration, to "smoke marijuana" or "use an illegal drug." Alternatively, the phrase could be viewed as celebrating drug use—"bong hits [are a good thing]," or "[we take] bong hits"—and we discern no meaningful distinction between celebrating illegal drug use in the midst of fellow students and outright advocacy or promotion. See *Guiles v. Marineau,* 461 F. 3d 320, 328 (CA2 2006) (discussing the present case and describing the sign as "a clearly pro-drug banner").

The pro-drug interpretation of the banner gains further plausibility given the paucity of alternative meanings the banner might bear. The best Frederick can come up with is that the banner is "meaningless and funny." 439 F. 3d, at 1116. The dissent similarly refers to the sign's message as "curious," *post,* at 1, "ambiguous," *ibid.,* "nonsense," *post,* at 2, "ridiculous," *post,* at 6, "obscure," *post,* at 7, "silly," *post,* at 12, "quixotic," *post,* at 13, and "stupid," *ibid.* Gibberish is surely a possible interpretation of the words on the banner, but it is not the only one, and dismissing the banner as meaningless ignores its undeniable reference to illegal drugs.

The dissent mentions Frederick's "credible and uncontradicted explanation for the message—he just wanted to get on television." . . . But that is a description of Frederick's *motive* for displaying the banner; it is not an interpretation of what the banner says. The *way* Frederick was going to fulfill his ambition of appearing on television was by unfurling a pro-drug banner at a school event, in the presence of teachers and fellow students.

Elsewhere in its opinion, the dissent emphasizes the importance of political speech and the need to foster "national debate about a serious issue," . . . as if to suggest that the banner is political speech. But not even Frederick argues that the banner conveys any sort of political or religious message. Contrary to the dissent's suggestion, . . . this is plainly not a case about political debate over the criminalization of drug use or possession.

IV

The question thus becomes whether a principal may, consistent with the First Amendment, restrict student speech at a school event, when that speech is reasonably viewed as promoting illegal drug use. We hold that she may.

In *Tinker,* this Court made clear that "First Amendment rights, applied in light of the special characteristics of the school environment, are available to teachers and students." 393 U.S., at 506. *Tinker* involved a group of high school students who decided to wear black armbands to protest the Vietnam War. School officials learned of the plan and then adopted a policy prohibiting students from wearing armbands. When several students nonetheless wore armbands to school, they were suspended. *Id.,* at 504. The students sued, claiming that their First Amendment rights had been violated, and this Court agreed.

Tinker held that student expression may not be suppressed unless school officials reasonably conclude that it will "materially and substantially disrupt the work and discipline of the school." . . . The essential facts of *Tinker* are quite stark, implicating concerns at the heart of the First Amendment. The students sought to engage in political speech, using the armbands to express their "disapproval of the Vietnam hostilities and their advocacy of a truce, to make their views known, and, by their example, to influence others to adopt them." . . . Political speech, of course, is "at the core of what the First Amendment is designed to protect." *Virginia v. Black,* 538 U.S. 343, 365 (2003). The only interest the Court discerned underlying the school's actions was the "mere desire to avoid the discomfort and unpleasantness that always accompany an unpopular viewpoint," or "an urgent wish to avoid the controversy which might result from the expression." *Tinker,* 393 U.S., at 509, 510. That interest was not enough to justify banning "a silent, passive expression of opinion, unaccompanied by any disorder or disturbance." *Id.,* at 508.

This Court's next student speech case was *Fraser,* 478 U.S. 675. Matthew Fraser was suspended for delivering a speech before a high school assembly in which he employed what this Court called "an elaborate, graphic, and explicit sexual metaphor." . . . Analyzing the case under *Tinker,* the District Court and Court of Appeals found no disruption, and therefore no basis for disciplining Fraser. 478 U.S., at 679–680. This Court reversed, holding that the "School District acted entirely within its permissible authority in imposing sanctions upon Fraser in response to his offensively lewd and indecent speech." . . .

The mode of analysis employed in *Fraser* is not entirely clear. The Court was plainly attuned to the content of Fraser's speech, citing the "marked distinction between the political 'message' of the armbands in *Tinker* and the sexual content of [Fraser's] speech." . . . But the Court also reasoned that school boards have the authority to determine "what manner of speech in the classroom or in school assembly is inappropriate." *Id.,* at 683. Cf. *id.,* at 689 (Brennan, J., concurring in judgment) ("In the present case, school officials sought only to ensure that a high school assembly proceed in an orderly manner. There is no suggestion that school officials attempted to regulate [Fraser's] speech because they disagreed with the views he sought to express").

We need not resolve this debate to decide this case. For present purposes, it is enough to distill from *Fraser* two basic principles. First, *Fraser's* holding demonstrates that "the constitutional rights of students in public school are not automatically coextensive with the rights of adults in other settings." . . . Had Fraser delivered the same speech in a public forum outside the school context, it would have been protected. See *Cohen v. California,* 403 U.S. 15 (1971); *Fraser, supra,* at 682–683. In school, however, Fraser's First Amendment rights were circumscribed "in light of the special characteristics of the school environment." *Tinker, supra,* at 506. Second, *Fraser* established that the mode of analysis set forth in *Tinker* is not absolute. Whatever approach *Fraser* employed, it certainly did not conduct the "substantial disruption" analysis prescribed by *Tinker, supra,* at 514. See *Kuhlmeier,* 484 U.S., at 271, n. 4 (disagreeing with the proposition that there is "no difference between the First Amendment analysis applied in *Tinker* and that applied in *Fraser,*" and noting that the holding in *Fraser* was not based on any showing of substantial disruption).

Our most recent student speech case, *Kuhlmeier,* concerned "expressive activities that students, parents, and members of the public might reasonably perceive to bear the imprimatur of the school." 484 U.S., at 271. Staff members of a high school newspaper sued their school when it chose not to publish two of their articles. The Court of Appeals analyzed the case under *Tinker,* ruling in favor of the students because it found no evidence of material disruption to classwork or school discipline. 795 F. 2d 1368, 1375 (CA8 1986). This Court reversed, holding that "educators do not offend the First Amendment by exercising editorial control over the style and content of student speech in school-sponsored expressive activities so long as their actions are reasonably related to legitimate pedagogical concerns." *Kuhlmeier, supra,* at 273.

Kuhlmeier does not control this case because no one would reasonably believe that Frederick's banner bore the school's imprimatur. The case is nevertheless instructive because it confirms both principles cited above. *Kuhlmeier* acknowledged that schools may regulate some speech "even though the government could not censor similar speech outside the school." *Id.,* at 266. And, like *Fraser,* it confirms that the rule of *Tinker* is not the only basis for restricting student speech.

Drawing on the principles applied in our student speech cases, we have held in the Fourth Amendment context that "while children assuredly do not 'shed their constitutional rights . . . at the schoolhouse gate,' . . . the nature of those rights is what is appropriate for children in school." *Vernonia School Dist. 47J v. Acton,* 515 U.S. 646, 655–656 (1995) (quoting *Tinker, supra,* at 506). In particular, "the school setting requires some easing of the restrictions to which searches by public authorities are ordinarily subject." *New Jersey v. T. L. O.,* 469 U.S. 325, 340 (1985). See *Vernonia, supra,* at 656 ("Fourth Amendment rights, no less than First and Fourteenth Amendment rights, are different in public schools than elsewhere . . ."); *Board of Ed. of Independent School Dist. No. 92 of Pottawatomie Cty. v. Earls,* 536 U.S. 822, 829–830 (2002) ("'special needs' inhere in the public school context"; "[w]hile schoolchildren do not shed their constitutional rights when they enter the schoolhouse, Fourth Amendment rights . . . are different in public schools than elsewhere; the 'reasonableness' inquiry cannot disregard the schools' custodial and tutelary responsibility for children" (quoting *Vernonia,* 515 U.S., at 656; citation and some internal quotation marks omitted).

Even more to the point, these cases also recognize that deterring drug use by schoolchildren is an "important—indeed, perhaps compelling" interest. *Id.,* at 661. Drug abuse can cause severe and permanent damage to the health and well-being of young people:

> "School years are the time when the physical, psychological, and addictive effects of drugs are most severe. Maturing nervous systems are more critically impaired by intoxicants than mature ones are; childhood losses in learning are lifelong and profound; children grow chemically dependent more quickly than adults, and their record of recovery is depressingly poor. And of course the effects of a drug-infested school are visited not just upon the users, but upon the entire student body and faculty, as the educational process is disrupted." *Id.,* at 661–662 (citations and internal quotation marks omitted).

Just five years ago, we wrote: "The drug abuse problem among our Nation's youth has hardly abated since *Vernonia* was decided in 1995. In fact, evidence suggests that it has only grown worse." *Earls, supra,* at 834, and n. 5.

The problem remains serious today. See generally 1 National Institute on Drug Abuse, National Institutes of Health, Monitoring the Future: National Survey Results on Drug Use, 1975–2005, Secondary School Students (2006). About half of American 12th graders have used an illicit drug, as have more than a third of 10th graders and about one-fifth of 8th graders. *Id.,* at 99. Nearly one in four 12th graders has used an illicit drug in the past month. *Id.,* at 101. Some 25% of high schoolers say that they have been offered, sold, or given an illegal drug on school property within the past year. Dept. of Health and Human Services, Centers for Disease Control and Prevention, Youth Risk Behavior Surveillance—United States, 2005, 55 Morbidity and Mortality Weekly Report, Surveillance Summaries, No. SS-5, p. 19 (June 9, 2006).

Congress has declared that part of a school's job is educating students about the dangers of illegal drug use. It has provided billions of dollars to support state and local drug-prevention programs, . . . and required that schools receiving federal funds under the Safe and Drug-Free Schools and Communities Act of 1994 certify that their drug prevention programs "convey a clear and consistent message that . . . the illegal use of drugs [is] wrong and harmful." 20 U.S.C. §7114(d)(6) (2000 ed., Supp. IV).

Thousands of school boards throughout the country—including JDHS—have adopted policies aimed at effectuating this message. . . . Those school boards know that peer pressure is perhaps "the single most important factor leading schoolchildren to take drugs," and that students are more likely to use drugs when the norms in school appear to tolerate such behavior. . . . Student speech celebrating illegal drug use at a school event, in the presence of school administrators and teachers, thus poses a particular challenge for school officials working to protect those entrusted to their care from the dangers of drug abuse.

The "special characteristics of the school environment," *Tinker,* 393 U.S., at 506, and the governmental interest in stopping student drug abuse—reflected in the policies of Congress and myriad school boards, including JDHS—allow schools to restrict student expression that they reasonably regard as promoting illegal drug use. *Tinker* warned that schools may not prohibit student speech because of "undifferentiated fear or apprehension of disturbance" or "a mere desire to avoid the discomfort and unpleasantness that always accompany an unpopular viewpoint." *Id.,* at 508, 509. The danger here is far more serious and palpable. The particular concern to prevent student drug abuse at issue here, embodied in established school policy, . . . extends well beyond an abstract desire to avoid controversy.

Petitioners urge us to adopt the broader rule that Frederick's speech is proscribable because it is plainly "offensive" as that term is used in *Fraser.* . . . We think this stretches *Fraser* too far; that case should not be read to encompass any speech that could fit under some definition of "offensive." After all, much political and religious speech might be perceived as offensive to some. The concern here is not that Frederick's speech was offensive, but that it was reasonably viewed as promoting illegal drug use.

Although accusing this decision of doing "serious violence to the First Amendment" by authorizing "viewpoint discrimination," *post,* at 2, 5 (opinion of STEVENS, J.), the dissent concludes that "it might well be appropriate to tolerate some targeted viewpoint discrimination in this unique setting," *post,* at 6–7. Nor do we understand the dissent to take the position that schools are required to tolerate student advocacy of illegal drug use at school events, even if that advocacy falls short of inviting "imminent" lawless action. See *post,* at 7 ("[I]t is possible that our rigid imminence requirement ought to be relaxed at schools"). And even the dissent recognizes that the issues here are close enough that the principal should not be held liable in damages, but should instead enjoy qualified immunity for her actions. . . . Stripped of rhetorical flourishes, then, the debate between the dissent and this opinion is less about constitutional first principles than about whether Frederick's banner constitutes promotion of illegal drug use. We have explained our view that it does. The dissent's contrary view on that relatively narrow question hardly justifies sounding the First Amendment bugle.

⤶☙⤷

School principals have a difficult job, and a vitally important one. When Frederick suddenly and unexpectedly unfurled his banner, Morse had to decide to act—or not act—on the spot. It was reasonable for her to conclude that the banner promoted illegal drug use—in violation of established school policy—and that failing to act would send a powerful message to the students in her charge, including Frederick, about how serious the school was about the dangers of illegal drug use. The First Amendment does not require schools to tolerate at school events student expression that contributes to those dangers.

The judgment of the United States Court of Appeals for the Ninth Circuit is reversed, and the case is remanded for further proceedings consistent with this opinion.

It is so ordered.

Dissenting Opinion, *Deborah Morse et al. v. Joseph Frederick*

JUSTICE STEVENS, with whom JUSTICE SOUTER and JUSTICE GINSBURG join, dissenting.

A significant fact barely mentioned by the Court sheds a revelatory light on the motives of both the students and the principal of Juneau-Douglas High School (JDHS). On January 24, 2002, the Olympic Torch Relay gave those Alaska residents a rare chance to appear on national television. As Joseph Frederick repeatedly explained, he did not address the curious message—"BONG HiTS 4 JESUS"—to his fellow students. He just wanted to get the camera crews' attention. Moreover, concern about a nationwide evaluation of the conduct of the JDHS student body would have justified the principal's decision to remove an attention-grabbing 14-foot banner, even if it had merely proclaimed "Glaciers Melt!"

I agree with the Court that the principal should not be held liable for pulling down Frederick's banner. See *Harlow v. Fitzgerald,* 457 U.S. 800, 818 (1982). I would hold, however, that the school's interest in protecting its students from exposure to speech "reasonably regarded as promoting illegal drug use," *ante,* at 1, cannot justify disciplining Frederick for his attempt to make an ambiguous statement to a television audience simply because it contained an oblique reference to drugs. The First Amendment demands more, indeed, much more.

The Court holds otherwise only after laboring to establish two uncontroversial propositions: first, that the constitutional rights of students in school settings are not coextensive with the rights of adults, . . . and second, that deterring drug use by schoolchildren is a valid and terribly important interest. . . . As to the first, I take the Court's point that the message on Frederick's banner is not *necessarily* protected speech, even though it unquestionably would have been had the banner been unfurled elsewhere. As to the second, I am willing to assume that the Court is correct that the pressing need to deter drug use supports JDHS's rule prohibiting willful conduct that expressly "advocates the use of substances that are illegal to minors." App. to Pet. for Cert. 53a. But it is a gross non sequitur to draw from these two unremarkable propositions the remarkable conclusion that the school may suppress student speech that was never meant to persuade anyone to do anything.

From Supreme Court of the United States, June 25, 2007.

In my judgment, the First Amendment protects student speech if the message itself neither violates a permissible rule nor expressly advocates conduct that is illegal and harmful to students. This nonsense banner does neither, and the Court does serious violence to the First Amendment in upholding—indeed, lauding—a school's decision to punish Frederick for expressing a view with which it disagreed.

I

In December 1965, we were engaged in a controversial war, a war that "divided this country as few other issues ever have." *Tinker v. Des Moines Independent Community School Dist.*, 393 U.S. 503, 524 (1969) (Black, J., dissenting). Having learned that some students planned to wear black armbands as a symbol of opposition to the country's involvement in Vietnam, officials of the Des Moines public school district adopted a policy calling for the suspension of any student who refused to remove the armband. As we explained when we considered the propriety of that policy, "[t]he school officials banned and sought to punish petitioners for a silent, passive expression of opinion, unaccompanied by any disorder or disturbance on the part of petitioners." *Id.*, at 508. The district justified its censorship on the ground that it feared that the expression of a controversial and unpopular opinion would generate disturbances. Because the school officials had insufficient reason to believe that those disturbances would "materially and substantially interfere with the requirements of discipline in the operation of the school," we found the justification for the rule to lack any foundation and therefore held that the censorship violated the First Amendment. . . .

Justice Harlan dissented, but not because he thought the school district could censor a message with which it disagreed. Rather, he would have upheld the district's rule only because the students never cast doubt on the district's anti-disruption justification by proving that the rule was motivated "by other than legitimate school concerns—for example, a desire to prohibit the expression of an unpopular point of view while permitting expression of the dominant opinion." *Id.*, at 526.

Two cardinal First Amendment principles animate both the Court's opinion in *Tinker* and Justice Harlan's dissent. First, censorship based on the content of speech, particularly censorship that depends on the viewpoint of the speaker, is subject to the most rigorous burden of justification:

> "Discrimination against speech because of its message is presumed to be unconstitutional. . . . When the government targets not subject matter, but particular views taken by speakers on a subject, the violation of the First Amendment is all the more blatant. View-point discrimination is thus an egregious form of content discrimination. The government must abstain from regulating speech when the specific motivating ideology or the opinion or perspective of the speaker is the rationale for the restriction." *Rosenberger v. Rector and Visitors of Univ. of Va.*, 515 U.S. 819, 828–829 (1995) (citation omitted).

Second, punishing someone for advocating illegal conduct is constitutional only when the advocacy is likely to provoke the harm that the government seeks to avoid. See *Brandenburg v. Ohio,* 395 U.S. 444, 449 (1969) (*per curiam*) (distinguishing "mere advocacy" of illegal conduct from "incitement to imminent lawless action").

However necessary it may be to modify those principles in the school setting, *Tinker* affirmed their continuing vitality. 393 U.S., at 509 ("In order for the State in the person of school officials to justify prohibition of a particular expression of opinion, it must be able to show that its action was caused by something more than a mere desire to avoid the discomfort and unpleasantness that always accompany an unpopular viewpoint. Certainly where there is no finding and no showing that engaging in that conduct would materially and substantially interfere with the requirements of appropriate discipline in the operation of the school, the prohibition cannot be sustained" [internal quotation marks omitted]). As other federal courts have long recognized, under *Tinker,*

> "regulation of student speech is generally permissible only when the speech would substantially disrupt or interfere with the work of the school or the rights of other students. . . . *Tinker* requires a specific and significant fear of disruption, *not just some remote apprehension of disturbance.*" *Saxe v. State College Area School Dist.,* 240 F. 3d 200, 211 (CA3 2001) (ALITO, J.) (emphasis added).

Yet today the Court fashions a test that trivializes the two cardinal principles upon which *Tinker* rests . . . ("[S]chools [may] restrict student expression that they reasonably regard as promoting illegal drug use"). The Court's test invites stark viewpoint discrimination. In this case, for example, the principal has unabashedly acknowledged that she disciplined Frederick because she disagreed with the pro-drug viewpoint she ascribed to the message on the banner . . . —a viewpoint, incidentally, that Frederick has disavowed. . . . Unlike our recent decision in *Tennessee Secondary School Athletic Assn. v. Brentwood Academy,* 551 U.S. __, __ (2007) . . . (ALITO, J., concurring), the Court's holding in this case strikes at "the heart of the First Amendment" because it upholds a punishment meted out on the basis of a listener's disagreement with her understanding (or, more likely, misunderstanding) of the speaker's viewpoint. "If there is a bedrock principle underlying the First Amendment, it is that the Government may not prohibit the expression of an idea simply because society finds the idea itself offensive or disagreeable." *Texas v. Johnson,* 491 U.S. 397, 414 (1989).

It is also perfectly clear that "promoting illegal drug use" . . . comes nowhere close to proscribable "incitement to imminent lawless action." *Brandenburg,* 395 U.S., at 447. Encouraging drug use might well increase the likelihood that a listener will try an illegal drug, but that hardly justifies censorship:

> "Every denunciation of existing law tends in some measure to increase the probability that there will be violation of it. Condonation of a

breach enhances the probability. Expressions of approval add to the probability. . . . Advocacy of law-breaking heightens it still further. But even advocacy of violation, however reprehensible morally, is not a justification for denying free speech where the advocacy falls short of incitement and there is nothing to indicate that the advocacy would be immediately acted upon." *Whitney v. California*, 274 U.S. 357, 376 (1927) (Brandeis, J., concurring).

No one seriously maintains that drug advocacy (much less Frederick's ridiculous sign) comes within the vanishingly small category of speech that can be prohibited because of its feared consequences. Such advocacy, to borrow from Justice Holmes, "ha[s] no chance of starting a present conflagration." *Gitlow v. New York*, 268 U.S. 652, 673 (1925) (dissenting opinion).

II

The Court rejects outright these twin foundations of *Tinker* because, in its view, the unusual importance of protecting children from the scourge of drugs supports a ban on all speech in the school environment that promotes drug use. Whether or not such a rule is sensible as a matter of policy, carving out pro-drug speech for uniquely harsh treatment finds no support in our case law and is inimical to the values protected by the First Amendment. . . .

I will nevertheless assume for the sake of argument that the school's concededly powerful interest in protecting its students adequately supports its restriction on "any assembly or public expression that . . . advocates the use of substances that are illegal to minors . . . ." App. to Pet. for Cert. 53a. Given that the relationship between schools and students "is custodial and tutelary, permitting a degree of supervision and control that could not be exercised over free adults," *Vernonia School Dist. 47J v. Acton*, 515 U.S. 646, 655 (1995), it might well be appropriate to tolerate some targeted viewpoint discrimination in this unique setting. And while conventional speech may be restricted only when likely to "incit[e] imminent lawless action," *Brandenburg*, 395 U.S., at 449, it is possible that our rigid imminence requirement ought to be relaxed at schools. See *Bethel School Dist. No. 403 v. Fraser*, 478 U.S. 675, 682 (1986) ("[T]he constitutional rights of students in public school are not automatically coextensive with the rights of adults in other settings").

But it is one thing to restrict speech that *advocates* drug use. It is another thing entirely to prohibit an obscure message with a drug theme that a third party subjectively—and not very reasonably—thinks is tantamount to express advocacy. Cf. *Masses Publishing Co. v. Patten*, 244 F. 535, 540, 541 (SDNY 1917) (Hand, J.) (distinguishing sharply between "agitation, legitimate as such" and "the direct advocacy" of unlawful conduct). Even the school recognizes the paramount need to hold the line between, on the one hand, non-disruptive speech that merely expresses a viewpoint that is unpopular or contrary to the school's preferred message, and on the other hand, advocacy of an illegal or unsafe course of conduct. The district's prohibition of drug advocacy is a gloss on a more general rule that is otherwise quite tolerant of non-disruptive student speech:

"Students will not be disturbed in the exercise of their constitutionally guaranteed rights to assemble peaceably and to express ideas and opinions, privately or publicly, provided that their activities do not infringe on the rights of others and do not interfere with the operation of the educational program.

"The Board will not permit the conduct on school premises of any willful activity . . . that interferes with the orderly operation of the educational program or offends the rights of others. The Board specifically prohibits . . . any assembly or public expression that . . . advocates the use of substances that are illegal to minors. . . ." App. to Pet. for Cert. 53a; see also *ante*, at 3 (quoting rule in part).

There is absolutely no evidence that Frederick's banner's reference to drug paraphernalia "willful[ly]" infringed on anyone's rights or interfered with any of the school's educational programs.[1] On its face, then, the rule gave Frederick wide berth "to express [his] ideas and opinions" so long as they did not amount to "advoca[cy]" of drug use. . . . If the school's rule is, by hypothesis, a valid one, it is valid only insofar as it scrupulously preserves adequate space for constitutionally protected speech. When First Amendment rights are at stake, a rule that "sweep[s] in a great variety of conduct under a general and indefinite characterization" may not leave "too wide a discretion in its application." *Cantwell v. Connecticut*, 310 U.S. 296, 308 (1940). Therefore, just as we insisted in *Tinker* that the school establish some likely connection between the armbands and their feared consequences, so too JDHS must show that Frederick's supposed advocacy stands a meaningful chance of making otherwise-abstemious students try marijuana.

But instead of demanding that the school make such a showing, the Court punts. Figuring out just *how* it punts is tricky; "[t]he mode of analysis [it] employ[s] is not entirely clear," see *ante*, at 9. On occasion, the Court suggests it is deferring to the principal's "reasonable" judgment that Frederick's sign qualified as drug advocacy.[2] At other times, the Court seems to say that *it* thinks the banner's message constitutes express advocacy.[3] Either way, its approach is indefensible.

To the extent the Court defers to the principal's ostensibly reasonable judgment, it abdicates its constitutional responsibility. The beliefs of third parties, reasonable or otherwise, have never dictated which messages amount to proscribable advocacy. Indeed, it would be a strange constitutional doctrine that would allow the prohibition of only the narrowest category of speech advocating unlawful conduct, . . . yet would permit a listener's perceptions to determine which speech deserved constitutional protection.[4]

Such a peculiar doctrine is alien to our case law. In *Abrams v. United States*, 250 U.S. 616 (1919), this Court affirmed the conviction of a group of Russian "rebels, revolutionists, [and] anarchists," . . . on the ground that the leaflets they distributed were thought to "incite, provoke, and encourage resistance to the United States," *id.*, at 617 (internal quotation marks omitted). Yet Justice Holmes' dissent—which has emphatically carried the day—never inquired into the reasonableness of the United States' judgment that the leaflets would likely undermine the war effort. The dissent instead ridiculed that judgment:

"nobody can suppose that the surreptitious publishing of a silly leaflet by an unknown man, without more, would present any immediate danger that its opinions would hinder the success of the government arms or have any appreciable tendency to do so." *Id.,* at 628. In *Thomas v. Collins,* 323 U.S. 516 (1945) (opinion for the Court by Rutledge, J.), we overturned the conviction of a union organizer who violated a restraining order forbidding him from exhorting workers. In so doing, we held that the distinction between advocacy and incitement could not depend on how one of those workers might have understood the organizer's speech. That would "pu[t] the speaker in these circumstances wholly at the mercy of the varied understanding of his hearers and consequently of whatever inference may be drawn as to his intent and meaning." *Id.,* at 535. In *Cox v. Louisiana,* 379 U.S. 536, 543 (1965), we vacated a civil rights leader's conviction for disturbing the peace, even though a Baton Rouge sheriff had "deem[ed]" the leader's "appeal to . . . students to sit in at the lunch counters to be 'inflammatory.'" We never asked if the sheriff's in-person, on-the-spot judgment was "reasonable." Even in *Fraser,* we made no inquiry into whether the school administrators reasonably thought the student's speech was obscene or profane; we rather satisfied ourselves that "[t]he pervasive sexual innuendo in Fraser's speech was plainly offensive to both teachers and students—indeed, to any mature person." 478 U.S., at 683. Cf. *Bose Corp. v. Consumers Union of United States, Inc.,* 466 U.S. 485, 499 (1984) ("[I]n cases raising First Amendment issues we have repeatedly held that an appellate court has an obligation to make an independent examination of the whole record in order to make sure that the judgment does not constitute a forbidden intrusion on the field of free expression" (internal quotation marks omitted)).[5]

To the extent the Court independently finds that "BONG HiTS 4 JESUS" *objectively* amounts to the advocacy of illegal drug use—in other words, that it can *most* reasonably be interpreted as such—that conclusion practically refutes itself. This is a nonsense message, not advocacy. The Court's feeble effort to divine its hidden meaning is strong evidence of that . . . (positing that the banner might mean, alternatively, "'[Take] bong hits,'" "'bong hits [are a good thing],'" or "'[we take] bong hits'"). Frederick's credible and uncontradicted explanation for the message—he just wanted to get on television—is also relevant because a speaker who does not intend to persuade his audience can hardly be said to be advocating anything.[6] But most importantly, it takes real imagination to read a "cryptic" message (the Court's characterization, not mine, see *ibid.,* at 6) with a slanting drug reference as an incitement to drug use. Admittedly, some high school students (including those who use drugs) are dumb. Most students, however, do not shed their brains at the schoolhouse gate, and most students know dumb advocacy when they see it. The notion that the message on this banner would actually persuade either the average student or even the dumbest one to change his or her behavior is most implausible. That the Court believes such a silly message can be proscribed as advocacy underscores the novelty of its position, and suggests that the principle it articulates has no stopping point.

Even if advocacy could somehow be wedged into Frederick's obtuse reference to marijuana, that advocacy was at best subtle and ambiguous.

There is abundant precedent, including another opinion THE CHIEF JUSTICE announces today, for the proposition that when the "First Amendment is implicated, the tie goes to the speaker," *Federal Election Comm'n v. Wisconsin Right to Life, Inc.*, 551 U.S. _____ (2007) (slip op., at 21) and that "when it comes to defining what speech qualifies as the functional equivalent of express advocacy . . . we give the benefit of the doubt to speech, not censorship," *post*, at 29. If this were a close case, the tie would have to go to Frederick's speech, not to the principal's strained reading of his quixotic message.

Among other things, the Court's ham-handed, categorical approach is deaf to the constitutional imperative to permit unfettered debate, even among high-school students, about the wisdom of the war on drugs or of legalizing marijuana for medicinal use.[7] See *Tinker*, 393 U.S., at 511 ("[Students] may not be confined to the expression of those sentiments that are officially approved"). If Frederick's stupid reference to marijuana can in the Court's view justify censorship, then high school students everywhere could be forgiven for zipping their mouths about drugs at school lest some "reasonable" observer censor and then punish them for promoting drugs. . . .

Consider, too, that the school district's rule draws no distinction between alcohol and marijuana, but applies evenhandedly to all "substances that are illegal to minors." App. to Pet. for Cert. 53a; see also App. 83 (expressly defining "'drugs'" to include "all alcoholic beverages"). Given the tragic consequences of teenage alcohol consumption—drinking causes far more fatal accidents than the misuse of marijuana—the school district's interest in deterring teenage alcohol use is at least comparable to its interest in preventing marijuana use. Under the Court's reasoning, must the First Amendment give way whenever a school seeks to punish a student for any speech mentioning beer, or indeed anything else that might be deemed risky to teenagers? While I find it hard to believe the Court would support punishing Frederick for flying a "WINE SiPS 4 JESUS" banner—which could quite reasonably be construed either as a protected religious message or as a pro-alcohol message—the breathtaking sweep of its opinion suggests it would.

III

Although this case began with a silly, nonsensical banner, it ends with the Court inventing out of whole cloth a special First Amendment rule permitting the censorship of any student speech that mentions drugs, at least so long as someone could perceive that speech to contain a latent pro-drug message. Our First Amendment jurisprudence has identified some categories of expression that are less deserving of protection than others—fighting words, obscenity, and commercial speech, to name a few. Rather than reviewing our opinions discussing such categories, I mention two personal recollections that have no doubt influenced my conclusion that it would be profoundly unwise to create special rules for speech about drug and alcohol use.

The Vietnam War is remembered today as an unpopular war. During its early stages, however, "the dominant opinion" that Justice Harlan mentioned in his *Tinker* dissent regarded opposition to the war as unpatriotic, if not treason. 393 U.S., at 526. That dominant opinion strongly supported the pros-ecution of several of those who demonstrated in Grant Park during the 1968 Democratic Convention in Chicago, see *United States v. Dellinger,* 472 F. 2d 340 (CA7 1972), and the vilification of vocal opponents of the war like Julian Bond, cf. *Bond v. Floyd,* 385 U.S. 116 (1966). In 1965, when the Des Moines students wore their armbands, the school district's fear that they might "start an argument or cause a disturbance" was well founded. *Tinker,* 393 U.S., at 508. Given that context, there is special force to the Court's insistence that "our Constitution says we must take that risk; and our history says that it is this sort of hazardous freedom—this kind of openness—that is the basis of our national strength and of the independence and vigor of Americans who grow up and live in this relatively permissive, often disputatious, society." *Id.,* at 508–509 (citation omitted). As we now know, the then-dominant opinion about the Vietnam War was not etched in stone.

Reaching back still further, the current dominant opinion supporting the war on drugs in general, and our anti-marijuana laws in particular, is reminis-cent of the opinion that supported the nationwide ban on alcohol consumption when I was a student. While alcoholic beverages are now regarded as ordinary articles of commerce, their use was then condemned with the same moral fer-vor that now supports the war on drugs. The ensuing change in public opinion occurred much more slowly than the relatively rapid shift in Americans' views on the Vietnam War, and progressed on a state-by-state basis over a period of many years. But just as prohibition in the 1920's and early 1930's was secretly questioned by thousands of otherwise law-abiding patrons of bootleggers and speakeasies, today the actions of literally millions of otherwise law-abiding users of marijuana,[8] and of the majority of voters in each of the several States that tolerate medicinal uses of the product,[9] lead me to wonder whether the fear of disapproval by those in the majority is silencing opponents of the war on drugs. Surely our national experience with alcohol should make us wary of dampening speech suggesting—however inarticulately—that it would be better to tax and regulate marijuana than to persevere in a futile effort to ban its use entirely.

Even in high school, a rule that permits only one point of view to be expressed is less likely to produce correct answers than the open discussion of countervailing views. *Whitney,* 274 U.S., at 377 (Brandeis, J., concurring); *Abrams,* 250 U.S., at 630 (Holmes, J., dissenting); *Tinker,* 393 U.S., at 512. In the national debate about a serious issue, it is the expression of the minori-ty's viewpoint that most demands the protection of the First Amendment. Whatever the better policy may be, a full and frank discussion of the costs and benefits of the attempt to prohibit the use of marijuana is far wiser than sup-pression of speech because it is unpopular.

I respectfully dissent.

Notes

[1.] It is also relevant that the display did not take place "on school premises," as the rule contemplates. App. to Pet. for Cert. 53a. While a separate dis-trict rule does make the policy applicable to "social events and class trips," *id.,* at 58a, Frederick might well have thought that the Olympic Torch Relay was neither a "social event" (for example, prom) nor a "class trip."

[2.] See *ante,* at 1 (stating that the principal "reasonably regarded" Frederick's banner as "promoting illegal drug use"); *ante,* at 6 (explaining that "Principal Morse thought the banner would be interpreted by those viewing it as promoting illegal drug use, and that interpretation is plainly a reasonable one"); *ante,* at 8 (asking whether "a principal may . . . restrict student speech . . . when that speech is reasonably viewed as promoting illegal drug use"); *ante,* at 14 (holding that "schools [may] restrict student expression that they reasonably regard as promoting illegal drug use"); see also *ante,* at 1 (ALITO, J., concurring) ("[A] public school may restrict speech that a reasonable observer would interpret as advocating illegal drug use").

[3.] See *ante,* at 7 ("We agree with Morse. At least two interpretations of the words on the banner demonstrate that the sign advocated the use of illegal drugs"); *ante,* at 15 (observing that "[w]e have explained our view" that "Frederick's banner constitutes promotion of illegal drug use").

[4.] The reasonableness of the view that Frederick's message was unprotected speech is relevant to ascertaining whether qualified immunity should shield the principal from liability, not to whether her actions violated Frederick's constitutional rights. Cf. *Saucier v. Katz,* 533 U.S. 194, 202 (2001) ("The relevant, dispositive inquiry in determining whether a right is clearly established is whether it would be clear to a reasonable officer that his conduct was unlawful in the situation he confronted").

[5.] This same reasoning applies when the interpreter is not just a listener, but a legislature. We have repeatedly held that "[d]eference to a legislative finding" that certain types of speech are inherently harmful "cannot limit judicial inquiry when First Amendment rights are at stake," reasoning that "the judicial function commands analysis of whether the specific conduct charged falls within the reach of the statute and if so whether the legislation is consonant with the Constitution." *Landmark Communications, Inc. v. Virginia,* 435 U.S. 829, 843, 844 (1978); see also *Whitney v. California,* 274 U.S. 357, 378–379 (1927) (Brandeis, J., concurring) ("[A legislative declaration] does not preclude enquiry into the question whether, at the time and under the circumstances, the conditions existed which are essential to validity under the Federal Constitution. . . . Whenever the fundamental rights of free speech and assembly are alleged to have been invaded, it must remain open to a defendant to present the issue whether there actually did exist at the time a clear danger; whether the danger, if any, was imminent; and whether the evil apprehended was so substantial as to justify the stringent restriction interposed by the legislature"). When legislatures are entitled to no deference as to whether particular speech amounts to a "clear and present danger," *id.,* at 379, it is hard to understand why the Court would so blithely defer to the judgment of a single school principal.

[6.] In affirming Frederick's suspension, the JDHS superintendent acknowledged that Frederick displayed his message "for the benefit of television cameras covering the Torch Relay." App. to Pet. for Cert. 62a.

[7.] The Court's opinion ignores the fact that the legalization of marijuana is an issue of considerable public concern in Alaska. The State Supreme Court held in 1975 that Alaska's constitution protects the right of adults to possess less than four ounces of marijuana for personal use. *Ravin v. State,* 537 P. 2d 494 (Alaska). In 1990, the voters of Alaska attempted to undo that decision by voting for a ballot initiative recriminalizing marijuana possession. Initiative Proposal No. 2, §§1–2 (effective Mar. 3, 1991), 11 Alaska Stat., p. 872 (Lexis 2006). At the time Frederick unfurled his banner, the constitutionality of that referendum had yet to be tested. It was subsequently struck down as unconstitutional. See *Noy v. State,* 83 P. 3d 538 (Alaska App. 2003). In the meantime, Alaska voters had approved a ballot measure decriminalizing the use of marijuana for medicinal purposes, 1998 Ballot Measure No. 8 (approved Nov. 3, 1998), 11 Alaska Stat., p. 882 (codified at Alaska Stat. §§11.71.090, 17.37.010–17.37.080), and had rejected a much broader measure that would have decriminalized marijuana possession and granted amnesty to anyone convicted of marijuana-related crimes, see 2000 Ballot Measure No. 5 (failed Nov. 7, 2000), 11 Alaska Stat., p. 886.

[8.] See *Gonzales v. Raich,* 545 U.S. 1, 21, n. 31 (2005) (citing a Government estimate "that in 2000 American users spent $10.5 *billion* on the purchase of marijuana").

[9.] *Id.,* at 5 (noting that "at least nine States . . . authorize the use of marijuana for medicinal purposes").

POSTSCRIPT

Can a School Punish a Student for Speech That Is Reasonably Viewed as Promoting Illegal Drug Use?

*H*azelwood gave school administrators fairly broad authority to intervene in school newspapers, and *Fraser* was a case about the spoken word. In addition to these cases, one dealing with press and the other with speech, the Vietnam-era case of *Tinker v. Des Moines* involved an armband, a kind of silent protest. The future is likely to generate more cases about control of expression involving students and different kinds of cases. The reason for this is simple, namely that there are new ways to communicate, the number of new forms of communication is growing, and whether something communicated electronically occurred in school or out of school may not be clear. Although the three most important precedents involve armbands, speech, and a printed newspaper, three very traditional modes of expression, we are now in an era of ever-increasing forms of communication. We have cell phones that have the processing power of some computers, bloggers who wish to be recognized as journalists, and virtual worlds like SecondLife that allow us to reshape our identities.

In *Morse v. Frederick,* the Court could have provided some clarification of the important question of when school officials can punish students for off-campus behavior. There have been increasing numbers of such cases in recent years. The earliest cases tended to involve underground newspapers that were critical of teachers or administrators and were not written and published in or during school. More recent cases have involved new problems like cyberbullying and the creation of Web sites or Facebook pages that criticize teachers or use offensive language.

Consider, for example, the following:

- Anthony Latour was expelled from school because of four rap songs he wrote over a four-year period. The songs, which contained profanity and violent imagery, were put on the Internet. The District Court ruled in favor of the student. *Latour v. Riverside Beaver Sch. Dist.* (August 24, 2005, http://www.aclupa.org/downloads/LatourPIOrder.pdf).
- Justin Layshock posted a parody profile of his school's principal on MySpace. The profile was created outside of school but proved to be so popular that the computer system in school could not be used for several days. In *Layshock v. Hermitage School District,* the District Court for the Western District of Pennsylvania (http://www.citmedialaw .org/threats/hermitage-school-district-v-layshock), the federal District Court

ruled that Justin Layshock's rights were not violated when he was suspended because of the disruption caused in the school. A copy of the Web site can be found at http://www.aclupa.org/downloads/Justinswebsite .pdf. The case is currently on appeal to the federal Court of Appeals for the Third Circuit.

Some Web sites touching on these examples are http://www.aclu.org/studentsrights/ index.html, http://www.citmedialaw.org/threats/hermitage-school-district-v-layshock# description, and http://www.aclupa.org/legal/legaldocket/middleschoolrapperexpelled. An actual picture of the armband worn by John Tinker is at http://www.bandofrights .org/bandimages/armbands.jpg. Recent articles include Rita J. Verga, "Policing Their Space: The First Amendment Parameters of School Discipline of Student Cyberspeech," 23 *Santa Clara Computer & High Tech. L. J.* 727 (May, 2007); Mary-Rose Papandrea, "Student Speech Rights in the Digital Age," 60 *Fla. L. Rev.* 1027 (2008); and Brannon P. Denning and Molly C. Taylor, "*Morse v. Frederick* and the Regulation of Student Cyberspeech," 35 *Hastings Const. L. Q.* 835 (2008).

Internet References . . .

National Conference of State Legislators

"Legislative Term Limits: An Overview"

http://www.ncsl.org/default.aspx?tabid=14849

U.S. Term Limits

Grassroots information and lobbying organization

http://www.termlimits.org/

The ReDistricting Game

Fun yet informative resource from the USC Annenberg Center

http://www.redistrictinggame.org/

U.S. Census Bureau

U.S. Census Bureau's Redistricting Data page

http://www.census.gov/rdo/

League of Women Voters

Redistricting Reform

**http://www.lwv.org/AM/Template.cfm?Section=Redistricting&Template=/
TaggedPage/TaggedPageDisplay.cfm&TPLID=144&ContentID=13902**

State Legislatures

*L*ike governors, voters are often skeptical of government and promote a limited function for state legislators. However, state legislative roles have transformed from "sometime" legislators almost exclusively controlled by rural white males, to a more urban and diverse demographic. Many of these legislators also meet annually today with support staffs and have higher salaries than before. However, skepticism of state legislators still exists because of careerism, corruption, and their intense focus on re-election.

- Should State Legislators Have Term Limits?
- Should Legislators Have the Responsibility for Redistricting?

ISSUE 10

Should State Legislators Have Term Limits?

YES: Patrick Basham, from "Assessing the Term Limits Experiment: California and Beyond," Cato Institute (August 31, 2001)

NO: Bruce Cain, John Hanley, and Thad Kousser, from "Term Limits: A Recipe for More Competition?" in *The Marketplace of Democracy* (McDonald and Samples, 2006)

ISSUE SUMMARY

YES: Patrick Basham contends that the term-limits movement is one of the most successful grassroots political efforts in U.S. history.

NO: Bruce Cain and his colleagues find that the premises of the term-limits movement are largely false.

Basham and Cain et al. have different views not only on the outcome of the term-limits movement after a few electoral cycles, but on whether to keep state legislative term limits going. Term limits first took effect in 1996.[1] By 1998, more than 200 legislators from California, Colorado, Maine, Arkansas, Michigan, and Oregon, as well as the Missouri Senate, all had term limits take effect, according to the National Conference of State Legislatures. For example, Arkansas and Michigan legislatures found themselves involved in huge turnovers as 100 Arkansas House members and 64 of 110 Michigan members could not run for re-election. Two years later, term limits took effect in five other states—Arizona, Florida, Montana, Ohio, and South Dakota.

In 2002, term limits started for both the Missouri legislature and the Michigan Senate. In Missouri, 45 percent (23 members) of its legislature were termed out, while in the Michigan Senate it was more than 70 percent (73 members).[2] Michigan had 44 members termed out and Missouri only 21 in 2008.[3]

From 1990 to 1995, Basham finds legislative term limits passed in 18 states, with an average of 68 percent voter support. Currently, there are 15 states with state legislative term limits with 6 others nullifying theirs through the courts.[4]

By the end of 2000, Basham notes, those term limits were wide ranging, influencing more than 700 state legislative seats. He argues further that term limits had attained the goal of ending careerism among state legislators and that research backs this up.

Conversely, Cain et al. use their research to find that term-limit movement claims are, for the most part, unfounded. Their research does find an increase in "descriptive turnover" by an average of 14 percent. Likewise, political competition is increased, bringing not only a greater number of women and minorities into the political arena, but also into other professions besides political aides and lawyers, Basham contends. He also argues that term limits also brings in new faces who challenge the legislative leadership, decreasing their power. Cain et al., though, dispute this finding that while legislative experience and committee seniority, more power is put in leaders' hands.

Cain et al. do find some increase in Latino and other minority representatives. However, they argue that this change would have occurred anyway, but term limits made this change happen more quickly. Although minorities have increased, as Basham has also noted, these authors diverge in their findings in that women do not seem to have increased because of term limits.

Cain et al., much like Basham, also find some increase in the level of contesting among both incumbent and open seats. However, term limits have failed in making races closer or creating greater party turnover. It may be that incumbency advantages—name recognition, staff, money, constituency service—are apparently learned quickly.

Although some studies find little extra confidence in reaction to term limits, Basham reminds readers of polls in Missouri and California; both were more than 69 percent positive on the question relating to term limits. People like term limits regardless of the actual outcomes. However, Cain et al. find that the real problem is that term limits are only a partial solution to a much larger problem—the lack of political competition, especially against many incumbency advantages. They argue further that term limits do little because other factors such as primary system incentives, voter polarization, redistricting, and the influence of money from outside groups will persist. To address these issues means greater reform than term limits alone, they assert. Basham, on the other hand, finds that the evidence points to term limits working nationwide and that we should endorse and extend them to more states rather than ending this experiment.

Notes

1. National Conference on State Legislatures, "Coping with Term Limits: A Practical Guide," Legislative Term Limits: An Overview.

   http://www.ncsl.org/LegislaturesElections/LegislatorsLegislativeStaffData/LegislativeTermLimitsOverview/tabid/14849/Default.aspx

2. *Ibid*.

3. National Conference on State Legislatures, "Members Termed Out: 1996–2008," http://www.ncsl.org/Default.aspx?TabId=14842

4. Statistics according to the U.S. Term Limits Web page, http://www.ustl.org/

YES

Patrick Basham

Assessing the Term Limits Experiment: California and Beyond

The term limits movement is one of the most successful grassroots political efforts in U.S. history. From 1990 to 1995 legislative term limits passed in 18 states with an average of 68 percent voter support. By the end of 2000 those term limits had affected more than 700 legislative seats.

Term limits were intended to end careerism among state legislators. Academic and other research on the effects of term limits suggests that they have substantially attained that goal. Current research supports the following conclusions:

- Term limits remain popular with state electorates long after their introduction.
- Term limits stimulate electoral competition in state legislative elections.
- Term limits enable nontraditional candidates to run for seats in state legislatures. Female, Hispanic-American, and Asian-American candidates find it easier to enter term-limited legislatures than non-term-limited bodies. The record is more mixed for African Americans.
- Term limits weaken seniority systems in state legislatures.
- Term limits tend to weaken the leadership of a state legislature.
- Term limits have not strengthened interest groups, state bureaucracies, or legislative staffs as predicted by critics of term limits.
- Some evidence suggests that term limits foster public policies compatible with limited government.

Introduction

Term limits are perhaps the most far-reaching change in state legislatures in recent decades. If we find that they hurt the quality of representation, states may want to rethink them. But if we find that term limits, on balance, are beneficial, it might persuade some additional states to enact them.

Richard Niemi
University of Rochester

From *Policy Analysis*, no. 413, August 31, 2001, pp. 1–21. Copyright © 2001 by Cato Institute. Reprinted by permission via Copyright Clearance Center.

The term limits movement is one of the most successful grassroots political efforts in U.S. history. From 1990 to 1995 legislative term limits passed in 18 states with an average of 68 percent voter support. In November 2000 Nebraska became the 19th state to limit the terms of state legislators. By the end of 2000 term limits had affected more than 700 legislative seats. However, only 11 states (California, Maine, Colorado, Arkansas, Michigan, Oregon, Arizona, Montana, South Dakota, Ohio, and Florida) have actually put term limits into practice during the past five years. The last five of those states did not come on board until last year. A further seven states (Missouri, Idaho, Oklahoma, Utah, Wyoming, Louisiana, and Nevada) will put term limits into effect by 2008. Term limits in the states have had a broad but unknown impact. For that reason, this paper seeks to assess the measurable effects of state term limits in light of the intentions of their proponents.

Term limits continue to be opposed by a majority of politicians and by a majority of the legislative staff, bureaucrats, journalists, and interest groups that depend on politicians for employment, patronage, sources, and votes. Interest groups (especially large, heavily regulated corporations as well as unions that rely on government intervention in the labor market) view term limits as anathema to their interests. A 1990 survey of 302 state legislators found only 41 percent in favor of term limits. Inside the Beltway, the *Washington Post* regularly editorializes to the effect that "term limits are a terrible idea." On the West Coast, the *San Francisco Chronicle* concluded that "term limits at the legislative level have ill-served California." Yet, despite a steady onslaught of negative commentary emanating from the political and media establishments, public opinion remains solidly in favor of term limits. During last year's elections, local term limits passed in California, Florida, Maryland, and New Mexico, adding to the total of nearly 3,000 municipal offices and more than 17,000 local politicians already subject to term limits.

On March 23, 1998, the U.S. Supreme Court let stand term limits for California's state legislators, ensuring the survival of comparable term limit provisions in other states. That decision permitted ongoing testing of the hypothesis that "there are systemic explanations . . . for our collective woes." Almost 11 years after the passage of the first term limit provisions, researchers are now able to move, albeit cautiously, from speculation to analysis. Caution is warranted, given the well-documented difficulty in tracking the effects of term limits. After all, "even in states like Maine and California that have been under term limits for a few years, they're in . . . a transition period right now." Research and analysis are complicated by the different influences of term limits on the respective state legislatures and by a variety of compounding factors, including the vagaries of term limit legislation and the differences between so-called citizen and professional legislatures. Therefore, it is apparent that term limits will produce different outputs in different states. Bruce E. Cain and Marc A. Levin note that "term limits vary in features that may have causal significance." They summarize:

Most important, there are variations in the length of the limits imposed, ranging from 6 to 12 years. Shorter terms . . . should have more pronounced effects than longer ones. Twelve states limit by consecutive years of service, whereas the others do not. Some states, like California, include a lifetime ban, but others merely require that the office holder rotate out for a period of time. In most states, limits apply to service in a given chamber of the legislature, but in Oklahoma, limits apply to legislative service in either or both chambers.

"Citizen legislatures" (e.g., those of Maine, Montana, and South Dakota) feature politicians with relatively short tenure. They possess small staffs, are paid relatively low salaries, largely act as part-time legislators, and attend short legislative sessions. In contrast, "professional legislatures" (e.g., those of California, Colorado, and Michigan) feature politicians who enjoy relatively lengthy tenure, are usually full-time legislators, are paid middle-class salaries, employ full-time staff, and attend yearlong legislative sessions. The professionalization of state legislatures began to gather momentum in the 1960s. That development has significant implications for both the politics and the analysis of term limits. For example, as economists Stephanie Owings and Rainald Borck note, "It seems clear that the incentives for professional legislatures to legislate to the benefit of special interest groups and to strike logrolling deals differ from the incentives faced by citizen legislators." Hence, the prediction of Rader, Elder, and Elling:

> The full impact of term limits will probably not be realized until they have been in place for a number of years. The coercive or expulsion effects of term limits come into play only as the first cohort of legislators exhaust their allowable terms. Such effects are yet to be experienced in some states or have only recently been experienced in others.

This paper is both a review of existing and forthcoming studies of term limits in state legislatures and an original analysis of existing or obtainable data about both term-limited and non-term-limited state legislatures. I attempt to provide preliminary answers to several research questions directly related to the influence of term limits on representative democracy and contemporary legislative politics. Those questions include the following:

- Do term limits make campaigns more competitive?
- Are campaigns more costly under term limits?
- Have term limits changed who runs for state legislatures?
- Do term limits increase the occupational and demographic diversity of officeholders and, if so, how?
- Have term limits changed the way state legislatures work?
- Have term limits made legislators more willing to act independently in defense of either their states' or constituents' interests?
- Have term limits weakened the political class at the state level or have they simply shifted power to bureaucrats, legislative staff, or interest groups?
- What quality of legislation is produced by term-limited legislatures?

Throughout, I emphasize California's term limits experience. California is described by Michael Barone as "the great laboratory of America." Moreover, the state is the largest term-limited jurisdiction, has one of the oldest term-limited legislatures, epitomizes the professional legislature model, and therefore provides the most extensive source of relevant research material.

A Historical Overview of Term Limits

> In free governments, the rulers are the servants, and the people their superiors. . . . For the former to return among the latter does not degrade, but promote them.
>
> Benjamin Franklin

As Steven Millman reminds us, "The concept of term limits is by no means new." The historical roots of term limits go as far back as Athenian democracy in the fifth century B.C. and are grounded in traditional republican and classical liberal models of limited, democratic government. In Colonial America term limits were referred to as the "rotary system," or the principle of "rotation in office." The New England Colony's charter provided for the rotation of public officials and a limit on years of office-holding. By 1777, 7 (of the 10) new state constitutions provided for rotation in office. Convened in 1777, the Continental Congress approved the Articles of Confederation that became the nation's first constitution in 1781. The articles included rotation of offices and limited federal legislators to a maximum of three years in Congress.

In 1787 the Constitutional Convention in Philadelphia revised the Articles of Confederation, thereby producing the nation's second constitution. Clearly, the Framers intended the country to be governed by successive citizen congresses. After all:

> The Framers . . . lived in a different time. Congress as they envisioned it did not need term limits, because Congressional service as they envisioned it was always going to be a part-time job. . . . That assumption, understandable in its day, allowed the Framers to believe that Congress would just naturally remain a citizen legislature, without any Constitutional requirement that those serving in Congress not spend their entire lives there.

The Framers debated the idea of mandatory rotation but, confident that sufficient safeguards (such as short terms in office and voluntary retirements) were in place to forestall careerism, and concerned that its inclusion meant "entering into too much detail" for a short document, they set aside the arguments of the anti-Federalists and chose not to include a term limits provision in the new Constitution. Moreover, President George Washington's voluntary retirement after his second term in office established a precedent that held among occupants of the White House until the mid-20th century administration of Franklin D. Roosevelt.

As Mark P. Petracca establishes, "A general aversion to making a career of legislative service also characterized state and local politicians." At the state level, gubernatorial term limits have been commonplace throughout our nation's history. Municipal term limits have been in place since 1851 when the Indiana Constitution prescribed county-level limits. At the federal level, a tradition of voluntary retirement after only one or two terms in the U.S. House of Representatives lasted until nearly the end of the 19th century. From 1830 to 1850, turnover in the House averaged 51.5 percent. After the Civil War, legislative tenure gained new importance when the introduction of the seniority principle for congressional committee membership changed the dynamics of obtaining leadership positions. Consequently, between 1860 and 1920 House members' average tenure increased from four to eight years, and it has continued to rise ever since.

In the 1960s and 1970s the average state legislature experienced the turnover of one-third of its members every two years. During the 1980s, however, turnover declined considerably, and by 1988 average turnover had fallen to only 16 percent of state legislators. Overall, during the 1980s 99.3 percent of unindicted congressional and state legislative incumbents won reelection. In California the tenure of Assembly members averaged 2.5 terms in the 1940s and rose steadily to reach 4.5 terms by the 1980s. During the California elections of 1984, 1986, and 1988, 267 of 270 incumbents successfully sought reelection. In 1988 incumbent state senators had a 100 percent reelection rate, and incumbent members of the state Assembly had a 96 percent reelection rate. Unsurprisingly, then, the state Assembly's turnover rate fell by more than 50 percent during the 1980s.

On the East Coast, Maine's incumbent reelection rate varied from 88 to 94 percent in the modern pre–term limits period. To the south, in North Carolina 81 percent of state Assembly incumbents were reelected in 1994. Further west, during the pre–term limits period of 1982 to 1988, no incumbent Colorado state senator lost his or her legislative seat. During that period only 8.4 percent of Colorado's state legislative elections resulted in changes of party representation. In 1994 only 3 of 65 Colorado state House seats up for election had contested primaries, and 83 percent of incumbents were reelected by more than 55 percent of the vote.

As a political movement, term limits first achieved statewide success in September 1990 when Oklahoma limited the terms of its state legislators. Later that year, California did the same—an influential move, given the state's size. In 1994 Utah's legislature earned the distinction of being the only state legislature in the country to pass term limits, preempting passage by voter initiative. Term limits were first put into practice in 1996 in California's professional legislature and Maine's part-time legislature; Maine was the first state to term limit both legislative chambers.

Between 1990 and 1996, 21 states adopted term limits (the state supreme courts of Massachusetts, Nebraska, and Washington nullified term limits). Those term limits ranged from 6 to 12 years for lower houses and from 8 to 12 years for upper houses; the more stringent limits were enacted in Arkansas, California, Michigan, and Ohio. The term limits in each state differ in important ways. Some laws involve ballot access restrictions, some are lifetime limits, and others place limits on consecutive terms. During the next four years, term limits went into effect in six states; five more states put term limits into practice in 2000. Seven more states will be subjected to term limits by 2008. In November 1999 Mississippi voters rejected term limits, becoming the first statewide electorate to oppose this reform measure. Term limits also currently affect 40 governors. The appeal of limiting the terms of elected officials is also evident in the passage of term limits for hundreds of cities across the country, including Los Angeles, New York City, and the District of Columbia.

Goals and Projected Benefits of Term Limits

> When politicians know they must return to civil society and live under the laws passed while they were in office, they will think more carefully about the long-term effects of the programs they support.

> Lawrence W. Reed

Term limits seek to improve American democracy by addressing the problem of careerism. Skepticism about and distaste for long-term political careerism are central to the American experience. As state legislatures have become more professional, they have attracted candidates who can and do spend their entire careers in the state capital. Careerism flourishes because incumbents are virtually certain to be reelected, largely because of the inherent advantages of holding office. In the opinion of proponents of term limits, careerism poses several problems for our system of representative democracy. Once in office, careerist legislators pay less attention to the needs and wishes of their constituents. As Petracca observes:

> Representative democracy requires electoral competition and the dependence of legislators on the people. But electoral competition is no longer possible in a system where the benefits and power of incumbency virtually guarantee a lifelong career as a legislator. The problem is not individual incumbents, but rather, chronic incumbency.

Moreover, careerist elected officials became a political class attentive to their own interests. As term limits activist Eric O'Keefe views it:

> The problem, quite simply, is that our representatives are not representative. They are a separate class, identifying their interests with those of the government, not the people. When the interests of the government in which they serve and the people they putatively serve conflict . . . they invariably side with the government.

Substantial and continuing public support for term limits suggests widespread distaste for careerism in politics, as well as a conviction that the continual infusion of fresh blood into state legislatures will improve American government. By mandating frequent legislative turnover, term limits may bring new perspectives to state legislatures, reduce the concentration on reelection, and thereby diminish the incentive for wasteful election-related pork-barrel spending that flourishes in a careerist legislative culture.

Proponents of term limits expect them to deal with the problem of careerism in two ways. First, the prospect of shorter political careers should change the characteristics of people who choose to seek public office, encouraging political participation by non-professional politicians. Potential candidates may view a few terms in the legislature more as a civic obligation than as an outlet for private ambition. Second, legislators would be closer to the world outside politics, the world where most people live their lives. Making the legislature closer to the private sector would also familiarize legislators with the complex consequences of laws and regulations. Overall, a legislature composed of average citizens would be a legislature that looked more like America and less like a political class of arrogant and ambitious politicians intent on self-aggrandizement.

Advocates of term limits have advanced two arguably incompatible reasons why increasing competition will improve our political system. Some advocates argue that increasing competition in the political marketplace, as in the economic marketplace, leads to greater consumer choice and satisfaction. In politics, greater competition might force candidates to adhere more closely to the will of the people regarding the composition of laws and regulations. Other advocates argue that opening the political system to more competition will attract candidates who are not career minded and hence are willing to exercise independent judgment or take an independent stand for the good of their state, nation, or society.

Other arguments for term limits focus on how they might change the outputs of legislatures. Studies show that the longer an individual stays in office, the greater his support for increased government spending. Limiting terms may lead to limited government, or at least a smaller government than would have existed in their absence. It is possible, of course, that term limits may simply reduce pork-barrel spending without affecting the overall expenditures of government. Consequently, the long-term budgetary effects of term limits merit close examination.

Political Competition and Term Limits

The problem is . . . chronic incumbency.

Hendrik Hertzberg

Opponents of term limits are technically correct when they assert that "we already have term limits—they're called elections." Unfortunately, American politics has fewer and fewer competitive elections. Simply put, our electoral system is unfair; it has been described as "a stacked deck that needed a corrective." Term limits constitute, in large measure, an attempt to overcome the problem of the costs of the so-called incumbency advantage. In federal politics, for example, incumbency is worth an 11 percent increase in expected vote share to the average officeholder. Cox and Morgenstern found a comparable advantage accruing to incumbents at the state level. The advantages of incumbency include access to the media, franked constituent mailings, name recognition, subsidized staff and travel, pork-barrel spending, and lawmaking power. Those advantages are further fueled by the fact that incumbent politicians raise, on average, more than twice the amount of campaign contributions that their challengers do. For example, political action committees contribute nearly eight times more money to incumbents than to challengers. The incumbency advantage is not only important; its importance has risen over time.

A decade ago, conservative author and commentator George F. Will referred to "a perpetual incumbency machine" that "has become today's swollen government operating with no limits on the incontinent spending and regulating that is undertaken to perpetuate in office the spenders and regulators." Hence, in Will's view, "term limits are needed as an auxiliary precaution against the perennial lust for power," as "careerism is the shared creed of Democrats and Republicrats." Clearly, by the 1990s Americans had "grown increasingly weary and distrustful of the permanent government . . . in state capitals around the nation." Therefore, the argument was successfully made that "the only effective way to level the political playing field is to limit terms."

As the long odds against ousting an incumbent may deter better qualified potential candidates from running for office, it was forecast that term limits would attract a different kind of candidate and, consequently, would provide "fresh faces more attuned to the people's needs, more responsive, less career-oriented," that is, citizen legislators. In late 1990, before the passage of California's term limits initiative, journalist John H. Fund wrote:

> Term limitation would create a climate in which talented men and women from businesses and professions would want to run . . . since they would know they would reach a position of significant influence in a few short years instead of having to make a career of politics if they wanted to play a major role. . . . Citizen-legislators would come to government briefly, then many would return to private life and live with the consequences of the laws they had passed.

The distinction between professional and citizen legislators is an important one as "the movement for imposed term limits in part rests on the belief that term limits would make legislatures more like citizen legislatures," and differences in the types of state legislatures affect turnover rates. Turnover is much higher in citizen legislatures than in professional legislatures. For example, in citizen legislatures the turnover rate in lower houses after 6 years was 15 percent higher, and after 12 years 21 percent higher, than in professional legislatures; meanwhile, in upper houses, citizen legislatures had a turnover rate that was 14.5 percent higher after 6 years, and 14 percent higher after 12 years, than did professional legislatures.

Term limits were expected to reduce barriers to entry to politics. That is, term limits were expected to produce more open seats. It was reasonable to forecast that more candidates for office and the increased turnover of state legislatures would produce better choices for voters.

Term Limits in Practice

What happened? According to John Hood, president of the John Locke Foundation, "One undeniable fact is that they [term limits] have made state and local elections more competitive." As expected, turnover rates increased. In 1996, 52 state legislators left office because of term limits; in 1998, more than 200 state legislators were forced to step down. In 2000, 369 state legislators were forced out by term limits. On average, term-limited legislatures have lost a third of their pre–term limits incumbents. The number of special elections increased as term-limited incumbents left office early to take private-sector positions or to begin campaigning for other, usually higher, offices.

Since 1996 California has experienced crowded, competitive state primaries and general elections. The prospective imposition of term limits on the California state legislature more than doubled voluntary turnover (from 11 to 25 percent) in two years. In this manner, according to Rader, Elder, and Elling, "the effects of term limits . . . arise not only as a direct consequence of members being forced from office but also indirectly as a consequence of the anticipation of that eventuality on the part of both current office holders and would-be office holders." It appears that term limits "contributed to increased levels of turnover in the states that adopted such limits even before they took effect." The projected tendency of lame-duck, term-limited legislators to shirk their duties appears to be mitigated by the fact that term limits may "merely focus the reelection goals of legislators on other offices. Legislators might attempt to move up to statewide office, run for congressional seats, or even drop down from a legislature's upper house to its lower chamber." As economists John R. Lott Jr. and Kermit Daniel explain:

> Making the date that incumbents leave office more certain encourages the entry by challengers even before the seat becomes vacant, if only to be better positioned once the incumbent does leave. Incumbents may also more frequently be pitted against politicians who hold other offices but who do not want to wait for the incumbents to retire, as these challengers may be facing the end of their terms. Reducing the importance of seniority may also lower the returns to running for reelection. Term limits may thus make elections more competitive even before politicians find them binding.

In California the average turnover rate between 1972 and 1992 was 20 percent in the state Assembly and 12 percent in the state Senate. Since 1990 the Assembly's turnover rate has grown to 36 percent and the Senate's has risen to 17 percent. Stanley M. Caress found a 20 percent increase in the number of voluntary retirements and an increase in the number of special elections from an average of 1 per year between 1980 and 1989 to an average of 10 per year between 1990 and 1993. Research by Lott and Daniel on California's state Assembly and Senate races between 1976 and 1994 addressed the effect of term limits on four areas: campaign expenditures, the closeness of races, the number of candidates running for office, and whether candidates run unopposed. Lott and Daniel concluded:

California's legislative term limits have dramatically reduced campaign expenditures. Real expenditures during the three general elections after the term limits initiative passed in 1990 were lower than in even 1976. This drop has occurred at the same time that races have become closer contests and more candidates are running for office. By any measure, term limits have coincided with large changes in the level of political competition, even before term limits have forcibly removed a single politician from office. The changes are so large that more incumbents are being defeated, races are closer, more candidates are running, and fewer single candidate races occur than at any other time during our sample period.

Further evidence that California has experienced lower campaign expenditures in the term limits era is the fact that, after 1992, state Assembly and Senate campaign spending dropped 44 percent compared with the period from 1984 to 1988.

Traditionally, incumbents have been able to insulate themselves from serious competition. However, experience at the state level suggests that voter choice is increased by term limits. In California, for example, the imposition of state-level term limits in 1990 led to a 1992 increase of more than 25 percent in candidate filings for the state Senate and more than 50 percent for the state Assembly; Senate candidate filings for 1994 reflected yet another increase, and, although Assembly candidate filings dropped from 1992, they remained 15 percent higher than in 1990.

Maine's term limits also came into effect in 1996 and caused a 40 percent turnover of the state legislature. In Colorado, in the nine term-limited state Senate elections, the number of candidates per seat was 35 percent higher than in the non-term-limited state Senate races. In Michigan 67 of 110 House legislators ended their final terms in 1998; 64 new legislators entered the House after the 1998 elections. In the South half of the 100-seat Arkansas House opened up in 1998 as a result of the 1992 term limits law. Meanwhile, in Florida last year 55 of 120 House members and 11 of 40 state senators were term limited out of office. During the 1992–2000 electoral cycle, Floridians observed an unusually high number of long-time incumbents either retire or run for higher office. On November 7, 2000, Florida's voters elected first-time legislators to 63 of 120 House seats.

Ohio's term limits also did not come into effect until 2000. Last year 43 of 99 House members and 6 of 33 state senators were term limited out of office. That resulted in one-third of term-limited representatives leaving for either private- or public-sector positions. Earlier last year Ohio experienced what was described as the state's "Big Bang" primary season. Four safe Republican seats in Ohio's Hamilton County drew 50 candidates. Such enthusiasm helped to ensure that Ohio's March 2000 primary slate was the most crowded in 20 years with an uncharacteristically high number of nominations (56 House and 16 Senate) unresolved until primary day.

The Maine 2000 Results

As part of a larger, forthcoming Cato Institute study of public financing of state elections, I analyzed the results of both the Maine state House and the Maine state Senate races in the 1998 and 2000 elections. For the purposes of this paper, I attempted to assess the influence of term limits on the competitiveness of Maine's recent election. The data suggest that, overall, term limits were relatively effective at opening up the state's electoral process.

I compared the number of incumbents who ran unopposed in the two elections. As shown in Table 1, in 1998 five state Senators ran unopposed, four more than in 2000, indicating a more competitive electoral environment last year. Table 2 reveals that two of the four newly competitive Senate seats resulted from term limits coming into effect last year. In the state House 34 representatives ran unopposed in 1998; in 2000 the number fell by 2 to 32— and 4 of the seats were term limited.

Table 1

Unopposed Incumbents

Chamber	Unopposed Incumbents	
	2000	1998
Senate	1	5
House	32	34

Source: Author's calculations.

Table 2

Term Limits and Unopposed Incumbents

Chamber	Newly Competitive Seats as a Result of Term Limits, 2000
Senate	2
House	4

Source: Author's calculations.

In the 2000 election 7 of 13 open Senate seats were the result of term limits. Four of those seven open seats switched to the other party (two went Democratic, two went Republican). Also interesting is the fact that just one of the six remaining non-term-limited open seats switched to the other party.

In the state House 15 of 34 open seats were the result of term limits. Five (33.3 percent) of those 15 seats switched to the other party (4 went Democratic, 1 went Republican). Six (31.6 percent) of the 19 non-term-limited seats switched to the other party (5 went Democratic, 1 went Republican). The statistical proximity of term-limited and non-term-limited seats with regard to partisan gains should not overshadow the fundamental contribution of term limits to producing an additional 15 open seats.

Figure 1

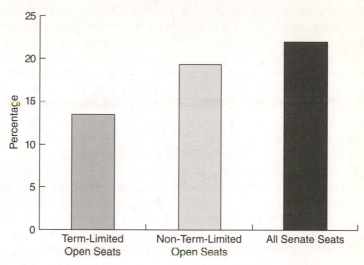

Average Winning Margin: Term-Limited and Non-Term-Limited Open Senate Seats, 2000

Furthermore, as shown in Figure 1, the average winning margin for the term-limited open seats was only 13.5 percent, compared with a statewide average of 22 percent. The average winning margin for the non-term-limited open seats was 19.4 percent, a differential much closer to the statewide average. Term limits seemed to have produced more competitive elections in specific contests.

Less favorable for term limits, the average winning margin for the term-limited open House seats was 24.9 percent, compared with a statewide average of 22.4 percent. The average winning margin for the non-term-limited open House seats was 17.3 percent, 5 percent lower than the statewide average. Those results may be a function of the particular seats that were open in 2000.

Overall, term limits were relatively effective at opening up Maine's electoral process to greater competition. Moreover, as my forthcoming study details, it appears that electoral competitiveness in Maine's 2000 races benefited more from the introduction of term limits than from the introduction of public funding.

Diversity and Representation under Term Limits

How successful were the efforts to bring about more representative legislatures through term limits? The preliminary indications are that legislatures are becoming more representative of the electorate, with a more realistic attitude toward legislative affairs.The California legislature, for example, now "looks more like California, both demographically and ideologically." In 1992 one-third of California's first term-limited state Assembly was freshmen legislators, the largest share since 1946. Petracca investigated the new state legislators' occupational backgrounds. Interestingly, in 1995 there were only 3.4 percent self-described full-time legislators, down from 36 percent in 1986. However, there was an increase in the number of local government officials holding state-level positions, confirming a trend discussed in the preceding section.

In California three times more legislators are now businesspeople than were previously. Furthermore, former legislative staffers—a principal source of new legislators in the pre–term limits era—are a small proportion of new legislators. Petracca's findings are confirmed elsewhere. For example, a *Los Angeles Times* survey of the 1992 state legislature found a plethora of different occupations represented. Throughout California there has been an increase in the number of candidates from outside the political establishment. However, Jean-Philippe Faletta and colleagues found that the backgrounds of pre– and post–term limits Michigan state legislators were comparable.

As predicted by proponents of term limits, the number of successful female and minority candidates has risen. That has significant implications for the distribution of power within state legislatures. Studying Michigan (where term limits went into effect for the state House in 1998), Jovan Trpovski et al. found that term limits also "might increase the electoral opportunities for men of different races and ethnicities." Apparently, that increase has occurred. A recent survey of the term-limited Michigan legislature documents a 42 percent increase in female state House members and a 65 percent increase in African-American state House members. In California the regular availability of open seats has increased the electoral successes of both women and minorities, and "even critics concede that term limits have been a major factor in the growth of Hispanic representation—which is up from only 6 percent of the legislature in 1990 to about 23 percent in 2001."

The 1992 California state legislature contained one-third more female legislators than the pre–term limits legislature as well as the first elected Asian American in 12 years. Between 1990 and 1996, 4 more females, 10 more Hispanics, and 2 Asian Americans were elected to the California state Assembly. Females now constitute 25 percent of California legislators, up from 17 percent in 1990. According to Katches and Weintraub, female legislators have ascended to several leadership positions in the Assembly for the first time as a result of term limits–fostered turnover. Caress asks: "How much of this movement is the direct product of term limits? . . . California's experience does suggest a potential link." Although in California females and Hispanics made major gains in power, the influence of African Americans declined as fewer were elected (down from seven in 1990 to four in 1996).

The relative success of female candidates appears to be more than a Californian phenomenon. After surveying nearly 3,000 legislators in 50 states and interviewing 22 legislative leaders in four term-limited states, Carey, Niemi, and Powell concluded that "term limits might help a few more women win office." Bernstein and Chadha's study of six state legislatures also found that term limits improved advancement opportunities for female legislators. Kathleen Bratton and Kerry Haynie's research suggests that "term limits may well bring about an increase in the number of women and minorities in the leadership." Other research confirms that females are more likely to gain leadership positions in high-turnover legislatures.

Clearly, it is now easier for women to be elected as seats open up at regular intervals. The 1996 implementation of term limits in Maine allowed for the election of the state House's first female speaker. After two elections under full term limits, 50 percent of the legislature's leadership is female. According to Susan J. Carroll and Krista Jenkins, "The gains made by women in term-limited state senate seats [in California, Colorado, and Maine] demonstrate that term limits can lead to increased numbers of women in office if women candidates . . . come forward to take advantage of the opportunities which term limits provide."

The Institutional Impact of Term Limits

The legislative process is remarkably adaptable and resilient.

Douglas G. Brown, director, Colorado's
Office of Legislative Legal Services

Proponents of term limits saw their potential institutional effects as highly important. The primary goal was to change the political culture within the legislative environment. Term limits, it was believed, would change the face of state legislatures, break up the political class, and inject new ideas into the political mainstream. Furthermore, the faster turnover of legislators would weaken the relationship between careerist politicians and the lobbyists employed by special-interest groups. Overall, it was felt that "a regular infusion of new leadership . . . would be a spur to brisk accomplishment."

The contrary forecasts of opponents of term limits emphasized the benefits of seniority and experience. Critics lamented the projected loss of experienced legislators. In short, "some critics . . . believe that the important transmission of institutional norms would cease, causing institutional memory to be lost." It was predicted that this could lead to less effective legislatures, with some suggestion that "public policy is likely to suffer from a lack of careful deliberation and compromise." Critics predicted a significant rise in the influence of the remaining tenured actors—bureaucrats, lobbyists, and legislative staffers—who would run institutional rings around the rookie legislators.

The Loss of Knowledge and Experience

In Missouri, the impact of term limits is only just now being felt. So far, the state doesn't seem any the worse for wear and new legislators aren't spending most of their time walking around the hallowed halls of Jefferson City looking for restrooms, as critics had warned.

Joplin Globe

Critics of term limits maintain that extended legislative service is essential to understanding the highly complex legislative process. According to

Sacramento Bee political columnist Peter Schrag, term limits "take some of government's toughest decisions out of the hands of legislators with long experience and deliver them into the hands of amateurs." Schrag informs us that "no one who has been there [California's state Assembly] four years or less has learned enough about California's complicated system of government. . . . Term limits themselves send the message that experience is not as important as ideological purity and faithful representation of the voters of one's district." In much the same vein, the *San Francisco Chronicle* bemoaned the fact that "institutional memory has disappeared" in Sacramento.

Has the alleged loss of knowledge and experience dealt a devastating blow to the term-limited state legislatures? Here, normative issues raise their head in the term limits debate. My reading of such criticism is influenced by my preference for limited, constitutional government. As Cain and Levin point out:

> To the populists and libertarians, these developments, if true, are not normatively problematic. Populists would say that being responsive to what the people want is more important than recalling what was done in the past, and libertarians would say that the less legislators know about the past, the better. This trend—less institutional memory and expertise—is a problem only for deliberationists and professionalists, who want the legislature to be transformative.

And they note:

> Agreeing about likely effects is hard enough, but people often do not agree on the many values and goals implicit in the debate—e.g. what representatives should do in office, how expert they need to be about policies, and the role of new faces in the legislature. . . . To someone who thinks that less government is better governance, diminished legislative expertise (if that is the effect of term limits) may be a good fact.

Viewed through that prism, the evidence accumulated to date suggests that the fears of critics are unwarranted. The critics' claim that the legislative process takes many years to master is less an indictment of inexperienced legislators than of the legislative process. The workings of America's state legislatures are far more complex than is necessary. Arguably, many of the states are better off without some of this vaunted experience. After all, state legislatures are not the only place to gain useful experience. The private-sector experience that many newcomers are bringing to the term-limited legislatures may prove more valuable for the general welfare. Clearly, political experience is no guarantor of staff-free effective legislating. In non-term-limited professional legislatures, federal and state, most legislation is in fact written by staff members, not by the politicians themselves. In practice, the more senior the legislator, the more dependent he or she is likely to be on staff.

It is important not to underestimate the counter-argument that term-limited legislators are more likely to have a fresh outlook. There is a growing body of evidence that term-limited legislatures perform the state's business more efficiently than do non-term-limited legislatures. It is worth recalling that, prior to term limits, California's state Senate was referred to as "the geriatric ward of California." Now California's legislature works more quickly than before term limits were put into practice, even going so far as to pass state budgets on time. According to the *Sacramento Bee*'s Dan Walters, "One would have to go back a long way, perhaps decades, to find a legislative session that produced as much" as the 1997 session. Also in 1997, Maine's new term-limited legislature passed the state budget in record time.

There also appears to be less rubber-stamping of legislation in a term limits environment. For example, before term limits nearly all bills reported out of Maine's legislative committees had unanimous support; under term limits, however, the proportion of unanimous reports fell to 70 percent. The actual number of bills enacted into law has steadily fallen since the introduction of term limits.

The introduction of an arguably higher quality, more richly experienced, and more diverse pool of candidates and legislators has led to an infusion of new blood and ideas. Michigan House Speaker Chuck Perricone says that, "while critics of term limits may portray a scenario of experienced, knowledgeable people being pushed out of office, only to be replaced by inexperienced newcomers[,] I believe those naysayers fail to appreciate the benefits resulting from a new infusion of capable leaders." The research of Trpovski et al. on Michigan's term-limited legislature indicates that the new legislators exhibit more energy and enthusiasm than did their predecessors. According to the *Detroit News*'s B. G. Gregg, in Michigan "the volume of measures enacted into law already this year [June 1999] surprised many observers who feared a House with so many newcomers would be slow to act as rookies took their time getting up to speed." Most recently, Florida's newly term-limited legislature handled a constitutional crisis, passed election reform legislation, and generally performed without serious error or mistake.

There are also indications that a new relationship may be developing between inexperienced legislators and their constituents. Rader, Elder, and Elling found that legislators elected after the passage of term limits spent more time communicating with their constituents and attending meetings in their districts than did their veteran peers during the course of the same legislative session.

Seniority and the Committee System

> With relentless efficiency, the seniority system empowers the country's most politically sluggish precincts at the expense of its politically more lively ones. That is perverse.
>
> Hendrik Hertzberg

In state legislatures, as on Capitol Hill, "the chairs of important committees are elevated by a decades-long, quasi-feudal process of favor-trading, personal-alliance-building, ladder-climbing and seat-warming." Because legislators know that their professional advancement is dependent in large part on repeated election to the same office, they tend to succumb to "static ambition." Traditionally, the selection of state legislative leaders was based on seniority.

Hence, in 1993 the average tenure of lower house leaders was 12 years; it was 11 years for state senate leaders. As a consequence of term limits, changes are occurring on the traditional leadership career path.

However, term limit laws strike directly at the entrenched power of seniority, unquestionably reducing its importance. Term limits eliminate the possibility of entrenched legislative leaders dominating a legislative chamber. As Caress reminds us, in the California state Assembly of the 1980s, dominated as it was by Speaker Willie Brown, it was "an accepted fact that it was virtually impossible to pass a bill unless the Speaker approved it, and any legislation the Speaker favored was likely to be enacted." Unfortunately, before term limits, "the tendency for state legislative leaders to maintain their grip on power for prolonged periods of time . . . is certainly not unique to California." In Georgia, for example, Speaker Tom Murphy tightly controlled the legislative agenda for more than two decades. As a result of California's term limits, "the potential for long term domination by a single individual no longer exists in either chamber." Even critic Peter Schrag acknowledges:

> It will become much harder for Assembly speakers or Senate presidents, none of whom is likely to serve more than two years, to accumulate either the power that their predecessors had or the dispensable political campaign funds on which much of that power was based. The personal arrogance and indifference of some long-term members may become a thing of the past.

According to a 1997 national survey of state legislators conducted by the Council of State Governments, term limits have provided greater access to leadership positions for freshman legislators. Today there is an accelerated career path for legislators. Generally speaking, freshman legislators are more assertive, more vocal, and more powerful than in the past. In addition, they tend to ask tougher questions of bureaucrats and demand a higher level of performance from government agencies than did their predecessors. Carey, Niemi, and Powell's 50-state survey found that party leaders and committee chairs lost some influence in term-limited legislatures. Thompson and Moncrief replicate this finding. In fact, "the explanatory power of seniority . . . is more than twice as great for state legislatures without term limits." In term-limited legislatures, advancement is now far more frequently based on merit.

Term-limited legislators have almost instant influence, unlike their predecessors who frequently waited decades to climb the seniority ladder. Raymond La Raja and Dorie Apollonio found that, in the term-limited California legislature, "power is decentralized in the Assembly and the influence of caucus leaders has diminished . . . [in the Senate] the power of committee chairs is waning." In Michigan, "today, active participation by new legislators is the rule, not the exception." The term-limited Arkansas legislature was bolder than most and simply abolished the seniority system for selecting committee chairs. Committee chairs are now selected from the floor. Under a more merit-based approach to committee assignments, political philosophy is now as important as personal loyalty.

Therefore, it is becoming increasingly clear that term limits weaken the power of party leaders. While political scientists who adhere to the "party government" model may argue that strong partisan leadership is a prerequisite of legislative accomplishment, the contemporary experience of states as diverse as California and Maine highlights the potential of term-limited legislatures to overcome such alleged handicaps. Weakened legislative leaderships are opening up the budget process. Such is the finding of the 1999–2000 National Conference of State Legislatures' study of five term-limited states. Weaker party leaders make possible stronger, more independent legislators. Independent term-limited legislators are operating in a far more secure environment than their predecessors could ever have envisioned. The reason: "There is no punishment the leadership can inflict. . . . And the leadership knows it, too."

The Bureaucracy

Pessimistic forecasters cautioned that, under term limits, the bureaucracy would gain influence. Simply put, unelected civil servants would run state government. Unfortunately, in practice, in far too many state legislatures the bureaucrats already run the day-to-day government. As Rader, Elder, and Elling found in Michigan, "The post term limit cohort is no more likely to rely upon state agencies." Hence, the downward slope into unaccountable governance as envisioned by critics was nonexistent—most states were already in that undesirable position. Critics who stress the specter of bureaucratic influence inadvertently address a symptom of a poor system while ignoring the disease afflicting the body politic. The source of the bureaucratic problem is not term limits; rather, the source of the problem is the growth of government programs and regulations that create thickets of red tape, through which the average taxpayer, businessperson, *and* legislator find it all but impossible to wade successfully. As legal scholar James Bond reminds us,

> If the . . . government were truly one of delegated, enumerated, and thus limited powers, citizen representatives who served a maximum of three two-year terms would be wholly adequate to the task of deciding the general public policy questions that are appropriately within the purview of the national government.

It remains true that "legislators control the purse and the power to govern the bureaucrats any time they want to." Over the past generation, however, there has been a lack of legislative appetite for exercising such power. Irresponsible legislatures permitted the bureaucracy to grow; therefore, it can only be hoped that more responsible term-limited legislatures will act swiftly to prune back the bureaucracy.

The Influence of Lobbyists and Legislative Staff

In 1991 Nelson Polsby predicted that term limits would transfer power from legislators to interest groups. Five years later Schrag intoned that "the winners from term limits will be . . . the lobbyists, who are never termed out." One is tempted to respond with "the more things change . . . ," especially when one considers that, as Fund wrote at the onset of term limits, "it is . . . difficult to see how the special interests will readily gain more access and influence than they have now." Referring to the California state Assembly in the weeks before the 1990 term limits initiative, former state assemblyman Peter Schabarum pointed out to term limits critics that "special interests already run this legislature." At that time interest groups spent $3.3 million in an unsuccessful attempt to prevent passage of California's 1990 term limits initiative. It is difficult to comprehend why such self-interested actors would so aggressively object to a political development so clearly favorable to their professional well-being.

Fortunately, we are now able to move beyond mere speculation and assess certain developments within the available sample of term-limited states. In practice, term limits appear to act as a rather natural campaign finance reform. Term limits diminish the value of a legislative seat to lobbyists and the special interests they represent in state capitals. According to economist Alexander Tabarrok, "Term limits increase the cost of lobbying through individual politicians." That reduces the incentive for lobbyists to raise and to distribute the large "soft money" contributions so disliked by the political establishment. As economist Stephen Moore points out: "This result is quite predictable. Lobbyists are not likely to invest tens of thousands of dollars in candidates if the citizen legislator is likely to be in [office] for only a short while." Furthermore, term-limited politicians are far more likely to have nonpolitical sources of income. Therefore, they are less likely to succumb to the enticements of lobbyists. Hood succinctly describes the alteration to the incumbent-lobbyist dynamic:

> Lobbyists . . . frequently gain power by developing longtime, symbiotic relationships with key legislative leaders or committee heads . . . those who view legislative service as an interruption in their lives . . . simply have less to gain by ingratiating themselves with lobbyists, reporters, and other governmental insiders.

Schrag forecast that, under term limits, "the flow of money . . . will be less subject to the control of a powerful speaker like [Willie] Brown. There simply isn't time for anyone to develop the long-term relationships that Brown, for better or worse, managed with trial lawyers, public employee unions, land developers, and other major lobbies." It is unsurprising, then, that there is now evidence that lobbyists are unsettled by the term limits–induced need to build new relationships from scratch. Moncrief and Thompson's recent survey of lobbyists in Arkansas, California, Colorado, Maine, and Michigan found that "lobbyists . . . feel that term limits has changed the nature of the lobbying task itself; they consistently report more of their time is devoted to communication, coalition building, and just generally getting their job done."

In Maine term limits have made it more difficult to lobby legislators. According to Maine state Senator Jane Amero, "Lobbyists are having to work harder because of the changing faces in leadership." In the Midwest, Ohio lobbyist Dennis Wojtanowski commented that "the future belongs to those who deal in substance, as opposed to those who deal in relationships." Ohio's term limits "opponents feared lobbyists would gain even more influence"; however, in practice, "lobbyists struggled as their long-term relationships with veteran pols became meaningless." In Michigan Rader, Elder, and Elling found term-limited legislators "less likely to rely on lobbyists for information and guidance."

It was predicted by proponents of term limits that, as the priority of the average legislator shifted from short-term electioneering to long-term public policy, staff would spend less time on constituent work in order to focus more on issue research. The truth of that prediction is supported by much of the available evidence. However, Rader, Elder, and Elling found that, in Michigan, "the post term limit cohort tend to be more reliant on staff" generally than were their pre–term limit predecessors. That finding may reflect state-specific factors, given that Timothy Hodson found that the turnover rate for California state legislative committee staff more than doubled under term limits. In post–term limits California, 73 percent of legislative staff remain in their positions for three years or less, thereby reducing the staff's value to legislators as purveyors of institutional knowledge.

A decade later it remains true that "the most zealous opponents (of term limits) are . . . staffers, career bureaucrats and corporate lobbyists." Seventy-eight percent of state legislative staffers, for example, continue to oppose term limits. As legal scholar Einer Elhauge suggests, it seems unlikely that those nonpolitical institutional actors would oppose term limits if they thought term limits strongly increased their own influence.

Term Limits and Limited Government

It's going to bring about better government.

Jeb Bush, Governor of Florida

May it be argued from a limited-government perspective that term limits benefit the policymaking process? In support of the term limits concept, Nobel laureate economist Friedrich Hayek, and later Amihai Glazer and Martin P. Wattenberg, predicted that more policy-oriented legislators would produce more general interest legislation and, consequently, less pork-barrel spending targeted at specific electoral districts. It was surmised that a decline in political parochialism would halt, or at least reduce, the growth in the size and scope of government. George Will, espousing a preference for a Burkean representative legislature composed of trustees rather than delegates, similarly forecast that term limits would produce less parochially oriented legislators. According to Will, term limits "would change the motives and behavior of legislators." Pre–term limits, "careerism is the dominant motive of most legislators. By removing that motive, term limits would make [politicians] less subservient to public opinion and more deliberative." Although insufficient time has passed to judge fully the consequences of term limits, there is now some evidence that this is what is happening in term-limited state legislatures.

For a decade we have known that there is a positive relationship between the length of an elected official's legislative service and his or her votes in favor of higher government spending. Long-term occupants of elected office become socialized to favor the higher spending advocated by special-interest lobbyists. In part, that results from the fact that witnesses before congressional and legislative committees, along with lobbyists and constituents, almost always favor higher levels of spending. In terms of the political culture, "experience in government tends to produce legislators who are . . . interested in defending government." Furthermore, as Owings and Borck explain: "Professional legislators . . . invest more time and money in pork barrel spending to secure support from their home district. This too would tend to increase the tendency of professional legislatures to have higher spending." In addition, the legislative logrolling so cannily practiced by veteran politicians results in higher government spending. Hence, it is reasonable to conclude that "any . . . structure which shortens tenure should result in decreased government spending."

During the decade of the term limits experiment, numerous empirical studies confirmed earlier work correlating tenure with spending. The Cato Institute's Stephen Moore and Aaron Steelman studied congressional voting records and concluded "that the longer members serve in Congress, the more pro-tax-and-spend they become." That study's findings are comparable to those of the National Taxpayers Union and the Competitive Enterprise Institute. Aaron Steelman's analysis of the voting behavior of members of Congress on the most significant budget, tax, and regulatory issues before the 104th and 105th Congresses found that, among Republicans, tenure in office is positively associated with a member's propensity to tax and spend. In 27 of the 31 documented votes, those Republicans with three or fewer terms in the House and two or fewer terms in the Senate voted far more fiscally conservatively than did senior Republicans. While Republicans tax and spend more the longer they are in elected office, Democrats (who generally arrive in Congress already favoring more spending and higher taxes) tend not to tax and spend more as they remain in office. According to Steelman, "If the public wants . . . to reduce the size and scope of government, term limits may be imperative." It is reasonable to assume, therefore, that senior state legislators are more likely to vote for higher taxes and higher spending than are their junior colleagues.

That assertion about the relationship between term limits and limited government is strengthened by research provided for this paper by the Cato Institute's Michael J. New. An analysis of the changes in state taxes during fiscal year 2000 provides some enlightening data. Looking first at "old" term limit states (Maine, California, Colorado, and Oregon), New found that all four cut taxes. Maine's legislature reduced taxes by 3.8 percent, the largest tax cut among the New England states. In California state taxes fell by 1.9 percent, which in nominal terms constituted the largest tax cut in the 50 states. There was a 3.4 percent reduction in taxes in Colorado, the largest tax cut in the Rocky Mountain states. During 2000 the Oregon state legislature passed a tax cut that will be effective in fiscal year 2002.

Next, analyzing the changes in state taxes in the five "new" (i.e., states with term limit laws that took effect in 2000) term limit states (Florida, Ohio, South Dakota, Montana, and Arizona), New found that in two of the states, South Dakota and Montana, taxes remained at 1999 levels. However, in

Florida taxes fell by 1.7 percent, in Arizona they dropped by 1.3 percent, and the Ohio legislature reduced state taxes by 3.1 percent. It is also noteworthy that, although Montana did not reduce taxes for fiscal year 2000, in 2001 the state legislature passed a tax and expenditure limitation that, if it becomes law, will be one of the three most stringent such limitations in the country (along with Washington's and Colorado's). Montana's is the *only* legislature to enact so stringent a tax and expenditure limitation; it provides a preliminary indication that term-limited legislatures may be willing to constrain their own behavior.

In the fall of 1991 author and columnist David S. Broder stated that "no one knows whether term limits would induce tighter budgets." Five years later, Broder reminded his readers that "the proposition that the term-limits advocates ask us to accept is that by shortening the tenure of people in office, we will lengthen their perspective. Those who serve briefly, they say, will give greater weight to the long-term needs of the nation." Carey, Niemi, and Powell found that, indeed, "term limits are associated with less-district-oriented electioneering activities" and tend to make legislators more interested in statewide concerns. More specifically, term limits lead to less pork-barrel spending. The national survey of the effects of term limits on state legislators conducted by Carey, Niemi, and Powell found that "term limits decrease the time legislators spend on activities for which they are roundly criticized—most notably the time they devote to securing pork for their districts." The researchers conclude, "If the goal is to discourage district parochialism . . . the reform shows signs of success." That supports Moore's conclusion that "there's mounting evidence that term limits lead to smaller government and better legislating."

For example, term limits help to achieve limited government through the tendency to deprofessionalize state legislatures. During the past four decades the professionalization of state legislatures has had a stimulating effect on state government spending. Owings and Borck found that "professionalism is a significant determinant of government spending . . . legislatures tend to spend more the more professional their members." Unsurprisingly, therefore, Owings and Borck also noted that "our findings indicate that government spending in states with citizen legislatures is significantly lower than in states with professional legislatures. By reducing the professionalism of their legislators, citizens, if they so wish, can effectively constrain the size of government." Hence numerous proponents of limited government aim "to restore and preserve part-time citizen decision making at the state" level.

There is a pattern developing across the country in term-limited states. In California, "with the ranks of career politicians dwindling and the legislature dominated by members with strong(er) ties to their constituents . . . than to the special interests . . . the amateur politicians . . . managed to pass the largest state tax cut in a generation." In neighboring Arizona, term limited in 2000, even before term limits took effect the composition of the legislature changed from higher spending professional legislators to more fiscally conservative citizen legislators. In Michigan the term-limited state House cut the state income tax, is phasing out the state Single Business Tax, and created a reform board to take over Detroit's failing public school system. Earlier this year, after the

Ohio Supreme Court ruled that the state's public school funding system was inequitable and ordered increased spending on education, the state's media and political elites pushed for a tax increase to fill the revenue void. However, term-limited freshmen conservatives in the state House successfully fought for offsetting cuts in higher education and welfare programs. Former Ohio House speaker Jo Ann Davidson revealingly commented about the freshmen legislators that, "if they had more experience, they probably would have been less eager to cut." Indeed.

Conclusion

Eleven years after the passage of the first initiative, what preliminary conclusions may be drawn about the term limits experiment? From the vantage point of those opposed to term limits, lawyer and columnist Bruce Fein recently offered a reasonable barometer of opposition sentiment when he observed,

> Where term limits persist, proponents have assembled no evidence of an increase in public welfare or a lessening of disgruntlement . . . the approximately two dozen states sporting legislative term limits have witnessed no climb in public confidence or satisfaction with state laws or legislative oversight relative to non-term-limit jurisdictions.

Fein and his fellow critics either ignore or dismiss the public's approval of term limits in practice. For example, when Missouri voters were asked last year whether they would vote for the same term limits initiative that passed in 1992, 74 percent answered yes. In a June 1999 poll 73 percent of Californians agreed that term limits had been good for their state; in a June 2000 poll 69 percent of Californians said they still approved of the original (1990) term limits initiative. Therefore, it should not surprise anyone that the California legislature's public approval ratings are higher than before the introduction of term limits. As Figure 2 illustrates, term limits on state legislators remain popular nationwide.

The evidence offered in this paper suggests that critics also underestimate the positive developments that to date accompany term limits. First, it is increasingly clear that term limits stimulate political competition. That is accomplished in a variety of ways, from increasing the number of open seats and special elections to lowering the reelection rates of incumbents. There is also evidence to suggest that campaigns may be less costly in a term-limited electoral environment. Many former incumbents return to private life, and a significant number run for other offices thereby stimulating political competition at other levels.

Second, term limits provide incentives (e.g., open seats and limited tenure) for non-traditional candidates to run for seats in state legislatures. The occupational makeup of state legislatures is gradually moving away from the traditional preponderance of ex-lawyers and ex-political aides. Greater occupational diversity is paralleled by greater gender and racial diversity. Female candidates seem to find it easier to gain entry to term-limited legislatures than to non-term-limited legislatures. The same is true for Hispanic and Asian Americans; the record to date is more mixed for African Americans.

Figure 2

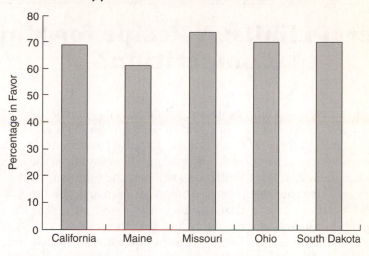

Public Support for Term Limits at the State Level

Sources: California, Diversified Research, Inc., poll, June 6, 2000; Maine, U.S. Term Limits poll, cited in Kerry A. Flatley, "First Rumblings of a Backlash to Term Limits," *Christian Science Monitor*, April 12, 1999; Missouri, Diversified Research, Inc., poll, April 27, 2000; Ohio, Ohio poll, Institute for Policy Research, University of Cincinnati, May 11–23, 1999; and South Dakota, Rasmussen Research poll, January 31, 2000.

Third, term-limited state legislatures undergo significant changes, many of which are positive in nature. As institutions, they become more merit based and less governed by an outdated seniority system. Leadership positions (especially that of Speaker) become less powerful as a more decentralized power structure evolves in response to the growing independence of newer legislative entrants. Term-limited legislatures certainly appear to be no less efficient than their predecessors. In many instances, the loss of institutional memory, legislative knowledge, and political experience has fostered a more energetic, more ideological, and more effective deliberative body. There is little evidence to suggest that (contrary to the predictions of critics of term limits) the bureaucracy, the interest group lobbyists, or the legislative staffs have filled the "experience void" to the detriment of state-level democracy or public policy. Overall, the term limits experiment shows sign of weakening the careerism that characterized postwar legislative life and suffocated nearly all attempts at significant policy innovation. There are clear indications that term limits foster institutional settings that are favorable to the advancement of public policies compatible with the idea of limited government.

In 1990 Oklahoma became the first state in the nation to term limit its legislators. Eleven years later a majority of term-limited states are experiencing campaigns to modify or repeal those laws. That is regrettable, as the balance of the available evidence strongly endorses extending, rather than ending, the term limits experiment.

Bruce Cain, John Hanley,
and Thad Kousser

 **NO**

Term Limits: A Recipe for More Competition?

One of the promises term-limits proponents made was that restrictions on time in office would foster greater electoral competition. A ballot argument for California's Proposition 140, for instance, stated: "Limiting terms will create more competitive elections, so good legislators will always have the opportunity to move up the ladder. Term limitations will end the ingrown, political nature of both houses—to the benefit of every man, woman and child in California." Amidst widespread concern that the incumbency advantage at all levels of government had increased measurably and that the political system was insulated from changing electoral swings, twenty-one states adopted state legislative term limits by 2000 (twelve of them between 1990 and 1992 alone). Six states subsequently repealed or had their term limits invalidated by the courts, leaving fifteen states to carry through their imposed limits on legislative tenure. Even though most of these laws were passed before 1996, over half of the term-limited state legislatures did not fully experience the first effects on any house until 2000. But now that all but two lower houses and three upper houses have fully implemented one cycle of term limits, we can try to shed some light on the proposition that term limits enhance political competition.

Why would people believe that term limits foster political competition? Limiting an incumbent's term of service to a specified number of years guarantees a minimum level of legislator turnover, in effect compensating for inadequate levels of electoral competition by creating more "open seats" (that is, seats without incumbents) than the electoral process would otherwise do. In an ideal electoral model, competitive elections produce regular turnover of both incumbents (descriptive turnover) and parties (party turnover). Theoretically, this should increase electoral responsiveness (the rate at which electoral shifts result in seat changes) and possibly reduce systemic partisan bias (a party holding a higher share of seats than the other party would if it had the same electoral share).

In practice, incumbency advantages of various sorts mute the value of competition by reducing both descriptive and party turnover, thereby weakening electoral responsiveness and increasing systemic bias. Campaign finance and redistricting reforms have tried to lessen incumbent advantages, but to little or no effect. Hence, the reasoning goes, if incumbency effects cannot be lessened, they can at least be eliminated periodically through formal limits.

From *The Marketplace of Democracy* by John Samples and Michael P. McDonald (Brookings Institute, 2006), pp. 199–201, 204–208, 216–221. Copyright © 2006 by Brookings Institution Press. Reprinted by permission.

Actual turnover might exceed the minimum if there is a higher rate of antici-patory or office-jumping retirements, but the rate can never drop below the legal minimum. Whether that minimum is constraining depends upon the length and permanence of the term limitation. A limit of six years is guar-anteed to produce more descriptive turnover than a limit of twelve years. A lifetime ban from a given office will prevent recidivism completely whereas a temporary ban only makes returning to office more difficult.

The guaranteed effect of legislative term limits is regularized descriptive turnover, but what about the competitive effects? Does the imposition of term limits increase the overall proportion of open seats, creating a new mixture of contests that is a recipe for more competition? If so, does the higher number of open-seat races lead only to more descriptive turnover or does it increase party turnover as well? Do term limits increase the share of contested races, on average? Do they make races closer, on average? In short, how well do term limits compensate for the failure of normal electoral processes to produce competition?

In this chapter we will first review what the political science literature, largely produced since the mid-1990s, says about the competitive effects of term limits. Then we look at data across a broad range of states to see whether the indicators of competitive state legislative elections increased or decreased as the term limits were implemented. Next we examine the unique natural experiment of Oregon, where term limits operated briefly before being aban-doned. To explore the theoretical basis of some of our findings, we then compare data on the strategic entry of candidates with prior elective office experience into California legislative contests before and after the implemen-tation of term limits. Finally, we analyze levels of primary election competi-tiveness in California and Colorado.

In general, our analyses reveal that the effects of term limits on competi-tion are mild to nonexistent. Descriptive turnover has increased, but party turnover and the margins of victory in races have shown little or no change. The reasons for this, we believe, are the other trends in the electoral environ-ment and the strategic behavior of incumbents. As to the first, term limits might have worked if other factors, such as redistricting and rising electoral polarization, had not occurred at the same time. In addition, since the odds of defeating an incumbent are long, serious challengers wait for open-seat oppor-tunities. Competition is lessened in incumbent seats and concentrated in the open ones. While term limits opened up more seats, the overall pattern of competition reflects the common strategic assessment that it is usually better to wait for a member to "term out" before running for a seat. . . .

Cross-State Analysis

Our analysis of state legislative election results uses general election data pro-duced under the direction of James Snyder (MIT), Richard Niemi (University of Rochester), and Thomas Carsey and William Berry (Florida State University). Our data set of primary elections was compiled by research assistants at the University of California, Berkeley. Because of the preliminary nature of some of the data, not all states could be used. Maine, a term-limits state, was removed from our analysis for this reason. In addition, we removed from our analysis states in which one or both houses of the state legislature had multi-member districts over some portion of our study window. This restriction eliminated three term-limits states, Arizona, North Dakota, and South Dakota.

Aggregating candidate general election returns up to the district level for each state in the years 1991–2003 produced one case for every district up for election in a given year. These were then coded for whether the general election featured candidates from both the Republican and Democratic parties, and also whether an incumbent was ineligible for reelection due to term limits. We also coded district elections based on whether or not they were held in a term-limits environment, a concept that is critical to our analysis. The phrase "term-limits environment" means that some portion of a chamber's membership was ineligible for reelection in a given year. To take an example, while the lower houses of the legislatures in Michigan and Arkansas became term-limits environments in 1998, their senates did not become term-limits environments for our purposes until later (2000 in Arkansas, 2002 in Michigan). States that never enacted term limits, such as New York and Massachusetts, are categorized as no-term-limits environments throughout our period of study. This means that the term-limits effects that we observe are generated both by variation across states (comparing states with and without term limits) and across time (comparing states before and after their term-limits laws were implemented). Other scholars have constructed this category more broadly, considering a term-limits environment to exist from the moment that term limits are legally enacted. Our purpose in adhering to a stricter conceptualization is to capture more purely the effects that term limits had on the election outcomes by focusing on the results after term limits were implemented rather than before.

We then computed mean rates of two-party competition for term-limits and no-term-limits environments for open seats and seats with incumbents running for reelection. Using our data on which incumbents were termed out, we further broke down the open-seat category for term-limits states in order to separate districts in which an incumbent chose not to run from those in which he or she was *ineligible* to run. For the districts where two-party competition existed, we calculated the mean margin of victory for open seats and seats featuring an incumbent, in both the term-limits and no-term-limits environments, again distinguishing further between open seats where the incumbent was ineligible for reelection and those where the incumbent was eligible but did not run. Last, we computed the rate at which state legislative seats changed party over the period 1993–2000.

Our analysis . . . shows a number of statistically significant effects. First, the rates of two-party contestation of legislative seats are higher in term-limits environments than in no-term-limits environments. This result holds for both open seats and seats with incumbents. Under term limits, incumbents are challenged in the general election by the opposite major party in almost 70 percent of cases; where term limits have not been enacted, or have been enacted but not yet begun to bar individuals from seeking reelection, only 55 percent of incumbents were challenged. Looking exclusively at open seats, we see again that rates of two-party contestation were higher in term-limits environments, though this difference is approximately half of that observed where incumbents were present. Eighty-one percent of all open seat races in term-limits environments featured head-to-head competition between a Democrat and a Republican, while only 74 percent of open seat races outside of term limits were a contest between the major parties. Averaging across the two types of seats, the rate of major-party contestation is about 15 percentage points higher under term limits.

The news for competition is not so sunny, however, when we look at the average margin of victory in these contested seats. Comparing the average margin for all seats in a term-limits environment (26.80 percent) with all seats without term limits (26.84 percent) shows that limits have absolutely no aggregate effect. Yet underneath this overall stasis are some important changes of the type found in single-state studies in the existing literature. Term limits bring a larger percentage of open seats, our analysis shows. But for each type of seat, margins of victory are not as close under term limits as they are in a no-term-limits environment. In open seats with term limits, the spread between the two candidates is significantly *larger* than it is in the absence of term limits, meaning that contested seats become less competitive. Incumbent-held seats also feature slightly higher winning margins, though the effect is not statistically significant. These increases in the margin for each category of seat have almost perfectly counterbalanced the term-limits effect of creating more open seats.

For similar reasons, our measure of turnover in party control of seats shows no overall difference between those districts that are in term-limits environments and those that are not. While total rates of party turnover are the same, incumbents do better in term-limits environments, losing only 2.8 percent of races, as opposed to 5.3 percent in no-term-limits environments. Parties looking to hold on to open term-limited seats also do better in term-limits environments, losing 13.8 percent of seats versus 19.1 percent in no-term-limits environments. Both of these results are statistically significant. That the overall rate of party turnover is nearly equal between the two environments is explained by a greater number of seats becoming open in term-limits environments.

Imagine two legislative chambers: one without term limits, and the other with a four-term, eight-year limit. Were we to pretend that in the term-limited legislature no members ever left before being termed out, and that in the limitless chamber members served an average of six terms, we would expect the limitless chamber to produce more party turnover than the term-limited chamber. Though our assumptions of this hypothetical are somewhat unrealistic, it illustrates that a sizable proportion of the gain in the absolute number of open seats under term limits is taken away by the lower rate at which seats opened by term limits change party control.

Our result is reinforced by another finding from the data, specifically that the margin of victory in open, contested seats is higher in the term-limits environments than in chambers without term limits. Higher margins of victory, of course, imply that the candidates are less evenly matched in term-limits environments than in traditional two-party races. What the data suggest, therefore, is that candidates in term-limits environments may be entering legislative contests in greater numbers, even though their chances of winning are smaller. Since legislative term limits are a relatively new innovation, it remains to be seen whether the higher rates of contestation present in term-limits environments result from the novelty of large numbers of open seats, or whether the new strategic environment truly encourages increased contestation. . . .

Conclusion

A fundamental premise of the term-limits movement turns out to be mostly untrue in several important senses. What is clearly true is that term limits increase descriptive turnover by about 14 percent on average. Even so, the level varies from state to state depending upon the length of the term limit. Term limits also appear to increase the level of contestation in both open and incumbent seats. But term limits have not made races closer or led to more party turnover. What do we make of all this?

The increase in descriptive turnover cannot be dismissed out of hand. New faces count for something. The JPTL has documented that some term-limited states have seen dramatic increases in the number of Latino representatives, a trend that would have likely occurred eventually, but happened more quickly because of the higher level of churning caused by limiting incumbency. Curiously, term limits do not seem to have increased the number of women in office relative to the number in non-term-limited legislatures.

Beyond gender and racial differences, new members have come in with different perspectives, and the legislatures they work in have been transformed in important ways. Committee seniority and experience have declined, and in many states this has put more power in the hands of party leaders and more action on the floor. There is less deference to committees in some states, and weaker leadership in the lower houses. Where the effects are most dramatic, legislative oversight has declined and executive control of the budget has increased. In short, term-limited legislatures tend to be less powerful, and executives more so. To put it another way, more descriptive turnover has altered important institutional structures and the perspectives that representatives bring to lawmaking.

The lack of effect on party turnover rates is unfortunate. Ideally, by creating more open seats, term limits would have heightened legislative responsiveness and lessened bias. There is no sign that this has happened. It is certainly a good thing that the level of contestation has gone up. An incumbent who faces even a weak opponent is more accountable than one with no challenger, and may be forced to take up the issues championed by the challenger. But the fact that party turnover rates are at best no better and possibly worse than in states without term limits is not encouraging. The margin of victory being no lower (and in some instances higher) suggests that capping incumbency does not matter: the main advantages of being an incumbent are apparently realized very quickly. In addition, primary contests have not become more competitive after the implementation of term limits either.

In hindsight, these findings make sense. Using term limits to tackle the problems of lower competition in America is a partial equilibrium solution to a general equilibrium problem. Yes, incumbency is part of the reason that legislative races have become less competitive, but short of eliminating incumbents every two years, the advantages of incumbency (name recognition, money, staff, projects, constituency service, and others) will still be there. Moreover, other factors such as redistricting, the incentives of primary systems, the influence of groups with money, and the general trend of voter polarization and social sorting are pushing in the opposite direction of safer seats. Opening up more seats could have led to more competition if everything else had stayed the same, but that was not the case. Indeed, it is possible that weakened incumbents might have let the underlying partisan forces matter more. In the 1980s, some Democratic incumbents held on to seats that were politically and demographically Republican by virtue of their incumbency and tailored moderation. But as they have been termed out, the underlying partisan makeup has become even more the controlling factor. Hence descriptive turnover has no effect on party turnover.

A serious attempt to increase party turnover in American legislative elections would require a muitipronged attack on several causes at once. And even it this were politically and constitutionally possible (which it is not), there is the question raised by others in this volume of whether a system that is jiggered to create more close races and enhance party turnover is any better than the one we have. In the end, term-limits laws succeeded in bringing more descriptive turnover, but failed to create more competition either through closer races or increased party turnover.

References

Allebaugh, Dalene, and Neil Pinney. 2003. "The Real Costs of Term Limits: Comparative Study of Competition and Electoral Costs." In *The Test of Time: Coping with Legislative Term Limits,* edited by Rick Farmer, John David Rausch, and John C. Green. Lanham, Md.: Lexington Books.

Barcellona, Miriam M., and Andrew P. Grose. 1994. *Term Limits: A Political Dilemma.* San Francisco: Council of State Governments.

Cain, Bruce E., and Thad Kousser. 2004. *Adapting to Term Limits: Recent Experiences and New Directions.* San Francisco: Public Policy Institute of California.

California Journal. 1982. "Assembly," *California Journal* (July). Sacramento: StateNet.

———. 1984. "The Assembly," *California Journal* (July). Sacramento: StateNet.

Council of State Governments. 2004. *The Book of the States, 2004 Edition.* Vol. 36. Lexington, Ky.: Council of State Governments.

Cromwell, Oliver, II. 1991. "Yes: A Reform Whose Time Has Come." *Annual Report of the Cosmos Club:* 89–90.

Daniel, Kermit, and John R. Lott Jr. 1997. "Term Limits and Electoral Competitiveness: Evidence from California's State Legislative Races." *Public Choice* 90:165–84.

Fowler, Linda. 1992. "A Comment on Competition and Careers." In *Limiting Legislative Terms,* edited by Gerald Benjamin and Michael J. Malbin. Washington: CQ Press.

Fund, John. 1991. "Term Limitation: An Idea Whose Time Has Come." In *Limiting Legislative Terms,* edited by Gerald Benjamin and Michael J. Malbin. Washington: CQ Press.

Hoffenblum, Alan, ed. 2004. *The California Target Book, Volume 4, 2004 General Election Edition.* Los Angeles: Alan Hoffenblum and Associates.

Jacobson, Gary C., and Samuel Kernell. 1983. *Strategy and Choice in Congressional Elections.* 2nd ed. Yale University Press.

Kousser, Thad. 2005. *Term Limits and the Dismantling of State Legislative Professionalism.* Cambridge University Press.

Masket, Seth, and Jeffrey B. Lewis. Forthcoming 2006. "A Return to Normalcy? Revisiting the Effects of Term Limits on Competitiveness and Spending in California Assembly Elections." *State Politics and Policy Quarterly.*

Moncrief, Gary, Lynda Powell, and Tim Storey. Forthcoming. "Term Limits and the Composition of Legislatures." In *Institutional Change in American Politics: The Case of Term Limits,* edited by Karl Kurtz, Bruce Cain, and Richard Niemi. University of Michigan Press.

Petracca, Mark P. 1991. "The Poison of Professional Politics." Policy Analysis 151. Washington: Cato Institute.

Pinney, Neil, George Serra, and Dalene Sprick. 2004. "The Costs of Reform: Consequences of Limits Terms of Service." *Party Politics* 10: 69–84.

Squire, Peverill. 1992. "Legislative Professionalization and Membership Diversity in State Legislatures." *Legislative Studies Quarterly* 17:69–79.

Sulkin, Tracy. 2005. *Issue Politics in Congress.* Cambridge University Press.

Thompson, Joel A., and Gary F. Moncrief. 1998. *Campaign Finance in State Legislative Elections.* Washington: CQ Press.

POSTSCRIPT

Should State Legislators Have Term Limits?

The term-limit debate on the state legislative level started about 1990 with initiatives passed in three states—California, Colorado, and Oklahoma.[1] Over time, 18 states later adopted term limits; however, it seems that, although the term-limit movement briefly flourished in the nineties, the trend was not only slowing down, but halting in some states.[2] Four states had their supreme courts throw out term limits—Massachusetts, Oregon, Washington, and Wyoming; additionally, term limits have been repealed by legislatures in Idaho and Utah.

For example, in Washington and Massachusetts, legislative limits on terms were tossed out in the 1990s. Both states established term-limits through the initiative process; however, their states' supreme courts rejected the initiative change of state statutes regarding qualifications for office.

A few years later in Wyoming, a 2004 case also invalidated the state's limits. Wyoming overwhelmingly passed term-limits law through an initiative in 1992, with a 77 percent approval.[3] Wyoming had to pass term limits through statutory law, meaning through the legislature, because this state is one of the few sates without an initiative procedure to amend its state constitution. Subsequent to term limits taking effect 12 years later in November 2004, 13 legislators were forced from office because of the change. The change was not popular with the state legislature at the time, and as a result, two voters and two legislators challenged the limits in court. Justices held term limits as just another qualification for office, according to the Wyoming Supreme Court's ruling. Therefore, additional qualifications are unconstitutional, according to the Wyoming state constitution, because they are not enumerated, or listed specifically. The court did not consider whether term limits themselves are constitutional, but instead ruled that the way they were imposed was questionable at best, as was the case in similar state cases in Oregon, Washington, and Massachusetts. What is interesting is that, even though term limits were passed by a wide margin of voters (77 percent) in Wyoming, the court said, "The fact that 77 percent of the voters favored a particular measure does not make that measure constitutional. Either we live under a constitutional government or we do not."[4]

Both Washington and Massachusetts state supreme courts deemed term limits unconstitutional.[5] These state courts rejected their state's limits because the limits covered multiple parts of their state constitutions, violating their states' requirement to have only a single subject on initiatives.

The Idaho Supreme Court upheld term limits, calling them constitutional in 2001.[6] In January 2002, Idaho made a surprising and unprecedented move, when it became the first state whose state legislature killed term limits imposed through the initiative process eight years earlier.[7] The initiative had limited legislators to eight years in office. The Republican-led legislature passed House Bill 425, striking down term limits, but created a showdown with the governor of their own party, Dirk Kempthorne, who advocated for term limits. Governor Kempthorne vetoed the bill, stating he could not "in good conscience allow this act of direct democracy to be wiped off the books by the mere stroke of my pen."[8] However, the next day, both chambers of the Idaho state legislature overrode the governor's veto with a two-thirds supermajority.

Although the term-limit movement's heyday is largely over, 15 states still have term limits. The effects have been mixed, and they have been challenged, probably not for the last time.

Notes

1. "Legislative Term Limits: An Overview," National Conference of State Legislators, 2006. Accessed December 4, 2009, http://www.ncsl.org/LegislaturesElections/LegislatorsLegislativeStaffData/LegislativeTermLimitsOverview/tabid/14849/Default.aspx

2. *Ibid.*

3. "Wyoming High Court Nixes Term Limits." (May 4, 2004). Accessed December 4, 2009, http://www.ncsl.org/Default.aspx?TabId=14820

4. *Ibid.*

5. *Ibid.*

6. "State Legislative Term Limits," U.S. Term Limits. Accessed December 4, 2009, http://www.termlimits.org/content.asp?pl=18&sl=19&contentid=19

7. Vincent J. Schodolski, "Term Limits under Assault from Idaho GOP," *Chicago Tribune* (May 1, 2009). Accessed December 9, 2009. http://www.encyclopedia.com/doc/1G1-120412267.html

8. Dirk, Kempthorne, "Veto of House Bill 425" (January 31, 2002). Accessed December 4, 2009, at www2.state.id.us/legislat/vetoed.html

ISSUE 11

Should Legislators Have the Responsibility for Redistricting?

YES: Dean Murphy, from "Who Should Redistrict?" *New York Times Magazine* (October 23, 2005)

NO: Scott M. Lesowitz, from "Recent Development: Independent Redistricting Commissions," *Harvard Journal on Legislation* (Summer 2006)

ISSUE SUMMARY

YES: Dean Murphy argues that the state legislature should keep redistricting under its power because that is what democracy is all about.

NO: Scott Lesowitz argues that state legislators are biased and the only way to create compact and competitive districts is to create a commission comprised of people who will not benefit from the outcome of redistricting.

Dean Murphy and Scott Lesowitz both agree that the persistent gerrymandering, or creating legislative district lines for partisan advantage, is wrong.

Lesowitz relates the story of Governor Arnold Schwarzenegger's push to have an independent redistricting commission. The governor colorfully illustrated why he thought the state needed Proposition 77, moving redistricting of legislative lines outside lawmakers' hands and into those of a panel of judges. Governor Schwarzenegger spoke at a press conference strategically positioned at the intersection of two assembly districts, nos. 10 and 15, designated with thick red ribbon. "The politicians have divided a neighborhood. They have divided cities, towns and people, and this is what we what to eliminate. And, this is why we need redistricting, because the district lines were drawn to favor the incumbents rather than to favor the voters."

Likewise, Murphy relates a story of how the Texas state legislature, in 2001, was in gridlock over drawing congressional district lines and had to take their case to court. The court created a compromise plan. As a result, 17 Democrats were elected and 15 Republicans were seated in the Texas' congressional delegation. However, on the state level the Republicans took over. And, in an unprecedented move, the Texas state legislature redrew a new redistricting plan. As a result, by 2004 only 11 Democrats and 21 Republicans took office. Miller argues that, although it is hard to say how important this election was, six seats turned over to Republicans. He states, "This election does demonstrate the potential power of a legislature to adjust political outcomes through the redistricting process—a practice employed by Democrats and Republicans alike."

Lesowitz says that an independent redistricting commission would prevent public officials from redrawing district lines that give themselves a political advantage. Both Proposition 77 in California and State Issue 4 in Ohio create commissions that are as nonbiased as possible. It would be comprised of people who do not have a conflict of interest in government or a political party and would not be seeking office themselves. These members would be variously chosen by judges, who would come from both parties. Also, votes would have to be unanimous to ratify a redistricting plan.

Lesowitz argues that, although there are problems with the electoral process, complaints about the redistricting process would not disappear by taking it out of the state legislature. He states specifically that like-minded people tend to live near like-minded people. San Francisco, for example, is a Democratic safe haven, and, similarly, Bakersfield, California, is remarkably secure for Republicans. If you drew squares around these two towns, they would illustrate compactness; this is often a critique by those who say we should reform redistricting to have fewer lines that seem to meander, capturing similar people for a legislator to gain an electoral advantage. But a compact district might not necessarily be competitive, Murphy points out. He illustrates Arizona's experience with an independent redistricting commission, where half of the state senate seats were not contested in 2004. In another example, Murphy points to Iowa's use of an independent commission where Congress members still won 98 percent of the time.

Murphy argues further that it makes no sense to place such important, wide-ranging political questions in the hands of unelected officials without accountability. Lesowitz retorts that there is an assumption that elected politicians with political agendas would somehow work out better. "In fact, elected politicians may calculate that the political gains from gerrymandering are potentially so great that they outweigh any potential backlash from voters." Lesowitz explains, moreover, that even if a redistricting commission is less responsive to voters, the political system itself might be more accountable by making elections more competitive.

Murphy quotes Bruce Cain, a former special master for Arizona's redistricting, who says, "The problem is that people have different expectations about the outcomes. You can change the process, but you can't take away the controversy."

Both authors agree that gerrymandering has its problems, but how to fix it is another matter. Lesowitz argues for a redistricting commission to take bias out of legislators' hands because they have an incentive to create safe seats for themselves. Murphy contends that keeping a redistricting commission in legislators' hands keeps such an important political matter democratically accountable.

YES

Dean E. Murphy

Who Should Redistrict?

Rising out of the farmland south of Sacramento, Elk Grove is a pleasant, unremarkable collection of scrubbed subdivisions with artificial lakes and velveteen lawns. What makes Elk Grove special—and of intense interest to politicians—is that in a state where political segregation is the norm, Democrats and Republicans live side by side in almost equal numbers.

When the residents of Elk Grove choose their state legislators, however, their votes are divided into two improbable assembly districts that meander into outlying rural areas and give each a Republican majority. Those districts are the legacy of a statewide redistricting in California in 2001 from which both parties benefited. The Democrats retained firm control of the State Legislature and the 53-member Congressional delegation, while Republicans were assured 20 safe seats in Congress and a spoiler's share of the seats in the state Capitol.

And so, on a sunny May afternoon, Elk Grove was the natural backdrop for the Republican governor, Arnold Schwarzenegger, to stump for Proposition 77, an ostensibly politically neutral ballot initiative that would take the power to set voting districts away from state lawmakers and give it to an independent panel of retired judges. Schwarzenegger stood in the center of a neighborhood of half-million-dollar homes where aides had put down hundreds of feet of red ribbon. The ribbon bisected the street, turning at a right angle on the asphalt in front of the governor's lectern and continuing through the sprinkler-fed turf between homes owned by Darren and Nichola Denney and Garry and Susan Darms, who were standing, Let's-Make-A-Deal fashion, in front of them. A pair of blue signs posted on either side of the red line said "15th Assembly District" and "10th Assembly District."

"The politicians have divided a neighborhood," Schwarzenegger intoned. "They have divided cities, towns and people, and this is what we want to eliminate. And this is why we need redistricting, because the district lines were drawn to favor the incumbents rather than to favor the voters." One of the assemblymen with the governor, Guy Houston, complained that his district stretched across four counties from suburban San Francisco to Elk Grove, 80 miles to the northeast. "I love Elk Grove," said Houston, who lives in San Ramon, on the western fringe of the district. "The people here are so nice, great to represent. But shouldn't we have districts that are more compact and competitive?"

The short answer to Houston's rhetorical question is yes. Politicians tend to be held to account when they represent communities where social ties and common institutions make people more likely to be politically active. Gerrymandered districts like Houston's have been blamed for a host of ills: complacent incumbents, polarized politics, cynical voters, dull elections. The arguments for taking the politics out of drawing political boundaries have been mounting. California and Ohio voters will go to the polls Nov. 8 to decide whether to let outside panels determine how electoral districts—both for State Legislature and for the United States House of Representatives—will be drawn. More than a dozen other states are thinking of doing the same.

And yet, how many of the complaints about elections would really disappear simply by taking the redistricting process out of the hands of elected officials? Houston says districts should be compact and competitive, but in California, like-minded people tend to cluster. Draw a box around San Francisco and you create a safe haven for Democrats; do the same around Bakersfield and Republicans benefit. The districts would have less sinister shapes, but they would not necessarily lead to more meaningful elections. So which is more important to democracy? Compactness or competitiveness? Or something entirely different?

The two Elk Grove districts are neither compact nor particularly competitive, so no doubt there is room for improvement there. As it turned out, the red ribbon running up Grand Point Lane did not divide the 10th from the 15th district; the real boundary was blocks away. But nobody noticed it at the time, not the elected officials nor the residents, and that can't be good for democracy either.

The drawing of legislative boundaries is one of the most politicized and corruptible practices in American-style government, and few people will say they approve of the gerrymandering it has unleashed. Boundary-rigging infamously kept blacks from gaining political power in the South. (One Mississippi district, mapped in the late 1870's with the single purpose of preventing the re-election of a black congressman, was 500 miles long and 40 miles wide.) In the early part of the 20th century, rural lawmakers held onto power by simply ignoring their obligation to draw new boundaries as people migrated to the cities and populations shifted, thus denying the swelling cities the political representation their numbers warranted.

The passage of the Voting Rights Act in 1965 and various rulings by the Supreme Court curtailed such egregious gerrymandering, but the practice endures—sometimes to favor incumbents, sometimes to favor one political party over the other. Lawmakers now use finely tuned demographic information and advanced computer programs to create "safe but slim victory margins in the maximum number of districts, with little risk of cutting their margins too thin," as the Supreme Court justice Stephen G. Breyer wrote last year in a dissenting opinion in a gerrymandering case, *Vieth v. Jubelirer*. That is what happened in California, where the deal worked out between the two parties created safe seats for incumbents. There was also, of course, the spectacle two years ago in which Tom DeLay, then the Republican majority leader in the House, orchestrated a mid-decade partisan gerrymander in his home state of

Texas, which Democratic lawmakers tried to thwart by fleeing to Oklahoma and New Mexico. They failed, and of the seven incumbents defeated in Congress in 2004, four of them were Texas Democrats who had been placed in the newly rigged districts.

But while it's easy to make a case against gerrymandering, it's much harder to say how districts should be drawn. Most states require that district boundaries be revisited every 10 years, after the release of new census data and the reapportionment of the country's Congressional seats. The creation of contiguous districts is the most widely accepted and uncontroversial criterion. Every state requires contiguity, and in 1842, Congress passed the first federal law that mandated the drawing of contiguous Congressional districts. A few other rules apply: the Supreme Court decisions of the 1960's forced Congressional districts to be roughly equal in population. The Voting Rights Act also prohibits "retrogression" in minority voting rights in certain states and the diluting of the political strength of minority communities anywhere. But beyond these piecemeal and often vague criteria—contiguity, after all, can accommodate serpentine shapes—legislators are free to create the maps as they see fit.

The Supreme Court has been little help in separating raw politics from mapmaking, with the justices disagreeing on how to deal with even obvious partisan boundary-rigging. In *Vieth v. Jubelirer*, Pennsylvania Democrats asked the court to overturn the state's redistricting plan, which was drafted by a Republican-led State Legislature and signed into law by a Republican governor. The new map gave Republicans the advantage in 12 of 19 Congressional districts, even though Democrats outnumbered Republicans statewide. Four of the justices held that redistricting was a political matter that could never be decided by the courts. Five justices agreed that excessive partisanship in redistricting could be unconstitutional, but they didn't settle on a standard for deciding when a party had gone too far. Ultimately, the court allowed the Pennsylvania map to stand.

The Vieth case helped push the issue of gerrymandering into the hands of activists who are pursuing reform one state at a time. Even before Vieth, six states had assigned the task of redistricting Congressional seats to officials outside the State Legislature, and 12 had done so for state legislative districts. In California, Proposition 77 would give mapmaking power to three retired judges chosen in a multistep, excruciatingly choreographed process meant to ensure that both parties are represented; in Ohio, the redistricting power would go to five citizens, with a judge from each of the two major parties choosing one of the panelists. Voters in Florida are expected to take up a redistricting measure next year that would create a 15-member citizen commission.

If these initiatives succeed, people who do not hold elected office will be the ones to weigh and balance competing interests. But as Larry M. Bartels, director of the Center for the Study of Democratic Politics at Princeton, points out, changing the mapmakers does not eliminate the vexing philosophical questions behind the mechanics of electoral mapmaking. "Should they attempt to maximize the number of competitive races or to ensure that the partisan distribution of seats in the legislature appropriately reflects the partisan distribution of votes?" he wrote in an e-mail message. "Is it more important for districts to have precisely equal populations or to reflect 'natural communities' defined by political boundaries, media markets or other criteria? Should they attempt to keep as many people as possible in the same districts in order to facilitate accountability, or should each redistricting cycle be treated as a blank slate?"

In other words, what are the electoral building blocks of a representative democracy? The answers are not always obvious. In Arizona, an independent commission was given the power to create "fair and competitive" districts. That commission drew some districts with large Latino populations, with the stated goal of giving a historically underrepresented group a stronger voice. Some Democratic and Latino groups complained that the real intention was to dilute their strength in other districts. First the Department of Justice, and later the courts, sent the mapmakers back to the drawing board. "The problem is that people have different expectations about the outcomes," Bruce E. Cain, who served as a special master for the Arizona redistricting, told me. "You can change the process, but you can't take away the controversy."

Independent redistricting wears the cloak of a good-government reform movement, but like most things in politics, its proponents have many motives. Schwarzenegger may truly believe that it's an affront to democracy to carve the state into safe districts for incumbents, but he would also benefit from a quick change in the cast of characters in the Democratic-controlled State Legislature—preferably in time for a hoped-for second term. (He called a special election—costing the state $45 million—rather than waiting until the regular statewide elections next year.) In Ohio, the group pushing redistricting is a nonpartisan organization called Reform Ohio Now. But the Democrats and union officials who dominate the group also view new boundaries as a way to break the Republican hold on both the statehouse and the Congressional delegation, and to revive a lackluster Democratic Party.

In any case, engineering districts for the benefit of incumbents or political parties seems easier to accomplish than creating more competition. Despite all the work on a new Arizona map done by the independent commission, nearly half of the State Senate seats weren't even contested in last year's election, according to the Center for Voting and Democracy, which promotes competitive elections. In Iowa, where an independent commission serves in an advisory role and is often cited as a reform model, the group found that Congressional incumbents have still won 98 percent of their re-election bids since 1982. In the end, the process had changed but the results were much the same.

Nicole Boyle is known around the University of California at Berkeley's Institute of Governmental Studies as the "G.I.S. queen." For nine years, starting when she was an undergraduate, she has analyzed election data with a technology known as Geographic Information Systems. On a morning in late August, Boyle was typing on her keyboard in front of an oversize screen covered with thousands of shapes splashed in multiple colors. Since the mid-1990's, the institute has maintained California's official redistricting data. With funding from a private grant, the institute is now using the data to test a central premise of the redistricting reform movement: Can you draw districts that increase competitiveness while also accommodating other desires, like compactness? Boyle has been crunching demographic and census numbers since the spring trying to come up with an answer.

On this morning, she had run into a brick wall with an experimental version of Congressional District 29 in Los Angeles County, as she used the keyboard to move the boundaries, dropping some census tracts and adding others. "This district has almost no chance of being a competitive district," Boyle conceded with some frustration.

Bruce Cain, who also runs the Berkeley institute, says that competitiveness comes down to which factors are given priority—and that, ultimately, is a political determination. How much weight, for example, should mapmakers give to so-called communities of interest—areas where people work in the same industry or use the same reservoir, say, but don't live within the same political boundaries? Where you begin drawing lines even makes a difference because, like a stone dropped in a pond, the ripples of one district's boundaries affect others. Boyle and Karin Mac Donald, the statewide database director, demonstrated that the final map for California would be different if you just started drawing upward from the Mexican border instead of downward from the Oregon one. "Good luck finding 24 willing judges," Mac Donald said, referring to the the independent panel from which the three California mapmakers would be picked. "I can't imagine they're lining the streets saying 'Pick me!'"

A top priority of Proposition 77 is to keep cities and counties whole. That would make it very difficult to create many competitive districts because Californians—and most Americans, for that matter—don't live in politically integrated communities. "It's not going to lead to a massive transformation, with 50 percent of the seats being competitive, because the state isn't laid out that way," Cain said of the measure. The institute's computer modeling shows, so far, that at most a dozen or so of the state's 53 Congressional districts could have competitive races.

The problem is not unique to California. Last year, The Austin American-Statesman conducted a county-by-county statistical analysis of presidential election returns since 1948. The survey found that Americans increasingly reside in "landslide counties"—in which a presidential candidate receives at least 60 percent of the vote—and that "political segregation" in counties had grown by 47 percent from 1976 to 2000. The Ohio measure tries to get around partisan clustering by requiring that competitiveness, rather than keeping cities and counties whole, be the most important consideration in drawing a redistricting plan. It even includes a mathematical formula for determining competitiveness.

To achieve districts with a political-party balance in California would require, in some instances, extending lines from the Pacific Ocean to the Nevada border—contortions that conflict with the goal of compactness. Even trying to draw the most competitive map that conformed to the basic principles of equal population and contiguity would require "waiting until the sun exploded for us to find a solution," as Michael P. McDonald, a redistricting expert and a visiting scholar at the Brookings Institution, told me.

When I visited Berkeley, Karin Mac Donald had just returned from giving a talk on redistricting, this one to the League of Women Voters, which considers Proposition 77 flawed because the panel of retired judges would be too small to reflect the state's diversity. One lesson that she has taken from the lecture circuit is that many Americans, no matter how much they complain about the poison of partisanship, are comfortable with their like-minded communities. "People always say it would be great to have competitive districts," Mac Donald explained. "But you talk to them for two minutes about what that would mean, and in the end they say, 'I don't want to live in a competitive district, but everyone else should.'" Why, I asked? "Because in a competitive district they might not get what they want."

Scott M. Lesowitz  **NO**

Recent Development: Independent Redistricting Commissions

In 2001, a divided Texas legislature deadlocked over the drawing of congressional districts. In response, a panel of federal judges instituted a compromise redistricting plan. In the following election, using the congressional districts drawn by these judges, Texas voters elected seventeen Democrats and fifteen Republicans to the United States House of Representatives. At the state level, Republicans fared better, winning control of both houses of the Texas legislature. Then, in 2003, those Texas legislature Republicans broke with tradition and began a campaign to perform a second round of redistricting based on the 2000 census data.

A struggle ensued between Texas Democrats and Republicans, but the new redistricting plan eventually passed. The results of the 2004 election using the new redistricting plan were drastically different from the results of the 2002 election: whereas Texans elected seventeen Democrats and fifteen Republicans in 2002 to the U.S. House of Representatives, in 2004 they elected eleven Democrats and twenty-one Republicans. While it is debatable just how egregious the Republican-led redistricting plan was, this election does demonstrate the potential power of a legislature to adjust political outcomes through the redistricting process—a practice that has been employed by Democrats and Republicans alike.

Shortly after these events in Texas, on June 13, 2005, California Governor Arnold Schwarzenegger called a special election in which Californians would vote on four propositions designed to address California's budgetary woes and reform the political process in the state. One of the four measures, Proposition 77, called for the creation of an independent commission, composed of three retired judges, to replace the state legislature as the chief body in charge of performing redistricting in California. Californians rejected Proposition 77 by a fairly sizeable margin.

On the same day, Ohio voters also decisively defeated State Issue 4, a ballot measure that would have created an independent redistricting commission there.

However, the defeat of Proposition 77 and State Issue 4 does not necessarily mean that the public does not support redistricting reform. For instance, Arizona voters passed an initiative creating an independent redistricting commission in 2000. Also, there were numerous factors weighing against the

From *Harvard Journal on Legislation,* vol. 43, issue 2, Summer 2006, pp. 535–550. Copyright © 2006 by Harvard Law School. Reprinted by permission.

two doomed ballot propositions. For instance, Proposition 77's fate was likely tied to the unpopularity of its chief supporter, Governor Schwarzenegger; public disapproval of the special election and its expense in general; efforts by both major political parties against the measure; and historic skepticism toward redistricting commissions in California. State Issue 4 was likely harmed by perceptions that it was a ploy by Democrats to increase their political power and that it used a confusing formula to perform redistricting, producing sample redistricting plans that "looked like strands of spaghetti thrown against a wall." Further, while California voters rejected Proposition 77, polls indicated that a majority of likely California voters supported making some sort of change in the redistricting process. In addition, numerous other states are considering adopting independent commissions to perform redistricting in the future. The lessons that the stories of Proposition 77 and State Issue 4 provide are pertinent to future redistricting reform efforts.

I. Overview of Proposition 77 and State Issue 4

Proposition 77 called for the creation of a commission composed of three retired judges to perform redistricting. While redistricting under the plan would normally have occurred once per decade, a special one-time redistricting would have followed passage of the proposition.

According to the measure, the process for selection of the three retired judges would have begun with the Judicial Council's nominating twenty-four retired judges willing to serve as special masters to perform redistricting. No more than twelve of the retired judges could have been from a single political party. From the pool of twenty-four nominated judges, the speaker and the minority leader of the State Assembly and the president pro tempore and the minority leader of the State Senate each would have nominated three retired judges to serve as special masters, for a total of twelve. The proposed statute would have forbidden nominators from selecting judges who share his or her party affliation. Each politician then would have had the opportunity to peremptorily strike one remaining retired judge from consideration. The chief clerk of the State Assembly would have drawn the special masters from the remaining pool of candidates by lot, continuing to draw until pulling a special master from each of the two largest political parties. A retired judge would not have been permitted to serve as a special master if he or she had ever held elected partisan public office or a political party office, changed political party affiliation since becoming a judge, or received income in the past year from certain political entities.

Districts drawn by the commission would have had to conform to the geographic boundaries of counties and cities to the "greatest extent practicable" and to have been as compact as possible while respecting those boundaries. The special masters would have been forbidden from considering the potential effects that a redistricting plan would have on incumbents or political parties. Additionally, they could not have considered the residence of any candidate, or the party affiliation and voting history of the electorate, except as required by federal law.

Meetings of the commission would have been subject to a number of provisions, and the special masters would have had to approve the anal redistricting plan by a unanimous vote. The plan would have gone into effect for the next primary and general election, when voters would have had the opportunity to either accept or reject by majority vote the continued use of the redistricting plan adopted by the special masters.

Ohio's State Issue 4 would have created an independent redistricting commission consisting of five members. A special redistricting would have followed the passage of the proposition, with subsequent redistricting occurring only in the year following a national census. The two longest continually serving judges on the state district court of appeals who had been nominated by members of different political parties each would have appointed to the redistricting commission one person who shares his or her political affliation. These two appointees then would have selected the three other members of the commission. One of these three subsequent appointees would have to have been an independent, while the other two would have been forbidden from belonging to the same political party. Regional, gender, and racial diversity would have been requisite considerations in the appointment process.

The measure would have spelled out a long list of requirements to bar candidates with close partisan connections. There also would have been strict prohibitions on future possible conflicts of interest, including restrictions on future political activity and dealings with government. State Issue 4 also would have provided a complicated array of procedures and formulas in an attempt to ensure a maximum number of competitive races. The measure also would have encouraged parity in the number of both competitive and uncompetitive districts that support each political party. The commission would have been allowed to adjust a prevailing plan to preserve "communities of interest based on geography, economics or race," as long as there would be little change in competitiveness.

II. Rating the Anti-Bias Mechanisms

One of the primary reasons to employ an independent commission to perform redistricting is to prevent officials from drawing district lines in a manner designed to achieve political gain. When creating a redistricting system, it is important that the system ensure the highest level of impartiality.

The regimes envisioned by Proposition 77 and State Issue 4 would have gone to great lengths to ensure that redistricting commission members would not have had conflicts of interests with either the government or a political party. State Issue 4 would have placed restrictions on political activity and business with political actors after service on the commission. Such restrictive policies seem crucial to ensuring that members of redistricting commissions will be as nonpartisan as possible and not tempted by the possibility of future political or financial gain. Even if a commission is balanced in partisanship, if the commission members are too politically connected, they may sponsor a plan that helps to ensure electoral victory for incumbents from both parties; both parties would be interested in ensuring easy re-election for their incumbents.

State Issue 4 also would have attempted to limit bias by giving the members of the redistricting commission very little personal leeway in the redistricting process. The measure enumerated very specific criteria to be followed. In fact, most of the process could have been performed by a computer. However, while such a system can help to prevent abuses, it also creates inflexibility and inhibits honest commissioners from better implementing comments from the public and from avoiding previously unanticipated problems.

Proposition 77 also would have employed commission member selection mechanisms that might have lessened the chance of bias and partisanship. One mechanism employed by Proposition 77 was that the four state legislators involved in the selection process would have evenly represented the minority and majority parties. Also, each partisan politician could only have nominated candidates for the commission who did not belong to the same political party as he did. Presumably, a politician would not pick someone from the other party who is known as a partisan ideologue or who is likely to be unfair. A commission of neutral members is less likely to be biased and more likely to compromise than an evenly divided commission of partisans.

Another safeguard was that each major political party would have to have been represented on the commission and a unanimous vote would have been required for ratification of a redistricting plan. Thus, a member of each major party would have to have supported the plan, preventing supporters of one political party from taking over the process, though this also could have led to deadlocks. Additionally, the Judicial Council would have picked the twenty-four people from which the four legislators would have chosen. While judges are not always apolitical, presumably a judicial body would be less political in its selections than a legislative body. Also, allowing each of the four legislators involved in the selection process to strike a nominee from consideration would have helped to ferret out problematic candidates.

One peculiar provision of Proposition 77's selection process was that the three members of the redistricting commission would have been chosen at random from the remaining pool of nominees after each legislator was afforded an opportunity to strike a nominee. Problematic candidates could have survived the lottery. Also, immensely qualified and fair candidates, who would enjoy universal approval, could have been removed by the lottery. A better mechanism to achieve neutrality would have been to have the legislators initially nominate eleven candidates and then require each legislator to strike two candidates.

III. Democratic Accountability

Drawing legislative districts carries significant political ramifications that affect the average citizen. One common critique of creating independent redistricting commissions is that it puts redistricting in the hands of unelected officials who have little or no accountability to the voters. A related argument is that the independent redistricting commissions will be unrepresentative of the diverse population of a state.

One problem with the arguments that independent redistricting commissions are too unaccountable is that they assume elected politicians are more accountable. In fact, elected politicians may calculate that the political gains from gerrymandering are potentially so great that they outweigh any potential backlash from voters.

Also, even if the redistricting commissions are less responsive to some of the concerns of voters, the political system overall may become more accountable. If an independent redistricting commission is well designed, the plan it produces should make elections more competitive. Since more competitive elections should make politicians more accountable generally, this increased responsiveness may outweigh any loss of accountability in the redistricting process.

Both Proposition 77 and State Issue 4 would have required the commissions to have public meetings where citizens could have an opportunity to voice their ideas and concerns. Redistricting business must also be conducted in public, helping to keep the process transparent and facilitating public discourse with the commission. In turn, it is important that a redistricting commission have enough flexibility that it can incorporate public opinion.

One challenge is determining the way in which a redistricting commission will be implemented. In the case of implementation through a ballot referendum that alters the state constitution, the actions of the commission could not be controlled without additional constitutional change. In contrast, many key actions made by administrative agencies can be overturned by the legislature. On the other hand, the problem with a redistricting commission created through a legislative action and not a state constitutional amendment is that one political party may take control of the legislature and the governorship and then dissolve the redistricting commission or otherwise disregard its work.

The problem of democratic accountability may seem especially pertinent to women and minorities, who might be inadequately represented on the redistricting commission. This concern was especially pertinent with respect to Proposition 77 for two reasons. First, the commission would have had only three members. Those three members could not have represented every ethnic group in an incredibly diverse state like California. Second, retired judges are likely to be white males. State Issue 4 addressed this concern over the lack of minority and female representation by stating that regional, gender, and racial diversity should be considered in the appointment process. However, it is equally doubtful, with only five members on the Ohio commission, that all pertinent racial, ethnic, and regional groups would have been represented, even if the selectors had made a good faith effort to include women and minorities.

However, while a redistricting commission may inevitably not reflect the diversity of the population as well as the state legislature can, it is debatable how big of a problem this is. First, individual politicians may care more about making their districts as easy to win as possible and protecting their political party's fortunes than about the interests of various groups. Second, the Voting Rights Act ensures that minority groups will have districts where they are able to pick representatives of their own choice. Third, the criteria directing the redistricting commission's work can be drafted in a manner to protect the interests of minorities or other groups. Provisions can be included to allow (or in some cases require) the preservation of communities of interest, but too many of such districts may lead to heavy bias for one party. Fourth, many administrative agencies do not adequately reflect the ethnic, gender, and regional differences of the citizens they govern, and yet administrative agencies are allowed to make many vital decisions. Fifth, state legislatures often do not adequately reflect the diversity of the state, either.

Proposition 77 did attempt an additional safeguard; while any newly created redistricting plan would have been used in the next scheduled election, voter approval of the plan at that election would have been required for the plan to continue to be utilized in subsequent elections. This measure seemingly would have ameliorated the problem of democratic accountability in measures like Proposition 77. If a plan did not reflect the wishes of the voters, it would be rejected. However, it must be acknowledged that redistricting is a technical and seemingly mundane issue. It might be difficult and costly to educate voters about the ramifications of a redistricting plan. Voters may be more concerned about issues that seem more pertinent to them, such as healthcare, the economy, and national security. Unless there were large and obvious problems with a plan, such as adverse impacts on large portions of the state or on a major political party, it could be difficult to defeat a plan.

IV. Special One-Time Redistricting

One common criticism of both Proposition 77 and State Issue 4 is that the measures called for a special, one-time redistricting to occur after passage by the voters. Some contend that a special mid-decade redistricting is unfair because such a redistricting uses old data from the last census. For instance, if a special redistricting were to occur in 2006, as was called for by Proposition 77, the data used would be from the 2000 census. This means that population changes that had occurred since 2000 would not be taken into account, which might especially hurt the representation of minorities when their populations grow more quickly than the rest of the population.

This critique has one major flaw: regardless of whether a special redistricting occurs, data from the last census will still govern the election. For example, if no special redistricting occurs, the previously drawn districts will be used, which were based on data from the last census. Therefore, mid-decade population shifts would not be reflected anyway. Another criticism of a special redistricting for the next election is that it would be very difficult logistically to perform redistricting that quickly. This concern seems especially warranted considering that it would be the first redistricting performed under the new plan. Presumably, the first time employing any plan will take longer than later uses, as there would be no previous experience using the plan. Calling for redistricting to occur in an election two or more years away would likely provide more time.

If the negative effects of political gerrymandering still exist when redistricting reform occurs, it would be desirable to perform a special one-time redistricting. However, unless the current maps are particularly unfair, no special redistricting should be proposed in a redistricting reform measure. The inclusion of the special redistricting reform in the measures was one possible reason for the lack of support for both Proposition 77 and State Issue 4. In both cases, there was a sense that the redistricting reform measures were motivated by the out-of-power party's desire to change its political fortunes. Calling for immediate redistricting is likely to increase the perception that the party proposing the reform simply wants a quick change to help it in the next election.

Conclusion

There has long been concern about allowing legislators to draw the districts in which they face reelection. There is potential for legislators to collude to draw safe districts that incumbents can win easily. Also, there is the possibility that one political party will control the state legislature and the governorship and will use their power to gerrymander the state's districts to enhance their future electoral prospects at the expense of their opponents and the democratic process.

Designers of redistricting commissions need to be aware of the potential ramifications of their system and of its possible flaws. Even if the only goal of a commission system is to remove the possibility of the worst abuses of gerrymandering, designers must be careful not to introduce unintended consequences. Using seemingly apolitical redistricting criteria may unfairly harm the political prospects of one political party and result in low levels of competition. Partisan voting data and preferences would have to be utilized to adjust district lines to achieve minimum levels of competition and results that are not unduly biased against one political party. This Article posits that redistricting commissions can be created without significant problems with political bias. An ideal system should not just rely on bipartisanship to achieve neutrality. A collection of neutral people should be better at both working together and achieving fairness than a politically balanced group of ideologues. Efforts to keep politically connected people off of the commission, to curtail potential abuse of discretion, and to limit dealings with political figures after service on the panel will minimize the costs of entrusting commissions with political data. While there are legitimate concerns about the democratic accountability of independent redistricting commissions, on balance a well-designed redistricting commission should better represent the interests of the public than legislators, who may allow potential political gain to dictate their actions. Also, federal law protects minorities in the redistricting process, and the new statute or amendment creating the redistricting commission can provide extra guarantees to minorities if federal law is deemed inadequate. The redistricting commission should be required to take public input, as was the case in both Proposition 77 and State Issue 4, and the redistricting commission should be given enough flexibility to take this input into account.

On the whole, the complex issues that are raised by creating a redistricting commission may make the endeavor impracticable, especially since the negative effects of political gerrymandering can be exaggerated. However, if a commission is crafted with enough thought, care, help from statisticians, and input from the public about its views on what a fair redistricting system would achieve, a fairer redistricting commission system should result.

POSTSCRIPT

Should Legislators Have the Responsibility for Redistricting?

It seems that political equality among the two major parties may have come to an end on the state level.[1] Although both parties had nearly the same number of chambers and seats nationwide, recent elections in 2006 and 2008 have given Democrats a large electoral advantage that will challenge Republicans in the foreseeable future because of something called "redistricting." Democrats currently control both chambers in 27 states, but Republicans only control 14 others, largely in the South. Only 9 states are divided so that each party controls only one chamber, the lowest number since 1982.

States are also becoming more polarized, argues Alan Rosenthal, a Rutgers University political scientist.[2] "The blue states are getting bluer, but there aren't many red states left that are really, totally red."

This single-party Democratic ascendancy is mounting right in time for the wave of redistricting in response to changes in the census of 2010.[3] Party control is really important because the party in the driver's seat will lock in its power and majority control for the next decade.

The take-home message for Republicans is that it is "important for Republicans to do better in 2010 than they have in the last two elections," says Michael McDonald, George Mason University political scientist, "because they don't want to feel the cruel cut of the redistricting knife."[4]

Redistricting is the process of redrawing electoral and constituency boundaries every 10 years in response to the census.[5] There are three basic ways that states' constitutions and laws allow them to go about creating state legislative boundaries. First, typically the state legislature is responsible for initiating and implementing a redistricting plan in 36 different states, many of which need the governor's approval. Second, five states—Arizona, Idaho, New Jersey, Washington, Hawaii—perform redistricting through an independent or bipartisan commission.[6] Third, in two states—Iowa and Maine—independent organizations recommend redistricting plans, but with approval by the state legislatures.

District lines are important because they can help or hurt a candidate or party.[7] Party control of the state legislature and the governorship is usually at stake. Each district line must be redrawn, in response to the census, to encompass equal populations, and shifts in lines should reflect changes in populations, such as individuals moving to rural areas to cities to find jobs. However, redrawing lines is always controversial because the majority party draws lines to keep itself in control. When redistricting lines are created for partisan control, it is called "gerrymandering."

Gerrymandering is considered a negative concept. The word itself is derived from two other words, "Gerry" and "salamander." "Gerry" refers to former Massachusetts Governor Elbridge Gerry; "salamander" refers to the shape of the district he created to benefit his party in the election of 1812.[8]

A recent controversy, called "prison-based gerrymandering,"[9] occurred when prisoners were counted as "residents" in a specific district, unfairly padding the district's population and inflating the voice of other residents allowed to vote in the district. Giving some people more power violates the fundamental concept of "one person, one vote"; in other districts that not have such prisons, voters' political power is thereby diluted, especially in cities.

After the census in 2010, new debates are expected as each party works to gain advantages in population count and political voice.

Notes

1. Alan Greenblatt, "Undoing the Split: Closely Divided Legislatures Are Getting Hard to Find," *Governing* magazine (February 2009). Accessed December 5, 2009, http://www.governing.com/archive/archive/2009/feb/observer.txt

2. *Ibid.*

3. *Ibid.*

4. *Ibid.*

5. "What Is the Census? When We All Answer the Census, Our Needs Are Heard," Census.gov. Accessed December 4, 2009, http://2010.census.gov/2010census/how/index.php

6. David Magleby, David O'Brien, Paul Light, James MacGregor Burns, J. W. Peltason, and Thomas Cronin, *State and Local Politics: Government by the People* (Pearson, 2007), p. 65.

7. *Ibid.*

8. Losco and Ralph Baker, *Am Gov* (McGraw Hill, 2009).

9. "Prison-Based Gerrymandering," *New York Times* (May 20, 2006). Accessed December 5, 2009, http://www.prisonersofthecensus.org/news/2006/05/20/NYT-gerrymandering/

Internet References . . .

Window on State Government: Susan Combs, Texas Comptroller of Public Accounts

"Property Taxpayers' Bill of Rights"

http://www.window.state.tx.us/taxinfo/proptax/bill_of_rights.html

Tax Foundation

"Property Taxes on Owner-Occupied Housing by State, 2004–2008"

http://www.taxfoundation.org/publications/show/1913.html

Low Tax Rate.com

"FAQs: You may be paying too much property tax!"

http://www.lowtaxrate.com/page/faq

Greenbelt Alliance: Open Spaces & Vibrant Places

http://www.greenbelt.org/

Natural Resources Defense Council

"Smart Growth"

http://www.nrdc.org/smartgrowth/default.asp

Sprawl Busters

http://www.sprawl-busters.com/

Heartland Institute

"Report: Urban Sprawl Fears Largely Unfounded"

**http://www.heartland.org/publications/environment%20climate/article/13355/
Report_Urban_Sprawl_Fears_Largely_Unfounded.html**

Suburbs, Cities, and Schools

*H*istorically, the American population migrated from the country-side to the cities by the 1920s and eventually to the urban sprawl of the suburbs by the 1970s. Property tax often goes hand in hand with urban sprawl, or the movement of people toward the suburbs. Good public schools are still the way we move forward as a society. However, governing schools is a preoccupation no matter where the school is located. And issues such as how to pay for schools and how to deal with population growth in suburbs where schools are bursting at the seams often create conflict too.

- Is Property Tax an Appropriate Revenue Source for State and Local Governments?

- Should Municipal Governments Limit Urban Sprawl?

- Are School Boards Necessary?

- Do Religious Groups Have a Right to Use Public School Facilities after Hours?

ISSUE 12

Is Property Tax an Appropriate Revenue Source for State and Local Governments?

YES: Steven Ginsberg, from "Two Cheers for the Property Tax," *Washington Monthly* (October 1997)

NO: Gerald Prante, "The Property Tax Rebellion," *American Legion Magazine* (April 2008)

ISSUE SUMMARY

YES: Gerald Prante and Steven Ginsburg agree, property tax is not popular among taxpayers. Ginsburg describes its unpopularity as "about as revered as communism and as popular as a pro-lifer at a NOW rally." He finds that this revulsion to property tax is because it seems unreasonable, arbitrary, and even unfair.

NO: Prante describes it this way: "Even for a famously anti-tax nation like the U.S., it's surprising how much Americans hate property taxes." He adds that more than seven years after 2000, property taxes have shot up 26 percent per person, a much higher rate than other types of taxes.

This hatred for property taxes is not helped by the fact that assessments are very infrequent, often only every 10 years, Ginsburg finds. Therefore, estimates are often unreliable. It is even worse in California, where properties are only reassessed when they are sold, which means new housing is slapped with the current rate of taxes, whereas a property in a family for years hardly pays anything.

Prante adds that local governments see property taxes as windfalls and spend as fast as they can to build schools, create and expand new services, and raise city employment salaries.

However, Ginsburg says, maligned as property taxes are, this revenue source is important not only to supplement other taxes, but also to collect from the most wealthy in a community. "The property tax picks up where the income tax leaves off. Even if they manage to downplay their annual income, chances are, rich folks are going to buy property." Ginsburg further notes that property tax can more properly reflect the ability for the elderly to pay with limited incomes. But exemptions can be made for those who cannot even pay this tax. Prante notes, this is why homeowners with fixed incomes are the first and often most loud opponents to property taxes.

Prante also counters that if property taxes are high, prospective buyers are less likely to pay as much for a house and fewer people will invest in property. In essence, if there are fewer property venues to do business, it could mean that will translate into losing jobs in the area.

Without property taxes, schools would be crippled, Ginsburg argues, because they receive a majority of their revenue from property taxes. He points out that, although the rich would likely not care because they can easily pay for private school, most school budgets would be devastated. Without the property tax, Ginsburg argues that we would find other sources of revenue to keep schools going. The problem here is that other taxes are not as egalitarian and would certainly shift the burden on to the poor and the middle class. Ginsburg also admits that the property tax is not perfect and says that property taxes must be less arbitrary and more transparent.

Prante admits that "there is no such thing as a free lunch." If a community cuts property taxes, equal cuts in spending or raises in other taxes sources would appear. Also, it could damage local control because the federal government would probably take over the reins and hence more control. Also, no property tax would mean no federal deductions off taxes.

Prante says reforms to shift the tax burden from property taxes are led in states such as Florida, Georgia, Connecticut, New York, and Indiana. In Georgia, although outright repeal of property taxes was defeated, there has been a push to expand sales taxes to many consumer and business services. Additionally, Florida has pushed for a 3 percent cap each year to fight a tax increase creep.

Ginsburg contends that Florida's system of recent reforms has resulted in "a maze of slimmed-down services and hidden 'non-tax' fees that end up unfairly shackling the middle class." He finds that these methods fail to raise the same amount that property tax did and quotes Kurt Wenner of Florida TaxWatch: "The schools don't have much of a chance." In another example, in Texas, Proposition 1 lowered property taxes statewide by $1 billion; as a consequence, Texas schools had to raise other taxes to pay bills.

Ginsburg and Prante agree property taxes are a paradox: No one likes them, but taxes are a necessary evil. Whether to cap property taxes and reduce spending, or reform property taxes to make them more transparent and less arbitrary, the debate fumes over America's most vilified tax revenue.

YES

Steven Ginsberg

Two Cheers for the Property Tax

To most Americans, the property tax is about as revered as communism and as popular as a pro-lifer at a NOW rally. The reasons are not hard to understand. At first glance, the property tax system seems arbitrary, unreasonable, and just plain unfair. Every year property owners are hit with a large tax bill, demanding a nearly immediate lump-sum payment. In many jurisdictions, including our nation's capital, the government isn't even required to do you the courtesy of mailing that bill; if you miss the deadline, you must pay late fees whether you received your notice or not. Furthermore, as far as many homeowners are concerned, the manner by which both tax rates and individual property values are determined could not be more random if they were plucked out of a hat. In some cases this is because on-site assessments are only done infrequently—like every five or 10 years. This forces assessors to rely on unreliable estimation methods in the intervening years, such as setting the value of a property based on what neighboring real estate sold for that year, regardless of how the condition of those properties compares with that of the building being assessed. Thus a shack and a renovated loft in the same area can be valued at the same amount. In other communities, like those in California, property values are reassessed only when a building is sold. So a young family of four buying a home in San Francisco's pricey real estate market is slapped with an exorbitant tax bill, while the filthy-rich investment banker down the street is still paying the same amount in taxes as when he first purchased his home in 1979.

Property tax rates are just as varied. In each community, homeowners, businesses, and non-homestead residences (like apartment buildings) vie to lighten their portion of the tax load. Often, regardless of actual property values, whichever group happens to have the most lobbying clout gets a break, while the losing parties are left to shoulder more than their fair share of the burden. In Minnesota, for instance, between 1977 and 1990 homeowners were able to cut their share of property taxes from 45 to 36 percent, even as their share of real estate values rose from 51 to 56 percent. All of this financial finagling, of course, only strengthens taxpayers' conviction that the system is inherently unjust and highly politicized.

It's not surprising then that the property tax has earned such a bad rep among voters—and even less surprising that politicians have latched onto the issue. If you're looking to win votes, opposing the property tax is a no-brainer: It's like declaring that you're anti-drugs. Already, states as politically diverse as Oregon and New York have moved to defang the property tax.

From *Washington Monthly*, October 1997, pp. 33–35. Copyright © 1997 by Washington Monthly. Reprinted by permission.

But before we pop open the champagne to toast these developments, we need to take a close look at the upside of the property tax. (And, yes, there is a considerable one.) For although the list of the system's failures is long, people who advocate lowering or abolishing the tax outright are in many cases not considering the big picture.

For starters, contrary to popular belief, the property tax serves as a vital complement to other types of taxes. For instance, our income tax system may be geared to collect more from the affluent, but it also includes numerous loopholes that allow the rich to slip out of paying an amount of tax truly commensurate with their wealth. The property tax picks up where the income tax leaves off. Even if they manage to downplay their annual income, chances are, rich folks are going to buy property. They can't resist owning that summer home in Nantucket, that weekend home in the Hamptons, or that colonial mansion in Georgetown. After all, what's the point of having all that dough if you're not going to spend it? Thus the amount of property you own is as important an indicator of how well-off you are as the income you're officially pulling in each year.

Similarly, property taxes improve the accuracy with which the wealth of senior citizens—whose assets tend to dramatically outweigh their cash incomes—can be taxed. Without property taxes, many seniors would only be taxed on their fixed incomes—which often grossly underestimate how well-to-do they actually are. Now, we're not talking about the 70-year-old Brooklyn couple whose fixed income barely covers the taxes on the brownstone they bought 30 years ago. (An exemption can and should be made to ensure taxes don't force elderly people out of their homes.) But lots of seniors have invested in real estate other than their primary residences. Take the case of a retired speculator who bought property years ago and has watched gleefully as its value skyrocketed. He can enjoy the benefits of his good fortune long before he actually sells those investments. For instance, ownership of pricey real estate makes him eligible for large loans on which the interest is tax deductible. Furthermore, he can spend his fixed annual retirement income without a second thought—knowing that if he's ever low on funds, he can simply cash in his property. The property tax ensures that his tax bill reflects his good fortune. It's not surprising then, that the powerful AARP seniors lobby is pressuring states for an overhaul of the property tax system. And as baby boomers slide into their golden years, we can expect this branch of the anti-property tax lobby to grow even stronger.

Who Will Pick Up the Slack?

No doubt the rich and the elderly recognize that abolishing or lowering property taxes would deal a crushing blow to the schools in their communities—which is where the bulk of the tax's revenues go. But that's no skin off their noses: The rich can always send their kids to private school, and most old people's kids have already flown the nest. Of course, cash-strapped communities are unwilling to stand by as their schools are devastated and may raise other kinds of taxes—like sales taxes—to make up for lost revenue. But such taxes shift more of the burden onto the middle and lower classes, who must buy basic goods, even if they can't afford property.

If you have any doubts about the kind of fiscal havoc the elimination of the property tax can cause, you need only look at what's happened in the states that have "reformed" it. In Florida, the large and religiously anti-property tax seniors population has pushed lawmakers into reducing the property tax rates for some, and completely exempting others. The result is a maze of slimmed-down services and hidden "non-tax" fees that end up unfairly shackling the middle class. Worst of all, these alternative methods simply can't raise the same amount of revenue as the property taxes did. Consequently, notes Kurt Wenner, an economist with Florida TaxWatch, "the schools don't have much of a chance." Small wonder that Florida kids consistently place near the bottom in national reading and math tests, alongside much poorer states such as Louisiana.

In Texas, voters overwhelmingly approved Proposition 1, a ballot measure providing $1 billion in property tax "relief." The law's supporters in the legislature said they had to act "before there was a taxpayer revolt." Of course, almost immediately after the bill passed, school districts across the state announced that they would have to raise other taxes to make ends meet.

Taxpayers in Maine are looking to reduce their property tax bills by expanding the homestead exemption by $20,000, a measure that would rob the state of $200 million in funds. To compensate for the reduction in real estate taxes, Maine will be forced to extend its 6 percent sales tax to a wide range of everyday sources that directly hit middle-class wallets, including movie theaters, bowling alleys, beauticians, and barbers.

The situation is no different in New York; Governor Pataki, along with a slew of legislators, has vowed to cut property taxes. But as property taxes go down, local taxes, user fees, and college education prices continue to surge to make up the difference. The New York proposals are so unbalanced they prompted Patricia Woodworth, director of the budget for the State of New York, to complain to *Newsday* last April, "the benefits are going to go to those who have the greater monetary and financial interest in property holdings, which is not the average person. This plan is not truly tax relief."

But it is Oregon that gives us the most vivid example of what happens when property taxes are slashed. The northwestern state passed Measure 5 in 1990, putting a cap on all property tax increases. This, in turn, forced a massive transfer of state funds to support schools, which left the state with no choice but to cut spending on child welfare, prisons, and state police.

The bottom line: When property taxes are cut, other taxes must be raised to make up for lost revenues. And, as Chris Herbert, an economist at the Harvard-MIT Joint Center for Housing Studies, points out, the property tax is far more progressive than the alternatives. "Cutbacks in property tax have got to be made up and they're not going to be done by a more progressive tax," he says. "Localities can't get states to pick up the tab, so there's a big shift to user charges. You start getting taxes on trash collection and recreation facilities. With user fees things are becoming less progressive because you're paying as much as the next guy"—regardless of whether he happens to be a millionaire.

Mend It, Don't End It

But if we want to get the property tax off the political hit list, we need to address the legitimate problems with the current system. A handful of governments around the country have already started the ball rolling, instituting models that correct some of the more egregious flaws.

Washington state has perhaps the best system, having tackled the issue of favoritism head-on and passed a constitutional amendment declaring that statewide property tax rates must be uniform. For example, all real estate property is currently taxed at approximately 1.2 percent. In addition, all property tax revenues are split between the state and localities. This allows states to tap a deep vein of revenue and distribute it equitably. Under such a system, localities ultimately get to administer their portion of the pot, but the disparity between rich and poor districts is not so wide. "The real key is that the system is administered fairly," says Kriss Sjoblon, an economist at the Washington Research Council. "We have a good system of assessment that eliminates inequities, and the uniformity is vital. People should be treated fairly and folks shouldn't get deals."

Even jurisdictions with special needs can establish systems that are less arbitrary and that make sense to the average taxpayer. Pittsburgh, for instance, has initiated a "split-rate" system in an attempt to foster urban renewal. Property tax is really two separate taxes, one on land and one on building values; Pittsburgh simply separated these two values. The city then lowered the tax on buildings, giving property owners an incentive to maintain, build, and improve their properties, while at the same time increasing the levy on land values, thus discouraging land speculation and stemming urban sprawl. In Pittsburgh and other Pennsylvania cities where the "split-rate" is employed, 85 percent of homeowners pay less than they would with a flat rate, according to analysis by the *American Journal of Economics and Sociology*. The analysis also found that those who do pay more tend to be wealthier homeowners.

Most importantly, the system achieves its goal of encouraging economic growth in urban centers. A study conducted by University of Maryland economists Wallace Oates and Robert Schwab, comparing Pittsburgh to 14 other eastern cities during the decade before and the decade after Pittsburgh expanded its two-rate system, found that: "Pittsburgh had a 70.4 percent increase in the value of building permits, while the 14-city average decreased by 14.4 percent. These findings are especially remarkable when it is recalled that the city's basic industry—steel—was undergoing a severe crisis throughout the latter decade."

Aside from these more comprehensive systems, there are a number of basic steps localities could take to alter the perception of unfairness and ease the burden of property taxes:

- Use the property tax to pay for more than just schools. If seniors and the wealthy feel that the taxes support services they need, they will have reason to pause before directing their lobbying muscle against it.
- Raise the level of exemptions for people over 65. Property taxes do blindside some senior citizens, and there's no reason why they should

have to move out of their lifelong homes because the market value of the house has gone up. A moderate raise in the exemption level would prevent poorer seniors from losing their homes, while still raising revenue from the wealthy.

- Stagger payments. A major reason property tax is so unpopular is that it's administered in huge chunks and people aren't allowed much time before hefty late fees kick in. Distributing the burden over four or more payments a year, with more advanced notice, would take some of the sting out of the bill.
- Upgrade technology. Set it up so people can pay electronically. It's a small thing, but it will make a difference. Most cities allow offenders to pay parking tickets with credit cards, there's no reason they can't do the same with property tax.

Rooting out favoritism and slipshod assessment methods will help make the tax palatable to the majority of citizens. They will no longer see the property tax as a mindless ogre coming to swallow up their hard-earned money. Instead, they will see it as the soundest way to make sure that everyone, especially the wealthy, contributes his share to ensure a high level of public services. In short, they will see it for what it is.

Gerald Prante  **NO**

The Property Tax Rebellion

Even for a famously anti-tax nation like the U.S., it's surprising how much Americans hate property taxes. The Tax Foundation's annual survey consistently confirms this, finding that only gasoline taxes and estate taxes cause a similar revulsion.

Nevertheless, no tax has increased faster over the past seven years than the hated property tax. From 2000 through 2007, property tax revenue per capita has risen 26 percent after adjusting for inflation. That's much faster than real personal income (7.5 percent) or other tax sources like general sales taxes (5.7 percent) and income taxes (4.9 percent). This 26-percent surge has been all the more shocking to the nation's property owners because the 1990s had been so placid. The growth rate in real per capita property tax collections over the previous seven-year period (1993–2000) was only 2 percent. So if property taxes seem to rising more than 10 times faster than they used to, that's because they are!

As every homeowner knows, these soaring property tax collections coincided with an even more rapid increase in home values across the country. Skyrocketing real estate values have pushed up the property tax base, so unless local governments diligently ratcheted down their rates (or "millages" as property tax rates are sometimes called), then local government coffers were flooded with revenue.

Some city and county councils did lower rates, which we can confirm not by checking thousands of local budgetary documents but by identifying where local government spending growth has remained modest. On the other hand, many localities simply treated the rising real estate values as a windfall that they should spend as fast as they could, building new schools, expanding social services, or raising the salaries and retirement packages of government employees. Spending in those areas has increased quickly. Most local governments followed a middle course, offering rate cuts to their property owners but not commensurate with the rising real estate values. Overall, at least through the end of 2005, soaring real estate values made it easy for local governments to raise property taxes.

This recent, rapid increase still hasn't come close to restoring property taxes to what they were a century ago, the nation's biggest tax, back when state and local governments spent twice as much as the federal government. Since the early 20th century, local governments have relied more and more heavily upon other sources of revenue, especially transfers from federal and state governments who themselves were bringing in a lot more tax revenue from new income and sales taxes. There was a flurry of new state taxes on income and sales during the 1930s, and by 1970 most states had gotten around to taxing both.

Of all the traditionally local responsibilities, public schools have received the most new financing from federal and state governments. In 1960, the federal government's share of elementary and secondary education spending was only 2.3 percent, but by 2006 the feds were pitching in over 7 percent. That still may not seem like a huge share, but it's still a three-fold increase. Despite this growing federal share, property tax bills have still risen. That's how fast local spending on schools and other functions is rising.

Where Are Property Taxes Getting the Most Attention?

Even though most property taxes are still local, governors and state legislators have issued the loudest calls for property tax relief. This has been especially true in Florida, Georgia, New York, Connecticut and Indiana, where demands for property tax relief are reaching an almost irresistible level. The demands are louder now, but the public has always hated the property tax.

While the famous Proposition 13 in California from 1979 is still the most significant property tax limitation measure ever passed (it's still in effect today), some state legislators are now demanding more radical action than a cap on residential real estate assessments. Some have even demanded total repeal of their property taxes.

Such a statewide repeal, to be enforced on localities by the state, was proposed recently in Georgia, Indiana and Florida. Those proposals have all been replaced with less drastic plans to cut rates, cap assessments, or otherwise grant relief. But the fire hasn't been quenched, and even where caps or other tax relief mechanisms have been enacted, calls are still being heard for scaling property taxes back further.

The Wrong and Right Ways to Legislate Property Tax Relief

The obvious problem with many of these tax relief proposals is that they don't curtail spending, so the tax revenue must be raised from another source. Often those new, higher taxes are even enacted in the same bill or referendum that cut the property taxes, making it obvious that a tax swap is in the making, not overall tax relief. For example, in order to "pay for" property tax relief in Indiana, Gov. Mitch Daniels's property tax limitation proposal has called for a one percentage point increase in the general sales tax rate. The Indiana House of Representatives has passed that bill in a lopsided 93-1 vote, so Gov. Daniels's sales tax hike is apparently beating out the competing proposals that would have raised income taxes to fund property tax relief.

Georgians have witnessed the most radical proposals. Even after the plan for total repeal was abandoned, many legislators are still championing a plan that would repeal the education portion of the property tax for all homeowners by expanding the sales tax to many services, not just lawn care and auto repair, which are popular targets for sales tax expansion in many states, but to many business and consumer services, possibly even accounting and legal services.

Another Georgia proposal would put relatively strict spending limits on the amount that local governments can increase their spending each year. Although the "right way" to limit property taxes is for county and municipal citizens to enforce spending and tax discipline on their local governments, maintaining local authority over property taxes, this Georgia proposal is the "right way" to accomplish the same thing at the state level. Property tax relief without spending discipline is just a shell game.

Over the past 18 months, no state has seen the property tax debated more than the State of Florida. Even though the state has no income tax, Florida Gov. Charlie Crist went on a whirlwind tour of the Sunshine State in January, lobbying for voters to approve an amendment to the state constitution that would make portable the state's "Save Our Homes" provision. Crist's campaign was successful, gaining almost two-thirds of votes cast.

Here's how the new "portability" mechanism will work in Florida. For many years, "Save Our Homes" has restrained the growth of tax assessments on a homeowner's primary residence below the fair market value, capping it at 3 percent each year, similar to the way California's Proposition 13 prevents home values from rising more than 2 percent a year for tax purposes. Long-time homeowners benefit substantially from this system, but when they move, the "catch-up" occurs. The new owner starts paying property tax on the fair market value. As people who dislike this system always phrase it, identical homes right next door to each other can carry very different property tax burdens. Is that fair?

The new constitutional amendment now only preserves the "Save Our Homes" limit on assessments, but it also allows someone who's selling to use part of his accumulated property tax savings on a new home. Real estate agents are ecstatic because logically, people should find it easier to buy new homes. This property tax relief is on top of the property tax reductions that the Florida legislature passed in 2007, which totaled 13.55 billion per year.

Where Are Property Taxes Highest?

Of all the localities in the U.S., counties in Western New York are laying the heaviest property taxes on their residents. In 2006, the Tax Foundation calculated Niagara County, NY, as having the highest median property taxes on homeowners (as a percentage of the median home value). Frustrated Niagara property owner Lee Bordeleau was so irate that he put up a billboard on a county highway highlighting the county's unwanted distinction. In response to such anger from upstate homeowners, New York Gov. Elliot Spitzer is proposing legislation to expand the so-called STAR program that credits some fraction of property tax payments against income taxes. Ultimately, however, if New York wants to lower its property tax burden, it will have to raise taxes elsewhere or reduce its spending on public schools, currently close to the nation's highest.

Property Tax Reform Efforts: The Good and the Bad

American antipathy toward the property tax seems exaggerated to economists and political scientists who typically prefer property taxes to income and sales taxes. These experts worry that movements to limit the property tax can end up doing more harm than good.

The first principle taught to every freshman economics student is that there is no such thing as a free lunch. Limiting property taxes requires a commensurate cut in spending or a hike in other taxes. Also, if we value our federalist system of government, it might be dangerous to restrict the property tax because power could shift to higher levels of government willing to funnel money to local services, money derived from income and sales taxes that economists consider more detrimental than property taxes.

This can be a paradox for conservatives who typically favor cutting taxes at every opportunity. It may work in the short run, but if tax limitations shift power to state and federal governments, the local control that is a bedrock principle for most conservatives must diminish. Ordinary citizens may ultimately be able to control the property tax more *without* limitations imposed by state governments because it is much easier for an ordinary citizen to be heard and heeded at a local school board meeting than at the state capital.

Academics also point out this virtue of property taxes: it is one of the most transparent taxes. People know how much they pay more accurately than with sales taxes, often the alternative vehicle for funding. If we agree that sales taxes are more hidden and easily raised without riling the taxpayers, then this could be another reason that shifting from property taxes to sales taxes could ultimately make it easier for governments to raise taxes overall.

People on the political left naturally feel just the opposite. Though typically dubious of tax limitation, they favor the side effect, centralization of power in state capitals or Washington. They are especially keen on centralization in states with diverse geographies because funding from the state capital is more likely to be distributed in a manner that's proportionate to population instead of property value. Decades ago when education was financed solely by local property taxes, schools in poor areas could never extract as much tax revenue from their property owners as schools in wealthier areas could. The quaint little rural schoolhouse has a nostalgic appeal to Americans, but now the mere fact that it requires less money per pupil creates the impression of inequality in education. After all, schoolchildren are helpless, and their parents often have little ability to determine where their children attend school.

If property tax limitations do indeed push power up the governmental food chain, then local governments may become not only less powerful but less diverse. Homogenous tax and spending bundles will thereby limit choice among "tax consumers" as to where to live.

Finally, one obvious yet often overlooked disadvantage of shifting away from the property tax is the federal deduction for property taxes paid. From the self-interested perspective of a state's lawmakers, a state should not "leave money on the table" by arranging its state and local taxes in a way that doesn't take full advantage of federal tax deductions.

Of course, lowering property taxes is not all bad. After all, it's a tax cut, which by itself is a good thing. High property taxes lower the amount that prospective buyers are willing to pay for a house, everything else being equal. On the other hand, the property tax also discourages investments in property, especially structures. It is a tax on capital, which can decrease the supply of property, both residential and commercial. This has the secondary effect of decreasing the demand for local labor, which complements capital, thereby suppressing wages in areas with above-average property taxes. How big of a negative effect a high property tax has on an area varies though, depending upon different factors like how easily people and businesses can move to other jurisdictions, as well as the quality of the local government services provided.

Then there are the more obvious benefits of reducing property taxes in addition to the economic benefits. First, limits on the property tax can be a type of insurance against sudden changes in assessments, which is one of the main reasons Americans are so frustrated with the property tax recently. Similarly, although increased property values do represent changes in wealth for the homeowner, that wealth is "on paper" in the current year, and it is not the same as receiving a check in the mail for the amount of the home value change. In order to realize that "income," one would either have to sell the house or take out a home-equity loan. But the property tax is a tax that can increase significantly as a result of that change in wealth, and it is not sensitive to changes in cash incomes. This is why homeowners on fixed incomes, typically older homeowners, are often the most vociferous opponents of property taxes. Finally, continuing on this theme of unpredictability in property taxes, there is also the property tax assessment process. While the IRS is loathed by Americans, at least there is no doubt as to how much your salary is each year. With property taxes, however, people often dispute their assessment and hence their tax bill, which can lead to a fairly lengthy process requiring research on the assessments of comparable homes. This is because the assessment process itself is highly subjective, and having an assessor monitor changes in home values adds to the uncertainty and also brings up questions of privacy.

Conclusion

Americans do not like the property tax. So when property taxes increase dramatically as they have for the past seven years, it is no surprise that the public will call for and politicians will be proposing cutting this disliked tax. But while cutting property taxes does have its benefits, efforts to limit their impact do have their costs, such as higher taxes elsewhere. Ultimately, politicians and voters must face the reality that there is no free lunch. The only way to bring substantive tax relief to the people is to reduce spending on the government services that they receive.

POSTSCRIPT

Is Property Tax an Appropriate Revenue Source for State and Local Governments?

More often than not, the abrupt momentum behind the abolishment or reduction in property taxes is the steep rise in home prices.[1] Property taxes are not popular among the American public. According to a Gallup Poll in April 2005, the question was asked: "Which do you think is the worst tax, that is, the least fair: federal income tax, federal Social Security tax, state income tax, state sales tax, or local property tax?" Forty-two percent answered property tax, and the federal tax was next highest, with only 20 percent.[2]

In South Carolina, housing prices climbed as high as any place in the southern United States between 2002 and 2005. At the time, South Carolina median home prices increased 6 percent a year statewide, just short of the average of 7 percent in the South. In reaction, legislation was passed in 2006, replacing local residential property taxes to pay for local schools with a 1-cent increase in state sales taxes. This meant the tax burden turned from large homeowners to everyone who consumes goods—more of a burden on the poor. Additionally, the tax burden shifted to the already strapped state. States such as Oregon, California, and Michigan moved in a similar direction in the past.

Fiscal shortfalls have propelled such action on property taxes.[3] In a few states, the property tax, often rising inexorably to make up for some of these funding gaps, has led to property tax revolts.[4] As a result, a reliance on property taxes has declined. For example, from 1962 to 1992, cities' reliance on property taxes deteriorated from nearly 50 percent to 26.5 percent during those 30 years.[5] Florida and New Jersey, for example, took action in a public fury over their property tax by pushing for major tax reorganizations.

Property tax is also known as an *ad valorem* tax, a tax that an owner must pay based on the value of his or her property.[6] Bernard Ross and Myron Levine (2006) found property taxes have been around for more than 200 years. However, Glenn W. Fisher, Wichita State University, found that the property tax has a history beyond that.[7] Property tax based on ownership of land truly goes back to ancient times, when European kings taxed their serfs. British tax assessors, Fisher contended, used land occupancy or ownership to approximate a property holder's tax rate in the fourteenth and fifteenth centuries. Over time, this moved from a tax on the person to a tax on the property itself.

Whether to tax citizens via property tax or sales tax often provides a heated debate centered on individual philosophies concerning the nature of property tax. Some argue it is a regressive tax scheme and others a progressive system of raising revenue for state and local governments. This debate may explain why some states, such as Texas, rely heavily on property taxes, as do some cities, such as Portland and Boston. But this is not the case for all cities nationwide; Shreveport and Oklahoma City both focus on sales taxes.[8]

On the one hand, some believe property taxes are regressive, disproportionately hurting lower income individuals such as pensioners and others on a fixed income.[9] Pensioners have often accumulated property assets over time, but when they retire, their income becomes fixed, therefore a higher proportion of their personal income goes to taxes than when they were working.[10] This sentiment is used by those wanting either to reduce property taxes increases through caps or abolish them altogether and replace them with either a "fair" tax or sales tax. Sales tax could also serve school systems more fairly because it is more likely to be uniform rather than allowing rich neighborhoods with higher property valuations to determine the local school budget.

On the other hand, some people argue that property taxes are actually progressive, because basically the citizens with the highest incomes tend to own much more valuable property or properties.[11] Nearly a third of all households do not even own property and so are exempt from paying such taxes. The rich also have more intangible personal property—bonds, cash, and stocks—very often escaping any taxation, so property tax is at least one way to make them pay their fair share.

Notes

1. John Petersen, "Housing's Tax Bubble: Rising Property Values Fomented Tax Reform in South Carolina, but Restrictions in the New Law May Haunt the State," *Governing* magazine (November 2006). http://www.governing.com/archive/archive/2006/nov/finance.txt

2. Gallup Poll (April 5–7, 2005). (N=503, MoE ± 5). Accessed December 5, 2009, http://www.pollingreport.com/budget3.htm

3. Katherine Barrett, and Richard Greene. "State Tax Systems: A Special Report: Growth & Taxes: Why Outdated State Tax Systems Undercut Economic Vitality, and What States Can Do about It," *Governing* magazine (January 1). Accessed December 5, 2009, http://www.governing.com/column/growth-taxes

4. Bernard Ross and Myron Levine, *Urban Politics: Power in Metropolitan America*, 7th ed. (Thomson/Wadsworth, 2006).

5. *Ibid,* pp. 476–477.

6. *Ibid.*

7. Glenn W. Fisher, "History of Property Taxes in the United States," Economic History Association, EH.Net. Accessed December 5, 2009, http://eh.net/encyclopedia/article/fisher.property.tax.history.us

8. Ross and Levine, 2006.

9. *Ibid.*

10. *Ibid.*

11. "Land Value Tax: Progressive Revenue Flyer," Henry George Foundation of America (2009). Accessed December 4, 2005, http://www.scribd.com/doc/13541825/Land-Value-TaxProgressive-Revenue-Flyer

ISSUE 13

Should Municipal Governments Limit Urban Sprawl?

YES: Rob Gurwitt, from "Not-So-Smart Growth," *Governing* (October 2000)

NO: Thomas J. DiLorenzo, from "The Myth of Suburban Sprawl," *USA Today* (Society for the Advancement of Education, May 2000)

ISSUE SUMMARY

YES: Rob Gurwitt explains that communities annex to beat out other communities before they annex the same piece of land, but such behavior has a high cost.

NO: Thomas DiLorenzo argues that problems associated with urban sprawl are hysterically out of proportion and that market principles should prevail.

Rob Gurwitt describes annexation happening around the country; for example, he explains that in Florida competition and entrepreneurship dominate because there is a fear that some communities will be left out in the cold. "Welcome to annexation politics, Florida-style," he says. In Ohio, lawmakers are combating urban sprawl by shifting annexation power away from cities to counties and townships, which most often lose taxes when annexation occurs. He argues that annexation is not only about where land will be winding up:

> It's about who controls what happens on the land, who reaps the fiscal benefits and who pays the cost of shifting that control, whose government infrastructure can best handle the demands that development is bound to generate.

Gurwitt further explains that because annexation is about control, it is at the center of the suburban sprawl debate. He quotes Peter DetWiler, staff director for the California Senate Committee on Local Government: "The hand that controls boundaries also controls the location, timing, and cost of the public facilities and services upon which private development depends."

On the other hand, Thomas DiLorenzo pits average Americans who are living their American Dream in the suburbs with urban planners and environmentalists who reveal a "visceral hatred of it [suburban sprawl]." DiLorenzo derides the term "smart growth" as a euphemism for "centralized governmental planning," essentially taking away a family's free choice. There is a double standard, he contends. These families, he says, are thought to be "stupid" and destructive, whereas the environmentalist "coercive planning schemes" are considered "smart." DiLorenzo claims that the "Smart Growth Network" is a coalition that is trying to force these families back to the city to pay taxes to benefit local interests.

Gurwitt counters that urban sprawl is not a conspiracy, but that developers want to do business for two driving reasons: first, to pay the least amount of money for land as feasible and to develop it unimpeded, if at all possible, which typically means in unincorporated areas. Although Gurwitt says he understands why surburban sprawl happens, it creates problems, especially when it happens in a disparate and ad hoc manner. He argues, "Annexation should be one of the centerpieces of any serious growth-management reform."

"Unplanned" development is rather misleading, DiLorenzo says; developers build suburbs for people because that is what they want.

DiLorenzo argues further that those who claim suburban sprawl is a problem ignore both buyers' and sellers' preferences. He explains that these people who live away from city centers realize that they make a trade-off and that smart growth advocates want their preferences to trump those of 100 million Americans who have chosen to live in the suburbs.

Yet local governments are finding that pressure and frenzy to develop guarantees conflict over which towns should benefit and which will not, Gurwitt says.

Whereas Gurwitt sees destructive conflict among those scrambling to annex in a haphazard manner, DiLorenzo sees such development as the will of the people and a natural outgrowth of the American Dream.

YES

Rob Gurwitt

Not-So-Smart Growth

Largo, Florida, is a suburb of 65,000 people, just north of St. Petersburg. It is a comfortable place, with one major regret in life: It isn't located on the water. It sits in the middle of a peninsula, halfway between the Gulf of Mexico and Tampa Bay.

But Largo has a strategy for breaking out of its landlocked position. Between it and the Bay there's a strip of unincorporated territory that uses the Largo sewer system. Not long ago, town officials began contacting residents of this strip and handing them an ultimatum: Become part of Largo, or we turn off the sewer service.

Those tactics provoked a suit from the neighboring town of Pinellas Park. Also landlocked, Pinellas Park has an official goal of adding 150 acres a year to its territory. The Largo ploy was a threat to its dreams of expansion.

Welcome to annexation politics, Florida-style. Communities play it for one reason: to win. "It's always competition and always entrepreneurship," says Jack Schluckebier, city manager of the town of Casselberry, just outside Orlando. "You're either in it with that perspective, or if you don't have that perspective, others will, and pretty soon you'll be a footnote."

Pinellas County, in which both Largo and Pinellas Park are located, has done its best to bring order to the chaos. Earlier this year, the Pinellas County Planning Council brokered a peace. Its director, Dave Healey, worked out a map to which each of the county's 24 cities agreed—some of them reluctantly—showing where their growth would occur, based on existing service capabilities and what made the most sense. "All of the cities were forced into this competition," explains Healey. "With predetermined, logical limits, they could plan better for their future and avoid the race to see who could get there first." Next month, the new growth plan will be submitted to the county's voters as a charter amendment.

Florida's annexation wars may sound extreme, but they are not unusual. As jurisdictions all over the country come to terms with the torrid pace of development, they are discovering that annexation lies somewhere close to the heart of the matter.

California is currently trying to bring a measure of reason to the whole process by which communities and service districts draw and redraw their boundaries. A bill to strengthen the county-level agencies that oversee such activities has been working its way through the legislature. Meanwhile, Ohio lawmakers are working on a plan to shift the balance of annexation power away from cities, and to give more of a say to the jurisdictions—both township and counties—that lose tax base when land is annexed.

When it is done intelligently, annexation can impose order on complicated p1anning problems. It can bring a city and its existing service infrastructure to newly developed land that badly needs it. But annexation is also a potential flash-point, for all sorts of reasons. To begin with, one community's tax-base gain is inevitably another jurisdiction's loss. Yet any effort to control who can claim a particular piece of land is sure to bump up against home-rule sensitivities: Cities don't like other governments telling them how they can grow. And just as ticklish, annexation puts a crimp in the ability of developers to choose the jurisdiction with the friendliest zoning or the most cost-effective services.

In other words, annexation politics is not just about what piece of land will wind up in which jurisdiction. It's about who controls what happens on the land, who reaps the fiscal benefits and who pays the cost of shifting that control, and whose governmental infrastructure can best handle the demands that development is bound to generate.

"Drawing boundaries is more than an exercise in cartographic neatness," says Peter DetWiler, staff director for the California Senate Committee on Local Government. "The hand that controls boundaries also controls the location, timing and cost of the public facilities and services upon which private development depends." Small wonder that annexation law, arcane as it might seem, is fast becoming the newest front in the growth-control wars.

The most dramatic annexation flare-up in recent years occurred in Tennessee, where a law passed by the legislature in 1997 blocked virtually all cities in the state from annexing land, and encouraged even the tiniest subdivisions to incorporate. The law was eventually thrown out in court, but before the controversy died down, the state had enacted a sweeping new planning measure requiring cities and counties to get together and agree on cities' future growth boundaries.

Actually, states have been seeking to temper the excesses of the annexation issue for a long time. As far back as 1963, the California legislature created a set of 58 boundary watchdogs, one for each county, known as Local Agency Formation Commissions, or LAFCOs. Under their enabling legislation, LAFCOs were asked to rule on boundary changes—incorporations, annexations and the creation and expansion of special-service districts—for two purposes: to promote the orderly formation or extension of local governments, and to discourage urban sprawl.

Anyone who's spent some time on the outskirts of Los Angeles or San Francisco might well question whether LAFCOs have served the latter purpose, but what is especially clear is that the law now needs some sort of update. This point was driven home in January by the report of the state's Commission on Local Governance for the 21st Century—appointed by former Republican

Governor Pete Wilson and headed by the Republican mayor of San Diego, Susan Golding—which stated baldly that "there is no comprehensive strategy to determine how the burdens of growth will be shared, how resources benefiting more than one locality will be protected, and how necessary but locally undesirable facilities will be sited. As a result, farmland and open space continue to be swallowed up by sprawling suburban expansion." The report went on to suggest that the powers of LAFCOs to "prevent sprawl" be strengthened.

This is precisely what Robert Hertzberg, the speaker of the California Assembly, has set out to do. Hertzberg's interest was sparked by the San Fernando Valley's move to secede from Los Angeles and create a separate city, but the measure he ended up writing goes a good bit beyond that parochial dispute. In addition to making sure that LAFCOs become truly independent—they've usually been funded and staffed by the counties, even though cities and special districts are also represented on their boards—Hertzberg would empower LAFCOs to review each jurisdiction's so-called "sphere of influence"—its projection of future boundaries—every five years to ensure that they make sense.

Not surprisingly, the Hertzberg bill has aroused great antagonism among developers and municipalities. In particular, they objected to strong language in the original version promoting in-fill development and requiring LAFCOs to consider regional growth policies in making their decisions. The bill was rewritten to be neutral on infill development, and gives LAFCOs the option of considering regional policy, but does not require it. "Most of the provisions that we had the most concern with, in terms of a radical expansion of powers, have been modified to the point we can live with," says Dan Carrigg, the League of California Cities' lobbyist on land use issues. The bill passed the Assembly in June and at the end of the summer was still in committee in the Senate.

In Ohio, the annexation debate seems to be bringing cities and developers together, although it is far from clear how much of an impact they will have on a measure now working its way through the legislature. The big beneficiaries of that bill are counties and townships: County boards would get more of a say in whether or not unincorporated land could be annexed, and municipalities would be required to share tax revenues from territory they annexed with the township it was annexed from.

Ohio's townships—land outside incorporated cities in Ohio is divided into townships, which have a few governmental powers but mostly rely on the counties for government—have actually been pushing such a move for the better part of a decade, and three years ago came quite close to getting what they wanted. A bill tilted in their favor was defeated by a single vote in the Senate Rules Committee after the governor at the time, former Cleveland mayor George Voinovich, threatened a veto.

These days, however, the politics of local government in Ohio are quite different. Township trustees are an increasingly influential bloc, both in the legislature and at the county level. They have induced the County Commissioners Association of Ohio to flip its position on township-backed annexation reform. The commissioners have dropped their opposition of previous years and come out in favor of the current measure.

Although Ohio's townships portray the annexation issue as a matter of controlling growth and promoting farmland preservation, at base it's a question of who gets to say where growth occurs and who reaps its benefits. The central dilemma, as Susan Cave of the Ohio Municipal League, says, is this: "Developers want to do business in locations that provide two things: the least expensive way of doing it; and a regulatory and service climate that allows them to do their development in the best way they can. Well, the least expensive way is generally out in the unincorporated areas: The land is less expensive, and there are no old industrial sites to clean up. On the other hand, they also want services, and in Ohio, cities are the traditional providers of water and sewer." Moreover, township zoning often requires scattered development without density, whereas cities allow much greater density; not surprisingly, then, developers prefer to buy up unincorporated land and then petition for annexation into a nearby city. Where landowners want the annexation to occur, for the most part it does.

The new measure, though, would allow county commissioners to consider the interests of property owners within a half-mile of the land proposed for annexation, which essentially hands the property owners a veto. "Let's say that 10 years ago I built an expensive house, and now the land next to me is annexed and I've suddenly got a shopping center with a parking lot 30 feet from my house. There's something not right about that in our members' minds," says Larry Long, director of the county commissioners' association. "Development interests feel that if a majority of the people want to be in a city, it ought to be automatic. Our people say, 'OK, as long as you're not really messing up your next-door neighbor or breaking the bank of that township government.'" Under Ohio law, the counties don't actually lose tax revenue when a piece of land is incorporated, which is why the issue has been of less vital import for them than for cities and townships.

As Tom Hart, of the Building Industry Association of Central Ohio, puts it, "The public policy question is a tough one: How do you determine whose rights are greater, the right of the person to develop his or her land, or the person next to it who doesn't want to see it change?" Handing final say over annexations to neighbors affected by development or left behind by annexation may well put a crimp in development in Ohio, as Hart predicts. Or it may produce development that remains in townships, which will then have to acquire a service infrastructure that until now many have lacked.

⚹

It was precisely this sort of unplanned development that Dave Healey and the Pinellas County Planning Council in Florida wanted to end. Eager to capture land and new taxes, cities in Florida have bent over backwards to make themselves appealing to neighborhoods and developers. In the process, however, some cities have relaxed growth management plans—easing up, for example, on rules governing how intensely a given parcel can be developed, or waiving impact fees—and making costly plans to extend infrastructure. "We've had situations where a piece of property was in one community's water, sewer and fire district," says Healey, "and the community across the street offered to jack and bore its sewer system under the street to extend it. By getting to that parcel, it provided a leg in the door to get to the next one, but it wasn't a sound financial decision."

The "leg in the door" to which Healey refers is a provision in Florida law that says that only territory "contiguous" to a municipality's borders can be annexed, which explains why cities have an incentive to amass as much territory as possible: The parcel they annex this year may not be terribly important, but the parcel next to it could bring in a wealth of taxes. The problem with this, of course, is that it makes land use planning futile. "When annexation happens, it is in a disparate, ad hoc manner," Healey says. "It's when a city can get there and if they can get contiguous, and isn't rational when you look at service areas."

All of this may make it sound as if Florida law makes it easy for cities to annex land. In fact, just the opposite is true, which is why cities anxious to keep up with growth take whatever land they can get. "When you compare Florida to any other growth state," says Jack Schluckebier, "we're way down the list in terms of growth of population compared to growth of boundaries of cities in terms of land mass. The problem is, cities often confront the same demands for services whether someone is formally in their city or not. You could say you're not going to let folks outside your city use your services, but that's pretty difficult with parks and police and emergency services. So you end up with the worst of two worlds, which is having to plan for infrastructure but not being able to support it with the right population. There's fewer people paying the full tab." This is why, Schluckebier says, "the state should get into the heart of this like nobody's business. Annexation should be one of the centerpieces of any serious growth-management reform."

As it happens, Florida Governor Jeb Bush has just created a new Growth Management Study Commission, and asked it to look at the panoply of development issues affecting his state. The commission has not decided whether it will take up annexation reform or not. Schluckebier isn't optimistic. "The basic rules we operate under for annexation purposes have been established for almost 30 years," he says. "In that time there have been two or three growth management commissions that have come and gone, and they've managed to steer their way clear of dealing with that treacherous 'A' word." But you can only do that for so long. As state and local governments around the country are discovering, development pressures ultimately guarantee painful conflict over who can claim their benefits.

Thomas J. DiLorenzo  **NO**

The Myth of Suburban Sprawl

To millions of Americans, a house in the suburbs with a nice yard, garden, and a little open space is the American Dream. To environmentalists and urban planners, though, it is a nightmare. The invectives they use to describe suburbia reveal a visceral hatred of it:

Its critics have compiled a list of alleged disasters caused by suburban living that verges on the hysterical. They claim that it is responsible for profound environmental stress, intractable traffic congestion, expensive housing, loss of open space, the virtual destruction of U.S. cities, isolated lives, racial segregation, ugliness, destruction of wetlands and recreational areas, higher taxes, asthma among children, vehicular accidents, unemployment and poverty, destruction of the family farm, demise of the public schools, and, according to Sprawl Watch Clearinghouse, even the menacing spectacle of "neo-Nazi young people." Vice Pres. Gore has even stated that, in contrast to the calm serenity of, say, Manhattan traffic, driving in the suburbs is the root cause of "road rage."

Many of the problems the critics of suburbia are concerned with have been either greatly exaggerated or simply fabricated. Moreover, the proposed "solution" to these problems—centralized governmental planning of where people live and work and how they commute (i.e., regulatory sprawl) is bound to be economically inefficient, harmful to growth, and inherently inequitable.

Smart growth is the environmental movement's chosen euphemism for centralized governmental planning. The essential idea is that the free choices and careful lifestyle planning done by individual families in cooperation with the housing industry and local public officials are inherently "stupid" and socially destructive, whereas the coercive planning schemes favored by environmentalists and urban planners are "smart" and socially enlightened.

The "Smart Growth Network" is a coalition of environmental organizations, urban planners, and city politicians. The ultimate aim of the latter group is apparently to force people to move back into the metropolises where they can pay city, rather than suburban, taxes. It is a "bootleggers and Baptists" kind of coalition, to borrow economist Bruce Yandle's phrase that he used to describe the coalition in favor of alcohol prohibition in the 1920s. The Baptists favored prohibition for moral reasons, while the bootleggers wanted it for purely economic motives—it eliminated their competition. Similarly, the attack on suburbia is an important element of the secular "religion" of environmentalism, whereas urban politicians are in it for the (tax) money.

In order to correct all of the supposed inefficiencies of suburban development, smart growth proponents have proposed an ever-growing list of regulations, taxes, and myriad other governmental interventions. The charge that suburban development is economically inefficient ignores the most elementary of economic principles. Allocative efficiency means that, in competitive markets, resources tend to be used by those who value them most highly. Those people who value a particular parcel of land more than the current owners do, for example, will offer the owners a price they find too attractive to refuse. It is in this way that resources tend to be allocated to the most highly valued uses.

Smart growth advocates are using a bogus definition of "efficiency" that ignores the preferences of market participants (buyers and sellers), and simply reflects their personal preferences. Suburban residents who have moved out of the city clearly have decided that they are willing to endure more time spent in an automobile in exchange for a larger house with more open space. It is a trade-off they are willing to make. Smart growth advocates are expressing their disapproval of those choices and believe that their preferences are more important than those of the more than 100,000,000 Americans who live in the suburbs.

All the talk of "unplanned" suburban development is misleading. It is not a matter of planned vs. unplanned suburban development, but who is to do the planning. People who build or purchase homes in the suburbs do so as part of their work, lifestyle, and family planning. Developers who build houses and towns and shopping centers for them do so because that is what the people want. Thus, the profit motive provides powerful incentives for developers to cater to the preferences of consumers. Those who do the best job will prosper, while those who don't will fail. This is the very essence of economic efficiency and involves a great deal more planning (and more efficient planning, at that) than can be accomplished by any governmental planning board.

Some governmental policy actually fosters "sprawl." Examples include tax incentives that encourage businesses to locate in one place rather than another; minimum-lot zoning that artificially reduces land density; and governmental pricing of such services as water and electricity at average, rather than marginal, cost, artificially enhancing dispersed development. The latter can create nuisances, such as congestion, crowding, or environmental degradation, but these are inefficiencies that can be altered through privatization, tax and regulatory reform, or common-law remedies, without effectively eliminating the private suburban real estate market and replacing it with a bureaucratic, command-and-control, central planning scheme.

When smart growth advocates argue that suburban development imposes costs on cities by allegedly creating poverty and unemployment and harming public schools, they have their causation backwards. It is the destructive policies of the past generation of urban planners that have led to escalating crime, unemployment, and poverty in the cities as well as the decline of the public schools. The handiwork of urban planners over the past 30 years—and the heavy tax burdens that have accumulated to pay for all their schemes—has encouraged millions of Americans to leave the cities for the suburbs.

In his landmark book, The Federal Bulldozer, Martin Anderson documented in great detail how, as early as 1962, Federal urban renewal programs (in force since 1949) had been "a thundering failure." They forcibly displaced millions of Americans, seizing homes, businesses, and property—sometimes with no compensation. The process destroyed thousands of low-rent homes and squandered billions of tax dollars.

By 1963, more than 50,000 lower-income families had been evicted by Federal urban planners. Most were forced to find more expensive housing or live in government-subsidized housing projects that quickly turned into dilapidated, crime-ridden slums. Only half of these families received any kind of compensation for their property losses. Four times more housing units were destroyed by urban planners than were replaced, causing a housing crisis for the poor. Approximately 26,000 small businesses had their property "acquired" by the state. About one-fourth of them ended up going out of business altogether.

A case can be made that no city in the U.S. has been subjected to more urban planning over the past 35 years than Washington, D.C. The results have been disastrous and are undoubtedly the reason why thousands of former residents have migrated from the nation's capital to the nearby suburbs. This model of urban planning and social engineering now has the highest tax burden of any local government jurisdiction and, arguably, the worst public services.

Refuting Regulatory Rationales

Disappearing farms. One frequently cited rationale for smart growth regulation is that suburban development allegedly is eating up America's farmland, threatening the agriculture industry and even our ability to feed ourselves in the future. This purported market failure must be remedied by regulatory restrictions on suburban development.

The facts are that non-agriculture uses of land in the U.S.—cities, highways, railroads, airports—amount to just 3.6% (82,000,000 acres) of the total land, and cropland has remained virtually constant, at 24% of the U.S. land mass, since 1945. Over three-fourths of the states have more than 90% of their land in rural uses—including forests, cropland, pastures, wildlife reserves, and parks—and just 4.8% of the total land area of the U.S. is developed.

It is somewhat surprising that so much land remains devoted to agriculture, given the vast improvements in U.S. agricultural productivity during the last half-century. Today, the agricultural sector is approximately one and a half times more productive than it was 50 years ago. Thus, it is capable of producing more food on less land.

Though total agricultural land (not just that which is used to grow crops) is 20% less than it was in 1950, this is primarily a result of increased agricultural productivity, not sprawling suburbs. Moreover, the rate of loss of total agricultural land has significantly slowed in recent years, from a rate of 6.2% during the 1960s to 5.8% in the 1970s, five percent in the 1980s, and 2.7% in the 1990s. The U.S. Department of Agriculture's Economic Research Service concluded in 1997 that "losing farmland to urban uses does not threaten total cropland or the level of agricultural production which should be sufficient to meet food and fiber demand into the next century."

The main reason why even more agricultural land hasn't been disinvested is the massive governmental subsidies to agriculture, primarily in the form of Federal low-interest loans and grants, price supports, and quotas and tariffs on imported agricultural products. Because of these subsidies, there are many farm businesses that are inefficiently operated and that would not (and should not) survive were it not for the subsidies. There are too many farms and too many farmers if economic efficiency is the criterion to be applied.

The notion that the conversion of farmland to suburban development is necessarily harmful to nature and the environment is questionable. Geologist James R. Dunn has rejected the Sierra Club's assertion that suburbanization is "the biggest threat to America's wildlife heritage." He notes that, in many areas, abandoned farmland reforests naturally, and, when people move to the suburbs, they tend to plant abundant amounts of trees and vegetation, which often make better animal habitat than what was provided by farmland.

Traffic congestion. Politicians promoting smart growth usually claim to sympathize with suburban commuters who are annoyed by too much traffic congestion and propose to do something about it. However, the types of policies they advocate would increase traffic congestion and exacerbate air pollution.

Smart growth advocates do not want to build any more highways—in the cities or the suburbs. Their goal is to pack the population into the cities or more densely populated suburban areas. This may lead to a slight reduction in driving time, but, combined with a large percentage increase in population, the inevitable result is more traffic congestion, not less. In fact, urban planners in Portland, Ore., have openly stated that their objective is to increase traffic congestion so much and make life so miserable for that city's commuters that they will abandon their vehicles. "Congestion signals positive urban development," they announced in 1999.

In contrast, the U.S. Department of Transportation's Nationwide Transportation Survey shows that, as people and jobs have moved to the suburbs, commuting times decreased from an average of 22 minutes per commute in 1969 to 20.7 in 1995. Contrary to the impression most Americans have of the Los Angeles "commuting nightmare," the typical resident has just a 20-minute commute to one of myriad suburban employment locations.

Air pollution has also declined as America has suburbanized. Conversely, according to the Federal government's Roadway Congestion Index, urban areas with higher population densities have higher levels of traffic congestion and air pollution, contrary to what smart growth proponents would have us believe.

Soaring housing prices. The principal objective of smart growth advocates is to reduce significantly the supply of housing in the suburbs and to use the tax and regulatory powers of the state to force a segment of the population back into the cities. The effect of such a scheme on housing markets would be to slash the supply of housing in the suburbs, thereby making it more expensive there, while increasing the demand (and price) for urban housing. In addition, the myriad building code and other regulations that are proposed for urban areas would raise the cost of housing. The end result would be higher-priced housing in urban areas as well as in suburbia. Higher housing prices triggered by smart growth would effectively constitute a regressive tax on lower-income families, who can least afford the higher housing costs.

A variety of techniques are promoted ostensibly to control growth. States provide subsidies to local governments that grant property tax abatements to the owners of farms or purchase land and place it off-limits to development. Agricultural zoning that prohibits development altogether and minimum-lot zoning, including "superzoning" such as exists in parts of Marin County, Calif., where 60-acre lots are required, are also advocated. Moratoria on new connections to public utility systems and higher development charges, whereby developers are assessed hefty fees to subsidize local governmental budgets are other tools in the tinkers' toolboxes. Ecological hurdles such as environmental impact statements and lawsuits to protect "endangered" species such as the spotted owl or the kangaroo rat can be used to block development.

Mass transit. Another key element of the smart growth agenda is increased government subsidies for mass transit, particularly buses and light rail systems (i.e., streetcars). Though proposed in the name of economic efficiency, mass transit subsidies are among the most inefficient of all uses of taxpayer dollars.

Public transit ridership peaked during the World War II years and has declined by about two-thirds (from 23,000,000,000 trips annually to about 8,000,000,000) since that time, despite the tens of billions of dollars in government subsidies. Public transit's share of urban passenger miles has fallen from more than 30% in 1945 to barely two percent today. The free market worked quite efficiently as consumers chose to travel more by automobile and the auto industry accommodated them with better cars.

Smart growth advocates complain that automobile travel has been subsidized by the government and that their proposals seek to correct this government-induced distortion. While it is true that building the interstate highway system subsidized automobile travel, it is not at all clear that government policy has artificially stimulated automobile travel above what it would otherwise have been. Drivers have been paying heavy Federal and state gasoline taxes for decades, which tend to reduce the number of miles driven. Other governmental policies such as environmental and safety regulations have increased the price of cars and, thus, the cost of auto travel. It is impossible to know what kinds of roads might have been built had private entrepreneurs been given more leeway in building interstate highways, much as financier James J. Hill built a transcontinental railroad in the 19th century without a dime of government subsidy, not even land grants.

Government subsidies to public transit have been a futile, wasteful, and sometimes corrupt attempt to foil the efficiency of the marketplace by subsidizing less-efficient means of transportation, amounting to more than $155,000,000,000 since 1964. Despite this influx of funding, every U.S. public transit system with a rail element operates at a loss, according to the American Public Transit Association. In no city do riders pay even half the cost of their own transportation.

Mass transit not only costs more than automobile travel, it is slower. The average time spent commuting to work by car is 21 minutes, compared to an average 38-minute bus trip or 45 minutes by rail or subway. Public transit systems with a rail component even consume 22% more BTUs per person-mile than automobiles.

Monopoly Government

Smart growth policies are inherently undemocratic, because a key component of the overall strategy is the creation of governmental authorities in metropolitan areas vested with more-or-less-authoritarian land-use powers over entire regions. These governmental bodies are not referred to by smart growth advocates as monopolistic, of course. Euphemisms such as "consolidated," "metropolitan," or "regional" government are used instead.

Since 1925, the idea of monopoly government for metropolitan areas has been known by political scientists as the urban "reform tradition." The key elements, first championed by Pres. Woodrow Wilson, are a single government in every urban area, few elected officials in governments run mostly by unelected bureaucrats, no separation of powers within the government, and an exceptionally powerful chief executive.

The idea is to substitute the rule of experts for individual choice. Yet, in a metropolitan area with several competing governmental jurisdictions, if one imposes land-use or other policies that are not to the liking of a majority of the voting population, the result will be out-migration of population, industry, and the tax base to more favorable jurisdictions. Citizens' ability to "vote with their feet" imposes a degree of discipline on government. If one's objective is to have a government that is the servant, rather than master, of the people, decentralized metropolitan government is much more conducive to that end than is one large, monopolistic government that is mainly detached from electoral pressures.

There is much empirical support for this proposition in the economics literature. Writing in the National Tax Journal, for instance, David L. Sjoquist reported the results of an econometric study that concluded that "expenditures per capita in the central city fall as the number of jurisdictions in a metropolitan area increases."

Smart growth advocates persistently push for annexation, consolidation, and regional "tax-base sharing" that deprives citizens of the benefits of greater autonomy and creates an inherently inefficient and uncontrollable (by taxpayers) governmental system. Then again, that is apparently the idea for smart growth proponents, who want as little citizen interference with their plans as possible.

POSTSCRIPT

Should Municipal Governments Limit Urban Sprawl?

John Dellinger said, "smart growth," or anti-urban sprawl schemes, are limits on consumer choice, trampling on property rights.[1] Additionally, smart growth plans discriminate against newer and lesser well-off homeowners, who are forced to pay more for houses when restrictions on land use are the basis for skyrocketing property values.

Peter Gordon, a professor of planning and economics at the University of Southern California's School of Urban Planning and Development, argues that compact cities are a thing of the past, because businesses are starting to move to where their workers prefer to live[2] and people do not have to live next to where they work. Gordon adds that people are gaining their own sense of social capital in the suburbs, where traffic has subsided somewhat. Gordon says that it is really a matter of freedom to live where you want.

However, the U.S. Bureau of Census Data on Urbanized Areas defined urban sprawl as "the spreading out of a city and its suburbs over more and more rural land at the periphery of an urban area."[3] This means that rural land converts to urban landscape over time.

Although shopping center and recreational development are near suburban areas, sprawl is often blamed for several negative environmental and public health effects, with the key consequence being a greater dependence on automobiles.[4] This impact is lessened by the fact that many people still do live in cities because that is where they work.

There are five major criticisms of urban sprawl: (1) environmental and associated health impacts, (2) pollution, (3) traffic-related problems, (4) decreased physical activity, and (5) falling social capital.

Urban housing developments, dubbed "garden cities," were seen as the panacea to congested cities, where disease spread too easily and crime was often pervasive.[5] Pollution concerns became apparent after World War II, with the advent of pervasive automobile ownership.[6] Cities became infested with soot and industrial pollutants; however, as suburbs grew more prevalent, highway traffic out into the suburbs spread pollution there. Today, residences in suburban areas actually create more pollutants per person than those in cities because of more traffic. Traffic has also increased other problems beyond air pollution, such as more vehicle crashes and associated injuries to pedestrians. For individuals between 5 and 24 years old, vehicle collisions are a primary cause of death.[7] Death rates for those between 15 to 24 are 29.2 per hundred thousand, second only to those of the elderly 85 years and older, at 30.1 per hundred thousand.[8] Vehicle crashes are more of a threat to those in sprawling areas than for citizens who live in cities.[9]

Urban sprawl has also played havoc with many people's waist lines. There is a significant relationship among hypertension, overweight, and urban sprawl, according to leading journals in the area of health.[10] This is likely due to decreased walking in urban developments. Less walking, a result of this urban-sprawling development away from cities, creates a "car-centered culture," resulting in fewer health benefits and more weight gain than occurs for people who are living in urban environments.[11]

Julie Van Pelt, of the *Cascadia Scorecard 2006,* argues that urban sprawl is partly accountable for the weakening of social capital in the United States.[12] Neighborhoods in urban areas, which are dense, cultivate informal social connections among neighbors, whereas urban sprawl creates walls because of distance, and public spaces are transformed into private areas such as fenced backyards.

It seems urban sprawl has its pros and cons, but it is a phenomenon that will stay with us for the long term.

Notes

1. Amy Ridenour, "Smart Growth Legislation Discriminates Against Less Affluent Homeowners," National Center Blog, National Center for Public Policy Research (December 5, 2006). Accessed December 6, 2009, http://www.nationalcenter.org/2006/12/smart-growth-legislation-discriminates.html

2. Adrian Moore and Rick Henderson, "Plan Obsolescence: Urban Planning Skeptic Peter Gordon on the Benefits of Sprawl, the War Against Cars, and the Future of American Cities" (2008). Accessed December 6, 2009, http://reason.com/archives/1998/06/01/plan-obsolescence

3. U.S. Bureau of Census Data on Urbanized Areas, "What Is Sprawl?" (2009). Accessed December 5, 2009, http://www.sprawlcity.org/hbis/wis.html

4. Howard Frumkin, "Urban Sprawl and Public Health," *Centers for Disease Control and Prevention* May–June, http://www.cdc.gov/healthyplaces/articles/Urban20Sprawl20and20Public20Health20-20PHR.pdf

5. "Elements of Smart Growth: Health," *Smart Growth America.* Accessed December 6, 2009, http://www.smartgrowthamerica.org/health.html

6. Frumkin (2002).

7. "U.S. Death Statistic," The Disaster Center. Accessed December 6, 2009, http://www.disastercenter.com/cdc/

8. *Ibid.*

9. "Elements of Smart Growth: Health."

10. Bradford McKee, "As Suburbs Grow, so Do Waistlines," *New York Times* (September 4, 2003). Accessed February 7, 2008, http://www.nytimes.com/2003/09/04/garden/as-suburbs-grow-so-do-waistlines.html?pagewanted=1.

11. Barbara McCann and Reid Ewing. "Measuring the Health Effects of Sprawl: A National Analysis of Physical Activity, Obesity and Chronic Disease 2003," Smart Growth America, Surface Transportation Policy Project. Accessed December 6, 2009, http://www.smartgrowthamerica.org/report/HealthSprawl8.03.pdf

12. Julie Van Pelt, *Cascadia Scorecard 2006* (Seattle, WA: Sightline Institute, 2006).

ISSUE 14

Are School Boards Necessary?

YES: Rob Gurwitt, "Battered School Boards," *Governing* (May 2006)

NO: Matt Miller, from "First, Kill All the School Boards: A Modest Proposal to Fix the Schools," *The Atlantic* (January/February 2008)

ISSUE SUMMARY

YES: Rob Gurwitt argues that school boards, when working well, can help reform schools.

NO: Matt Miller argues that school boards are largely worthless and other reforms such as mayoral control should be pursued instead.

Both Gurwitt and Miller call our current school systems a failure and in need of reform. However, the authors see it in different ways.

Gurwitt tells the story of Gail Littlejohn, a retired executive of a publishing company, who found three other "likeminded civic do-gooders" and engineered a takeover of her local school board in Dayton, Ohio. Currently the board president, Littlejohn has pushed for reform.

Miller contends that school boards are not the answer because these governing bodies are rife with incompetence and union dominance, and they do nothing for the problem of financial inequality across school districts. Maybe it would be best, he argues, to "scrap them."

So, although Gurwitt writes that Littlejohn views school boards as platforms for reform, Miller argues that they should be scrapped for possible mayoral control, which would give the mayor the power to appoint school board members. Such mayor-controlled systems currently prevail in New York, Chicago, Oakland, and Boston. Miller contends that candidates for the school board otherwise have to raise a great deal of money for an unpaid job with a high volume of work. In balance, Miller quotes Francis Shen, a Harvard Kennedy School of Government researcher, who has studied the issue and who believes that mayoral control is certainly "not a silver bullet. It doesn't work everywhere."

Gurwitt's article quotes Don McAdams, who directs the Center for Reform of School Systems and who argues that school board elections are still important:

> This takes patience, the voters don't always send us ideal candidates, but democracy's a messy business. Where else is it working ideally? In

Washington? In the state capitals? I don't see anyone saying, "Let's replace Congress with an appointed body." We say, "This is democracy, this is the way it works."

Littlejohn, according to Miller's article, turned Dayton schools around, and she says the school board was key. It (1) brought more money into the classroom; (2) created an all-boys school and an all-girls school; (3) instituted a new reading program; and also (4) placed math and reading coaches in classrooms. Littlejohn attributes this change partly to her school board giving board members time to read documents, even taking the subject off the agenda if members did not have time to digest the material. Additionally, she made the superintendent give updates at every board meeting on how their reforms were progressing. She stressed that board members had to continually educate themselves in order to avoid micromanagement and reinforce their role in governance; and finally, board members could not use their position as a platform for higher office but had to promise never to run for any other office.

Miller, however, argues that local board control has kept schools from attracting research and development, because 15,000 fragmented boards across the country could not pool enough resources.

In addition to the issue of fragmentation, school board members are not prepared for the complexity and political nature of the board, Miller says, which drives quality candidates away from seeking positions in the first place. This lack of preparation for such complicated jobs has also pitted board members against the powerful teachers' unions—a losing position. Board members are at a disadvantage because of the unions' greater monetary power and capability to mobilize at the state and national levels when negotiating staffing changes, curriculum, compensation, and so on. Miller continues that "common-sense reforms," such as higher salaries in tough to recruit areas—special education, science, and math—are nonstarters because of unions.

Miller wants reform in the form of either more mayor control or strengthened national control by creating standards for grades 3–12 in core subjects, such as science, math, and reading, with more controversial subjects focused on later. He notes further that subsidies by the federal government only account for a paltry 9 percent of the education pie but should be increased to closer to 25–30 percent, bringing the per-pupil minimum funding up. Additionally, grants could be used as an incentive to make such reforms as connecting teacher pay to performance.

Gurwitt and Miller agree that schools are often failing. But does this mean we need more effective local control by school boards to give local citizens flexibility and voice over how their children are learning? Or does it mean abandoning elected school boards for more nationalized or mayoral control, which may be more efficient and equitable?

YES

Rob Gurwitt

Battered School Boards

Not long after Gail Littlejohn retired from an 18-year career as an executive with the Lexis-Nexis publishing company in Dayton, Ohio, she started getting calls from community groups hoping she'd join their boards. One group, which advocated vouchers as a cure for Dayton's chronically ailing school system, was especially persistent. Eventually, she agreed at least to read up on the city's schools. When she did, she was horrified.

Littlejohn discovered that Dayton ranked at the bottom of Ohio's 611 school districts. Test scores were abysmal, superintendents came and went, finances seemed out of control and the school board—like many of its counterparts in other cities—was derided as a squabble-prone holding pen for people trying to make their political name in town. Littlejohn decided this was the cause for her. She recruited a slate of three like-minded civic do-gooders, raised a great deal of money from the local business community and took over the school board. That was a bit over four years ago, and she has been its president ever since. The schools—although still in a state of academic emergency—have made measurable progress.

As sensible a step as Littlejohn's might sound, in the education world these days it's an unusual one. Pretty much everywhere you look, people unhappy with public schooling stand outside the system and pepper it with prescriptions for change: vouchers, charter schools, smaller schools, strict state standards, strict federal standards, regular assessment of pupils, regular assessment of teachers, market-based experiments, mayoral or state takeovers—the list of remedies is almost endless. The one idea that rarely seems to come up is using the school board—the official governing body of K–12 education all over America—as an engine of change. Yet, as Gail Littlejohn learned, that may be the simplest way to bring about significant improvement. Reformers have been stubbornly resistant to seizing the weapon that lies open to them. "When I first got on the board, none of the work I was familiar with focused on school boards as levers of change," comments Nancy Broner, a reform-minded school board member in Duval County (Jacksonville), Florida. "They're pretty much in the way most of the time, and you either tolerate them or get rid of them." The idea that school boards are irrelevant has been promoted by Chester E. Finn, the president of the market-oriented Fordham Foundation, who was assistant secretary of education in the Reagan administration. Three years ago, in his most widely quoted broadside, Finn wrote that "in the parts of

U.S. education that cause the greatest concern, namely cities large and small, today's typical elected local school board resembles a dysfunctional family." It's undeniable that policy decisions over the past couple of decades have made life almost impossibly difficult for many school boards. Their sway over the districts they govern has been curtailed at every turn. Congress, the Supreme Court, state legislatures, state boards of education, teachers' unions, state and federal courts, governors—all have put in place agreements and regulations that govern how schools and school districts are to function.

In some larger cities, such as Boston, Chicago, New York and Philadelphia, mayors or state commissions have simply brushed aside local school boards and taken over. Choice initiatives have placed schooling decisions in parents' hands and forced individual schools to compete for students. Finally, of course, the academic standards movement—begun in the states and federalized by No Child Left Behind—makes an end-run around school boards by requiring them to advance a set of educational goals picked for them by state and federal bureaucrats.

Harvard University political scientist William Howell wrote in a recent book that "school boards defend a status quo that is quickly slipping out of their grasp." Even the National School Boards Association, in publishing a riposte to its critics a few years ago, gave it the wistful title, "Do School Boards Matter?" Yet for all the assertions that the day of the school board has passed, a look around the country also raises the intriguing possibility that Gail Littlejohn and her colleagues on the Dayton board are not behind the times but right in tune with them. Elected reform slates have taken over in Dayton, St. Louis, and Portland, Oregon. Appointed boards in Philadelphia, Oakland, New York City and Boston have helped wring great improvement out of school systems given up for dead. In Florida's Duval County and North Carolina's Charlotte-Mecklenburg, elected boards are rewriting what they themselves do and how they operate so they can make similar changes to their school systems. And in New Orleans, the one city in the country with a chance to redesign its school system from scratch, the role of its school board—elected or appointed—is the subject of intense current debate. The effort to revive school boards as an instrument of change is being guided by Don McAdams, a school board member in Houston from 1990 to 2002, who now directs the Center for Reform of School Systems, and trains new school board members under a grant from the Los Angeles-based Broad Foundation. McAdams, who is probably involved with more urban school boards than anyone else in the country, argues that far from being irrelevant or impediments to reforming public education, boards—whether elected or appointed—are vital. "School districts are essential units of change," he says. "They're the ones that have to build civic capacity and sustain it over time." And if school districts are to play that role, the boards that run them have to lead the way. In the end, there really isn't much choice.

Staying Power

That's true largely because school boards are not going to give way to some other form of management anytime soon. School boards govern the overwhelming majority of the more than 15,000 school districts in America; they make up fully one-sixth of all the local governments in the country. Thomas Glass, a professor of educational leadership at the University of Memphis, points out that, with an average of seven or eight members on each, "that makes for an awful lot of elected officials. And how many elected officials have we ever eliminated in this country?"

School boards also retain, at least in the abstract, broad popular support. They are how Americans have been accustomed to seeing their school districts governed for the past century and the means through which parents and community members gain access to the school bureaucracy. "A key function of school boards," Howell says, "is to figure out how we effectively translate broad mandates so they can address the particular needs of the particular children we have in our community."

That, at least, is the ideal. In practice, it has been getting pretty ugly the past few years. There's the charge of aggravated assault against the president of the Paterson, New Jersey, school board, for instance, after he allegedly threw a ceramic mug at a fellow member. Or the shouting matches that have broken out on the North Kingstown, Rhode Island, board, leading in at least one instance to school officials requesting police help in escorting a board member from the room. The flight of black families from the Minneapolis public schools is being blamed on the chaos currently gripping the school board there. You can go around the country and find no shortage of similar instances.

Indeed, critics of school boards have a long and legitimate list of grievances. Turnout in school board elections is often quite low, making it easier for special interests—often groups with single-focus ideological agendas or factions interested mostly in steering contracts to themselves and their friends— to get candidates elected. In many places, the very nature of school-board politics seems to draw people with axes to grind, rather than disinterested civic leaders. "You see so many urban boards where board members are in conflict with the district," says the University of Memphis' Tom Glass. "They're supposed to be setting policy for the organization, but they themselves are in conflict with it."

Even when they are able to put ideology, partisanship and personal gain aside, today's school boards face a daunting set of challenges: federal laws on special education and the new assessment and racial reporting requirements imposed by No Child Left Behind; federal court decisions on the rights of religious groups and the need to accommodate students with disabilities; state laws setting academic standards, advancing charter schools and reshuffling school finances; negotiations on union contracts that govern pay scales, class sizes, teacher assessment, hiring and firing procedures. All of these fall into the laps of school board members. That's in addition to choosing and monitoring a superintendent, opening and closing schools, approving or disapproving charters, making decisions on buying or selling property, formulating and then trying to sell bond measures to the voters. As McAdams says, "Good governance is not easy; it is time-consuming even if your district is a high-performing one." Into this mix, we throw people who often have no background in finance, administration, consensus-building, political leadership or even education—all skills that the job of school board member practically demands. Only 18 states require some sort of training for new members, and even then it is often cursory or quickly forgotten in the hurly-burly of meetings and decision making. "It's a frightening spectacle," comments Howard Good, a former school board member who teaches journalism at SUNY-New Paltz. "You could argue that these are the people in charge of America's future, and they don't know why they're there or what they're doing once they are there. It's a close-up horror."

Consensus Approach

Which is what makes the story in Dayton so interesting. Dismayed by the strife, lack of focus and antagonistic relationship between school board members and school officials, Littlejohn decided not only to run for the board herself but to try to rebuild it. "One person couldn't drive reform," she says. "There had to be like-minded people on the board for some term of longevity."

By "like-minded," she did not mean people with the same recipe for fixing schools; she wanted colleagues interested in making the board function as a responsible public institution. "They had to have a track record of making good decisions," she says. "They had to support their own continuous learning—that is, they'd dig in and read about school reform. And they had to commit that they would not run for another public office. They had to really want to be a school board member." Combing Dayton's business, religious and higher-education communities, Littlejohn found three candidates who fit her bill of particulars. Campaigning as the "Kids First" team, they raised more than $120,000—an unheard-of amount for a Dayton school board election—and were swept into office in November 2001, defeating five other candidates.

Even before the election, Littlejohn and her group had begun meeting once a month with Don McAdams to talk about school reform and reforming board practices, and the sessions continued afterward. With four out of the seven board members, Littlejohn and her allies not only formed the board majority but also set the tone for how it would operate. They agreed that it was crucial to rebuild the board's public image by avoiding, as Littlejohn puts it, "all of the behaviors that detracted from getting business done: public embarrassment, not focusing on academic reform, spending most of your meeting fighting with people coming to speak from the public—anything that would have detracted from the image that we were about the business of academic reform."

They agreed to operate, as much as they could, by consensus: They agreed that any board member who wanted more time to study an issue could ask that it be removed from the agenda for a week or two. They instituted an update from the superintendent on reform progress at every meeting. And, perhaps most important, they agreed to undergo training aimed at reinforcing the board's governance role and eliminating micromanagement. "There is a different feeling there," says Tom Lasley, dean of the education school at the University of Dayton. "These are people who've said, 'We're here, we're staying here, we're not trying to go anywhere else, we believe in the schools, we're not trying to run for political office, and these are the priorities we're going to set.'"

The new board replaced the superintendent and entirely remade the district's finance office. It funneled more money to classroom instruction, created a new reading program, put math and reading coaches in classrooms and reconstituted low-performing schools. It created an all-girls school, an all-boys school and, with the University of Dayton, set up an academically rigorous high school that has begun attracting students who would otherwise have gone to private or charter schools.

The result of all this is that test scores in the district have begun to rise and, more important, there is a general sense among people who watch the schools closely that they are now in position to improve more. After a 2002 report saying that Dayton schools were in "crisis," for instance, the Council of the Great City Schools last year reported on their turnaround. "There are very few urban school districts any place in the country," the council's executive director commented at the time, "that have made the kind of progress in building the architecture for a good instructional system as the Dayton Public Schools."

No Silver Bullet

Similar changes, if less dramatic ones, have been taking place in other cities. Houston and St. Louis both have had reform-minded, consensus-oriented school boards for the past several years. In Portland, Oregon, where a combination of changing demographics, new state standards and reduced state funding all served to draw attention to a board that seemed manifestly incapable of dealing with the schools' problems, a political action committee led by five former school board presidents—and with the help of a coalition of business and civic leaders—helped sweep a new majority into place in 2002.

Admittedly, the electoral process is a dicey method of building a school board with the right set of skills to transform a troubled system. "With these school systems really needing reinvention and transformation, can cities by the electoral process elect the right portfolio of skills and experience, the right mix of people to serve together?" asks Cynthia Guyer, who runs the Portland Schools Foundation and who helped lead the effort to recruit reform candidates in 2002. "Portland has a lot of civic will to address these issues, but even here, it's really hard each year to find the right people who have that mix of skills, then to persuade the people you would want on a board to run for the office, serve in office, and work unpaid. And then you have to say, 'Oh, and you have to raise $25,000 or $50,000 and spend the next three months campaigning.'"

The political excesses of elected school boards around the country in recent years have been the principal factor driving some cities toward a radically different approach: direct mayoral control of the schools, with all or most of the board members serving by mayoral appointment. The mayors of Boston, Chicago, New York and Oakland have all put such systems in place. The Bring New Orleans Back Education Commission—the body charged by Mayor Ray Nagin with redesigning that city's school system—called early this year for an appointed board to oversee the radically redesigned system of school "networks" it envisions. It then backed off the idea of an appointed board in the face of intense political pressure, and now will say only that the system requires a "single, aligned governing body." But the commission's thinking was obvious: Given all the other problems a school board has to confront these days, and especially given the unique problems of New Orleans, electoral rivalry is one distraction the newly constituted board would be better off avoiding.

Mayoral control "is not a silver bullet," says Francis Shen, a researcher at Harvard's Kennedy School of Government who has studied the issue. "It doesn't work everywhere." But under the right circumstances—such as being able to appoint a majority of the board; having a city and school district that are coterminous; and having a mayor who actively wants to add education to his portfolio—Shen and his colleague, Brown University political scientist Kenneth Wong, have found that it makes a difference. "If the question is, over-all has this approach been positive for overall student achievement, we think the answer is yes," Shen says.

As promising as the system of mayoral control and appointment has shown itself to be in some cities, however, the fact still remains that the vast majority of school board members in America are elected, and will continue to be. So the question is whether an elected board, in a troubled urban system badly in need of reform, can do what is needed to redesign the system.

That is essentially the question that McAdams is trying to answer. With funding from the Broad Foundation, he is trying out his ideas in four districts: Charlotte-Mecklenburg, North Carolina; Duval County, Florida; Christina (Wilmington), Delaware; and Denver. All of them have elected school boards. For the past year, the members of these boards have gone through an intensive training process aimed at coming up with a "theory of action," a set of beliefs about what the board must do to create schools capable of turning out high-performing students regardless of income or race. "I can give you an analogy," says McAdams. "If you take a vacation in your car, there are lots of small things that are important: that the car is running well, that you have reservations, that you have a map. But the critical thing is, where are you going to go and why? Why do you want to go there?" The boards are now turning to debating which particular policies they will need to put in place to guide school administrators as they move forward.

The process has not always been easy. "We have a full range of belief systems on the board, from the far left to the far right and everything in between," says Kit Cramer, who sits on the Charlotte-Mecklenburg school board. "There are some who believe that by raising hell you can get things done and others who really want to work toward change. Most of our votes have gone the right way, but it's an ugly process. Unfortunately, we've become more the story than what we're doing." Even in Charlotte, though, the board has been able to agree on its core beliefs and to start drawing up new policies for district operations, academic performance and ways to grant more autonomy to schools performing at high levels.

The challenge for Charlotte-Mecklenburg, and for any school district with an elected board, is to be able to sustain reform efforts beyond the first blush of enthusiasm. Dayton learned this last November, when one of Gail

Littlejohn's allies was unseated by a union-backed candidate unhappy with the new board's priorities. Although Littlejohn still has a majority of backers, the election was a reminder that a reformist school board trying dramatic change risks being reined in abruptly.

Still, says McAdams, that is how the system works. "This takes patience," he argues. "The voters don't always send us ideal candidates, but democracy's a messy business. Where else is it working ideally? In Washington? In the state capitals? I don't see anyone saying, 'Let's replace Congress with an appointed body.' We say, 'This is democracy, this is the way it works.'"

Matt Miller

First, Kill All the School Boards

It wasn't just the slate and pencil on every desk, or the absence of daily beatings. As Horace Mann sat in a Leipzig classroom in the summer of 1843, it was the entire Prussian system of schools that impressed him. Mann was six years into the work as Massachusetts secretary of education that would earn him lasting fame as the "father of public education." He had sailed from Boston to England several weeks earlier with his new wife, combining a European honeymoon with educational fact-finding. In England, the couple had been startled by the luxury and refinement of the upper classes, which exceeded anything they had seen in America and stood in stark contrast to the poverty and ignorance of the masses. If the United States was to avoid this awful chasm and the social upheaval it seemed sure to create, he thought, education was the answer. Now he was seeing firsthand the Prussian schools that were the talk of reformers on both sides of the Atlantic.

In Massachusetts, Mann's vision of "common schools," publicly funded and attended by all, represented an inspiring democratic advance over the state's hodgepodge of privately funded and charity schools. But beyond using the bully pulpit, Mann had little power to make his vision a reality. Prussia, by contrast, had a system designed from the center. School attendance was compulsory. Teachers were trained at national institutes with the same care that went into training military officers. Their enthusiasm for their subjects was contagious, and their devotion to students evoked reciprocal affection and respect, making Boston's routine resort to classroom whippings seem barbaric.

Mann also admired Prussia's rigorous national curriculum and tests. The results spoke for themselves: illiteracy had been vanquished. To be sure, Prussian schools sought to create obedient subjects of the kaiser—hardly Mann's aim. Yet the lessons were undeniable, and Mann returned home determined to share what he had seen. In the seventh of his legendary "Annual Reports" on education to the Commonwealth of Massachusetts, he touted the benefits of a national system and cautioned against the "calamities which result . . . from leaving this most important of all the functions of a government to chance."

Mann's epiphany that summer put him on the wrong side of America's tradition of radical localism when it came to schools. And although his efforts in the years that followed made Massachusetts a model for taxpayer-funded schools and state-sponsored teacher training, the obsession with local control—not incidentally, an almost uniquely American obsession—still dominates U.S. education to this day. For much of the 150 or so years between

Mann's era and now, the system served us adequately: during that time, we extended more schooling to more people than any nation had before and rose to superpower status. But let's look at what local control gives us today, in the "flat" world in which our students will have to compete.

The United States spends more than nearly every other nation on schools, but out of 29 developed countries in a 2003 assessment, we ranked 24th in math and in problem-solving, 18th in science, and 15th in reading. Half of all black and Latino students in the U.S. don't graduate on time (or ever) from high school. As of 2005, about 70 percent of eighth-graders were not proficient in reading. By the end of eighth grade, what passes for a math curriculum in America is two years behind that of other countries.

Dismal fact after dismal fact; by now, they are hardly news. But in the 25 years since the landmark report *A Nation at Risk* sounded the alarm about our educational mediocrity, America's response has been scattershot and ineffective, orchestrated mainly by some 15,000 school districts acting alone, with help more recently from the states. It's as if after Pearl Harbor, FDR had suggested we prepare for war through the uncoordinated efforts of thousands of small factories; they'd know what kinds of planes and tanks were needed, right?

When you look at what local control of education has wrought, the conclusion is inescapable: we must carry Mann's insights to their logical end and nationalize our schools, to some degree. But before delving into the details of why and how, let's back up for a moment and consider what brought us to this pass.

130,000 Little Red Schoolhouses

Our system is, more than anything, an artifact of our Colonial past. For the religious dissenters who came to the New World, literacy was essential to religious freedom, enabling them to teach their own beliefs. Religion and schooling moved in tandem across the Colonies. Many people who didn't like what the local minister was preaching would move on and found their own church, and generally their own school.

This preference for local control of education dovetailed with the broader ethos of the American Revolution and the Founders' distrust of distant, centralized authority. Education was left out of the Constitution; in the 10th Amendment, it is one of the unnamed powers reserved for the states, which in turn passed it on to local communities. Eventually the United States would have 130,000 school districts, most of them served by a one-room school. These little red schoolhouses, funded primarily through local property taxes, became the iconic symbols of democratic American learning.

Throughout the late 19th and early 20th centuries, nothing really challenged this basic structure. Eventually many rural districts were consolidated, and the states assumed a greater role in school funding; since the 1960s, the federal government has offered modest financial aid to poorer districts as well. But neither these steps, nor the standards-based reform movement inspired by *A Nation at Risk,* brought significant change.

Many reformers across the political spectrum agree that local control has become a disaster for our schools. But the case against it is almost never articulated. Public officials are loath to take on powerful school-board associations and teachers' unions; foundations and advocacy groups, who must work with the boards and unions, also pull their punches. For these reasons, as well as our natural preference for having things done nearby, support for local control still lingers, largely unexamined, among the public.

No Problem Left Behind

Why is local control such a failure when applied to our schools? After all, political decentralization has often served America well, allowing decisions to be made close to where their impact would be felt. But in education, it has spawned several crippling problems:

No way to know how children are doing.   "We're two decades into the standards movement in this country, and standards are still different by classroom, by school, by district, and by state," says Tom Vander Ark, who headed the education program at the Bill and Melinda Gates Foundation from 1999 through 2006. "Most teachers in America still pretty much teach whatever they want."

If you thought President Bush's 2001 No Child Left Behind legislation was fixing these problems, think again. True, NCLB requires states to establish standards in core subjects and to test children in grades 3–8 annually, with the aim of making all students "proficient" by 2014. But by leaving standards and definitions of "proficiency" to state discretion, it has actually made matters worse. *The Proficiency Illusion,* a report released in October by the conservative Thomas B. Fordham Foundation, details how. "'Proficiency' varies wildly from state to state, with 'passing scores' ranging from the 6th percentile to the 77th," the researchers found:

> Congress erred big-time when NCLB assigned each state to set its own standards and devise and score its own tests . . . this study underscores the folly of a big modern nation, worried about its global competitiveness, nodding with approval as Wisconsin sets its eighth-grade reading passing level at the 14th percentile while South Carolina sets its at the 71st percentile.

The lack of uniform evaluation creates a "tremendous risk of delusion about how well children are actually doing," says Chris Cerf, the deputy chancellor of schools in New York City. That delusion makes it far more difficult to enact reforms—and even to know where reforms are needed. "Schools may get an award from their state for high performance, and under federal guidelines they may be targeted for closure for low performance," Vander Ark says. This happens in California, he told me, all the time.

Stunted R&D.   Local control has kept education from attracting the research and development that drives progress, because benefits of scale are absent.

There are some 15,000 curriculum departments in this country—one for every district. None of them can afford to invest in deeply understanding what works best when it comes to teaching reading to English-language learners, or using computers to develop customized strategies for students with different learning styles. Local-control advocates would damn the federal government if it tried to take on such things. Perhaps more important, the private sector generally won't pursue them, either. Purchasing decisions are made by a complex mix of classroom, school, and school board official. The more complicated and fragmented the sale that a company has to make, the less willing it is to invest in product research and development.

Incompetent school boards and union dominance.   "In the first place, God made idiots," Mark Twain once wrote. "This was for practice. Then He made School Boards." Things don't appear to have improved much since Twain's time. "The job has become more difficult, more complicated, and more political, and as a result, it's driven out many of the good candidates," Vander Ark says. "So while teachers' unions have become more sophisticated and have smarter people who are better-equipped and prepared at the table, the quality of school-board members, particularly in urban areas, has decreased." Board members routinely spend their time on minor matters, from mid-level personnel decisions to bus routes. "The tradition goes back to the rural era, where the school board hired the schoolmarm and oversaw the repair of the roof, looked into the stove in the room, and deliberated on every detail of operating the schools," says Michael Kirst, an emeritus professor of education at Stanford University. "A lot of big-city school boards still do these kinds of things." Because of Progressive-era reforms meant to get school boards out of "politics," most urban school districts are independent, beyond the reach of mayors and city councils. Usually elected in off-year races that few people vote in or even notice, school boards are, in effect, accountable to no one.

Local control essentially surrenders power over the schools to the teachers' unions. Union money and mobilization are often decisive in board elections. And local unions have hefty intellectual and political backing from their state and national affiliates. Even when they're not in the unions' pockets, in other words, school boards are outmatched.

The unions are adept at negotiating new advantages for their members, spreading their negotiating strategies to other districts in the state, and getting these advantages embodied in state and sometimes federal law as well. This makes it extraordinarily difficult for superintendents to change staffing, compensation, curriculum, and other policies. Principals, for their part, are compliance machines, spending their days making sure that federal, state, and district programs are implemented. Meanwhile, common-sense reforms, like offering higher pay to attract teachers to underserved specialties such as math, science, and special education, can't get traction, because the unions say no.

Financial inequity.   The dirty little secret of local control is the enormous tax advantage it confers on better-off Americans: communities with high property wealth can tax themselves at low rates and still generate far more dollars per pupil than poor communities taxing themselves heavily. This wasn't always the case: in the 19th century, property taxes were rightly seen as the fairest way to pay for education, since property was the main form of wealth, and the rich and poor tended to live near one another. But the rise of commuter suburbs since World War II led to economically segregated communities; today, the spending gap between districts can be thousands of dollars per pupil.

But local taxes represent only 44 percent of overall school funding; the spending gaps between states, which contribute 47 percent of total spending, account for most of the financial inequity. Perversely, Title I, the federal aid program enacted in the 1960s to boost poor schools, has widened the gaps, because it distributes money largely according to how much states are already spending.

What Would Horace Do?

I asked Marc Tucker, the head of the New Commission on the Skills of the American Workforce (a 2006 bipartisan panel that called for an overhaul of the education system), how he convinces people that local control is hobbling our schools. He said he asks a simple question: If we have the second-most-expensive K–12 system of all those measured by the Organization for Economic Cooperation and Development, but consistently perform between the middle and the bottom of the pack, shouldn't we examine the systems of countries that spend less and get better results? "I then point out that the system of local control that we have is almost unique," Tucker says. "One then has to defend a practice that is uncharacteristic of the countries with the best performance.

"It's an industrial-benchmarking argument," he adds.

Horace Mann wouldn't have used this jargon, but his thinking was much the same. In his time, the challenge was to embrace a bigger role for the state; today, the challenge is to embrace a bigger role for the federal government in standards, funding, and other arenas.

The usual explanation for why national standards won't fly is that the right hates "national" and the left hates "standards." But that's changing. Two Republican former secretaries of education, Rod Paige and William Bennett, now support national standards and tests, writing in *The Washington Post:* "In a world of fierce economic competition, we can't afford to pretend that the current system is getting us where we need to go." On the Democratic side, John Podesta, a former chief of staff to President Clinton and the current president of the Center for American Progress (where I'm a senior fellow), told me that he believes the public is far ahead of the established political wisdom, which holds that the only safe way to discuss national standards is to stipulate that they are "optional" or "voluntary"—in other words, not "national" at all.

Recent polling suggests he's right. Two surveys conducted for the education campaign Strong American Schools, which I advised in 2006, found that a majority of Americans think there should be uniform national standards. Most proponents suggest we start by establishing standards and tests in grades 3–12 in the core subjects—reading, math, and science—and leave more-controversial subjects, such as history, until we have gotten our feet wet.

According to U.S. Department of Education statistics, the federal government accounts for 9 percent, or $42 billion, of our K–12 spending. If we're serious about improving our schools, and especially about raising up the lowest, Uncle Sam's contribution must rise to 25 or 30 percent of the total (a shift President Nixon considered). Goodwin Liu, a University of California at Berkeley law professor who has studied school financing, suggests that a higher federal contribution could be used in part to bring all states up to a certain minimum per-pupil funding. It could also, in my view, fund conditional grants to boost school performance. For example, federal aid could be offered to raise teachers' salaries in poor schools, provided that states or districts take measures such as linking pay to performance and deferring or eliminating tenure. Big grants might be given to states that adopt new national standards, making those standards "voluntary" but hard to refuse. The government also needs to invest much more heavily in research. It now spends $28 billion annually on research at the National Institutes of Health, but only $260 million—not even 1 percent of that amount—on R&D for education.

What of school boards? In an ideal world, we would scrap them—especially in big cities, where most poor children live. That's the impulse behind a growing drive for mayoral control of schools. New York and Boston have used mayoral authority to sustain what are among the most far-reaching reform agendas in the country, including more-rigorous curricula and a focus on better teaching and school leadership. Of course, the chances of eliminating school boards anytime soon are nil. But we can at least recast and limit their role.

In all of these efforts, we must understand one paradox: only by transcending local control can we create genuine autonomy for our schools. "If you visit schools in many other parts of the world," Marc Tucker says, "you're struck almost immediately . . . by a sense of autonomy on the part of the school staff and principal that you don't find in the United States." Research in 46 countries by Ludger Woessmann of the University of Munich has shown that setting clear external standards while granting real discretion to schools in how to meet them is the most effective way to run a system. We need to give schools one set of national expectations, free educators and parents to collaborate locally in whatever ways work, and get everything else out of the way.

Nationalizing our schools even a little goes against every cultural tradition we have, save the one that matters most: our capacity to renew ourselves to meet new challenges. Once upon a time a national role in retirement funding was anathema; then suddenly, after the Depression, we had Social Security. Once, a federal role in health care would have been rejected as socialism; now, federal money accounts for half of what we spend on health care. We started down this road on schooling a long time ago. Time now to finish the journey.

POSTSCRIPT

Are School Boards Necessary?

"**H**ey hey, ho ho, one-man-rule has got to go!" chanted protesters in the middle of a monthly Stuyvesant High School board meeting in Lower Manhattan.[1] These protesters from the Campaign for Better Schools (CBS) are an alliance of community groups pushing the state legislature to curb the mayor's power over public schools. Following years of financial problems, poor administration, and falling academic performance, New York City changed from an elected school board to one appointed by the Mayor's office.[2]

The CBS contends that the newly mayoral-appointed school board, known as the Panel for Educational Policy, is only a "rubber stamp" for Mayor Bloomberg's guiding principles regarding schools.[3] Mayor Bloomberg's power is obvious because the panel usually votes unanimously with the administration ever since Mayor Bloomberg fired three members who indicated they would oppose a 2005 third-grade promotion policy.

However, Mayor Bloomberg contends that after the schools fell under his control, schools have prospered.[4] "We've cut $350 million from the bureaucracy and put it back into the classroom where it belongs," Dawn Walker, a Mayor Bloomberg spokeswoman, wrote in an e-mail. The administration

> created bonuses for high-performing teachers and principals; closed dozens of failing schools and opened 354 new ones, including 63 charter schools. We've created 66,000 new classroom seats. We've added 25 minutes to the school day—the equivalent of about 25 more school days a year, and we've cut school crime by 34 percent. Equally important, we've ended the disastrous policy of social promotion, which continued to put our students at a disadvantage by promoting them without them having mastered the basics.

More U.S. cities are considering ridding themselves of their school boards and are choosing instead to allow mayors to rule over what is in the classroom.[5] Milwaukee and Dallas, for example, are presently considering mayoral control of their city schools. A dozen major school systems, such as those in D.C., Boston, Chicago, and New York City, have a form of mayoral control already.

Today, a considerable majority of school systems still have elected school boards, most of which work out well.[6] Nearly 95 percent of the 14,500 school districts in the United States are presently supervised by elected school boards, which is not likely to change in the near future.

Arne Duncan, Secretary of Education, finds that "The ironic truth is that modern-day school boards evolved a century ago to control many of the abuses of mayoral control in earlier eras."[7] He notes that for 70 years, from 1850 until the 1920s, mayors normally expressed control over city schools. However, this arrangement had to change because mayors typically divvied out school board appointments by party allegiance and patronage. The Progressive Era saw this change when boards predominated, with the idea that they should be freed from politics.

As concerns school boards, Percy Bysshe Shelley said it well: "History is a cyclic poem written by time upon the memories of man."[8]

Notes

1. Phillisa Cramer, "Mayoral Control Critics Give School Board Literal-Rubber Stamps" (May 19, 2009). Accessed December 5, 2009, Gothamschools .com, http://gothamschools.org/2009/05/19/mayoral-control-critics-give-school-board-literal-rubber-stamps/

2. Angela Carella, "Should the Mayor Control the School Board?" (September 16, 2009). Accessed December 6, 2009, http://www.connpost.com/ci_13277813

3. Phillisa Cramer (2009).

4. Angela Carella (2009).

5. John Hechinger and Suzanne Sataline, "For More Mayors, School Takeovers Are a No-Brainer," *Wall Street Journal* (December 6, 2006). http://online .wsj.com/article/SB123682041297603203.html

6. Arne Duncan, "Education Secretary Arne Duncan: The Importance of Board and Mayor Partnerships." http://www.asbj.com/MainMenuCategory/ Archive/2009/October/Education-Secretary-Arne-Duncan-The-Importance-of-Board-and-Mayor-Partnerships.aspx

7. Arne Duncan (2009).

8. Percy Bysshe Shelley, "A Defence of Poetry" (1840). Accessed December 5, 2009, http://www.bartleby.com/27/23.html

ISSUE 15

Do Religious Groups Have a Right to Use Public School Facilities after Hours?

YES: Clarence Thomas, from Majority Opinion, *Good News Club et al. v. Milford Central School,* U.S. Supreme Court (June 11, 2001)

NO: David Souter, from Dissenting Opinion, *Good News Club et al. v. Milford Central School,* U.S. Supreme Court (June 11, 2001)

ISSUE SUMMARY

YES: Supreme Court Justice Clarence Thomas affirms the right of religious groups to use school facilities after the school day ends, maintaining that restricting such use is a violation of free speech rights.

NO: Supreme Court Justice David Souter, dissenting from the Court's opinion, contends that the use of school facilities by religious groups blurs the line between public classroom instruction and private religious indoctrination and therefore violates the Establishment Clause of the Constitution.

An Easter egg hunt on the White House lawn. Christmas as a national holiday. Prayers opening legislative sessions of state legislatures. If you were a judge and the above practices were challenged as being unconstitutional, how would you rule?

The First Amendment to the Constitution states that "Congress shall make no law respecting an establishment of religion, or prohibiting the free exercise thereof." Interpreting these words and applying them in particular cases has been exceedingly difficult for the courts. What, for example, does "respecting an establishment of religion" mean? Is any governmental involvement or support for religion, direct or indirect, small or great, barred by this phrase?

Although the courts have struggled to keep church and state separate, they have also recognized that it would be impossible to have an absolute prohibition on the celebration of religious values and holidays. Therefore, cases continue to be brought, challenging the courts to determine how the words of the Constitution and the standards of prior cases should be applied to the facts of each new case.

The clearest and most well known of the establishment-of-religion cases are the school prayer decisions. In 1963, in *School District of Abington Township, Pennsylvania, v. Schempp, 374* U.S. 203, the Supreme Court ruled that it was unconstitutional to require students to open the school day by reading biblical passages and reciting the Lord's Prayer. A year earlier, in *Engel v. Vitale,* 370 U.S. 421 (1962), the Supreme Court had ruled that public recitation of the New York Regent's Prayer in New York public schools was unconstitutional. This prayer read, "Almighty God, we acknowledge our dependence upon Thee, and we beg thy blessings upon us, our parents, our teachers, and our country."

Although banning prayer in the schools, the courts have upheld some questionable practices, such as Sunday closing laws and the loaning of secular textbooks to parochial schools. Yet they have struck down other statutes, such as a Kentucky law that required posting the Ten Commandments in the classroom (see *Stone v. Graham,* 101 S. Ct. 192, 1980). More generally, the Court has upheld prayers at the beginning of legislative sessions and tuition tax credits for parochial schools. Yet it has held unconstitutional statutes requiring a moment of silence in public schools (*Wallace v. Jaffree,* 105 S. Ct. 2479, 1985) and the teaching of "creation science" whenever evolution is taught (*Edwards v. Aguillard,* 107 S. Ct. 2573, 1987).

The many cases involving religion that have been considered by the Supreme Court in the past 30 years indicate that the task of defining precisely what role religion should have in government-sponsored activities is extraordinarily difficult. Religion has not been banned from public life. "In God We Trust" appears on U.S. coins, prayers are said at presidential inaugurations, Christmas is a national holiday, the lighting of the national Christmas tree at the White House is a newsworthy event, and tax exemptions are given to religious institutions. It is probably still accurate, as Supreme Court justice William O. Douglas once wrote, that "we are a religious people whose institutions presuppose a Supreme Being." It is also true, however, that many religious activities may not be sponsored by the government.

The following case is one of the most recent Supreme Court decisions to consider the intersection between the free exercise of religion and the establishment of religion. Justice Clarence Thomas finds that the plaintiff, the Good News Club, has as much a right as anyone else to use school grounds. Justice David Souter dissents.

YES

Clarence Thomas

Majority Opinion, *Good News Club v. Milford Central School*

JUSTICE THOMAS delivered the opinion of the Court.

This case presents two questions. The first question is whether Milford Central School violated the free speech rights of the Good News Club when it excluded the Club from meeting after hours at the school. The second question is whether any such violation is justified by Milford's concern that permitting the Club's activities would violate the Establishment Clause. We conclude that Milford's restriction violates the Club's free speech rights and that no Establishment Clause concern justifies that violation.

I

The State of New York authorizes local school boards to adopt regulations governing the use of their school facilities. In particular, N.Y. Educ. Law §414 (McKinney 2000) enumerates several purposes for which local boards may open their schools to public use. In 1992, respondent Milford Central School (Milford) enacted a community use policy adopting seven of §414's purposes for which its building could be used after school. Two of the stated purposes are relevant here. First, district residents may use the school for "instruction in any branch of education, learning or the arts." Second, the school is available for "social, civic and recreational meetings and entertainment events, and other uses pertaining to the welfare of the community, provided that such uses shall be nonexclusive and shall be opened to the general public."

Stephen and Darleen Fournier reside within Milford's district and therefore are eligible to use the school's facilities as long as their proposed use is approved by the school. Together they are sponsors of the local Good News Club, a private Christian organization for children ages 6 to 12. Pursuant to Milford's policy, in September 1996 the Fourniers submitted a request to Dr. Robert McGruder, interim superintendent of the district, in which they sought permission to hold the Club's weekly afterschool meetings in the school cafeteria. The next month, McGruder formally denied the Fourniers' request on the grounds that the proposed use—to have "a fun time of singing songs, hearing a Bible lesson and memorizing scripture"—was "the equivalent of religious worship." According to McGruder, the community use policy, which prohibits use "by any individual or organization for religious purposes," foreclosed the Club's activities.

From Supreme Court of the United States, June 11, 2001.

In response to a letter submitted by the Club's counsel, Milford's attorney requested information to clarify the nature of the Club's activities. The Club sent a set of materials used or distributed at the meetings and the following description of its meeting:

"The Club opens its session with Ms. Fournier taking attendance. As she calls a child's name, if the child recites a Bible verse the child receives a treat. After attendance, the Club sings songs. Next Club members engage in games that involve, *inter alia,* learning Bible verses. Ms. Fournier then relates a Bible story and explains how it applies to Club members' lives. The Club closes with prayer. Finally, Ms. Fournier distributes treats and the Bible verses for memorization."

McGruder and Milford's attorney reviewed the materials and concluded that "the kinds of activities proposed to be engaged in by the Good News Club were not a discussion of secular subjects such as child rearing, development of character and development of morals from a religious perspective, but were in fact the equivalent of religious instruction itself." In February 1997, the Milford Board of Education adopted a resolution rejecting the Club's request to use Milford's facilities "for the purpose of conducting religious instruction and Bible study."

In March 1997, petitioners, the Good News Club, Ms. Fournier, and her daughter Andrea Fournier (collectively, the Club), filed an action under 42 U.S.C. §1983 against Milford in the United States District Court for the Northern District of New York. The Club alleged that Milford's denial of its application violated its free speech rights under the First and Fourteenth Amendments, its right to equal protection under the Fourteenth Amendment, and its right to religious freedom under the Religious Freedom Restoration Act of 1993, 107 Stat. 1488, 42 U.S.C. §2000bb *et seq.*

The Club moved for a preliminary injunction to prevent the school from enforcing its religious exclusion policy against the Club and thereby to permit the Club's use of the school facilities. On April 14, 1997, the District Court granted the injunction. The Club then held its weekly afterschool meetings from April 1997 until June 1998 in a high school resource and middle school special education room.

In August 1998, the District Court vacated the preliminary injunction and granted Milford's motion for summary judgment. 21 F. Supp. 2d 147 (NDNY 1998). The court found that the Club's "subject matter is decidedly religious in nature, and not merely a discussion of secular matters from a religious perspective that is otherwise permitted under [Milford's] use policies." Because the school had not permitted other groups that provided religious instruction to use its limited public forum, the court held that the school could deny access to the Club without engaging in unconstitutional viewpoint discrimination. The court also rejected the Club's equal protection claim.

The Club appealed, and a divided panel of the United States Court of Appeals for the Second Circuit affirmed. 202 F. 3d 502 (2000). First, the court rejected the Club's contention that Milford's restriction against allowing religious instruction in its facilities is unreasonable. Second, it held that, because the subject matter of the Club's activities is "quintessentially religious," and the activities "fall outside the bounds of pure 'moral and character development,'" Milford's policy of excluding the Club's meetings was constitutional subject discrimination, not unconstitutional viewpoint discrimination. Judge Jacobs filed a dissenting opinion in which he concluded that the school's restriction did constitute viewpoint discrimination under *Lamb's Chapel v. Center Moriches Union Free School Dist.*, 508 U.S. 384 (1993).

There is a conflict among the Courts of Appeals on the question of whether speech can be excluded from a limited public forum on the basis of the religious nature of the speech. Compare *Gentala v. Tucson,* 244 F. 3d 1065 (CA9 2001) (en banc) (holding that a city properly refused National Day of Prayer organizers' application to the city's civic events fund for coverage of costs for city services); *Campbell v. St. Tammany's School Bd.,* 206 F. 3d 482 (CA5 2000) (holding that a school's policy against permitting religious instruction in its limited public forum did not constitute viewpoint discrimination), cert. pending, No. 00-1194; *Bronx Household of Faith v. Community School Dist. No. 10,* 127 F. 3d 207 (CA2 1997) (concluding that a ban on religious services and instruction in the limited public forum was constitutional), with *Church on the Rock v. Albuquerque,* 84 F. 3d 1273 (CA10 1996) (holding that a city's denial of permission to show the film *Jesus* in a senior center was unconstitutional viewpoint discrimination); and *Good News/Good Sports Club v. School Dist. of Ladue,* 28 F. 3d 1501 (CA8 1994) (holding unconstitutional a school use policy that prohibited Good News Club from meeting during times when the Boy Scouts could meet). We granted certiorari to resolve this conflict. 531 U.S. 923 (2000).

II

The standards that we apply to determine whether a State has unconstitutionally excluded a private speaker from use of a public forum depend on the nature of the forum. See *Perry Ed. Assn. v. Perry Local Educators' Assn.,* 460 U.S. 37, 44 (1983). If the forum is a traditional or open public forum, the State's restrictions on speech are subject to stricter scrutiny than are restrictions in a limited public forum. *Id.,* at 45–46. We have previously declined to decide whether a school district's opening of its facilities pursuant to N.Y. Educ. Law §414 creates a limited or a traditional public forum. See *Lamb's Chapel, supra,* at 391–392. Because the parties have agreed that Milford created a limited public forum when it opened its facilities in 1992, we need not resolve the issue here. Instead, we simply will assume that Milford operates a limited public forum.

When the State establishes a limited public forum, the State is not required to and does not allow persons to engage in every type of speech. The State may be justified "in reserving [its forum] for certain groups or for the discussion of certain topics." *Rosenberger v. Rector and Visitors of Univ. of Va.,* 515 U.S. 819, 829 (1995); see also *Lamb's Chapel, supra,* at 392–393. The State's power to restrict speech, however, is not without limits. The restriction must not discriminate against speech on the basis of viewpoint, *Rosenberger, supra,* at 829, and the restriction must be "reasonable in light of the purpose served by the forum," *Cornelius v. NAACP Legal Defense & Ed. Fund, Inc.*, 473 U.S. 788, 806 (1985).

III

Applying this test, we first address whether the exclusion constituted viewpoint discrimination. We are guided in our analysis by two of our prior opinions, *Lamb's Chapel* and *Rosenberger.* In *Lamb's Chapel,* we held that a school district violated the Free Speech Clause of the First Amendment when it excluded a private group from presenting films at the school based solely on the films' discussions of family values from a religious perspective. Likewise, in *Rosenberger,* we held that a university's refusal to fund a student publication because the publication addressed issues from a religious perspective violated the Free Speech Clause. Concluding that Milford's exclusion of the Good News Club based on its religious nature is indistinguishable from the exclusions in these cases, we hold that the exclusion constitutes viewpoint discrimination. Because the restriction is viewpoint discriminatory, we need not decide whether it is unreasonable in light of the purposes served by the forum.

Milford has opened its limited public forum to activities that serve a variety of purposes, including events "pertaining to the welfare of the community." Milford interprets its policy to permit discussions of subjects such as child rearing, and of "the development of character and morals from a religious perspective." Brief for Appellee in No. 98-9494 (CA2), p. 6. For example, this policy would allow someone to use Aesop's Fables to teach children moral values. Additionally, a group could sponsor a debate on whether there should be a constitutional amendment to permit prayer in public schools, and the Boy Scouts could meet "to influence a boy's character, development and spiritual growth." In short, any group that "promote[s] the moral and character development of children" is eligible to use the school building.

Just as there is no question that teaching morals and character development to children is a permissible purpose under Milford's policy, it is clear that the Club teaches morals and character development to children. For example, no one disputes that the Club instructs children to overcome feelings of jealousy, to treat others well regardless of how they treat the children, and to be obedient, even if it does so in a nonsecular way. Nonetheless, because Milford found the Club's activities to be religious in nature—"the equivalent of religious instruction itself," 202 F. 3d, at 507—it excluded the Club from use of its facilities.

Applying *Lamb's Chapel*,[1] we find it quite clear that Milford engaged in viewpoint discrimination when it excluded the Club from the afterschool forum. In *Lamb's Chapel,* the local New York school district similarly had adopted §414's "social, civic or recreational use" category as a permitted use in its limited public forum. The district also prohibited use "by any group for religious purposes." 508 U.S., at 387. Citing this prohibition, the school district excluded a church that wanted to present films teaching family values from a Christian perspective. We held that, because the films "no doubt dealt with a subject otherwise permissible" under the rule, the teaching of family values, the district's exclusion of the church was unconstitutional viewpoint discrimination. *Id.*, at 394.

Like the church in *Lamb's Chapel* the Club seeks to address a subject otherwise permitted under the rule, the teaching of morals and character, from a religious standpoint. Certainly, one could have characterized the film presentations in *Lamb's Chapel* as a religious use, as the Court of Appeals did, *Lamb's Chapel v. Center Moriches Union Free School Dist.*, 959 F. 2d 381, 388–389 (CA2 1992). And one easily could conclude that the films' purpose to instruct that "'society's slide toward humanism . . . can only be counterbalanced by a loving home where Christian values are instilled from an early age,'" *id.*, at 384, was "quintessentially religious," 202 F. 3d, at 510. The only apparent difference between the activity of Lamb's Chapel and the activities of the Good News Club is that the Club chooses to teach moral lessons from a Christian perspective through live storytelling and prayer, whereas Lamb's Chapel taught lessons through films. This distinction is inconsequential. Both modes of speech use a religious viewpoint. Thus, the exclusion of the Good News Club's activities, like the exclusion of Lamb's Chapel's films, constitutes unconstitutional viewpoint discrimination.

Our opinion in *Rosenberger* also is dispositive. In *Rosenberger,* a student organization at the University of Virginia was denied funding for printing expenses because its publication, *Wide Awake,* offered a Christian viewpoint. Just as the Club emphasizes the role of Christianity in students' morals and character, *Wide Awake* "'challenge[d] Christians to live, in word and deed, according to the faith they proclaim and . . . encourage[d] students to consider what a personal relationship with Jesus Christ means.'" 515 U.S., at 826. Because the university "select[ed] for disfavored treatment those student journalistic efforts with religious editorial viewpoints," we held that the denial of funding was unconstitutional. *Id.*, at 831. Although in *Rosenberger* there was no prohibition on religion as a subject matter, our holding did not rely on this factor. Instead, we concluded simply that the university's denial of funding to print *Wide Awake* was viewpoint discrimination, just as the school district's refusal to allow Lamb's Chapel to show its films was viewpoint discrimination. Given the obvious religious content of *Wide Awake,* we cannot say that the Club's activities are any more "religious" or deserve any less First Amendment protection than did the publication of *Wide Awake* in *Rosenberger.*

Despite our holdings in *Lamb's Chapel* and *Rosenberger,* the Court of Appeals, like Milford, believed that its characterization of the Club's activities as religious in nature warranted treating the Club's activities as different in kind from the other activities permitted by the school. See 202 F. 3d, at 510 (the Club "is doing something other than simply teaching moral values"). The "Christian viewpoint" is unique, according to the court, because it contains an "additional layer" that other kinds of viewpoints do not. *Id.*, at 509. That is, the Club "is focused on teaching children how to cultivate their relationship with God through Jesus Christ," which it characterized as "quintessentially religious." *Id.*, at 510. With these observations, the court concluded that, because the Club's activities "fall outside the bounds of pure 'moral and character development,'" the exclusion did not constitute viewpoint discrimination. *Id.*, at 511.

We disagree that something that is "quintessentially religious" or "decidedly religious in nature" cannot also be characterized properly as the teaching of morals and character development from a particular viewpoint. See 202 F. 3d, at 512 (Jacobs, J., dissenting) ("[W]hen the subject matter is morals and character, it is quixotic to attempt a distinction between religious viewpoints and religious subject matters"). What matters for purposes of the Free Speech Clause is that we can see no logical difference in kind between the invocation of Christianity by the Club and the invocation of teamwork, loyalty, or patriotism by other associations to provide a foundation for their lessons. It is apparent that the unstated principle of the Court of Appeals' reasoning is its conclusion that any time religious instruction and prayer are used to discuss morals and character, the discussion is simply not a "pure" discussion of those issues. According to the Court of Appeals, reliance on Christian principles taints moral and character instruction in a way that other foundations for thought or viewpoints do not. We, however, have never reached such a conclusion. Instead, we reaffirm our holdings in *Lamb's Chapel* and *Rosenberger* that speech discussing otherwise permissible subjects cannot be excluded from a limited public forum on the ground that the subject is discussed from a religious viewpoint. Thus, we conclude that Milford's exclusion of the Club from use of the school, pursuant to its community use policy, constitutes impermissible viewpoint discrimination.

IV

Milford argues that, even if its restriction constitutes viewpoint discrimination, its interest in not violating the Establishment Clause outweighs the Club's interest in gaining equal access to the school's facilities. In other words, according to Milford, its restriction was required to avoid violating the Establishment Clause. We disagree.

We have said that a state interest in avoiding an Establishment Clause violation "may be characterized as compelling," and therefore may justify content-based discrimination. *Widmar v. Vincent,* 454 U.S. 263, 271 (1981). However, it is not clear whether a State's interest in avoiding an Establishment Clause violation would justify viewpoint discrimination. See *Lamb's Chapel*, 508 U.S., at 394–395 (noting the suggestion in *Widmar* but ultimately not finding an Establishment Clause problem). We need not, however, confront the issue in this case, because we conclude that the school has no valid Establishment Clause interest.

We rejected Establishment Clause defenses similar to Milford's in two previous free speech cases, *Lamb's Chapel* and *Widmar*. In particular, in *Lamb's Chapel*, we explained that "[t]he showing of th[e] film series would not have been during school hours, would not have been sponsored by the school, and would have been open to the public, not just to church members." 508 U.S., at 395. Accordingly, we found that "there would have been no realistic danger that the community would think that the District was endorsing religion or any particular creed." *Ibid.* Likewise, in *Widmar,* where the university's forum was already available to other groups, this Court concluded that there was no Establishment Clause problem. 454 U.S., at 272–273, and n. 13.

The Establishment Clause defense fares no better in this case. As in *Lamb's Chapel,* the Club's meetings were held after school hours, not sponsored by the school, and open to any student who obtained parental consent, not just to Club members. As in *Widmar,* Milford made its forum available to other organizations. The Club's activities are materially indistinguishable from those in *Lamb's Chapel* and *Widmar.* Thus, Milford's reliance on the Establishment Clause is unavailing.

Milford attempts to distinguish *Lamb's Chapel* and *Widmar* by emphasizing that Milford's policy involves elementary school children. According to Milford, children will perceive that the school is endorsing the Club and will feel coercive pressure to participate, because the Club's activities take place on school grounds, even though they occur during nonschool hours. This argument is unpersuasive.

First, we have held that "a significant factor in upholding governmental programs in the face of Establishment Clause attack is their *neutrality* towards religion." *Rosenberger,* 515 U.S., at 839 (emphasis added). See also *Mitchell v. Helms,* 530 U.S. 793 (2000) (slip op., at 10) (plurality opinion) ("In distinguishing between indoctrination that is attributable to the State and indoctrination that is not, [the Court has] consistently turned to the principle of neutrality, upholding aid that is offered to a broad range of groups or persons without regard to their religion" (emphasis added)); (O'CONNOR, J., concurring in judgment) ("[N]eutrality is an important reason for upholding government-aid programs against Establishment Clause challenges"). Milford's implication that granting access to the Club would do damage to the neutrality principle defies logic. For the "guarantee of neutrality is respected, not offended, when the government, following neutral criteria and evenhanded policies, extends benefits to recipients whose ideologies and viewpoints, including religious ones, are broad and diverse." *Rosenberger, supra,* at 839. The Good News Club seeks nothing more than to be treated neutrally and given access to speak about the same topics as are other groups. Because allowing the Club to speak on school grounds would ensure neutrality, not threaten it, Milford faces an uphill battle in arguing that the Establishment Clause compels it to exclude the Good News Club.

Second, to the extent we consider whether the community would feel coercive pressure to engage in the Club's activities, cf. *Lee v. Weisman,* 505 U.S. 577, 592–593 (1992), the relevant community would be the parents, not the elementary school children. It is the parents who choose whether their children will attend the Good News Club meetings. Because the children cannot attend without their parents' permission, they cannot be coerced into engaging in the Good News Club's religious activities. Milford does not suggest that the parents of elementary school children would be confused about whether the school was endorsing religion. Nor do we believe that such an argument could be reasonably advanced.

Third, whatever significance we may have assigned in the Establishment Clause context to the suggestion that elementary school children are more impressionable than adults, cf., *e.g., Lee, supra,* at 592; *School Dist. of Grand Rapids v. Ball,* 473 U.S. 373, 390 (1985) (stating that "symbolism of a union between church and state is most likely to influence children of tender years, whose experience is limited and whose beliefs consequently are the function of environment as much as of free and voluntary choice"), we have never extended our Establishment Clause jurisprudence to foreclose private religious conduct during nonschool hours merely because it takes place on school premises where elementary school children may be present.

None of the cases discussed by Milford persuades us that our Establishment Clause jurisprudence has gone this far. For example, Milford cites *Lee v. Weisman* for the proposition that "there are heightened concerns with protecting freedom of conscience from subtle coercive pressure in the elementary and secondary public schools," 505 U.S., at 592. In *Lee,* however, we concluded that attendance at the graduation exercise was obligatory. *Id.,* at 586. See also *Santa Fe Independent School Dist. v. Doe,* 530 U.S. 290 (2000) (holding the school's policy of permitting prayer at football games unconstitutional where the activity took place during a school-sponsored event and not in a public forum). We did not place independent significance on the fact that the graduation exercise might take place on school premises, *Lee, supra,* at 583. Here, where the school facilities are being used for a nonschool function and there is no government sponsorship of the Club's activities, *Lee* is inapposite.

Equally unsupportive is *Edwards v. Aguillard,* 482 U.S. 578 (1987), in which we held that a Louisiana law that proscribed the teaching of evolution as part of the public school curriculum, unless accompanied by a lesson on creationism, violated the Establishment Clause. In *Edwards,* we mentioned that students are susceptible to pressure in the classroom, particularly given their possible reliance on teachers as role models. See *id.,* at 584. But we did not discuss this concern in our application of the law to the facts. Moreover, we did note that mandatory attendance requirements meant that State advancement of religion in a school would be particularly harshly felt by impressionable students. But we did not suggest that, when the school was not actually advancing religion, the impressionability of students would be relevant to the Establishment Clause issue. Even if *Edwards* had articulated the principle Milford believes it did, the facts in *Edwards* are simply too remote from those here to give the principle any weight. *Edwards* involved the content of the curriculum taught by state teachers during the school-day to children required to attend. Obviously, when individuals who are not schoolteachers are giving lessons after school to children permitted to attend only with parental consent, the concerns expressed in *Edwards* are not present.

Fourth, even if we were to consider the possible misperceptions by school-children in deciding whether Milford's permitting the Club's activities would violate the Establishment Clause, the facts of this case simply do not support Milford's conclusion. There is no evidence that young children are permitted to loiter outside classrooms after the schoolday has ended. Surely even young children are aware of events for which their parents must sign permission forms. The meetings were held in a combined high school resource room and middle school special education room, not in an elementary school classroom. The instructors are not schoolteachers. And the children in the group are not all the same age as in the normal classroom setting; their ages range from 6 to 12. In sum, these circumstances simply do not support the theory that small children would perceive endorsement here.

Finally, even if we were to inquire into the minds of schoolchildren in this case, we cannot say the danger that children would misperceive the endorsement of religion is any greater than the danger that they would perceive a hostility toward the religious viewpoint if the Club were excluded from the public forum. This concern is particularly acute given the reality that Milford's building is not used only for elementary school children. Students, from kindergarten through the 12th grade, all attend school in the same building. There may be as many, if not more, upperclassmen than elementary school children who occupy the school after hours. For that matter, members of the public writ large are permitted in the school after hours pursuant to the community use policy. Any bystander could conceivably be aware of the school's use policy and its exclusion of the Good News Club, and could suffer as much from viewpoint discrimination as elementary school children could suffer from perceived endorsement. Cf. *Rosenberger,* 515 U.S., at 835–836 (expressing the concern that viewpoint discrimination can chill individual thought and expression).

We cannot operate, as Milford would have us do, under the assumption that any risk that small children would perceive endorsement should counsel in favor of excluding the Club's religious activity. We decline to employ Establishment Clause jurisprudence using a modified heckler's veto, in which a group's religious activity can be proscribed on the basis of what the youngest members of the audience might misperceive. Cf. *Capitol Square Review and Advisory Bd. v. Pinette,* 515 U.S. 753, 779–780 (1995) (O'CONNOR, J., concurring in part and concurring in judgment) ("[B]ecause our concern is with the political community writ large, the endorsement inquiry is *not about the perceptions of particular individuals* or saving isolated nonadherents from . . . discomfort. . . . It is for this reason that the reasonable observer in the endorsement inquiry must be deemed aware of the history and context of the community and forum in which the religious [speech takes place]" (emphasis added)). There are countervailing constitutional concerns related to rights of other individuals in the community. In this case, those countervailing concerns are the free speech rights of the Club and its members. Cf. *Rosenberger, supra,* at 835 ("Vital First Amendment speech principles are at stake here"). And, we have already found that those rights have been violated, not merely perceived to have been violated, by the school's actions toward the Club.

We are not convinced that there is any significance in this case to the possibility that elementary school children may witness the Good News Club's activities on school premises, and therefore we can find no reason to depart from our holdings in *Lamb's Chapel* and *Widmar.* Accordingly, we conclude that permitting the Club to meet on the school's premises would not have violated the Establishment Clause.

V

When Milford denied the Good News Club access to the school's limited public forum on the ground that the Club was religious in nature, it discriminated against the Club because of its religious viewpoint in violation of the Free Speech Clause of the First Amendment. Because Milford has not raised a valid

Establishment Clause claim, we do not address the question whether such a claim could excuse Milford's viewpoint discrimination.

The judgment of the Court of Appeals is reversed, and the case is remanded for further proceedings consistent with this opinion.

It is so ordered.

Note

1. We find it remarkable that the Court of Appeals majority did not cite *Lamb's Chapel,* despite its obvious relevance to the case. We do not necessarily expect a court of appeals to catalog every opinion that reverses one of its precedents. Nonetheless, this oversight is particularly incredible because the majority's attention was directed to it at every turn. See, *e.g.,* 202 F. 3d 502, 513 (CA2 2000) (JACOBS, J., dissenting) ("I cannot square the majority's analysis in this case with *Lamb's Chapel*"); 21 F. Supp. 2d, at 150; App. O9-O11 (District Court stating "that *Lamb's Chapel* and *Rosenberger* pinpoint the critical issue in this case"); Brief for Appellee in No. 98-9494 (CA2) at 36–39; Brief for Appellants in No. 98-9494 (CA2), pp. 15, 36.

 **NO**

Dissenting Opinion of David Souter

J USTICE SOUTER, with whom JUSTICE GINSBURG joins, dissenting.

The majority rules on two issues. First, it decides that the Court of Appeals failed to apply the rule in *Lambs's Chapel v. Center Moriches Union Free School Dist.*, 508 U.S. 384 (1993), which held that the government may not discriminate on the basis of viewpoint in operating a limited public forum. The majority applies that rule and concludes that Milford violated *Lambs's Chapel* in denying Good News the use of the school. The majority then goes on to determine that it would not violate the Establishment Clause of the First Amendment for the Milford School District to allow the Good News Club to hold its intended gatherings of public school children in Milford's elementary school. The majority is mistaken on both points. The Court of Appeals unmistakably distinguished this case from *Lamb's Chapel,* though not by name, and accordingly affirmed the application of a policy, unchallenged in the District Court, that Milford's public schools may not be used for religious purposes. As for the applicability of the Establishment Clause to the Good News Club's intended use of Milford's school, the majority commits error even in reaching the issue, which was addressed neither by the Court of Appeals nor by the District Court. I respectfully dissent.

I

Lamb's Chapel, a case that arose (as this one does) from application of N.Y. Educ. Law §414 (McKinney 2000) and local policy implementing it, built on the accepted rule that a government body may designate a public forum subject to a reasonable limitation on the scope of permitted subject matter and activity, so long as the government does not use the forum-defining restrictions to deny expression to a particular viewpoint on subjects open to discussion. Specifically, *Lamb's Chapel* held that the government could not "permit school property to be used for the presentation of all views about family issues and child rearing except those dealing with the subject matter from a religious standpoint." 508 U.S., at 393–394.

This case, like *Lamb's Chapel,* properly raises no issue about the reasonableness of Milford's criteria for restricting the scope of its designated public forum. Milford has opened school property for, among other things, "instruction in

From Supreme Court of the United States, June 11, 2001.

any branch of education, learning or the arts" and for "social, civic and recreational meetings and entertainment events and other uses pertaining to the welfare of the community, provided that such uses shall be nonexclusive and shall be opened to the general public." App. to Pet. for Cert. D1–D3. But Milford has done this subject to the restriction that "[s]chool premises shall not be used . . . for religious purposes." As the District Court stated, Good News did "not object to the reasonableness of [Milford]'s policy that prohibits the use of [its] facilities for religious purposes."

The sole question before the District Court was, therefore, whether, in refusing to allow Good News's intended use, Milford was misapplying its unchallenged restriction in a way that amounted to imposing a viewpoint-based restriction on what could be said or done by a group entitled to use the forum for an educational, civic, or other permitted purpose. The question was whether Good News was being disqualified when it merely sought to use the school property the same way that the Milford Boy and Girl Scouts and the 4-H Club did. The District Court held on the basis of undisputed facts that Good News's activity was essentially unlike the presentation of views on secular issues from a religious standpoint held to be protected in *Lamb's Chapel*, see App. to Pet. for Cert. C29–C31, and was instead activity precluded by Milford's unchallenged policy against religious use, even under the narrowest definition of that term.

The Court of Appeals understood the issue the same way. See 202 F. 3d 502, 508 (CA2 2000) (Good News argues that "to exclude the Club because it teaches morals and values from a Christian perspective constitutes unconstitutional viewpoint discrimination"); *id.*, at 509 ("The crux of the Good News Club's argument is that the Milford school's application of the Community Use Policy to exclude the Club from its facilities is not viewpoint neutral"). The Court of Appeals also realized that the *Lamb's Chapel* criterion was the appropriate measure: "The activities of the Good News Club do not involve merely a religious perspective on the secular subject of morality." 202 F. 3d, at 510. Cf. *Lamb's Chapel, supra*, at 393 (district could not exclude "religious standpoint" in discussion on childrearing and family values, an undisputed "use for social or civic purposes otherwise permitted" under the use policy).[1] The appeals court agreed with the District Court that the undisputed facts in this case differ from those in *Lamb's Chapel*, as night from day. A sampling of those facts shows why both courts were correct.

Good News's classes open and close with prayer. In a sample lesson considered by the District Court, children are instructed that "[t]he Bible tells us how we can have our sins forgiven by receiving the Lord Jesus Christ. It tells us how to live to please Him. . . . If you have received the Lord Jesus as your Saviour from sin, you belong to God's special group—His family." The lesson plan instructs the teacher to "lead a child to Christ," and, when reading a Bible verse, to "[e]mphasize that this verse is from the Bible, God's Word" and is "important—and true—because God said it." The lesson further exhorts the teacher to "[b]e sure to give an opportunity for the 'unsaved' children in your class to respond to the Gospel" and cautions against "neglect[ing] this responsibility."

While Good News's program utilizes songs and games, the heart of the meeting is the "challenge" and "invitation," which are repeated at various times throughout the lesson. During the challenge, "saved" children who "already believe in the Lord Jesus as their Savior" are challenged to "'stop and ask God for the strength and the "want" . . . to obey Him.'" *Ibid.* They are instructed that

> "[i]f you know Jesus as your Savior, you need to place God first in your life. And if you don't know Jesus as Savior and if you would like to, then we will—we will pray with you separately, individually. . . . And the challenge would be, those of you who know Jesus as Savior, you can rely on God's strength to obey Him." *Ibid.*

During the invitation, the teacher "invites" the "unsaved" children "'to trust the Lord Jesus to be your Savior from sin,'" and "'receiv[e] [him] as your Savior from sin.'" *Id.*, at C21. The children are then instructed that

> "[i]f you believe what God's Word says about your sin and how Jesus died and rose again for you, you can have His forever life today. Please bow your heads and close your eyes. If you have never believed on the Lord Jesus as your Savior and would like to do that, please show me by raising your hand. If you raised your hand to show me you want to believe on the Lord Jesus, please meet me so I can show you from God's Word how you can receive His everlasting life." *Ibid.*

It is beyond question that Good News intends to use the public school premises not for the mere discussion of a subject from a particular, Christian point of view, but for an evangelical service of worship calling children to commit themselves in an act of Christian conversion.[2] The majority avoids this reality only by resorting to the bland and general characterization of Good News's activity as "teaching of morals and character, from a religious standpoint." See *ante,* at 9. If the majority's statement ignores reality, as it surely does, then today's holding may be understood only in equally generic terms. Otherwise, indeed, this case would stand for the remarkable proposition that any public school opened for civic meetings must be opened for use as a church, synagogue, or mosque. . . .

This Court has accepted the independent obligation to obey the Establishment Clause as sufficiently compelling to satisfy strict scrutiny under the First Amendment. See *id.*, at 271 ("[T]he interest of the [government] in complying with its constitutional obligations may be characterized as compelling"); *Lamb's Chapel,* 508 U.S., at 394. Milford's actions would offend the Establishment Clause if they carried the message of endorsing religion under the circumstances, as viewed by a reasonable observer. See *Capitol Square Review and Advisory Bd. v. Pinette,* 515 U.S. 753, 777 (1995) (O'CONNOR, J., concurring). The majority concludes that such an endorsement effect is out of the question in Milford's case, because the context here is "materially indistinguishable" from the facts in *Lamb's Chapel* and *Widmar. Ante,* at 13. In fact, the majority is in no position to say that, for the principal grounds on which we based our Establishment Clause holdings in those cases are clearly absent here.

In *Widmar,* we held that the Establishment Clause did not bar a religious student group from using a public university's meeting space for worship as well as discussion. As for the reasonable observers who might perceive government endorsement of religion, we pointed out that the forum was used by university students, who "are, of course, young adults," and, as such, "are less impressionable than younger students and should be able to appreciate that the University's policy is one of neutrality toward religion." 454 U.S., at 274, n. 14. To the same effect, we remarked that the "large number of groups meeting on campus" negated "any reasonable inference of University support from the mere fact of a campus meeting place." *Ibid.* Not only was the forum "available to a broad class of nonreligious as well as religious speakers," but there were, in fact, over 100 recognized student groups at the University, and an "absence of empirical evidence that religious groups [would] dominate [the University's] open forum." *Id.,* at 274–275; see also *id.,* at 274 ("The provision of benefits to so broad a spectrum of groups is an important index of secular effect"). And if all that had not been enough to show that the university-student use would probably create no impression of religious endorsement, we pointed out that the university in that case had issued a student handbook with the explicit disclaimer that "the University's name will not 'be identified in any way with the aims, policies, programs, products, or opinions of any organization or its members.'" *Id.,* at 274, n. 14.

Lamb's Chapel involved an evening film series on childrearing open to the general public (and, given the subject matter, directed at an adult audience). See 508 U.S., at 387, 395. There, school property "had repeatedly been used by a wide variety of private organizations," and we could say with some assurance that "[u]nder these circumstances . . . there would have been no realistic danger that the community would think that the District was endorsing religion or any particular creed. . . ." *Id.,* at 395.

What we know about this case looks very little like *Widmar* or *Lamb's Chapel.* The cohort addressed by Good News is not university students with relative maturity, or even high school pupils, but elementary school children as young as six.[3] The Establishment Clause cases have consistently recognized the particular impressionability of schoolchildren, see *Edwards v. Aguillard,* 482 U.S. 578, 583–584 (1987), and the special protection required for those in the elementary grades in the school forum, see *County of Allegheny v. American Civil Liberties Union, Greater Pittsburgh Chapter,* 492 U.S. 573, 620, n. 69 (1989). We have held the difference between college students and grade school pupils to be a "distinction [that] warrants a difference in constitutional results," *Edwards v. Aguillard, supra,* at 584, n. 5 (internal quotation marks and citation omitted).

Nor is Milford's limited forum anything like the sites for wide-ranging intellectual exchange that were home to the challenged activities in *Widmar* and *Lamb's Chapel.* See also *Rosenberger,* 515 U.S., at 850, 836–837. In Widmar, the nature of the university campus and the sheer number of activities offered precluded the reasonable college observer from seeing government endorsement in any one of them, and so did the time and variety of community use in the *Lamb's Chapel* case. See also *Rosenberger,* 515 U.S., at 850 ("Given this wide array of nonreligious, antireligious and competing religious viewpoints in the forum supported by the University, any perception that the University endorses one particular viewpoint would be illogical"); *id.,* at 836–837, 850 (emphasizing the array of university-funded magazines containing "widely divergent viewpoints" and the fact that believers in Christian evangelism competed on equal footing in the University forum with aficionados of "Plato, Spinoza, and Descartes," as well as "Karl Marx, Bertrand Russell, and Jean-Paul Sartre"); *Board of Ed. of Westside Community Schools (Dist. 66) v. Mergens,* 496 U.S. 226, 252 (1990) (plurality opinion) ("To the extent that a religious club is merely one of many different student-initiated voluntary clubs, students should perceive no message of government endorsement of religion").

The timing and format of Good News's gatherings, on the other hand, may well affirmatively suggest the *imprimatur* of officialdom in the minds of the young children. The club is open solely to elementary students (not the entire community, as in *Lamb's Chapel*), only four outside groups have been identified as meeting in the school, and Good News is, seemingly, the only one whose instruction follows immediately on the conclusion of the official school day. See Brief for National School Boards Association et al. as *Amici Curiae* 6. Although school is out at 2:56 p.m., Good News apparently requested use of the school beginning at 2:30 on Tuesdays "during the school year," so that instruction could begin promptly at 3:00, at which time children who are compelled by law to attend school surely remain in the building. Good News's religious meeting follows regular school activities so closely that the Good News instructor must wait to begin until "the room is clear," and "people are out of the room," before starting proceedings in the classroom located next to the regular third- and fourth-grade rooms. In fact, the temporal and physical continuity of Good News's meetings with the regular school routine seems to be the whole point of using the school. When meetings were held in a community church, 8 or 10 children attended; after the school became the site, the number went up three-fold.

Even on the summary judgment record, then, a record lacking whatever supplementation the trial process might have led to, and devoid of such insight as the trial and appellate judges might have contributed in addressing the Establishment Clause, we can say this: there is a good case that Good News's exercises blur the line between public classroom instruction and private religious indoctrination, leaving a reasonable elementary school pupil unable to appreciate that the former instruction is the business of the school while the latter evangelism is not. Thus, the facts we know (or think we know) point away from the majority's conclusion, and while the consolation may be that nothing really gets resolved when the judicial process is so truncated, that is not much to recommend today's result.

Notes

1. It is true, as the majority notes, *ante,* at 8, n. 3, that the Court of Appeals did not cite *Lamb's Chapel* by name. But it followed it in substance, and it did cite an earlier opinion written by the author of the panel opinion here, *Bronx Household of Faith v. Community School Dist. No. 10,* 127 F. 3d 207 (CA2 1997), which discussed *Lamb's Chapel* at length.

2. The majority rejects Milford's contention that Good News's activities fall outside the purview of the limited forum because they constitute "religious worship" on the ground that the Court of Appeals made no such determination regarding the character of the club's program, see *ante,* at 11, n. 4. This distinction is merely semantic, in light of the Court of Appeals's conclusion that "[i]t is difficult to see how the Club's activities differ materially from the 'religious worship' described" in other case law, 202 F. 3d, at 510, and the record below.

JUSTICE STEVENS distinguishes between proselytizing and worship, *ante,* at 1 (dissenting opinion), and distinguishes each from discussion reflecting a religious point of view. I agree with Justice Stevens that Good News's activities may be characterized as proselytizing and therefore as outside the purpose of Milford's limited forum, *ante,* at 5. Like the Court of Appeals, I also believe Good News's meetings have elements of worship that put the club's activities further afield of Milford's limited forum policy, the legitimacy of which was unchallenged in the summary judgment proceeding.

3. It is certainly correct that parents are required to give permission for their children to attend Good News's classes, see *ante,* at 14 (as parents are often required to do for a host of official school extracurricular activities), and correct that those parents would likely not be confused as to the sponsorship of Good News's classes. But the proper focus of concern in assessing effects includes the elementary school pupils who are invited to meetings, Lodging, Exh. X2, who see peers heading into classrooms for religious instruction as other classes end, and who are addressed by the "challenge" and "invitation."

The fact that there may be no evidence in the record that individual students were confused during the time the Good News Club met on school premises pursuant to the District Court's preliminary injunction is immaterial, cf. Brief for Petitioners 38. As JUSTICE O'CONNOR explained in *Capitol Square Review and Advisory Bd. v. Pinette,* 515 U.S. 753 (1995), the endorsement test does not focus "on the actual perception of individual observers, who naturally have differing degrees of knowledge," but on "the perspective of a hypothetical observer." *Id.,* at 779–780 (opinion concurring in part and concurring in judgment).

POSTSCRIPT

Do Religious Groups Have a Right to Use Public School Facilities after Hours?

Why should church and state be separate? Is there any danger to be feared from public religious displays? It is probably fair to say that behind the debates over this issue and the ongoing controversy over prayer in the schools are differing interpretations of the benefits and dangers of religion in public life. Does religion bring us to a higher level of existence, one that can help us shape our society for the better, or is it a system that will oppress dissidents, nonbelievers, and members of minority faiths? Almost everyone has an opinion on this question, and most can find some historical support for their positions. Ironically, the same historical circumstance may even be used to support opposing points of view. For example, at a congressional hearing on school prayer, the following testimony was introduced:

> *When I was educated in German public schools, they provided as part of the regular curriculum separate religious instruction for children of the three major faiths. At that time, all children in public schools from the ages of 6 to 18 were required not merely to recite a prayer at the beginning of each school session but to receive religious instruction twice a week. That system continued in the following decades.*

> —Statement by Joachim Prinz, quoted in testimony of Nathan Dershowitz, Hearings on Prayer in Public Schools and Buildings, Committee on the Judiciary, House of Representatives, August 19,1980

Did that program effectively teach morality to the German people? If it did, it would be difficult to explain the rise of Hitler and the total moral collapse and even depravity of many Germans, which resulted in the torture and death of millions of Jews and other minorities.

Another witness, however, testifying in support of prayer in the schools, quoted the report of the President's Commission on the Holocaust, which stated,

> *The Holocaust could not have occurred without the collapse of certain religious norms; increasing secularity fueled a devaluation of the image of the human being created in the likeness of God.*

> —Statement of Judah Glasner, Hearings on Prayer in Public Schools and Buildings, Committee on the Judiciary, House of Representatives, July 30,1980

Relevant cases concerning religion in the public schools are *McCollum v. Board of Education,* 333 U.S. 203 (1948), about religious instruction on school property; *Zorach v. Clauson,* 343 U.S. 306 (1952), regarding free time from school for religious instruction off school property; and *Board of Education of the Westside Community Schools v. Mergens,* 110 S. Ct. 2356 (1990), regarding the use of school premises for an after-school religious club. *Rosenberger v. University of Virginia,* 115 S. Ct. 2510 (1995) involved funding of a student newspaper by a religious group. Recent cases involving the constitutionality of the pledge of allegiance are discussed by Steven G. Gey in "'Under God,' the Pledge of Allegiance, and Other Constitutional Trivia," 81 *North Carolina Law Review* 1865 (2003). For broader discussions about the separation of church and state in America, see Martha Nussbaum, *Liberty of Conscience: In Defense of America's Tradition of Religious Equality* (Basic Books, 2008); Christopher L. Eisengruber and Lawrence G. Sager, *Religious Freedom and the Constitution* (Harvard University Press, 2007); and Peter Irons, *God on Trial: Landmark Cases from America's Religious Battlefields* (Penguin, 2007).

In June 2005, the Supreme Court decided two cases involving the placing of the Ten Commandments in public places. In a Kentucky case, *McCreary County v. ACLU of Kentucky* (545 U.S. 844), the Court found the purpose for the display to be religious and prohibited it. In a Texas case, *Van Orden v. Perry* (545 U.S. 677), the Court found a secular purpose to the display and allowed it. Both decisions were by a 5-4 vote, indicating a significant difference of opinion among the justices and the possibility for further cases involving this issue in the future.

Internet References . . .

The Brady Campaign to Prevent Gun Violence

The Brady Campaign works to pass and enforce sensible federal and state gun laws, regulations, and public policies.

http://www.bradycampaign.org/

Gun Free Kids

This advocacy organization supports state-based candidates who favor sound gun violence prevention policies.

http://www.gunfreekids.org/multimedia

The National Rifle Association

The NRA is widely recognized today as a major lobbying force and as America's foremost defender of Second Amendment rights.

http://home.nra.org/#/home

State and Local Policymaking

*P*olicymaking is conflictual whether it pits different levels of government—local, state, or federal—or a range of groups. Disputes that start on the local level can leak onto the national scene and vice versa. Making policy is the process by which the government considers a specific problem and possibly engages in solving it on various levels. State and local governments are confronted with problems daily. Schools are often the center of these debates because they are charged with educating children for the future; these issues touch us personally because we are either in school or have children in the education system. The most intimate question is still progressing through state legislatures: Who can marry whom?

- Should Same-Sex Couples Receive State Constitutional Protection?
- Do Charter Schools Merit Public Support?
- Should "Concealed and Carry" Guns Be Allowed in the Classroom?
- Should Local Schools Have National Standards?

ISSUE 16

Should Same-Sex Couples Receive State Constitutional Protection?

YES: Margaret Marshall, from Majority Opinion, *Goodridge et al. v. Department of Public Health,* Massachusetts Supreme Judicial Court (2003)

NO: Robert Cordy, from Dissenting Opinion, *Goodridge et al. v. Department of Public Health,* Massachusetts Supreme Judicial Court (2003)

ISSUE SUMMARY

YES: Massachusetts Supreme Judicial Court Chief Justice Margaret Marshall rules that prohibiting same-sex couples from marrying causes hardship to a segment of the population for no rational reason.

NO: Massachusetts Supreme Judicial Court Justice Robert Cordy, in dissent, holds that a statute banning same-sex marriage is a valid exercise of the state's police power.

In spring 2001, seven same-sex couples in Massachusetts unsuccessfully applied for marriage licenses from their respective town clerks. The clerks all denied the requests because the applicants were same-sex couples. As a result, the couples filed suit in the Massachusetts Superior Court (trial court), claiming that the clerks' actions violated the equal protection clause of the Massachusetts Constitution. That clause provides, "All people are born free and equal and have certain natural, essential and unalienable rights; among which may be reckoned the right of enjoying and defending their lives and liberties; that of acquiring, possessing and protecting property; in fine, that of seeking and obtaining their safety and happiness. Equality under the law shall not be denied or abridged because of sex, race, color, creed or national origin" (Mass. Const. Pt. 1, Art. 1). The trial court rejected the same-sex couples' claims and held that the state's prohibition of same-sex marriages was constitutionally permissible because it advanced the state's interest in protecting the primary purpose of the institution of marriage: procreation.

All sides agreed that the issue's importance was of sufficient magnitude to warrant bypassing the intermediate appellate court and, instead, called for direct appeal to the Massachusetts Supreme Judicial Court. There, in a sharply divided 4-3 decision, the Supreme Judicial Court vacated the trial court's ruling, holding that the prohibition of same-sex marriages was unconstitutional. The high court did not, however, order the state to begin to issue marriage licenses to the same-sex applicants but, instead, remanded the case back to the Superior Court, with a stay for 180 days to allow the Massachusetts legislature to take appropriate action.

The Massachusetts Court was immediately caught up in the political storm surrounding the question of gay rights in particular and the question of "moral values" and contemporary society more generally. The Court was both reviled and praised. Little more than a year away from the presidential elections, the Court and its decision were pulled into the national political debates. Was this decision the fair and just thing to do, treating all, regardless of their sexual orientation, to the benefits of the institution of marriage? Or is marriage an historically unique social institution, intended to recognize only the union between a man and a woman? With upward of 50 percent of all marriages in the United States ending in divorce, would this decision further contribute to the fragility of a social institution that, historically, has been central to the organization and stability of society? Or would it have the opposite effect: reaffirming the centrality of marriage, whether it be formed by same- or opposite-sex couples? Finally, was this decision yet one more example of a highly politicized, "activist" judiciary usurping the lawmaking function and "legislating" from the bench? Or was this a situation where the judiciary properly used its power of judicial review to protect the rights of a traditionally marginalized minority group? These issues are contested in the following opinions by Justices Marshall and Cordy from the *Goodridge* decision.

YES

Margaret Marshall

Majority Opinion *Goodridge et al. v. Department of Public Health*

Marriage is a vital social institution. The exclusive commitment of two individuals to each other nurtures love and mutual support; it brings stability to our society. For those who choose to marry, and for their children, marriage provides an abundance of legal, financial, and social benefits. In return it imposes weighty legal, financial, and social obligations. The question before us is whether, consistent with the Massachusetts Constitution, the Commonwealth may deny the protections, benefits, and obligations conferred by civil marriage to two individuals of the same sex who wish to marry. We conclude that it may not. The Massachusetts Constitution affirms the dignity and equality of all individuals. It forbids the creation of second-class citizens. In reaching our conclusion we have given full deference to the arguments made by the Commonwealth. But it has failed to identify any constitutionally adequate reason for denying civil marriage to same-sex couples.

We are mindful that our decision marks a change in the history of our marriage law. Many people hold deep-seated religious, moral, and ethical convictions that marriage should be limited to the union of one man and one woman, and that homosexual conduct is immoral. Many hold equally strong religious, moral, and ethical convictions that same-sex couples are entitled to be married, and that homosexual persons should be treated no differently than their heterosexual neighbors. Neither view answers the question before us. Our concern is with the Massachusetts Constitution as a charter of governance for every person properly within its reach. "Our obligation is to define the liberty of all, not to mandate our own moral code." *Lawrence v. Texas,* 123 S.Ct. 2472, 2480 (2003) (*Lawrence*), quoting *Planned Parenthood of Southeastern Pa. v. Casey,* 505 U.S. 833, 850 (1992).

Whether the Commonwealth may use its formidable regulatory authority to bar same-sex couples from civil marriage is a question not previously addressed by a Massachusetts appellate court. It is a question the United States Supreme Court left open as a matter of Federal law in *Lawrence, supra* at 2484, where it was not an issue. There, the Court affirmed that the core concept of common human dignity protected by the Fourteenth Amendment to the United States Constitution precludes government intrusion into the deeply personal realms of consensual adult expressions of intimacy and one's choice of an intimate partner. The Court also reaffirmed the central role that decisions

Majority Opinion, SJC-08860, March 4, 2003–November 18, 2003. Some case citations omitted.

whether to marry or have children bear in shaping one's identity. *Id.* at 2481. The Massachusetts Constitution is, if anything, more protective of individual liberty and equality than the Federal Constitution; it may demand broader protection for fundamental rights; and it is less tolerant of government intrusion into the protected spheres of private life. . . .

Barred access to the protections, benefits, and obligations of civil marriage, a person who enters into an intimate, exclusive union with another of the same sex is arbitrarily deprived of membership in one of our community's most rewarding and cherished institutions. That exclusion is incompatible with the constitutional principles of respect for individual autonomy and equality under law. . . .

The plaintiffs include business executives, lawyers, an investment banker, educators, therapists, and a computer engineer. Many are active in church, community, and school groups. They have employed such legal means as are available to them—for example, joint adoption, powers of attorney, and joint ownership of real property—to secure aspects of their relationships. Each plaintiff attests a desire to marry his or her partner in order to affirm publicly their commitment to each other and to secure the legal protections and benefits afforded to married couples and their children. . . .

The department, represented by the Attorney General, admitted to a policy and practice of denying marriage licenses to same-sex couples. It denied that its actions violated any law or that the plaintiffs were entitled to relief. The parties filed cross motions for summary judgment.

A Superior Court judge ruled for the department. In a memorandum of decision and order dated May 7, 2002, he dismissed the plaintiffs' claim that the marriage statutes should be construed to permit marriage between persons of the same sex, holding that the plain wording of G.L. c. 207, as well as the wording of other marriage statutes, precluded that interpretation. Turning to the constitutional claims, he held that the marriage exclusion does not offend the liberty, freedom, equality, or due process provisions of the Massachusetts Constitution, and that the Massachusetts Declaration of Rights does not guarantee "the fundamental right to marry a person of the same sex." He concluded that prohibiting same-sex marriage rationally furthers the Legislature's legitimate interest in safeguarding the "primary purpose" of marriage, "procreation." The Legislature may rationally limit marriage to opposite-sex couples, he concluded, because those couples are "theoretically . . . capable of procreation," they do not rely on "inherently more cumbersome" noncoital means of reproduction, and they are more likely than same-sex couples to have children, or more children. . . .

In short, for all the joy and solemnity that normally attend a marriage, G.L. c. 207, governing entrance to marriage, is a licensing law. The plaintiffs argue that because nothing in that licensing law specifically prohibits marriages between persons of the same sex, we may interpret the statute to permit "qualified same sex couples" to obtain marriage licenses, thereby avoiding the question whether the law is constitutional. . . . This claim lacks merit. . . .

&

The larger question is whether, as the department claims, government action that bars same-sex couples from civil marriage constitutes a legitimate exercise of the State's authority to regulate conduct, or whether, as the plaintiffs claim, this categorical marriage exclusion violates the Massachusetts Constitution. We have recognized the long-standing statutory understanding, derived from the common law, that "marriage" means the lawful union of a woman and a man. But that history cannot and does not foreclose the constitutional question.

The plaintiffs' claim that the marriage restriction violates the Massachusetts Constitution can be analyzed in two ways. Does it offend the Constitution's guarantees of equality before the law? Or do the liberty and due process provisions of the Massachusetts Constitution secure the plaintiffs' right to marry their chosen partner? In matters implicating marriage, family life, and the upbringing of children, the two constitutional concepts frequently overlap, as they do here. . . .

We begin by considering the nature of civil marriage itself. Simply put, the government creates civil marriage. In Massachusetts, civil marriage is, and since pre-Colonial days has been, precisely what its name implies: a wholly secular institution. . . . No religious ceremony has ever been required to validate a Massachusetts marriage.

In a real sense, there are three partners to every civil marriage: two willing spouses and an approving State. . . . While only the parties can mutually assent to marriage, the terms of the marriage—who may marry and what obligations, benefits, and liabilities attach to civil marriage—are set by the Commonwealth. Conversely, while only the parties can agree to end the marriage (absent the death of one of them or a marriage void ab initio), the Commonwealth defines the exit terms.

Civil marriage is created and regulated through exercise of the police power. . . . "Police power" (now more commonly termed the State's regulatory authority) is an old-fashioned term for the Commonwealth's lawmaking authority, as bounded by the liberty and equality guarantees of the Massachusetts Constitution and its express delegation of power from the people to their government. In broad terms, it is the Legislature's power to enact rules to regulate conduct, to the extent that such laws are "necessary to secure the health, safety, good order, comfort, or general welfare of the community." . . .

Without question, civil marriage enhances the "welfare of the community." It is a "social institution of the highest importance." Civil marriage anchors an ordered society by encouraging stable relationships over transient ones. It is central to the way the Commonwealth identifies individuals, provides for the orderly distribution of property, ensures that children and adults are cared for and supported whenever possible from private rather than public funds, and tracks important epidemiological and demographic data.

Marriage also bestows enormous private and social advantages on those who choose to marry. Civil marriage is at once a deeply personal commitment to another human being and a highly public celebration of the ideals of mutuality, companionship, intimacy, fidelity, and family. "It is an association that promotes a way of life, not causes; a harmony in living, not political faiths; a bilateral loyalty, not commercial or social projects." *Griswold v. Connecticut,* 381 U.S. 479, 486 (1965). Because it fulfils yearnings for security, safe haven, and connection that express our common humanity, civil marriage is an esteemed institution, and the decision whether and whom to marry is among life's momentous acts of self-definition.

Tangible as well as intangible benefits flow from marriage. The marriage license grants valuable property rights to those who meet the entry requirements, and who agree to what might otherwise be a burdensome degree of government regulation of their activities. . . . The Legislature has conferred on "each party [in a civil marriage] substantial rights concerning the assets of the other which unmarried cohabitants do not have." . . .

⋅⊙⋅

For decades, indeed centuries, in much of this country (including Massachusetts) no lawful marriage was possible between white and black Americans. That long history availed not when the Supreme Court of California held in 1948 that a legislative prohibition against interracial marriage violated the due process and equality guarantees of the Fourteenth Amendment, *Perez v. Sharp,* 32 Cal.2d 711, 728 (1948), or when, nineteen years later, the United States Supreme Court also held that a statutory bar to interracial marriage violated the Fourteenth Amendment, *Loving v. Virginia,* 388 U.S. 1 (1967). As both *Perez* and *Loving* make clear, the right to marry means little if it does not include the right to marry the person of one's choice, subject to appropriate government restrictions in the interests of public health, safety, and welfare. See *Perez v. Sharp, supra* at 717 ("the essence of the right to marry is freedom to join in marriage with the person of one's choice"). See also *Loving v. Virginia, supra* at 12. In this case, as in *Perez* and *Loving,* a statute deprives individuals of access to an institution of fundamental legal, personal, and social significance—the institution of marriage—because of a single trait: skin color in *Perez* and *Loving,* sexual orientation here. As it did in *Perez* and *Loving,* history must yield to a more fully developed understanding of the invidious quality of the discrimination.

The Massachusetts Constitution protects matters of personal liberty against government incursion as zealously, and often more so, than does the Federal Constitution, even where both Constitutions employ essentially the same language. See *Planned Parenthood League of Mass., Inc., v. Attorney Gen.,* 424 Mass. 586, 590 (1997); *Corning Glass Works v. Ann & Hope, Inc., of Danvers,* 363 Mass. 409, 416 (1973). That the Massachusetts Constitution is in some instances more protective of individual liberty interests than is the Federal Constitution is not surprising. Fundamental to the vigor of our Federal system of government is that "state courts are absolutely free to interpret state constitutional provisions to accord greater protection to individual rights than do similar provisions of the United States Constitution." *Arizona v. Evans,* 514 U.S. 1, 8 (1995).

The individual liberty and equality safeguards of the Massachusetts Constitution protect both "freedom from" unwarranted government intrusion into protected spheres of life and "freedom to" partake in benefits created by the State for the common good. See *Bachrach v. Secretary of the Commonwealth,* 382 Mass. 268, 273 (1981); *Dalli v. Board of Educ.,* 358 Mass. 753, 759 (1971). Both freedoms are involved here. Whether and whom to marry, how to express sexual intimacy, and whether and how to establish a family—these are among the most basic of every individual's liberty and due process rights. See, e.g., *Lawrence, supra* at 2481; *Planned Parenthood of Southeastern Pa. v. Casey,* 505 U.S. 833, 851 (1992); *Zablocki v. Redhail,* 434 U.S. 374, 384 (1978); *Roe v. Wade,* 410 U.S. 113, 152–153 (1973); *Eisenstadt v. Baird,* 405 U.S. 438, 453 (1972); *Loving v. Virginia, supra.* And central to personal freedom and security is the assurance that the laws will apply equally to persons in similar situations. "Absolute equality before the law is a fundamental principle of our own Constitution." *Opinion of the Justices,* 211 Mass. 618, 619 (1912). The liberty interest in choosing whether and whom to marry would be hollow if the Commonwealth could, without sufficient justification, foreclose an individual from freely choosing the person with whom to share an exclusive commitment in the unique institution of civil marriage. . . .

The plaintiffs challenge the marriage statute on both equal protection and due process grounds. With respect to each such claim, we must first determine the appropriate standard of review. Where a statute implicates a fundamental right or uses a suspect classification, we employ "strict judicial scrutiny." *Lowell v. Kowalski,* 380 Mass. 663, 666 (1980). For all other statutes, we employ the "'rational basis' test." *English v. New England Med. Ctr.,* 405 Mass. 423, 428 (1989). For due process claims, rational basis analysis requires that statutes "bear[ ] a real and substantial relation to the public health, safety, morals, or some other phase of the general welfare." *Coffee-Rich, Inc., v. Commissioner of Pub. Health, supra,* quoting *Sperry & Hutchinson Co. v. Director of the Div. on the Necessaries of Life,* 307 Mass. 408, 418 (1940). For equal protection challenges, the rational basis test requires that "an impartial lawmaker could logically believe that the classification would serve a legitimate public purpose that transcends the harm to the members of the disadvantaged class." *English v. New England Med. Ctr., supra* at 429, quoting *Cleburne v. Cleburne Living Ctr., Inc.,* 473 U.S. 432, 452 (1985) (Stevens, J., concurring).

The department argues that no fundamental right or "suspect" class is at issue here, and rational basis is the appropriate standard of review. For the reasons we explain below, we conclude that the marriage ban does not meet the rational basis test for either due process or equal protection. Because the statute does not survive rational basis review, we do not consider the plaintiffs' arguments that this case merits strict judicial scrutiny.

The department posits three legislative rationales for prohibiting same-sex couples from marrying: (1) providing a "favorable setting for procreation";

(2) ensuring the optimal setting for child rearing, which the department defines as "a two-parent family with one parent of each sex"; and (3) preserving scarce State and private financial resources. We consider each in turn. . . .

Our laws of civil marriage do not privilege procreative heterosexual intercourse between married people above every other form of adult intimacy and every other means of creating a family. General Laws c. 207 contains no requirement that the applicants for a marriage license attest to their ability or intention to conceive children by coitus. Fertility is not a condition of marriage, nor is it grounds for divorce. People who have never consummated their marriage, and never plan to, may be and stay married. . . . People who cannot stir from their deathbed may marry. See G.L. c. 207, § 28A. While it is certainly true that many, perhaps most, married couples have children together (assisted or unassisted), it is the exclusive and permanent commitment of the marriage partners to one another, not the begetting of children, that is the sine qua non of civil marriage.

Moreover, the Commonwealth affirmatively facilitates bringing children into a family regardless of whether the intended parent is married or unmarried, whether the child is adopted or born into a family, whether assistive technology was used to conceive the child, and whether the parent or her partner is heterosexual, homosexual, or bisexual. If procreation were a necessary component of civil marriage, our statutes would draw a tighter circle around the permissible bounds of nonmarital child bearing and the creation of families by noncoital means. The attempt to isolate procreation as "the source of a fundamental right to marry," *post* at (Cordy, J., dissenting), overlooks the integrated way in which courts have examined the complex and overlapping realms of personal autonomy, marriage, family life, and child rearing. Our jurisprudence recognizes that, in these nuanced and fundamentally private areas of life, such a narrow focus is inappropriate.

The "marriage is procreation" argument singles out the one unbridgeable difference between same-sex and opposite-sex couples, and transforms that difference into the essence of legal marriage . . . and full access to the political process, the marriage restriction impermissibly "identifies persons by a single trait and then denies them protection across the board." *Romer v. Evans*, 517 U.S. 620, 633 (1996). In so doing, the State's action confers an official stamp of approval on the destructive stereotype that same-sex relationships are inherently unstable and inferior to opposite-sex relationships and are not worthy of respect.

The department's first stated rationale, equating marriage with unassisted heterosexual procreation, shades imperceptibly into its second: that confining marriage to opposite-sex couples ensures that children are raised in the "optimal" setting. Protecting the welfare of children is a paramount State policy. Restricting marriage to opposite-sex couples, however, cannot plausibly further this policy. . . .

The department has offered no evidence that forbidding marriage to people of the same sex will increase the number of couples choosing to enter into opposite-sex marriages in order to have and raise children. There is thus no rational relationship between the marriage statute and the Commonwealth's proffered goal of protecting the "optimal" child rearing unit. Moreover, the department readily concedes that people in same-sex couples may be "excellent" parents. These couples (including four of the plaintiff couples) have children for the reasons others do—to love them, to care for them, to nurture them. But the task of child rearing for same-sex couples is made infinitely harder by their status as outliers to the marriage laws. . . . Given the wide range of public benefits reserved only for married couples, we do not credit the department's contention that the absence of access to civil marriage amounts to little more than an inconvenience to same-sex couples and their children. Excluding same-sex couples from civil marriage will not make children of opposite-sex marriages more secure, but it does prevent children of same-sex couples from enjoying the immeasurable advantages that flow from the assurance of "a stable family structure in which children will be reared, educated, and socialized." . . .

In this case, we are confronted with an entire, sizeable class of parents raising children who have absolutely no access to civil marriage and its protections because they are forbidden from procuring a marriage license. It cannot be rational under our laws, and indeed it is not permitted, to penalize children by depriving them of State benefits because the State disapproves of their parents' sexual orientation.

The third rationale advanced by the department is that limiting marriage to opposite-sex couples furthers the Legislature's interest in conserving scarce State and private financial resources. The marriage restriction is rational, it argues, because the General Court logically could assume that same-sex couples are more financially independent than married couples and thus less needy of public marital benefits, such as tax advantages, or private marital benefits, such as employer-financed health plans that include spouses in their coverage.

An absolute statutory ban on same-sex marriage bears no rational relationship to the goal of economy. First, the department's conclusory generalization—that same-sex couples are less financially dependent on each other than opposite-sex couples—ignores that many same-sex couples, such as many of the plaintiffs in this case, have children and other dependents (here, aged parents) in their care. The department does not contend, nor could it, that these dependents are less needy or deserving than the dependents of married couples. Second, Massachusetts marriage laws do not condition receipt of public and private financial benefits to married individuals on a demonstration of financial dependence on each other; the benefits are available to married couples regardless of whether they mingle their finances or actually depend on each other for support. . . .

Here, the plaintiffs seek only to be married, not to undermine the institution of civil marriage. They do not want marriage abolished. They do not attack the binary nature of marriage, the consanguinity provisions, or any of the other gate-keeping provisions of the marriage licensing law. Recognizing the right of an individual to marry a person of the same sex will not diminish the validity or dignity of opposite-sex marriage, any more than recognizing the right of an individual to marry a person of a different race devalues the marriage of a person who marries someone of her own race. If anything, extending civil marriage to same-sex couples reinforces the importance of marriage to individuals and communities. That same-sex couples are willing to embrace marriage's solemn obligations of exclusivity, mutual support, and commitment to one another is a testament to the enduring place of marriage in our laws and in the human spirit. . . .

The marriage ban works a deep and scarring hardship on a very real segment of the community for no rational reason. The absence of any reasonable relationship between, on the one hand, an absolute disqualification of same-sex couples who wish to enter into civil marriage and, on the other, protection of public health, safety, or general welfare, suggests that the marriage restriction is rooted in persistent prejudices against persons who are (or who are believed to be) homosexual. "The Constitution cannot control such prejudices but neither can it tolerate them. Private biases may be outside the reach of the law, but the law cannot, directly or indirectly, give them effect." Limiting the protections, benefits, and obligations of civil marriage to opposite-sex couples violates the basic premises of individual liberty and equality under law protected by the Massachusetts Constitution.

<hr />

We consider next the plaintiffs' request for relief. We preserve as much of the statute as may be preserved in the face of the successful constitutional challenge. . . .

Here, no one argues that striking down the marriage laws is an appropriate form of relief. Eliminating civil marriage would be wholly inconsistent with the Legislature's deep commitment to fostering stable families and would dismantle a vital organizing principle of our society. . . .

We construe civil marriage to mean the voluntary union of two persons as spouses, to the exclusion of all others. This reformulation redresses the plaintiffs' constitutional injury and furthers the aim of marriage to promote stable, exclusive relationships. It advances the two legitimate State interests the department has identified: providing a stable setting for child rearing and conserving State resources. It leaves intact the Legislature's broad discretion to regulate marriage. . . .

So ordered. . . .

Robert Cordy

Minority Opinion *Goodridge v. Department of Public Health*

. . . The court's opinion concludes that the Department of Public Health has failed to identify any "constitutionally adequate reason" for limiting civil marriage to opposite-sex unions, and that there is no "reasonable relationship" between a disqualification of same-sex couples who wish to enter into a civil marriage and the protection of public health, safety, or general welfare. Consequently, it holds that the marriage statute cannot withstand scrutiny under the Massachusetts Constitution. Because I find these conclusions to be unsupportable in light of the nature of the rights and regulations at issue, the presumption of constitutional validity and significant deference afforded to legislative enactments, and the "undesirability of the judiciary substituting its notions of correct policy for that of a popularly elected Legislature" responsible for making such policy, *Zayre Corp. v. Attorney Gen.*, 372 Mass. 423, 433 (1977), I respectfully dissent. Although it may be desirable for many reasons to extend to same-sex couples the benefits and burdens of civil marriage (and the plaintiffs have made a powerfully reasoned case for that extension), that decision must be made by the Legislature, not the court. . . .

A. *Limiting marriage to the union of one man and one woman does not impair the exercise of a fundamental right.* Civil marriage is an institution created by the State. In Massachusetts, the marriage statutes are derived from English common law. . . . They were enacted to secure public interests and not for religious purposes or to promote personal interests or aspirations. As the court notes in its opinion, the institution of marriage is "the legal union of a man and woman as husband and wife," *ante* at, and it has always been so under Massachusetts law, colonial or otherwise.

The plaintiffs contend that because the right to choose to marry is a "fundamental" right, the right to marry the person of one's choice, including a member of the same sex, must also be a "fundamental" right. While the court stops short of deciding that the right to marry someone of the same sex is "fundamental" such that strict scrutiny must be applied to any statute that impairs it, it nevertheless agrees with the plaintiffs that the right to choose to marry is of fundamental importance . . . and would be "hollow" if an individual was foreclosed from "freely choosing the person with whom to share . . . the . . . institution of civil marriage." Hence, it concludes that a marriage license cannot be denied to an individual who wishes to marry someone of the same sex. In reaching this result the court has transmuted the "right" to marry into a right to change the

Minority Opinion, SJC-08860, March 4, 2003–November 18, 2003.

institution of marriage itself. This feat of reasoning succeeds only if one accepts the proposition that the definition of the institution of marriage as a union between a man and a woman is merely "conclusory," rather than the basis on which the "right" to partake in it has been deemed to be of fundamental importance. In other words, only by assuming that "marriage" includes the union of two persons of the same sex does the court conclude that restricting marriage to opposite-sex couples infringes on the "right" of same-sex couples to "marry."

The plaintiffs ground their contention that they have a fundamental right to marry a person of the same sex in a long line of Supreme Court decisions that discuss the importance of marriage. In context, all of these decisions and their discussions are about the "fundamental" nature of the institution of marriage as it has existed and been understood in this country, not as the court has redefined it today. Even in that context, its "fundamental" nature is derivative of the nature of the interests that underlie or are associated with it. An examination of those interests reveals that they are either not shared by same-sex couples or not implicated by the marriage statutes.

Supreme Court cases that have described marriage or the right to marry as "fundamental" have focused primarily on the underlying interest of every individual in procreation, which, historically, could only legally occur within the construct of marriage because sexual intercourse outside of marriage was a criminal act. . . . Because same-sex couples are unable to procreate on their own, any right to marriage they may possess cannot be based on their interest in procreation, which has been essential to the Supreme Court's denomination of the right to marry as fundamental.

Supreme Court cases recognizing a right to privacy in intimate decision-making . . . have also focused primarily on sexual relations and the decision whether or not to procreate, and have refused to recognize an "unlimited right" to privacy. . . .

What the *Griswold* Court found "repulsive to the notions of privacy surrounding the marriage relationship" was the prospect of "allow[ing] the police to search the sacred precincts of marital bedrooms for telltale signs of the use of contraceptives." . . . When Justice Goldberg spoke of "marital relations" in the context of finding it "difficult to imagine what is more private or more intimate than a husband and wife's marital relations[hip]," he was obviously referring to sexual relations. Similarly, in *Lawrence v. Texas,* 123 S. Ct. 2472 (2003), it was the criminalization of private sexual behavior that the Court found violative of the petitioners' liberty interest. . . .

The marriage statute, which regulates only the act of obtaining a marriage license, does not implicate privacy in the sense that it has found constitutional protection under Massachusetts and Federal law. . . . It does not intrude on any right that the plaintiffs have to privacy in their choices regarding procreation, an intimate partner or sexual relations. The plaintiffs' right to privacy in such matters does not require that the State officially endorse their choices in order for the right to be constitutionally vindicated.

Although some of the privacy cases also speak in terms of personal autonomy, no court has ever recognized such an open-ended right. "That many of the rights and liberties protected by the Due Process Clause sound in personal

autonomy does not warrant the sweeping conclusion that any and all important, intimate, and personal decisions are so protected. . . ." *Washington v.
Glucksberg,* 521 U.S. 702, 727 (1997). Such decisions are protected not because
they are important, intimate, and personal, but because the right or liberty
at stake is "so deeply rooted in our history and traditions, or so fundamental
to our concept of constitutionally ordered liberty" that it is protected by due
process. *Id.* Accordingly, the Supreme Court has concluded that while the decision to refuse unwanted medical treatment is fundamental, *Cruzan v. Director,
Mo. Dept. of Health,* 497 U.S. 261, 278 (1990), because it is deeply rooted in our
nation's history and tradition, the equally personal and profound decision
to commit suicide is not because of the absence of such roots. *Washington v.
Glucksberg, supra.*

While the institution of marriage is deeply rooted in the history and traditions of our country and our State, the right to marry someone of the same
sex is not. No matter how personal or intimate a decision to marry someone
of the same sex might be, the right to make it is not guaranteed by the right of
personal autonomy. . . .

Unlike opposite-sex marriages, which have deep historic roots, or the
parent-child relationship, which reflects a "strong tradition" founded on "the
history and culture of Western civilization" and "is now established beyond
debate as an enduring American tradition," or extended family relationships,
which have been "honored throughout our history," same-sex relationships,
although becoming more accepted, are certainly not so "deeply rooted in
this Nation's history and tradition" as to warrant such enhanced constitutional protection.

Although "expressions of emotional support and public commitment"
have been recognized as among the attributes of marriage, which, *"[t]aken
together* . . . form a constitutionally protected marital relationship," those interests, standing alone, are not the source of a fundamental right to marry. . . .

Finally, the constitutionally protected interest in child rearing . . . is not
implicated or infringed by the marriage statute here. The fact that the plaintiffs
cannot marry has no bearing on their independently protected constitutional
rights as parents which, as with opposite-sex parents, are limited only by their
continued fitness and the best interests of their children. . . .

Because the rights and interests discussed above do not afford the plaintiffs any fundamental right that would be impaired by a statute limiting marriage to members of the opposite sex, they have no fundamental right to be
declared "married" by the State.

Insofar as the right to marry someone of the same sex is neither found in
the unique historical context of our Constitution nor compelled by the meaning ascribed by this court to the liberty and due process protections contained
within it, should the court nevertheless recognize it as a fundamental right?
The consequences of deeming a right to be "fundamental" are profound, and
this court, as well as the Supreme Court, has been very cautious in recognizing them. Such caution is required by separation of powers principles. If a
right is found to be "fundamental," it is, to a great extent, removed from "the
arena of public debate and legislative action"; utmost care must be taken when

breaking new ground in this field "lest the liberty protected by the Due Process Clause be subtly transformed into the policy preferences of [judges]." . . .

Although public attitudes toward marriage in general and same-sex marriage in particular have changed and are still evolving, "the asserted contemporary concept of marriage and societal interests for which [plaintiffs] contend" are "manifestly [less] deeply founded" than the "historic institution" of marriage. . . .

Given this history and the current state of public opinion, as reflected in the actions of the people's elected representatives, it cannot be said that "a right to same-sex marriage is so rooted in the traditions and collective conscience of our people that failure to recognize it would violate the fundamental principles of liberty and justice that lie at the base of all our civil and political institutions. . . .

"[I]t is not the court's function to launch an inquiry to resolve a debate which has already been settled in the legislative forum. '[I]t [is] the judge's duty . . . to give effect to the will of the people as expressed in the statute by their representative body. It is in this way . . . that the doctrine of separation of powers is given meaning.'" . . .

The court's opinion concedes that the civil marriage statute serves legitimate State purposes . . .

Civil marriage is the institutional mechanism by which societies have sanctioned and recognized particular family structures, and the institution of marriage has existed as one of the fundamental organizing principles of human society. . . . Marriage has not been merely a contractual arrangement for legally defining the private relationship between two individuals (although that is certainly part of any marriage). Rather, on an institutional level, marriage is the "very basis of the whole fabric of civilized society," . . . and it serves many important political, economic, social, educational, procreational, and personal functions.

Paramount among its many important functions, the institution of marriage has systematically provided for the regulation of heterosexual behavior, brought order to the resulting procreation, and ensured a stable family structure in which children will be reared, educated, and socialized. Admittedly, heterosexual intercourse, procreation, and child care are not necessarily conjoined (particularly in the modern age of widespread effective contraception and supportive social welfare programs), but an orderly society requires some mechanism for coping with the fact that sexual intercourse commonly results in pregnancy and childbirth. The institution of marriage is that mechanism.

The institution of marriage provides the important legal and normative link between heterosexual intercourse and procreation on the one hand and family responsibilities on the other. The partners in a marriage are expected to engage in exclusive sexual relations, with children the probable result and paternity presumed. . . . Whereas the relationship between mother and child is demonstrably and predictably created and recognizable through the biological process of pregnancy and childbirth, there is no corresponding process for creating a relationship between father and child. Similarly, aside from an act of heterosexual intercourse nine months prior to childbirth, there is no process for creating a relationship between a man and a woman as the parents of a particular child. The institution of marriage fills this void by formally binding the husband-father to his wife and child, and imposing on him the responsibilities of fatherhood. . . . The alternative, a society without the institution of marriage, in which heterosexual intercourse, procreation, and child care are largely disconnected processes, would be chaotic.

The marital family is also the foremost setting for the education and socialization of children. Children learn about the world and their place in it primarily from those who raise them, and those children eventually grow up to exert some influence, great or small, positive or negative, on society. The institution of marriage encourages parents to remain committed to each other and to their children as they grow, thereby encouraging a stable venue for the education and socialization of children. See P. Blumstein & P. Schwartz, *supra* at 26; C.N. Degler, *supra* at 61; S.L. Nock, *supra* at 2–3; C. Lasch, *supra* at 81; M.A. Schwartz & B.M. Scott, *supra* at 6–7. More macroscopically, construction of a family through marriage also formalizes the bonds between people in an ordered and institutional manner, thereby facilitating a foundation of interconnectedness and interdependency on which more intricate stabilizing social structures might be built. See M. Grossberg, *Governing the Hearth: Law and Family in Nineteenth-Century America* 10 (1985); C. Lasch, *supra*; L. Saxton, *supra* at 260; J.Q. Wilson, *supra* at 221. . . .

It is undeniably true that dramatic historical shifts in our cultural, political, and economic landscape have altered some of our traditional notions about marriage, including the interpersonal dynamics within it, the range of responsibilities required of it as an institution, and the legal environment in which it exists. Nevertheless, the institution of marriage remains the principal weave of our social fabric. . . .

It is difficult to imagine a State purpose more important and legitimate than ensuring, promoting, and supporting an optimal social structure within which to bear and raise children. At the very least, the marriage statute continues to serve this important State purpose.

. . . The question we must turn to next is whether the statute, construed as limiting marriage to couples of the opposite sex, remains a rational way to further that purpose. Stated differently, we ask whether a conceivable rational basis exists on which the Legislature could conclude that continuing to limit the institution of civil marriage to members of the opposite sex furthers the legitimate purpose of ensuring, promoting, and supporting an optimal social structure for the bearing and raising of children.

In considering whether such a rational basis exists, we defer to the decision-making process of the Legislature, and must make deferential assumptions about the information that it might consider and on which it may rely. . . .

There is no reason to believe that legislative processes are inadequate to effectuate legal changes in response to evolving evidence, social values, and views of fairness on the subject of same-sex relationships. Deliberate consideration of, and incremental responses to rapidly evolving scientific and social understanding is the norm of the political process—that it may seem painfully slow to those who are already persuaded by the arguments in favor of change is not a sufficient basis to conclude that the processes are constitutionally infirm. . . . The Legislature is the appropriate branch, both constitutionally and practically, to consider and respond to it. It is not enough that we as Justices might be personally of the view that we have learned enough to decide what is best. So long as the question is at all debatable, it must be the Legislature that decides. The marriage statute thus meets the requirements of the rational basis test. . . .

POSTSCRIPT

Should Same-Sex Couples Receive State Constitutional Protection?

After the Massachusetts Supreme Judicial Court decided *Goodridge,* the state senate requested an advisory opinion from the Court as to whether a pending "civil union" bill would satisfy the requirements of the Massachusetts Constitution. The bill would provide same-sex couples with the same benefits, protections, and responsibilities that a traditional marriage then provided to opposite-sex couples. In response, the Court held that only the recognition of same-sex marriages would prove constitutionally satisfactory. In May 2004, Massachusetts began issuing marriage certificates to same-sex couples, becoming the first state in the nation to do so. Although same-sex-marriage opponents have vowed to override the *Goodridge* decision by amending the Massachusetts state constitution, they have repeatedly failed to get the necessary votes in the state legislature to put a constitutional amendment up for a vote in a ballot initiative.

Beyond the borders of Massachusetts, the *Goodridge* decision generated a wave of legal and political activity, much of it timed to the 2004 presidential election. Both major candidates, Bush and Kerry, voiced their opposition to same-sex marriage. Although the Massachusetts senator moderated his opposition by supporting the notion of same-sex civil unions, he insisted that a "marriage" must remain between a man and a woman. President Bush pushed the point further and, during the later phases of the campaign, called for a constitutional amendment (one that would seem to "constitutionalize" the basic points of the federal Defense of Marriage Act, 28 U.S.C. 1738C (2004)) declaring that a "marriage" was the union between a man and a woman. It was suggested that Bush's harder line was calculated for political appeal to an important part of his political base. Whether this issue played a decisive role in the election is much more difficult to determine. What we do know is that the November 2004 election saw 11 states (Arkansas, Georgia, Kentucky, Michigan, Mississippi, Montana, North Dakota, Oklahoma, Oregon, Ohio, and Utah) overwhelmingly pass ballot initiatives that contained same-sex marriage bans.

More recent developments have signaled greater acceptance of same-sex marriage. In particular, after same-sex marriage became legal in Iowa, Connecticut, and California through judicial decisions similar to *Goodridge,* three states—Vermont, Maine, and New Hampshire—successively instituted same-sex marriage through legislation. By relying on the legislatures to change the state marriage statutes, same-sex-marriage proponents in those states undercut one of the main arguments of many same-sex-marriage opponents:

that in decisions such as *Goodridge*, judges were "legislating from the bench" and usurping the prerogative of the legislature to set marriage policy. Same-sex-marriage opponents, however, won a large victory in the 2008 elections when Californian voters passed Proposition 8, amending the state constitution to limit marriage to heterosexual couples and overturning the California Supreme Court's 2007 decision extending marriage to same-sex couples. Opponents of Proposition 8 tried to challenge the amendment in court, but the California Supreme Court ruled it was a legal ballot initiative, almost guaranteeing a future ballot initiative by same-sex-marriage proponents eager to undo the change.

A comprehensive overview of the same-sex-marriage debate and the constitutional issues it raises is provided by Evan Gerstmann in *Same-Sex Marriage and the Constitution,* 2nd ed. (Cambridge University Press, 2008).

For an analysis of the virtues of marriage for both same- and opposite-sex couples, see Jonathan Rauch, *Gay Marriage: Why It Is Good for Gays, Good for Straights, and Good for America* (Times Books, 2004). A counterpoint from the conservative perspective is offered by Maggie Gallagher, "What Marriage Is For," *Weekly Standard* (August 4–11, 2003), and Stanley Kurtz, "The End of Marriage in Scandinavia," *Weekly Standard* (February 2, 2004). Finally, historian Stephanie Coontz provides an illuminating perspective on how the meaning of marriage has changed over time in *Marriage, A History: How Love Conquered Marriage* (Penguin, 2006).

ISSUE 17

Do Charter Schools Merit Public Support?

YES: Joe Williams, from "Games Charter Opponents Play," *Education Next* (Winter 2007)

NO: Marc F. Bernstein, from "Why I'm Wary of Charter Schools," *The School Administrator* (August 1999)

ISSUE SUMMARY

YES: Journalist Joe Williams, a senior fellow with Education Sector, reviews the development of the charter school movement and finds multiple unwarranted bureaucratic impediments to its acceptance.

NO: School superintendent Marc F. Bernstein sees increasing racial and social class segregation, church-state issues, and financial harm as outgrowths of the charter school movement.

"The public education system as currently structured is archaic." So say Diane Ravitch and Joseph Viteritti in "A New Vision for City Schools," *The Public Interest* (Winter 1996). "Instead of a school system that attempts to impose uniform rules and regulations," they contend, "we need a system that is dynamic, diverse, performance-based, and accountable. The school system that we now have may have been right for the age in which it was created; it is not right for the twenty-first century."

Currently, the hottest idea for providing alternatives to the usual public school offering is the charter school movement. Charter schools, which receive funding from the public school system but operate with a good deal of autonomy regarding staffing, curriculum, and spending, began in Minnesota in 1991 through legislative action prompted by grassroots advocates. Charter schools have gained wide support, all the way up to the White House. In the 1998–1999 school year, some 1,700 charter schools served about 350,000 students nationwide. The 2000–2001 year saw about 500 additional charters granted.

The movement has certainly brought variety to the school system menu and has expanded parental choice. Community groups, activists, and entrepreneurs seem to be clamoring for available charters for Core Knowledge schools, Paideia schools, fine arts academies, Afrocentric schools, schools for at-risk students and dropouts, technology schools, character education-based schools, job-training academies, and so on.

The National Commission on Governing America's Schools has recommended that every school become a charter school, which would bring an end to the era of centralized bureaucratic control of public school districts. The Sarasota County School District in Florida has already embarked on a decentralized organizational model offering a "100% School Choice Program" through newly conceived "conversion, deregulated, and commissioned schools."

There are obstacles to success, however, and indeed some have already failed. According to Alex Medler in "Charter Schools Are Here to Stay," *Principal* (March 1997), these obstacles include inadequate capital funding and facilities, cash flow and credit problems, regulations and paperwork, disputes with local school boards, and inadequate planning time. A recently released report by the Hudson Institute, *Charter Schools in Action*, indicates wide success in overcoming such obstacles.

Michael Kelly, in "Dangerous Minds," *The New Republic* (December 30, 1996), argues that in a pluralistic society public money is shared money to be used for shared values. He finds that too many of the charter schools are run by extremists who like the idea of using public money to support their ideological objectives. He cites the failed Marcus Garvey School in Washington, D.C., which spent $372,000 in public funds to bring an Afrocentric curriculum to 62 students. However, he notes that this case has not led to a wave of protests against the concept of charter schools.

In fact, *Washington Post* columnist William Raspberry recently declared that he finds himself slowly morphing into a supporter of charter schools and vouchers. "It isn't because I harbor any illusions that there is something magical about those alternatives," he explains. "It is because I am increasingly doubtful that the public schools can do (or at any rate *will* do) what is necessary to educate poor minority children."

An associated topic is privatization. This either involves turning public school management over to private companies, such as Educational Alternatives, Inc., or cooperating with entrepreneurs who want to develop low-cost private alternatives for students currently enrolled in public schools. The most talked-about of the latter is entrepreneur Chris Whittle's Edison Project, an attempt to build a nationwide network of innovative, for-profit schools.

In the following paired views, Joe Williams details some of the strategies that have been employed by charter school opponents to block the competition they represent. Contrarily, Marc F. Bernstein sounds a number of warning signals as the public rushes to embrace charter schools as a reform mechanism.

YES

Joe Williams

Games Charter Opponents Play

Considerable attention has been paid to the most blatant barriers that public charter schools face. By lobbying against good charter legislation and fair funding financing anti-charter studies and propaganda, filing lawsuits, and engaging the public battle of ideas, teacher unions and other charter opponents openly wage what might be called an "air war" against charters.

But there is also evidence of a perhaps more damaging "ground war." Interviews with more than 400 charter school operators from coast to coast have revealed widespread localized combat—what one administrator called "bureaucratic sand" that is often hurled in the faces of charter schools. Indeed, as a 2005 editorial in the *Washington Post* described charter school obstruction in Maryland, "It's guerilla turf war, with children caught in the middle. Attempts to establish public charter schools in Maryland have been thwarted at almost every turn by entrenched school boards, teachers unions and principals resistant to any competition."

The goal appears to be to stop charter schools any way possible. A decade after Massachusetts passed its charter school law as part of the Education Reform Act of 1993, city officials in North Adams, Massachusetts, sued the state Department of Education, challenging the constitutionality of charter schools. Citing a 150-year-old clause in the state constitution, the city claimed all public school money had to go to schools that are controlled by "public agents." The suit was later dismissed but shows the lengths to which local interests will go to stop the schools or at least slow them down.

Today, more than 1 million students are enrolled in public charter schools in the 41 states (and the District of Columbia) that have charter laws, with almost 4,000 charter schools in all. Most, if not all, of these schools have encountered some form of bureaucratic resistance at the local level. That resistance may take place at the school's inception, when it first looks to purchase a building and comply with municipal zoning laws. It may come when opponents play games with a school's transportation or funding, or when legal barriers are tossed in the way, or when false information about charter schools is widely disseminated. Despite the obstacles, many charter schools are thriving. It's worth taking a look at the forces on the ground that would have it otherwise and the myriad ways they attempt to stymie the charter school movement.

From *Education Next,* Winter 2007, pp. 13–18. Copyright © 2007 by Education Next. Reprinted by permission of Hoover Institution, Stanford University.

No-School Zone

Often the most painstaking and difficult parts of launching a charter school are locating, purchasing, and maintaining the school building. Many charter opponents believe that if they can sufficiently complicate this nascent stage of a charter school's life, they will have dealt a major blow to its future success.

In Albany, New York, opponents have used the city's zoning commission to halt charter school growth. When Albany Preparatory Charter School requested a variance on property it was eyeing, opponents appeared before a public hearing about the proposed school building and used the opportunity to argue against charter schools in general. Both the city and the board of zoning appeals denied the variance request in February 2005 on grounds that the proposed building was in a location that was not suitable for a school. It wasn't difficult for the charter school to prove that the decision was unfairly "arbitrary and capricious," however. The building that Albany had deemed unsuitable for a school had been, for more than 70 years, Albany's very own Public School 3. In December 2005, State Supreme Court Justice Thomas J. Spargo gave the city 60 days to approve the variance request.

That same month, the Albany school system discussed ways to prevent another school, the Green Tech Charter High School, from opening. The school board voted to have Superintendent Eva Joseph review possibilities for taking the property by eminent domain so the district could seize the land before the charter school could be built. As the *Albany Times Union* reported, M. Christian Bender, chair of the proposed school's board of directors, remarked, "Two words come to mind—laughable and desperate." The school is expected to open in September 2007.

Albany's story is not unusual. Playing games with facilities and zoning is a powerful way to get charter schools to delay or abandon plans to open. Certainly some zoning boards resist on principle any new land use that may increase traffic or noise, but blatant political hostility is quite common. Why are local boards hostile to charter schools? Some may view charter schools as a threat to local traditions and long-standing power-sharing arrangements. One Ohio charter school operator suggested that appointees to zoning commissions in her area tend to be eager political up-and-comers. To build political capital, they're often willing to deliver for the public school systems. And those systems don't want charter schools competing for students and dollars. "Especially if you are a Democrat, standing up to a charter school can help you make a name for yourself in the most important political circles," she said.

Charter opponents understand that zoning commissions and boards of appeal have the power to halt new charter schools in their tracks. All over the country, particularly in the suburbs, zoning issues have been used to thwart attempts to open charter schools. To be sure, some cases involve garden variety "Not In My Back Yard" resistance to the increased traffic flow and daily bustle new charter schools bring. But often the opposition is blatantly political. When Lyndhurst, New Jersey mayor, James Guida, an opponent of charter schools, proposed zoning changes in 2001 that would require school lots to be a minimum of 1.5 acres in size, it stymied at least one charter school plan.

Guida talked about the school with a *Bergen Record* reporter: "We didn't target it, but if [the zoning law] hits it, so be it."

In a similar scenario, Englewood, New Jersey, officials wreaked havoc on the Englewood Charter School by abruptly rezoning the site of a converted warehouse that the school was planning to use. The change prevented elementary schools from operating on the location. "They passed zoning changes to specifically exclude us from buildings," said charter school organizer Paul Raynault.

In 2000, California voters approved Proposition 39, which requires that unused public school buildings be made available to public charter schools. Some districts have simply chosen not to follow the law, which gives public charter schools the right of first refusal. Two charter schools in southeast San Diego, Fanno Academy and KIPP Adelante Academy, filed a lawsuit against the district in 2005, accusing school officials of "blatant noncompliance" because classroom space was denied to charter schools and given instead to private schools that could afford to pay higher rent.

The San Diego lawsuit, filed with the help of the California Charter Schools Association, contends that districts usually sabotage charter schools in one of three ways: claiming a facilities request is incomplete and therefore denying it; offering sites that are impractical; and outright denial of the facility request. Eight out of nine charter school applications for space in San Diego in 2005 were denied, even though all completed the necessary paperwork for requesting classroom space. Before suing the district, both Fanno and Adelante reportedly sought to hold meetings with the agency to discuss their options. After several months without a response, their requests were denied. Early in 2006, the district had declared invalid requests from 24 charter schools seeking space declaring that none properly explained how the school's projected enrollment was determined. That level of detail hadn't been required on previous applications.

"This feels like political posturing," said Luci Flowers, principal of the Albert Einstein Academy Charter School. "I feel like we are pawns in a political game."

Sometimes hurdles for charter school facilities are thrown up not by districts, but by competing private-school interests. In Brooklyn, New York, the founders of the Explore Charter School signed a 10-year lease in 2002 for a property across the street from the St. James Catholic Cathedral. The property was co-owned by a private landlord and the Diocese of Brooklyn. The private landlord signed off on the lease, but just weeks before the school was scheduled to open, the diocese began unraveling the deal. The 10-year lease was slashed to two years, forcing school leaders to go back to the nearly full-time job of finding a suitable long-term facility.

Why the sudden resistance from the diocese? The church said it had new concerns that sex education might be taught in the public charter school. But Morty Ballen, the charter school's founder, claimed that a lawyer for the diocese told him that it was not the church's policy to support charter schools. "It's a hunch that we represent competition to the parochial schools," Ballen said. "It's unfortunate, because we all have the same goal—to provide kids with a good, solid education."

You Can't Get Here from There

Using transportation as a weapon against charters is particularly harmful to those charter schools that have longer school days and years than traditional public schools. "Transportation is huge," commented Jamie Callendar, a former Ohio legislator. "In the first few years the districts would outright refuse to provide transportation. Now they make it as inconvenient as possible."

In Ohio, students attending non-public and charter/community schools are eligible to receive transportation services from the local district if they and the school they attend meet certain criteria. The local district can, however, declare providing eligible students with transportation "impractical" for a variety of reasons and issue payment instead. In July, the Columbus Public School district announced its intent to notify 1,384 private and charter school students that it would be "impractical" to transport them to school on district school buses. Instead, students would be given a $172 check toward providing their own transportation to and from school—less than $1 per school day.

Similar scenarios play out all over the country. For nearly four months of the 2005–06 school year, the school bus belonging to the Ross Montessori School in Carbondale, Colorado, sat unused in the school's parking lot, another victim of the below-the-radar war against public charter schools.

The K–6 school paid $25,000 for a 78-passenger turbo-diesel school bus in the fall of 2005 with high hopes that it would make it easier for students— particularly Latinos—who didn't live close to the school to enroll. Critics at the nearby Roaring Fork School District, who had long opposed the charter school's existence, had complained publicly that Ross Montessori didn't serve its share of Latino students. The administration of Ross Montessori believed the bus would make it easier for Latino families to select the school.

"I thought this would be a solution," said Mark Grice, the school's director. Instead, as the bus sat, unused in the lot, week after week, it became a symbol for the passive-aggressive relationship that existed between the independent public charter school approved by the state and the local school district.

Why weren't students allowed to ride on the Ross Montessori bus? In Colorado, as in many places, school buses may not carry student passengers unless the vehicles are regularly inspected by a specially licensed school-bus mechanic. Grice and his administrative team quickly learned that most of the licenses to conduct inspections in the region belonged to mechanics employed full time by a school district.

When the charter school leaders checked with the mechanic at the local district in early October 2005, they were given the bureaucratic cold shoulder. Grice and his team decided the best way to proceed would be to call the next closest school district to see if its certified school-bus mechanic would conduct the required inspection. Arrangements were made to do just that, until Grice got a return call shortly before the scheduled inspection informing him that the appointment had been cancelled.

"They said they didn't want to get involved in the politics of our district," Grice recalled. The charter pushed back, and eventually the neighboring district agreed to inspect the bus—but only if the school could produce a letter from the superintendent of the charter school's geographic district giving permission. Eventually, the Carbondale superintendent agreed to call the neighboring superintendent. "I should have had him put it in writing," Grice said. Whatever the superintendents may have said between themselves, it didn't result in a bus inspection.

By chance, several months later, the charter school stumbled upon both a certified school-bus mechanic who was employed at a nearby Chevrolet dealership and a Catholic school that was looking to share with another school the cost of bus transportation in the region. "It allowed us to share the cost of the bus and to pay the driver better," Grice said. "But as soon as the district found out about it, someone called the Colorado Department of Education to question the separation of church and state."

The bus eventually got rolling, but Grice said he hates to think of how much time was spent dealing with these clearly avoidable hassles, time that could have been better spent on education.

The Check Is in the Mail

When districts are the ones passing along funding to charter schools, they gain immense influence over those schools' basic operations, and the charters are placed in the undesirable position of having to rely on those who may oppose their very existence.

The Franklin Career Academy, of Franklin, New Hampshire, ultimately perished after the local school district and city council simply refused to pay the school the already-low $3,340 per child that was guaranteed under the state's charter school law. As in many locations, New Hampshire law requires the per-pupil funds to pass from the state through local school districts, and then to charter schools. But Franklin school and city officials argued that the money was needed in the traditional schools and, astonishingly, voted against giving it to the charter school in the city budget. In its first year, Career Academy served 35 at-risk students in grades 7 through 12, but ended the year being owed $77,000 by the local district. The financial uncertainty forced the charter school to shut its doors. "Nothing went wrong with the school," said the charter school's board chairman Bill Grimm. "We closed because we didn't see any other option." The New Hampshire legislature is currently considering funding charter schools directly.

Ohio has a similar process for funding charter schools. Ohio charters are paid through the districts with which they are competing. Those districts, in turn, have the right to question the validity of every student record, a practice called "flagging." Because charter schools can't be subsidized for a student whose record is "flagged," dozens of charter school leaders throughout Ohio charge that their local public-school districts have used excessive "flagging" with the specific intention of harming the often fragile finances of their schools.

Depending on the size of the school, and the aggressiveness with which local districts decide to "flag" students, individual charter schools can see tens of thousands of dollars in legitimate funding delayed or withheld each year. And charter school administrators report that their limited office staffs can be overwhelmed as they scramble to investigate the reasons behind the flagging.

One Toledo charter school leader said her school had twice been denied six weeks' worth of funding for enrolled students. In both cases, she said, the local district raised objections to student records just before the deadline for closing out monthly payments, making it impossible for the charter school to gather the supporting documentation in time for payment.

"We don't even know that we have a problem, then all of a sudden they'll put up a flag and say, 'We need proof of residence,'" the charter leader said. "We've had kids who were in the [Toledo Public] schools for their entire academic careers and suddenly the district wants to challenge where they live."

Another charter school administrator reported that an official with the Toledo Public Schools (TPS) often flags student entries, but doesn't make clear what is wrong. (In one case, he allegedly claimed the word "Toledo" was spelled incorrectly on the database, but the school insisted they had it right. To make matters worse, she said, the TPS official wouldn't return telephone calls or e-mails to discuss the flag he had thrown.)

Official Ohio Department of Education policy bans districts' use of flagging to harass the charter schools, but some charter operators complain that the state often looks the other way and insists that charter schools resolve the problem with the local districts. Others note that there is a financial incentive for districts to delay making payments for as long as possible, even if they eventually have to pay the charter schools what they are owed in later installments.

"The district gets to use our money for a while [before eventually reconciling the accounts and spreading back-payments over several months] and we go into debt," a Toledo charter leader said. "Meanwhile, they accuse us of sucking the system dry."

Slinging Mud

Charter schools that either escape or survive the bureaucratic messes are lucky—but they're not safe. In many districts, organized campaigns of disinformation and slander have been launched against charter schools. Like lawsuits, faux research, and campaign contributions, name calling has emerged as one more useful political tool.

Toledo Public Schools teachers handed out flyers outside the East Toledo Charter School in 2006 to parents attending an informational open house. The flyers suggested inaccurately that the school wasn't performing well.

In Massachusetts in 2004, where district hostility to charter schools got so bad that state education officials had to warn superintendents to moderate their anti-charter politicking, one district student reported being pressured to sign a petition opposing charter schools. She was told if she didn't sign, funding for the school band might be cut from the budget. Reported the *Boston Globe*, "Children say their public school teachers have pressed them to sign petitions protesting new charters. School committee members have repeatedly called neighbors, imploring them to step down from charter boards. And flyers have circulated, sounding the death of public schools if a charter school opens."

In 2003 in Waltham, Massachusetts, an elementary-school principal sent out e-mails to families urging them to oppose pending charter-school proposals. In nearby Framingham that same year, city officials included with tax bills letters explaining how much money was going to charter schools. And in Cambridge, school officials in 2005 mailed letters to 4,000 families questioning the academic effectiveness of a charter school that had yet to open. Those letters also warned that students who chose to attend the Community Charter School of Cambridge wouldn't be able to join sports and clubs that regular public schools offer.

Some of the tactics used by charter opponents amount to bluffing but reveal how far they are willing to go to stop a charter school from opening. As the University of Wisconsin-Milwaukee (UWM) considered authorizing charter schools for the first time in 1999, the local teachers union and top administrators in the Milwaukee Public Schools threatened to ban the college's student teachers from obtaining required classroom experience if UWM approved any charter schools that would be managed by the for-profit firm Edison Schools.

No Truce in Sight

This ground war is both expensive and demoralizing. As the Thomas B. Fordham Foundation's Terry Ryan described the reality in one state, "Charter schools, many working in Ohio's toughest neighborhoods to educate the state's neediest children, are also forced to live under a cloud of uncertainty, harassment and intimidation."

Many of the charter principals interviewed for this story report spending upward of a third or even half of their time fighting these battles. In truth, charter opponents can lose some battles and still win the war, as charter school operations continue to be hampered by endless attacks on so many fronts. One can only wonder how these distractions impede the efforts of charter schools to educate their students.

Truce cannot be expected anytime soon. The enemies of charter schools are motivated and well-financed. For charter supporters, then, there is only one choice: fight back and win.

Marc F. Bernstein

 **NO**

Why I'm Wary of Charter Schools

With its passage of the New York Charter Schools Act of 1998, New York . . . became the 34th state to authorize or implement charter schools.

As a result, roughly two-thirds of the school districts nationwide now are subject to an educational reform that has yet to prove its worth but has raised the most serious practical and philosophical challenges to the viability of public education in our country's history.

In New York, a charter school can be established through an application submitted by teachers, parents, school administrators, community residents or any combination thereof. Though charter schools are subject to the same health and safety, civil rights and student assessment requirements of other public schools, they are exempt from all other state regulations.

The Case for Charters

The case for charter schools is quite simple—the arguments typically revolve around the alleged failure of the public schools. Though many have contested the validity of these charges (educational researchers Gerald Bracey and David Berliner prime among them), the news media, the political establishment and a large segment of the public have become convinced that our schools are failing to serve the children with whom they've been entrusted.

The 15-year diatribe, beginning with the *Nation at Risk* report in 1984, has been translated in recent years into legislative action enabling students to attend alternative charter schools paid for by the school districts that the students would have otherwise attended. Charter schools, by law, are free of most state mandates and are not obligated to conform to teacher union work rules and hours.

Charter school proponents contend the freedom from state regulations and collective bargaining constraints will yield significant advantages:

- Charter schools will permit and encourage a more creative approach to teaching and learning;
- Charter schools will establish models of educational reform for other schools in the same community;
- Charter schools will be more reflective of parent and community priorities through the alternative programs that cater to special interests and needs;

From *The School Administrator,* August 1999. Copyright © 1999 by American Association of School Administrators. Reprinted by permission.

- Charter schools will operate in a more cost-effective manner; and
- Charter schools will be governed by boards consisting of parents, teachers and community members, making them more responsive than public schools.

Unrealized Gains

Not only have these benefits not accrued to most of the students attending existing charter schools, but charter school proponents neglect to address three overarching concerns regarding the potential consequences of this movement.

First, the public money used to fund charter schools must come from an existing source and that source is the budget of the public school district.

Second, charter school populations tend to be more homogeneous than most public schools in terms of ethnicity, religion or race. This homogeneity will have a Balkanizing effect when young children are most open to dealing with differences among people.

Third, the constitutional separation between school and religion will be compromised by people of goodwill (and others) who see opportunities to provide alternate education to children in need.

Before elaborating on these concerns, it is instructive to review the formal studies completed to date that have examined the progress of charter schools in fulfilling their stated goals. Charter school advocates, however, seem to show little or no interest in research data about charter schools.

The Case Not Made

In perhaps the most extensive study to date, "Beyond the Rhetoric of Charter School Reform: A Study of Ten California School Districts," researchers at UCLA, led by Professor Amy Stuart Wells, looked at 17 charter schools in 10 school districts. Their selection of districts were chosen for their diversity in order "to capture the range of experiences within this reform movement."

Among its 15 findings, the study concluded that California's charter schools have not lived up to proponents' claims. Four of the findings are most telling:

- California's charter schools, in most instances, are not yet being held accountable for enhanced academic achievement of their students;
- Charter schools exercise considerable control over the type of students they serve;
- The requirement that charter schools reflect the social/ethnic makeup of their districts has not been enforced;
- No mechanisms are in place for charter schools and regular public schools to learn from each other.

Moreover, the researchers found "no evidence that charter schools can do more with less" and that "regular public schools in districts with charter schools felt little to no pressure from the charter schools to change the way they do business." Thus, the UCLA study disputes in the strongest of terms that charter schools raise the academic achievement of their students in a more cost-effective manner and that nearby public schools will do a better job educating their children by adopting the innovations of the charter schools.

In a yearlong study of Michigan's charter school initiative, researchers at Western Michigan University concluded that charter schools may not be living up to their promise of educational innovation and more effective use of public money. The report, which was presented to the pro-charter state board of education . . . , characterized many charters as "cookie-cutter" schools run by for-profit companies and suggested that many administrators and charter school boards were ill-equipped to run a school.

These two studies are clear in their findings, yet the charter movement grows. If the spread of charter schools did not auger the most dangerous consequences, we could ignore it as yet another failed experiment in American education. But the risks here are too great, not only to America's public schools, but to our very society.

The gravest concerns fall into three categories: financial impact, Balkanization and religious intrusion.

Financial Harm

The most direct and immediate impact upon the public schools relates to financing. Money to operate the charter schools comes from the public schools, whether the financing mechanism be that (1) the public school draws a check to the charter; (2) the state forwards a proportion of what the public would have received to the charter; or (3) the state's discretionary resources that could have been used to improve the public schools are budgeted for charter schools.

Regardless of the process, public schools wind up with fewer dollars to improve the education of their students. Such reduced funding likely will lead to poorer academic results, which then will be used to strengthen the case that charter schools (or voucher programs) are the only recourse for failing public schools. Is this Orwellian in intent or merely ignorant in practice?

In New York, where I've worked as a superintendent for 13 years, the public schools are required to pay the charter schools the average operating expenditure per pupil as computed for the most recent school year based on the number of students the charter school claims it will serve in the forthcoming school year. When public school leaders suggested that their schools would be denied a disproportionate amount of money, charter school proponents (and legislators) responded that the money is merely following the student. As such, the public school would have the same percentage of money as students.

This simplistic argument totally ignores the economic concept of marginal cost. It costs less to educate the 24th student in the class than the initial 5, 10, 15 or 20. In my letter to the editor of *The New York Times* on this subject . . . , I wrote: "This means that if 10 students in each grade were to transfer to a charter school from a 1,000-student public elementary school, the public school would lose approximately $500,000. No teacher, custodian or secretary salaries can be eliminated as a result of the reduction in the number of students. However, the public school would have $500,000 less available to educate its remaining students."

Where is the public school to go to recoup this lost $500,000? There are but two choices—raise taxes or reduce programming. Either choice has serious consequences for public education. If we raise taxes, our taxpayers will be paying more to educate fewer students. They won't care to hear about the principle of marginal cost. They will see the public schools as inefficient and will scream for tax relief or increased accountability for the costly public schools. And, if we cut programming or classroom staffing, our parents will demand to know why we are shortchanging their children.

Clearly, the cost of educating some students is greater than it is for others. Few would question that it costs more to meet the needs of a child with disabilities or one who enters public school without speaking English. Research shows it is the knowledgeable parents who do their homework in terms of investigating alternatives to the public school. Therefore, charter schools are more likely to have a sufficient pool of "less costly" applicants leaving the public school with the more costly students to educate.

In addition to penalizing public schools by reducing operating funds, New York state will have fewer total dollars available for educating students.

One provision of the new charter school law requires the state to establish a fund to provide charter schools with loans for furniture, equipment and facilities. The reservoir of available state money is only so large. It can only drain in so many directions. Thus, public schools that are now required to meet higher academic standards will be told that the state lacks the resources to assist.

The only other source of revenue for the public schools is the local taxpayer. Of course, the alternative is to eliminate or cut back nonacademic offerings. Those programs most likely to be dropped or curtailed are those in art or music, the ones for which there is no bottom-line, quantitative assessment.

Either choice results in a no-win situation. We can alienate our taxpayers or we can jeopardize the support of our parents.

Moreover, citizens in this state have the opportunity to register their support or disagreement with a school district's educational program through their vote on the annual school budget. Inasmuch as the charter school's program is solely within the control of its board of directors, is there not a true gap between the public's right of the purse strings and the independence given to charter schools?

A Balkanizing Effect

Can separate be equal?

This question, we thought, had been answered in 1954 by the U.S. Supreme Court in *Brown vs. Board of Education* when racially segregated schools prevailed in parts of our country by the design of governmental entities.

Nearly a half century later, we now have a government-endorsed policy leading us back to that same situation. Surprisingly, charter schools seem to enjoy strong support among minority legislators and advocates, the same groups that rallied behind the Supreme Court's decision that "separate is not equal" in education.

This reversal may reflect the disenchantment of minority parents with America's inner-city schools, which serve the greatest percentage of minority students. For example, a recent poll by the Washington-based Joint Center for Political and Economic Studies reported that blacks are 11 percent less likely than whites to be satisfied with their local public schools.

Though charter school laws in most states attempt to address the matter of potential racial imbalancing, the charter schools nonetheless are becoming increasingly segregated. The Minnesota Charter Schools Evaluation, conducted in 1998 by the University of Minnesota, found that charter schools in that state typically enroll greater numbers of ethnic minorities than the regular schools in their home districts. Half of the charters have student populations that are more than 60 percent children of color.

In Michigan, a statewide study of charters by Western Michigan University identified a segregation pattern in which white children were opting out of local public schools. The percentage of minorities in charters declined by more than 22 percent between 1995 and 1998.

Two other detailed studies—one in North Carolina, the other in Arizona—concluded that their states' charter schools have become increasingly segregated by race. The North Carolina Office of Charter Schools found that 13 of 34 charter schools that opened in 1997 were disproportionately black, compared with their districts. And, the North Carolina Education Reform Foundation, which helps to start charter schools, says at least 9 of the 26 schools that opened last year violate the diversity clause.

Having anticipated the possibility of segregation, North Carolina's charter school law included a diversity clause requiring charter schools to "reasonably reflect" the demographics of their school districts. Even so, the opposite has occurred.

A study titled "Ethnic Segregation in Arizona Charter Schools," issued in January 1999 by Casey Cobb of University of New Hampshire and Gene Glass of Arizona State University, found that nearly half of the state's 215 charter schools (as of 1997) "exhibited evidence of substantial ethnic separation."

These studies describe but one type of segregation—racial—while the term Balkanization connotes the formal division of a geographic area along racial, ethnic and/or religious lines. How unfortunate it would be for our nation's communities to become more fractionalized than they already are.

The limited existing research points to this as a possible outcome as students' attendance is based upon factors other than the schools' academic performance, whether at the parents' choosing or the schools' selection.

America's public schools have as one of their primary goals to acculturate, sensitize and civilize our children to prepare them for their future roles in a democratic society. Will this goal be seriously compromised due to charter schools?

I believe it was René Descartes who wrote that the chief cause of human error is to be found in the prejudices picked up in childhood.

Religious Intrusion

Following our state's adoption of a charter school law, New York City religious leaders began enthusiastically preparing themselves to establish charter schools. They already had access to classroom space, an extremely rare commodity, and a significant presence in their communities, which could only help in attracting students. Plus, the religious leaders have been persistent critics of the city's schools.

The most vocal of the clergy, the Rev. Floyd H. Flake of Queens, N.Y., a former U.S. congressman, argued for "skirt(ing) the constitutional barriers between church and state by offering religious instruction outside school hours."

This creative thinking is not limited to New York City. *Education Week* reported . . . that the Rev. Michael Pfleger, a pastor on Chicago's South Side, "has discussed shutting down St. Sabina (its parish school) and, in its place, opening a publicly funded charter school run by a nonprofit board, possibly with links to the parish or the Catholic archdiocese." Both Flake and Pfleger see charter schools as an opportunity to use public money to subsidize their educational and religious efforts.

The U.S. Constitution speaks loudly and clearly against religious intrusion into the public schools. In spite of Supreme Court cases defining the nature of permissible involvements, the issue is never truly resolved. Litigation involving charter schools inevitably will require the court to rule on charter schools' use of church property, the participation of religious leaders on charter school governing boards and the attendance of charter school students at home and afterschool religious education programs when the church's facilities are used to house the charter school.

The court's decisions will significantly affect public school finances and the influence religion will have upon children attending the nation's public schools, whether they are charter or regular public schools.

Constant Monitoring

Though charter schools have yet to prove their academic worth, they are rapidly increasing in number across the country. They provide choices to parents for their children's education and level the playing field between higher and lower socioeconomic classes. Charter schools lend a warm feeling that government is doing something to fix our failing schools by turning the capitalistic engine of competition loose upon the schools.

In reality, charter schools are denying public schools the financial resources they require to address the needs of an increasingly disparate student population. Our communities will be further divided along racial, religious and ethnic lines as children attend their schools of choice, opting to be with children of similar backgrounds. And the never-ending battle to maintain the separation of church and state will suffer another setback as public money moves in the direction of religious (charter) schools, where children receive religious instruction under the guise of attending charter schools.

As educational leaders committed to the values of public education, we must be wary of these unintended consequences. We must continually monitor charter schools' academic performance, use of public money for religious instruction and adherence to diversity provisions.

Undoubtedly, many policymakers have prejudged the success of the charter schools movement. But we must assume the duty to inform the public about this most serious challenge to public education. As part of a professional leadership organization and as career educators, we must monitor the performance of charters in our communities and communicate our concerns to legislators.

POSTSCRIPT

Do Charter Schools Merit Public Support?

Charter schools—are they a source of innovation, inspiration, and revitalization in public education or a drain on human and fiscal resources that will leave regular public schools weaker than ever? The debate has just begun, and preliminary results are just beginning to trickle in. But the air is filled with predictions, opinions, and pontifications.

Alex Molnar offers some scathing commentary on the charter school and privatization movements in his article "Charter Schools: The Smiling Face of Disinvestment," *Educational Leadership* (October 1996), and in his book *Giving Kids the Business: The Commercialization of America's Schools* (1996). A more positive assessment is delivered by Joe Nathan in his book *Charter Schools: Creating Hope and Opportunity for American Schools* (1996) and in his article "Heat and Light in the Charter School Movement," *Phi Delta Kappan* (March 1998). Further positive descriptions are provided in James N. Goenner's "Charter Schools: The Revitalization of Public Education," *Phi Delta Kappan* (September 1996), and James K. Glassman's "Class Acts," *Reason* (April 1998).

Additional sources of ideas include *How to Create Alternative, Magnet, and Charter Schools That Work,* by Robert D. Barr and William H. Parrett (1997); "Homegrown," by Nathan Glazer, *The New Republic* (May 12, 1997); "Charter Schools: A Viable Public School Choice Option?" by Terry G. Geske et al., *Economics of Education Review* (February 1997); "A Closer Look at Charters," by Judith Brody Saks, *American School Board Journal* (January 1998); "Healthy Competition," by David Osborne, *The New Republic* (October 4, 1999); "Chinks in the Charter School Armor," by Tom Watkins, *American School Board Journal* (December 1999); and Seymour Sarason's *Charter Schools: Another Flawed Educational Reform* (1998).

Some recent provocative publications are Arthur Levine, "The Private Sector's Market Mentality," *The School Administrator* (May 2000); Bruce Fuller, ed., *Inside Charter Schools: The Paradox of Radical Decentralization* (2000); and Bruno V. Manno, "The Case Against Charter Schools," *The School Administrator* (May 2001), in which Manno responds to common complaints.

A few more articles worthy of note are "School Reform—Charter Schools," *Harvard Law Review* (May 1997); "The Political Challenge of Charter School Regulation," *Phi Delta Kappan* (March 2004), by Frederick M. Hess; David Moberg's "How Edison Survived," *The Nation* (March 15, 2004); and two articles in *Education Next* (Winter 2007) by Sana Mead and Nelson Smith.

ISSUE 18

Should "Concealed and Carry" Guns Be Allowed in the Classroom?

YES: National Rifle Association (NRA) of America, Institute for Legislative Action, from "The Outcry Over Campus Carry. The New Campus Revolt: Empty Holsters," NRA's *America's 1st Freedom* magazine and the NRA Institute for Legislative Action website (2007)

NO: Brady Center to Prevent Gun Violence, from "No Gun Left Behind: The Gun Lobby's Campaign to Push Guns into Colleges and Schools" www.bradycenter.org (May 2007)

ISSUE SUMMARY

YES: The NRA says it is a student's right to carry a gun to class to keep him or herself safe.

NO: The Brady Center says that guns just facilitate more violence and make a campus less safe.

The National Rifle Association (NRA) claims there is a movement afoot on college campuses nationwide in the wake of the Virginia Tech incident in April 2007. A lone gunman shot down 27 Virginia Tech students, including five faculty members, and wounded 17 others before turning the gun on himself.[1] This movement, the NRA says, wants people to have the freedom to possess conceal-and-carry weapons on campus for safety reasons. The NRA cites the example of Michael Flitcraft, a University of Cincinnati sophomore, who wore empty holsters to class in protest. According to the NRA, students at more than 100 colleges participated in empty-holster events like Michael's.

The Brady Center agrees that there need to be more guns on campus, but in the hands of security officers, not students. They argue that the Virginia Tech shooter was considered mentally defective but was still able to purchase guns because his mental record was not entered correctly. The Brady Bill would have stopped this shooter from obtaining guns, but the NRA fought this legislation vigorously.

The NRA contends that for them it is really a matter of freedom, and they ask, "Should you have less freedom and safety than anyone else simply because you go to college?"

In some states, allowing guns on campus is already a reality. Utah, for example, allows, "concealed-and-carry" or "right-to-carry" guns on their campuses. And, although the University of Utah challenged it, the Supreme Court upheld the law, according to the NRA.

The Brady Center counters that Utah is a ripe example of the NRA's push not just for the right to bring guns on campus, but to deregulate all guns anywhere. There is only one remaining restriction in Utah: Students can opt out of sharing a room with a gun-carrying roommate.

The NRA claims that guns on a campus make it safer. However, the *New York Times* reports that on August 30, 2006, for example, a student opened fire, injuring two students at his high school. Later, police found homemade pipe bombs, guns, and ammunition in the student's car. Strangely enough, the student had actually emailed the Principal of the Columbine High School, saying it was "time the world remembered" the Columbine shootings. Additionally, the NRA cites how guns saved the day on three different campuses. For example, a restaurant owner used a shotgun to stop a shooter in Edinboro, Pennsylvania, a 14-year old who wounded three students and killed his science teacher.

The Brady Center says the NRA does not tell the truth: that thousands of people who possess concealed-and-carry licenses have perpetrated appalling acts of gun violence. An example given by the Brady Center is that of Nathaniel Ferguson, 47, who obtained his concealed-and-carry license 18 months after shooting a 30-year-old woman in the parking lot outside a bar.

Although the Brady Center cites their rights as fundamental to this debate, the NRA touts that not only is their right to bear arms is being abridged, but additionally their freedom of speech is likewise ignored; therefore, there should be more of a debate on this issue; for example, the NRA points to a quote by Scott Lewis in *The Washington Times*:

> Whenever proponents of "concealed carry" point to the success of concealed-carry laws throughout the nation, as well as studies showing that concealed handgun license holders are significantly less likely than non-license holders to commit violent crimes, they are answered with mockery, rather than intelligent discourse. In the world of academia and intellectual free expression, some issues are apparently not open for discussion. (p. 4)

The Brady Center counters,

> If the rights of educational institutions can be trampled in the gun lobby's mad push to arm students and teachers, what places in our society will remain off-limits to guns?

Fundamental also to the NRA position is the freedom to choose to have a gun on campus for safety's sake. However, the Brady Center says that guns make life less safe on campus because guns increase violence in schools. Whatever the outcome, the debate will rage on among gun control and gun rights advocates.

Note

1. "Report of the Virginia Tech Review Panel". Commonwealth of Virginia. http://www.governor.virginia.gov/TempContent/techPanelReport.cfm. Retrieved November 16, 2009.

YES

Right-to-Carry. The New Campus Revolt: Empty Holsters

"**S**hould you have less freedom and safety than anyone else simply because you go to college?"

"Should society trust you less than your brothers and sisters of equal age simply because you attend college and they don't?"

"If you're mature enough and responsible enough to cast a vote, fight a war, own a gun, carry a gun and exercise every other right of citizenship that every other adult citizen enjoys, then why should you be disarmed and defenseless at institutions of higher learning?"

In the aftermath of the April 2007 massacre at Virginia Tech, in which an armed maniac killed 27 students and five faculty members before killing himself, more and more students are asking life-and-death questions like these of their politicians and professors.

It's a new national movement that's gathering momentum on college campuses across the country.

In late October, that movement took to the streets in the form of so-called "empty holster protests" at over 110 college campuses in 38 states and the District of Columbia.

Led by a group called "Students for Concealed Carry on Campus," students wore empty holsters to protest state laws and student codes of conduct that prohibit them from exercising the Right to Carry on campus—even if they have Right-to-Carry permits.

While lawmakers delay, debate and defend the status quo—in which college students basically are accorded the status of second-class citizenship—too many of those students are becoming victims of crime.

"As a college student and a concealed handgun license holder, when I step onto campus I am left unable to defend myself," group founder Chris Brown, a political science major at North Texas University, says on the organization's website. "My state allows me to carry a handgun in public, but there is some imaginary line drawn around college campuses for silly reasons. And those silly reasons are getting people killed, raped and robbed."

Or, as one of the group's leaders notes in an e-mail signature evoking the tragedy at Virginia Tech, "Campus policies left students shooting back with camera phones. Life's worth more than pictures."

Yet many state legislatures and college administrators don't seem to think that students' lives—or the lives of faculty, staff and visitors—are worth as much as their own.

When Good Intentions Empower Bad Men

Even though 40 states have fair Right-to-Carry laws, 36 states ban carrying firearms at schools, while 20 of those specifically outlaw firearms on college campuses.

So far, only one state—Utah—specifically and expressly allows the Right to Carry on public college campuses, thanks to a 2004 law allowing the Right to Carry on all state property. Although the University of Utah challenged the law, the state Supreme Court upheld it last year.

Even before the shootings at Virginia Tech, many were calling for the Right to Carry to be restored on college campuses. Ironically, a bill that would have required colleges in Virginia to allow Right-to-Carry permit holders to exercise that right on campuses failed in committee not long before the Virginia Tech tragedy.

After that crime, four states proposed bills to allow concealed firearm license holders to carry on college campuses. Such bills failed in Alabama and South Carolina, but at this writing a bill is still pending in Michigan and Ohio.

Additionally, Louisiana's legislature defeated a proposed ban on firearms in college dorms and Maine rejected legislation that would have allowed colleges to prohibit firearms.

While lawmakers delay, debate and defend the status quo—in which college students basically are accorded the status of second-class citizenship—too many of those students are becoming victims of crime.

In a one-week period in late September alone:

- A Delaware State University freshman was arrested for shooting two fellow students;
- An armed man on the University of Wisconsin campus "said he wished to commit suicide or be killed by police";
- A St. John's University freshman was arrested while wearing a George Bush mask and carrying a rifle at the New York college;
- An Ole Miss junior was shot to death;
- A junior at Tufts University in Massachusetts was robbed at gunpoint;
- And a University of Memphis junior was murdered.

Yet despite proclaiming their intention to stop "gun violence," the gun-ban lobby doesn't seem to have much sympathy for the victims of college campus disarmament. In response to a question regarding the empty holster protest, Peter Hamm, spokesman for the Brady Campaign, mocked, "You don't like the fact that you can't have a gun on your college campus? Drop out of school."

Silent Protest Opens Debate

Not to be thwarted, however, some college students aren't giving up the fight as easily as the gun-ban lobby would hope.

. . . a bill that would have required colleges in Virginia to allow Right-to-Carry permit holders to exercise that right on campuses died in committee not long before the Virginia Tech tragedy.

When a friend proposed the idea of carrying empty holsters to show how lawful students had been disarmed, Michael Flitcraft, a 23-year-old sophomore at the University of Cincinnati, says he took the idea and ran with it.

Soon dozens of students, and ultimately over 100 colleges, joined in the empty holster protest.

While drawing attention to the injustice of denying college students their constitutional rights, the protest also helped educate the public and open a constructive dialog on many campuses.

"People are under the impression that this is going to suddenly put guns in the hands of college students," said Scott Lewis, a media coordinator for Students for Concealed Carry on Campus. "We have to explain that, 'No, this isn't going to change the laws on who can get a gun, and it's not going to make it legal to carry a gun while under the influence. It's just going to give people on college campuses the same rights that they already have anywhere else.'"

"I had somebody tell me, 'I'd just be terrified if I knew somebody was carrying a gun.' So I asked them, 'Why?'" said Jay Adkins, a senior at East Tennessee State University who helped organize the empty holster protest at his school.

"They had this idea that guns would just randomly go off, or that people would break out into gunfights all the time," Adkins said. "But when you confront them with the facts that people do this in regular society every day, all the time, and nothing happens, they realize that college students can be just as responsible as any other adults.

"We're all adults. We just want people to realize that we don't suddenly become less responsible when we walk onto a campus."

Even if the media are biased in their coverage—the protest did draw some very negative press comments—many involved believe the publicity helps their cause more than the bias hurts it.

"If it's big enough to get the media's attention and warrant a story," said Flitcraft, "then it's going to get the word out. And that can only help."

The Siren Song of Security Schemes

In the wake of the mass murders at Virginia Tech, colleges have adopted various official responses while basically steering away from any serious, open-minded discussion of the firearms option.

Several schools now hold exercises akin to fire drills simulating a killer on campus. Some have fitted locks to classroom doors to keep killers at bay. New Jersey state Senator Barbara Buono plans legislation requiring a lock on every college and school classroom door in the state.

Virginia Tech installed sirens last spring that, ironically, got their first use on the day of the April 16 tragedy.

Technology companies are now selling schools mass notification systems based on e-mail, text-messaging, phone calls, RSS computer feeds, PA systems and digital billboards. One such company, Omnilert LLC, reported that the number of schools using its systems jumped from 25 to over 200 after the Virginia Tech tragedy.

For its part, the International Association of Campus Law Enforcement Administrators—whose members bank on being the only armed presence on campus—has warned that allowing students who have Right-to-Carry permits to carry on college grounds "has the potential to dramatically increase violence on our college and university campuses."

Indeed, despite assurances from some university authorities that everything is on the table when it comes to campus security, the options offered almost never include the only option that can even the odds by meeting force with equal force—good people carrying firearms to protect themselves against violent criminals.

Freedom Saves Lives on Campus

Though the gun-ban lobby will never admit it, and the anti-gun media are loath to report it, even though guns are banned at schools throughout most of the United States, firearms in the hands of peaceful, ordinary citizens have proven decisive in stopping some school shootings.

- In January 2002 at the Appalachian School of Law in Grundy, Va., a 43-year-old former student walked into the offices of two faculty members and shot them to death. Hearing the gunfire, two students immediately and independently ran to their separate cars, retrieved their firearms and returned to confront the killer and hold him at gunpoint for police, preventing any further murders.
- In Pearl, Miss., after stabbing his mother to death, a 16-year-old took a rifle to his high school, killed his former girlfriend and another girl, then began firing into the crowd. The killer was leaving to continue his rampage at a nearby school when the vice principal of his high school ran off campus to his parked vehicle, retrieved his Colt .45, stopped the rampage and held the murderer for police.
- In Edinboro, Pa., after a 14-year-old shot a science teacher to death and wounded three others at a school dance in April 1998, a restaurant owner pointed a shotgun at the shooter, forced him to surrender and held the killer for 11 minutes until police arrived.

Of course, the gun-ban lobby loves to raise the specter of minor disagreements escalating into free-for-all shootouts among Right-to-Carry permit holders. But after crying "Wolf!" for so many years as state after state adopted

Right to Carry—and seeing their dire predictions fall flat each and every time—the gun-ban lobby lost its credibility.

Consequently, gun haters shifted their story line from tragedy to comedy, ridiculing Right-to-Carry permit holders as juvenile would-be John Waynes or James Bonds, before suggesting, with infinite parental patience, that things don't work like they do in the movies, and that armed good guys would never be able to shoot as well as armed bad guys.

. . . the options offered almost never include the only option that can even the odds by meeting force with equal force—good people carrying firearms to protect themselves against violent criminals.

What's worse, though, is what such mockery and derision represent: an attempt to stifle the exchange of ideas and debate about a serious issue. In other words, hardly the kinds of things one would hope to "learn" at today's "institutes for higher learning."

As Scott Lewis pointed out in The Washington Times, "Whenever proponents of concealed carry point to its success throughout the nation, as well as studies showing that concealed handgun license holders are significantly less likely than non-license holders to commit violent crimes, they are answered with mockery, rather than intelligent discourse. In the world of academia and intellectual free expression, some issues are apparently not open for discussion."

In the end, the issue isn't so much whether the good guys prevail, or whether free speech is upheld. What really matters is whether the God-given right of self-defense is acknowledged and respected by the powers that be.

As Andrew Dysart, a senior at Virginia's George Mason University who organized that school's chapter of Students for Concealed Carry on Campus, argued, "There's no guarantee to know either way whether the Right to Carry could have changed anything at Virginia Tech. But I believe those students should have been allowed at least the choice to have a chance of saving themselves. That's what's at issue here: whether or not students should have that option."

No Gun Left Behind: The Gun Lobby's Campaign to Push Guns Into Colleges and Schools

On April 16, 2007, the day of the "Massacre at Virginia Tech," in which 32 innocent college students and faculty lost their lives to a crazed gunman armed with two semi-automatic pistols and a couple hundred rounds of ammunition, *the first reaction of the gun lobby was that we need more guns on the college campuses of our Nation*. That's correct. Before a single funeral was held for any of the victims of the Virginia Tech tragedy, and before anyone even knew who the victims were or the perpetrator was, the gun lobby called for college campuses to be turned into armed camps. The gun lobby also wants to repeal the Federal Gun-Free School Zones Act and arm public school teachers.

Was this your reaction to the horrific tragedy at Virginia Tech—to think society should eliminate gun-free schools and campuses? Do the students of the Nation want classrooms to be filled with guns? Will they feel safer knowing that the student sitting next to them could be packing? Would the parents of those students want to select schools for their children where the teachers and staff members, and even the students, were armed? Would putting guns into classrooms contribute to robust academic debate and foster a climate of learning? Do we really want to give guns to binge-drinking college kids, or let college sports fans bring them to stadiums? What about suicidal students or those in need of psychological counseling? How will more guns help them? Is "more guns on campus" the only answer our society can come up with in response to horrific gun violence on a college campus?

As it turns out, the Virginia Tech shooter had been "adjudicated as a mental defective" prior to purchasing the two handguns he used in his rampage. Thus, had records of mental health decrees been entered properly, the Brady background check would have barred him from purchasing those guns at a Roanoke gun store and Blacksburg pawn shop. The gun lobby, of course, vehemently opposed the Brady Bill.

Instead of accepting the straightforward solution of universal, thorough, background checks, the gun lobby clamors for legislation that would prohibit colleges and universities from maintaining rules or regulations that bar students from carrying handguns on campus. These statutes would preempt "gun free" policies on campus and allow students with carrying concealed weapons (CCW) licenses to be armed. Of course, the gun lobby fails to mention that thousands of people with CCW licenses have committed atrocious acts of gun violence. Moreover, a quick look behind this outrageous proposal reveals it to be a ruse. *The gun lobby's real aim is to prohibit colleges and universities from keeping ANY policies or rules that restrict gun access or use by students, regardless of whether the student is old enough to obtain a CCW license.*

This aim was revealed quite clearly in a letter issued by the National Rifle Association exactly two weeks prior to the massacre at Virginia Tech. *In the letter, dated April 2, 2007, the NRA's Institute for Legislative Action wrote to members of the Maine legislature in opposition to a bill that would "allow any college or university to regulate the possession of firearms on the property of the college or university."* Maine colleges and universities already have policies restricting firearms on campus, but the NRA maintains in its letter that state preemption law and the right-to-bear-arms provision of the Maine Constitution already prohibits such policies. In the absence of clarity on this point, the legislation opposed by the NRA was introduced. We have reprinted the letter in full in the **Introduction.**

In addition to opposing legislation that would affirm the rights of colleges and universities to control gun possession and use by students and faculty, the gun lobby is backing legislation to expressly prohibit such policies. In Utah, a law passed in 2004 prohibits public schools or state institutions of higher education from adopting or enforcing any "policy pertaining to firearms *that in any way inhibits or restricts the possession or use of firearms on either public or private property."* The law also explicitly prohibits those educational institutions from keeping guns out of dorm residences, or requiring students to have a "permit or license to purchase, own, possess, transport, or keep a firearm." Only one restriction remains—students can opt-out of rooming with a guncarrying student. Needless to say, that is no real restriction. *The bottom line is that college students in Utah appear to have the right to carry and use almost any type of firearm wherever they want, regardless of school policy.*

Once academic institutions are stripped of their right to set gun policies for students and faculty, almost no other barriers remain that would keep schools from becoming "gun-filled" zones. Federal law prohibits persons under 21 from *buying* handguns, but it does not prohibit kids as young as 18 from *possessing* them. Moreover, AK-47s and other assault rifles, with high-capacity detachable magazines that can deliver far more firepower than that of the Virginia Tech shooter, are completely legal for kids even younger than 18 to purchase and own.

One can only imagine the nightmarish scenarios that would become possible if the gun lobby were successful in forcing guns onto college campuses. Will students bring their AK-47 assault rifles with them to show off while guzzling beer at college keggers? Given that 90% of attempted suicides with guns are successful, how much more frequently will temporarily-depressed youths commit suicide if guns are available? Will gun thieves decide that college dorm rooms provide easier marks than private homes? The school-age years are among the most volatile times in every person's life. College students face severe social and academic pressure. Why would anyone want to introduce guns into the mix?

The gun lobby is not content, however, with guns on college campuses. It also wants to repeal the Gun-Free School Zones Act and arm teachers and other staff in our nation's elementary and secondary schools.

This report is intended to raise the alarm about the gun lobby's campaign to force educational institutions to accept guns. That campaign began before the massacre at Virginia Tech. Unbelievably, however, the voices in support of the campaign have become even louder in the wake of the most horrific gun violence tragedy in the history of our Nation. Yet the effect of any policy to arm students and teachers will be to undermine school safety and academic freedom and supplant it with a culture of gun carrying that is completely foreign to those institutions. . . .

◦◦◦

The gun lobby has launched a step-by-step campaign to force guns into every nook and cranny of American society. First, they pushed hard to prevent law enforcement from exercising its informed judgment as to who could carry concealed handguns. Next, they launched a 50-state campaign to force businesses to accept guns on company property. Now, in the wake of the worst mass shooting in American history—the "Massacre at Virginia Tech"—the gun lobby is making a renewed effort to force guns into college classrooms and schools across the United States. The gun lobby has already pushed through a bill in Utah that prohibits public schools and state institutions of higher education from enacting policies barring guns on campus. If the educational community does not respond, this type of legislation may well be enacted in more and more states.

The First Step: Expanding the Number of People Carrying Concealed Weapons

Over the last decade, the gun lobby has pushed hard in all 50 states to permit the carrying of concealed weapons by nearly everyone except convicted felons. These "shall-issue" carrying concealed weapons (CCW) laws require state authorities to issue CCW licenses to virtually anyone who applies, regardless of whether the applicant can demonstrate a need to carry a gun. As a result, millions of Americans are now licensed to carry concealed handguns in public.

The change in CCW laws has had serious security implications for institutions concerned about the welfare of their customers, employees, and students. Can such institutions trust that CCW licensees are law-abiding, nonviolent, well-trained citizens? Unfortunately, the answer is no. Many dangerous CCW applicants have slipped through faulty state background checks, while others have been marginal, highrisk applicants who nonetheless **must** be issued a CCW license because they do not fit within a narrow, pre-set list of excluded persons. In addition, state training in handgun safety is cursory at best, with no real training in nonviolent conflict resolution to help CCW licensees exercise proper judgment when carrying a firearm.

The Second Step: Forcing Guns onto Business Property

The gun lobby has not been satisfied, however, with achieving step one—passing shall-issue CCW laws—in a majority of states. It has now chosen to become even more aggressive in making guns ubiquitous in American society. In May 2005, the NRA pushed a law through the Oklahoma legislature that tramples on centuries-old rights of private property owners as well as the rights of businesses to control their workplaces.

The Oklahoma "forced-entry" law makes it a crime for *anyone*—"person, property owner, tenant, employer, or business entity"—to bar *any* person, except a convicted felon, from bringing a gun onto *any* property in Oklahoma that is "set aside for *any* motor vehicle." In addition to making violators subject to criminal penalties, the statute grants individuals a right of action to sue persons, property owners, tenants, employers or businesses to force them to accept guns into any place set aside for motor vehicles and collect court costs and attorneys fees if they prevail.

The breadth of the Oklahoma legislation is staggering. The owner of *any* place "set aside" for a motor vehicle—which is defined to include not only cars, trucks, minivans, and sport utility vehicles, but also motorcycles and motor scooters—*must* accept guns onto their private property. Moreover, there is no limitation on *who* property owners must allow to bring a gun onto their property, except that the person cannot be a *convicted* felon. The Oklahoma law is not restricted to persons who have obtained a CCW license or received training in firearms safety. Nor is there any limitation on the *type* or *number* of guns that can be brought onto someone's private property, including AK-47s, UZIs, Tec-9s, or other assault weapons, or .50 caliber sniper rifles powerful enough to bring down an airplane.

For now the Oklahoma law is in legal limbo. A lawsuit filed by several Oklahoma companies in Federal court argued the law was unconstitutional for two reasons. First, it tramples private property and due process rights in violation of the Fifth and Fourteenth Amendments of the United States Constitution. Second, the law conflicts with the overarching Federal duty established by the Occupational Safety and Health Act's General Duty Clause, which requires employers to provide a workplace free from hazards. Thus, the Oklahoma law should give way under the Supremacy Clause of the United States Constitution. The court granted plaintiffs a temporary restraining order and blocked enforcement of the law pending a final decision on the merits, which has not yet been issued.

In addition to Oklahoma, the gun lobby has attempted to pass similar legislation in Georgia, Florida, Texas, Virginia, Indiana, California, Utah, Tennessee, Montana, New Hampshire, and several other states. It has succeeded—albeit with weaker laws—in Alaska, Minnesota, Kentucky, Kansas and Mississippi. Solid opposition from the business community and numerous other groups, including the Brady Campaign, has so far largely held off the gun lobby's onslaught.

This legislation attempts to force guns across a critical threshold that has been fundamental to American culture and law for centuries—the right of property owners to control their private property. It would also gut the long-standing right of businesses to set the terms and conditions of the workplace. Unless the gun lobby's legislative campaigns are stopped, there is no telling how far it will go in its zeal to inject guns everywhere in American society.

The Third Step: Forcing Guns into Schools and Campuses

After the massacre at Virginia Tech, we are now beginning to see how far the gun lobby is prepared to go in its quest to bar any institutions from attempting to maintain gunfree zones. Before we even knew who the shooter was, or the identity of his victims, several gun groups had issued press releases calling for legislation to prohibit Virginia Tech and other colleges and universities across the country from maintaining gun-free campuses. Many of those press releases called for repeal of the Federal Gun-Free School Zones Act of 1996 that prohibits firearms within 1,000 feet of elementary and secondary schools.

In addition, the NRA Institute for Legislative Action sent a letter to Maine legislators two weeks prior to the massacre making it clear they thought the law of Maine *already* prohibited colleges and universities in that state from "regulat[ing] the possession of firearms on the property of the college or university."

How serious is this threat? Educational institutions need to take it *very* seriously. In addition to revealing its true intentions in Maine, the gun lobby has already convinced the state legislature in Utah to pass a law prohibiting public schools or state institutions of higher education from enforcing or enacting any rule or policy that in "any way inhibits or restricts the possession or use of firearms on either public or private property," including college campuses. This type of law could turn colleges and universities into armed camps—*"gun-filled zones"*—by permitting students as young as 18 to keep and carry handguns on or off campus, and kids even younger than 18 to keep and carry rifles and shotguns, including military-style assault-rifles with high-capacity magazines. The University of Utah sued to overturn the law on the grounds that it violated principles of academic freedom and autonomy, but lost its case before the Utah Supreme Court.

Moreover, over the last two years the gun lobby has resorted to extreme hardball tactics with even its most ardent supporters in lobbying for guns-at-work legislation, which suggests they would do the same here. In Georgia, for example, after the Virginia Tech massacre, the National Rifle Association threatened every member of the legislature who voted to block or defeat that state's guns-at-work measure with an "F" rating, regardless of whether they had accumulated "A+" ratings from the NRA for years. Similar pressure is being brought to bear on legislators in Florida and Texas. The NRA also purchased billboard space and launched a boycott of the companies that sued to block the Oklahoma law.

If the rights of educational institutions can be trampled in the gun lobby's mad push to arm students and teachers, what places in our society will remain off-limits to guns? If legislatures can be convinced to prohibit colleges and universities from barring 18-year-old students from carrying handguns to class or sports arenas, or filling their dorm rooms with military-style assault rifles and high-capacity ammunition clips, will anywhere remain a gun-free sanctuary? If elementary and secondary-school teachers are armed, what message does that convey to our children? Of course, the gun lobby's extremist campaign has come under fire, but this has not deterred them in the past from using scorched-earth tactics to pursue their agenda. The gun lobby's campaign forces educational institutions to make a choice. They can either stand on the sidelines and be run over in state legislatures, passing laws that trample on the rights of institutions and property owners to establish gun-free policies, or they can lobby aggressively to prevent such laws from being passed in the first place. . . .

◆

Despite the horrific massacre at Virginia Tech, college and university campuses are much safer than the communities that surround them. A U.S. Justice Department study found that from 1995 to 2002, college students aged 18 to 24 experienced violence at significantly lower average annual rates—almost 20% lower—than non-students in the same age group. Moreover, **93% of the violence against students occurs off campus.** Even 85% of the violent crimes against students who live on campus occur at locations off campus.

Elementary and secondary schools are also safer than society at large, as fewer than 1% of school-age homicide victims are killed on or around school grounds or on the way to and from school. Plus, in every year from 1992 to 2000, youths aged 5–19 were at least 70 times more likely to be murdered away from school than at a school. Even Gary Kleck, a researcher often cited by the gun lobby, notes these statistics and concludes: **"Both gun carrying and gun violence are thus phenomena almost entirely confined to the world outside schools."**

The discrepancy in violence rates on and off school grounds and on and off college campuses is no doubt due, in part, to the fact that nearly every academic institution—from elementary school through higher education—has adopted a policy that either tightly controls possession and use of student firearms or bans guns altogether. The overwhelming preference among Americans—94% according to one survey—is to keep it that way.

If the gun lobby is successful in getting state legislatures beyond Utah to upset these longstanding policies and prohibit colleges and schools from barring or controlling gun possession and use by their students, it is not difficult to imagine the increased dangers and risks that will follow. They would, at a minimum, include:

- Diminished safety for students, faculty, staff, and visitors;
- Greater potential for student-on-student and student-on-faculty violence, and more lethal results when such violence occurs.

POSTSCRIPT

Should "Concealed and Carry" Guns Be Allowed in the Classroom?

Brent Tenney, a 24-year-old business major, brought his fully loaded 9mm semi-automatic with him every day to class at the University of Utah because it made him feel safer.[1] "It's not that I run around scared all day long, but if something happens to me, I do want to be prepared," said Tenney, who has a concealed-weapons permit and boasts that he takes his handgun almost everywhere other than his church.[2] Utah is the only state that allows students to bring their guns to class.

Nationally, 38 states outlaw guns from schools, 16 of which unequivocally prohibit weapons on college campuses.[3] Other states allow all schools to devise their own gun-related policies.

There is momentum to loosen gun laws in other states; for example, in Oklahoma, state Representative Jason Murphey's bill, to allow "concealed and carry" guns into classrooms by active and nonactive military personnel, passed the Oklahoma State House in 2008.[4] Those who want to bring guns into the classroom have to prove they passed the Council on Law Enforcement Education training to possess a state concealed weapons license. This legislation, was approved 65-36 in the Oklahoma State House, but the bill that passed was much narrower than Murphey's initial proposal, allowing anyone older than 21 years old carrying rights to bring his or her concealed handgun on campus.[5] The bill was later killed in the state senate.[6]

This momentum to add guns to the classroom emanates from the NRA, which also questions state enforcement of background checks. On April 16, 2007, Seung-Hui Cho, 23, a senior in English at Virginia Tech, killed 32 people and wounded many others.[7] It was later found that Cho was diagnosed with a severe anxiety disorder. In the Virginia Tech Review Panel report, the Panel disparaged the mental health professionals and educators who came into contact with Cho during his time in college. The report is critical of their inability to perceive his worsening state and to aid him. The Panel also condemned the misconception of Virginia privacy laws and cracks in the state's mental health system as well as Virginia's lack of gun laws.[8]

That Cho was able to buy not just one but two guns, in spite of his mental health history, has produced a new awareness of the insufficiencies of background gun checks.[9] It is states who must enforce federal gun laws, but Virginia failed to identify mass murderer Cho. This brings to light the fact that states often have inadequate information to enforce these federal laws

> Federal law prohibits anyone who has been "adjudicated as a mental defective," as well as those who have been involuntarily committed to a mental health facility, from buying a gun.[10]

Currently, the FBI claims that only 22 states offer any mental health records to the federal National Instant Criminal Background Check System.[11] There is a disconnect, though, between federal statutes and the Virginia state law on mental health disqualifications for firearms purchases; the Virginia law differs slightly from the federal statute. Therefore, Virginia only addresses its own criteria, with two categories warranting warnings to the Virginia police: an individual who is considered (1) mentally "incapacitated" or (2) "involuntarily committed." Richard J. Bonnie, chairman of the Supreme Court of Virginia's Commission on Mental Health Law Reform, said, "It's clear we have an imperfect connection between state law and the application of the federal prohibition." The commission he leads was created by the state last year to examine the state's mental health laws.

As a result, New York Rep. Carolyn McCarthy sponsored the NICS Improvement Amendments Act, which was passed into law in 2008.[12] This fairly new law requires all federal agencies possessing records on persons who cannot legally purchase a firearm to supply these records to the Attorney General. The Attorney General, in turn, sends them to the National Instant Criminal Background Check System (NICS) for inclusion in their records, making them available to gun sellers.[13]

Will guns in the classroom save lives? The question is still being debated.

Notes

1. Utah Only State to Allow Guns at College: Some Students Legally Pack Concealed Weapons, Others Question Value." MSNBC. Accessed December 5, 2009, http://www.msnbc.msn.com/id/18355953/

2. *Ibid.*

3. *Ibid.*

4. "Bill Allowing Guns on College Campuses Approved by House in Oklahoma," Associated Press (March 14). Accessed December 6, 2009, http://www.foxnews.com/story/0,2933,337818,00.html

5. *Ibid.*

6. "Okla. Senate Shoots Down Bill to Allow Guns on Campuses," CBS News. Accessed December 5, 2009, http://www.cbsnews.com/stories/2008/04/03/politics/uwire/main3993003.shtml

7. Duncan Adams, "The Alienation and Anger of Seung-Hui Cho," *The Roanoke Times*. Accessed December 6, 2009, http://www.roanoke.com/vtinvestigation/wb/wb/xp-130177

8. "Mass Shootings at Virginia Tech," Report of the Virginia Tech Review Panel: Presented to Timothy M. Kaine, Governor Commonwealth of Virginia by the Virginia Tech Review Panel (August 2007), http://www.governor.virginia.gov/TempContent/techPanelReport.cfm

9. Michael Luo, "U.S. Rules Made Killer Ineligible to Purchase Gun, *New York Times* (April 21, 2007). http://www.nytimes.com/2007/04/21/us/21guns.html?_r=110

10. *Ibid.*

11. *Ibid.*

12. United States Representative Carolyn McCarthy's Web site. Accessed December 06, 2009, http://carolynmccarthy.house.gov/index.cfm?sectionid=253&sectiontree=18,253

13. H.R. 2640: NICS Improvement Amendments Act of 2007. Accessed December 6, 2009, http://www.govtrack.us/congress/bill.xpd?bill=h110-2640

ISSUE 19

Should Local Schools Have National Standards?

YES: Chester E. Finn Jr., Liam Julian, and Michael J. Petrilli, from "To Dream the Impossible Dream: Four Approaches to National Standards and Tests for America's Schools," Thomas B. Fordham Foundation (August 2006)

NO: Lawrence A. Uzzell, from "No Child Left Behind: The Dangers of Centralized Education Policy," Cato Institute (May 31, 2005)

ISSUE SUMMARY

YES: Chester E. Finn, president; Liam Julian, associate writer and editor; and Michael J. Petrilli, vice president for national programs and policy, all of the Thomas B. Fordham Foundation, state, "National standards and tests may no longer be politically taboo."

NO: Lawrence A. Uzzell, an independent researcher and former staff member of the U.S. Department of Education and U.S. House and Senate committees on education, believes that "the key to rescuing our children from the bureaucratized government schools is radical decentralization."

Historically, governance of public education in the United States has aptly been described as a "national interest, a state power, and a local responsibility." With the origin of our nationhood coming through a successful revolutionary struggle against a strong central government, it is not surprising that power and control of education was not vested in a new central government. Rather, that power, by way of the Tenth Amendment, devolved to the individual states that in turn delegated much responsibility for governance to local entities such as school boards. Through the years that decentralized approach has been the prevalent pattern of governance of public education. Certainly there have been notable exceptions to that pattern wherein the federal government has exercised power over public schools, but those occasions have been limited generally to constitutional issues adjudicated by the U.S. Supreme Court. Such instances include court rulings related to separation of church and state, desegregation, student rights of expression, and student privacy. On other occasions, federal legislation has tied federal funding to state adherence to provisions within that legislation. Examples include gender equity, support of special needs students, and most recently the No Child Left Behind Act (NCLB). Theoretically, states may avoid the provisions of such legislation by not taking the federal funding. Practically speaking, refusing federal funds is not generally seen as a viable option for schools and, in any event, such a decision would likely lead to court action.

It is the specificity of NCLB provisions related to traditional state-level control over issues such as teacher quality, content and strategies for reading instruction, and school accountability measures that have caused some critics to suggest that this may be the single greatest federal incursion into state power over education in our nation's history. As Lawrence Uzzell states in his response to this issue, "NCLB may end up giving us the worst possible scenario: unconstitutional consolidation of power in Washington over the schools, with that power being used to promote mediocrity rather than excellence."

Perhaps anticipating such criticism, the legislation has, thus far, left it to individual states to develop content standards and administer the assessments related to those standards in order to determine whether students are making adequate yearly progress. Yet some do not believe that having educational standards set by individual states is the right way to go. In their *Education Week* (March 7, 2007) article, Rudy Crew, Paul Vallas, and Michael Casserly argue that the widely disparate nature of 50 different sets of standards and related assessment systems may eventually doom any national reform effort. They state:

> In the absence of a clear and consistent set of national academic standards for what should be expected of all children, each state instead sets its own standards for what kids should know or be able to do. Sometimes these standards are high; often they are not. Either way, they drive the teaching and learning in America's classrooms and serve to perpetuate the nation's educational inequities at a time when we should be working to overcome them.

This indeed is a high-stakes debate because it has major implications for not only the children and teachers in our nation's public schools, but, more broadly for all citizens, with respect to how we will govern our public schools in the future.

YES

Chester E. Finn Jr., Liam Julian, and Michael J. Petrilli

To Dream the Impossible Dream: Four Approaches to National Standards and Tests for America's Schools

For the first time in almost a decade, people are seriously weighing the value of instituting national standards and tests in American K–12 education. Yet despite many pervasive and commonsense reasons (explained below) to support such a reform, two large obstacles loom. The first is political: a winning coalition must be assembled, probably by a presidential contender—no small challenge, considering that the failed attempts of the 1990s to create national standards and tests left a bad taste in many politicians' mouths. The second obstacle is substantive: until policymakers can envision what a system of national standards and tests might look like, how it would work, and how its various logistical challenges might be addressed, this idea will remain just that. This report addresses the second obstacle and, in so doing, also helps with the political challenge. Once the key design issues are hammered out, it will be easier to tackle ideology and votes.

To gather input on how a system of national standards and tests might be designed, we queried a bipartisan selection of prominent experts. We knew that we would not agree with all of their views, nor would they agree with all of ours. But we certainly benefited from their varied and informed opinions and we're profoundly grateful for their cooperation—and their willingness to tackle this topic in public view. We asked them to answer a series of questions ranging from the macro—should the federal government design the tests—to the micro (e.g., ought the tests be given annually?). As we pondered their responses, certain patterns became clear. Within their excellent advice and good ideas are four distinct approaches to national standards and tests that we describe and appraise in the following pages:

1. **The Whole Enchilada.** This is the most direct and aggressive approach. The federal government would create and enforce national standards and assessments, replacing the fifty state-level sets of standards and tests we have now. The United States would move to a national accountability system for K–12 education.

2. **If You Build It, They Will Come.** This is a voluntary version of the first model. Uncle Sam would develop national standards, tests and accountability metrics, and provide incentives to states (such as additional money or fewer regulations) to opt into such a system. A variant would have a private group frame the standards. Either way, participation would be optional for states.
3. **Let's All Hold Hands.** Under this approach, states would be encouraged to join together to develop common standards and tests or, at the least, common test items. Uncle Sam might provide incentives for such collaboration, but that's it.
4. **Sunshine and Shame.** This model, the least ambitious, would make state standards and tests more transparent by making them easier to compare to one another and to the National Assessment of Educational Progress (NAEP).

In this paper, we outline how each model might work in practice, and we evaluate the likelihood that each would:

- End the "race to the bottom";
- Result in rigorous standards rather than merely politically acceptable ones;
- Expand Washington's role in education;
- Prove politically feasible.

It's no secret that we, at the Thomas B. Fordham Foundation, favor national standards and tests—provided they are done right. We believe they are needed now more than ever. But as policy analysts have begun seriously to debate the idea in recent months and a few politicians have begun (at least privately) to flirt with it, a sure conversation stopper kept getting in the way. Someone would ask, "So how exactly would this work in practice?" Tumbling from their lips would be five, ten, a dozen legitimate and important questions about the implementation of this basic idea. Who would write the standards? The federal government? Congress or the Department of Education? What would happen to state standards and tests? Which subjects would you test? How often? Who would deliver the results? How would this intersect with No Child Left Behind? And on and on. We quickly realized that for this idea to advance beyond the domain of wishful thinking and knee jerk reacting, someone would have to take a stab at answering such questions. This is our attempt.

Recent history illustrates the need to address these design problems. Mistakes can be costly. President George H.W. Bush watched his ambitious plan for national standards sink after his administration outsourced the job to professional organizations of educators such as the National Council of Teachers of English. President Bill Clinton found his "voluntary national tests" proposal lampooned by concerns over student privacy, overweening government involvement, and "fuzzy" math. If tomorrow's political leaders are to tackle this topic, they will need a plan that's fully baked.

We knew we could not flesh out these design issues alone, so we called upon a dozen eminent colleagues from left, right, and center. Some are scholars, others policymakers. Some support national standards and tests while others abhor the notion. All, however, are thoughtful, creative, and experienced policy entrepreneurs. And they did not disappoint—their lucid and insightful comments are found throughout this report. . . .

We started by posing twelve important questions that one would have to answer if he or she were serious about actually implementing national standards and tests. . . . We sent these stumpers to our esteemed experts and solicited their responses. What we received surprised us. First, many of our colleagues showed themselves to be more skeptical about the project of national standards and tests than we—or even they—assumed they would be. Second, as we sifted through their answers, we noticed some patterns. Four distinct approaches to national standards and tests, rose to the surface, each with its own pluses and minuses. Fleshing out and evaluating this quartet of models became the purpose of this report:

1. **The Whole Enchilada.** This is the most direct and aggressive approach. The federal government would create and enforce national standards and assessments, replacing the fifty state-level sets of standards and tests we have now. The United States would move to a national accountability system for K–12 education.
2. **If You Build It, They Will Come.** This is a voluntary version of the first model. Uncle Sam would develop national standards, tests and accountability metrics, and provide incentives to states (such as additional money or fewer regulations) to opt into such a system. A variant would have a private group frame the standards. Either way, participation would be optional for states.
3. **Let's All Hold Hands.** Under this approach, states would be encouraged to join together to develop common standards and tests or, at the least, common test items. Uncle Sam might provide incentives for such collaboration, but that's it.
4. **Sunshine and Shame.** This model, the least ambitious, would make state standards and tests more transparent by making them easier to compare to one another and to the National Assessment of Educational Progress (NAEP).

Drawing heavily on our expert contributors, we describe what each of these models might look like in practice, with particular reference to these three design elements:

- **Politics & Process.** Who sets the standards? What is their relationship to the federal government? How are they developed? How do educators and the public weigh in?
- **Scope.** How many subjects get tested? How frequently?
- **Consequences.** How do these standards interact with state accountability systems? Is anyone held accountable for the standards' rigor?

Why National Standards and Tests?

Once this four-entree menu of options for policymakers took shape, we felt an obligation to provide an evaluation of each—a Zagat's review, if you will. What are their relative pros and cons?

Of course, this is a matter of values and judgment. Just as a food critic has her own biases (simple versus complex, classic versus cutting edge), so do we have our own policy preferences. We can cite plenty of reasons why one might support national standards and tests, but which do we find most compelling? In other words, which pressing problems do we think standards-based reform, and specifically national standards and tests, are needed to solve?

Let's start with standards-based reform. At a time when much of the No Child Left Behind debate centers around "teaching to the test," it's worth remembering why policymakers embarked on this reform agenda in the first place.

The first reason was educational: to create a more coherent and consistent educational experience for American children. Back in the day when teachers could simply close their doors and teach whatever they wanted, students faced a real risk of learning about dinosaurs every year and never encountering the solar system. Standards provided the opportunity for the system to map out a coherent curricular plan grade by grade, ideally culminating in the knowledge and skills needed for success in higher education, the workplace, and our democratic polity. As E.D. Hirsch, Jr., has masterfully explained, this curricular coherence in the schools is especially critical for poor children, who are least likely to develop the "cultural literacy" at home that will allow them to compete in a meritocracy. Standards also allow educators to work collaboratively on curriculum, professional development and so forth, though, importantly, standards are not themselves the curriculum. Done right, they focus on the results to be achieved and leave room for individual schools and educators to figure out the best way to reach them.

The second reason was moral and political: where standards existed, they tended to be higher for affluent children and lower for those living in poverty and for children of color. Schools (and parents) in leafy suburbs pushed their students (at least their affluent students) to tackle rigorous Advanced Placement courses; meanwhile, poor urban districts made excuses for their pupils and seemed content with basic literacy (or just school completion). Statewide standards, measured by standardized tests and linked to meaningful accountability, were seen as the antidote to inequitable expectations.

The final reason was organizational: it was hoped that, by focusing on results, states could scrap myriad input-and-process regulations that sought to improve the schools through the force of coercion. One of the earliest advocates of this approach was the National Governors Association (NGA). Led by Tennessee's Lamar Alexander, it embarked in 1985 on a multi-year education reform initiative—most unusual for an outfit that traditionally changed priorities as often as it changed chairs, i.e., annually. The keystone event was the governors' release and endorsement, during their annual summer meeting in 1986, of an Alexander-inspired report called *Time for Results*.

The governors accepted the post-Coleman reasoning that, if stronger achievement is what's needed, policymakers should focus on the results they seek and how to extract these from the education system, willing or not. They introduced a conceptual quid-pro-quo that foreshadowed charter schools and other potent structural innovations. Experts call it "tight-loose" management: being demanding with regard to outcomes but relaxed about how those outcomes are produced. In Alexander's more homespun phrasing, the governors declared themselves ready for "some old-fashioned horse-trading. We'll regulate less, if schools and school districts will produce better results."

We believe that although these arguments are still valid today, ultimately state standards and tests are inadequate to address four of America's greatest challenges:

1. Global competition
2. A fragmented education marketplace
3. The unwillingness of states to set and police their own rigorous standards
4. An overweening federal government

Global Competition

The United States faces unprecedented competition from nations around the planet. If all of our young people are to succeed in the "flat" global economy of the 21st century, they will need to achieve to world-class standards.

Globalization, outsourcing, and the Internet have created a worldwide marketplace. Fifty years ago, students graduating from our public school system faced competition from peers in their own town or region. Today, American students must compete with children from India, China, and Brazil.

Virtually all of the world's advanced nations recognize this challenge and have aligned their educational systems with a uniform set of nationwide academic expectations or requirements. Yet, in the United States, we continue to pretend that math in Birmingham is different than math in Boston, much less Bangalore. We cannot afford the parochialism of our current system if we want to maintain our economic position in the world. Plus, the United States is no longer a country in which people are born, live their lives, and die in the same town or even the same state. Americans move frequently, and that means children move frequently, too. National standards and tests could ensure high expectations from sea to shining sea.

A Fragmented Education Marketplace

One of the promises of standards-based reform was that it would allow for, even demand, the development and alignment of powerful educational resources: stronger teacher preparation, content-rich professional development, multimedia curricular materials, etc. Yet the variability and mediocrity of state-by-state standards have made the fruition of this promise much more challenging.

Take teacher training. While science teacher candidates in Ohio could conceivably be prepared to teach to Ohio's science standards, many of them will leave Ohio after graduation. The result? Teacher training stays at 30,000 feet rather than drilling down to specific content and concepts.

Or take curricular materials. While it's easy to imagine teachers using well-developed digital content in their classrooms instead of the shoddy textbooks available today, companies that could provide this content are hampered by the fractured educational marketplace that (understandably) demands alignment with state standards. Moving to national standards, and thus creating a national market, would create strong incentives for companies to invest in developing the successors to today's lackluster materials. Across all aspects of our educational system, common expectations would allow for a common conversation among educators and collaborative problem-solving.

Of course, the problem of varying standards is not faced by our education system alone. Take the technology sector: at key moments the industry has coalesced around common standards in order to improve efficiency and facilitate innovation. For instance, people around the world enjoy wireless Internet access when they travel because the industry agreed on a common wireless technology protocol. Rather than bickering over standards, technology companies and other providers can compete over the services and content they offer customers. This could happen in education, too.

The Unwillingness of States to Set and Police Their Own Rigorous Standards

The state standards movement has been in place for almost fifteen years. For almost ten of those years, we at the Thomas B. Fordham Foundation have reviewed the quality of state standards. Most were mediocre to bad ten years ago, and most are mediocre to bad today. They are generally vague, politicized, and awash in wrongheaded fads and nostrums. With a few exceptions, states have been incapable (or unwilling) to set clear, coherent standards, and develop tests with a rigorous definition of proficiency. By our lights, you can count on one hand the number of states with clear proficiency standards in reading and math and expectations even approaching those of the National Assessment of Educational Progress.

No Child Left Behind was supposed to improve on the situation, by taking the example of leading standards-based reform states such as Texas and North Carolina and applying their successful policies to the entire nation. But its designers made a critical mistake. Rather than settling on a common standard for school performance and allowing states and schools to meet that standard as they judged best, it developed a common timeline for achieving "universal proficiency" but allowed states to define "proficiency" in reading and math as they saw fit. The result: there is now heavy pressure on states to define "proficiency" downward and to make Swiss cheese out of NCLB's accountability provisions. Already many states, in order to explain the discrepancy between their passing rates on state tests and their students' performance on NAEP, are claiming that journalists and others should equate state "proficiency" with

NAEP's "basic" level. In other words, they are satisfied to get their students to "basic"—"proficiency" be damned. A system that allows such quibbling puts the entire standards-based-reform enterprise in peril.

An Overweening Federal Government

Finally, and counter-intuitively, we see national standards and tests as an opportunity to rein in the federal government. For forty years, Washington has sought to improve the nation's schools by regulating what they do. To date, scant evidence exists that this strategy works.

Common standards and tests could allow Washington to back away from its top-down, regulatory approach and settle instead for clarifying the objectives to be achieved and measuring (and publicizing) whether states, schools, and students are in fact meeting them. Many think that national standards entail an increased federal role. We see it in precisely the opposite way—that a good set of national standards will lead to a reduced and focused federal role that is also better suited to Uncle Sam's particular skill set.

Judging Each Approach

With those biases and objectives in mind, we evaluate each model against the following criteria:

- Is it likely to end the "race to the bottom"? As noted above, because NCLB requires states to adopt standards and tests, get all students to proficiency by 2014, and hold schools accountable for the results, states face great pressure to lower their standards and ease the rigor of their tests. A few states have done this in plain view; we worry that many more are doing so behind closed doors via the many, many ways that expectations can surreptitiously be softened. So a critical question to ask of the four approaches to national standards and testing is whether they will halt any backsliding and lead to world-class standards suited to the demands of the 21st century.
- Is it likely to result in rigorous standards rather than merely politically acceptable ones? As explained above, the ugly truth about standards-based reform is that most of the academic standards in use today are slipshod. A reasonable concern, then, is whether any of these approaches to national standards and tests will be able to get it right when it comes to the content and rigor of the standards themselves.
- Is it likely to lead to an expanded federal role in education? In other words, can we set national standards and tests without federalizing the U.S. education system and thereby doing it a disservice? To what degree do these four approaches require a stronger role for Uncle Sam? Do they make it more or less likely that Congress will intervene in a larger swath of issues or that federal courts will mandate spending levels supposedly needed to achieve the standards?
- Is it likely to prove politically feasible? We offer our best judgment about the odds that any of these four approaches could survive the political minefield. Of course, some will argue that any version of

national standards and tests are infeasible, even that this is a "third rail" type of political problem. We disagree and think this is the wrong reading of history. The evolution of bipartisan support for standards-based reform in American K–12 education can be traced from Charlottesville (1989) through the setting of national education goals (1990) to the National Assessment Governing Board's establishing of "achievement levels" (early 1990s). And further to the composition of the National Council on Education Standards and Testing (1991) and the National Education Goals Panel (1990) through the Goals 2000 and Improving America's Schools Acts (1994) and through any number of education "summits" to the enactment in 2001 of NCLB itself. What went wrong in the early 1990s wasn't the principle of national education standards; it was a misjudgment as to where and by whom these should be set. While one of us once said that "national testing is doomed because the right hates 'national' and the left hates 'testing,'" we believe that times are a changing. Business leaders' concerns about economic competitiveness and civil rights leaders' (belated) embrace of testing as a tool to close the achievement gap indicate that national standards and tests may no longer be politically taboo.

Lawrence A. Uzzell  **NO**

No Child Left Behind: The Dangers of Centralized Education Policy

The No Child Left Behind Act (NCLB), which the Bush administration claims as its proudest achievement in domestic policy, directly contradicts the principles of an "ownership society" which the administration is promoting in areas such as Social Security reform. The administration recognizes that the educational policies of the last four decades, a period of almost uninterrupted centralization, have failed, but its remedy is yet more centralization.

The NCLB statute is a reform strategy at war with itself. It virtually guarantees massive evasion of its own intent, ordering state education agencies to do things that they mostly don't want to do. Washington will be forced either to allow the states great leeway in how they implement NCLB or to make NCLB more detailed, prescriptive, and top-heavy. If Washington chooses the former, the statute might as well not exist; if the latter, federal policymakers will increasingly resemble Soviet central planners trying to improve economic performance by micromanaging decisions from Moscow. NCLB may end up giving us the worst possible scenario: unconstitutional consolidation of power in Washington over the schools, with that power being used to promote mediocrity rather than excellence.

It is too early to know for certain which scenario will prevail, but it is already clear that state and local education officials are skillfully protecting their interests in ways that undermine the intent of NCLB. Especially telling has been their widespread dishonest reporting in at least four areas: graduation rates, school violence, qualified teachers, and proficiency tests. As it becomes increasingly clear that the states can satisfy the requirements of NCLB by lowering their standards, there will likely be a "race to the bottom."

Instead of using centralized decrees to turn mediocre institutions into excellent ones, as they have been trying but failing to do for the last several decades, the state and federal governments should be empowering individual families to "vote with their feet" by transferring to the schools of their own choice.

The key locus for such revolutionary reforms is the states. The best contribution the national government can make to educational improvement is to avoid educational policymaking and allow states to experiment with school choice programs.

From *Policy Analysis*, no. 544, May 31, 2005, pp. 1–6, 16–18. Copyright © 2005 by Cato Institute. Reprinted by permission.

Introduction

In domestic policy, the No Child Left Behind (NCLB) education act is the Bush administration's top claim to visionary leadership. The president and his aides have compared NCLB to landmark programs such as the Social Security Act or the Homestead Act. In his acceptance speech at the 2004 Republican convention, President Bush stated that NCLB is "the most important federal education reform in history." Both during and since the 2004 election campaign, President Bush's speeches have depicted the 2002 act as an unqualified success; even before his second inauguration, the president proposed to extend its provisions from elementary schools to high schools.

Especially striking is the boast that Bush has increased federal spending on education faster than any president since Lyndon Johnson. That is a reversal as profound as the Clinton administration's embrace of sweeping welfare reform in 1996; in both cases the party in power accepted ideas long associated with its opponents. The Republican reversal is the more stunning of the two because most members of the president's party on Capitol Hill changed course with him. During the Republican Party's rise to majority status from the 1960s to the 1990s, by contrast, it usually opposed centralized federal programs in education as in other areas of governance. As recently as 1996, the party's platform pledged to abolish the U.S. Department of Education.

What ultimately matters is NCLB's success not as a one-shot campaign tactic but as a long-term strategy for bringing genuine reform to the country's dysfunctional public schools. With party loyalty keeping most congressional Republicans from criticizing the statute, its skeptics currently find themselves marginalized in Washington. But in the long run NCLB should and will be judged by its actual results.

Dangers of Centralization

No Child Left Behind was enacted in the form of a reauthorization of the 1965 Elementary and Secondary Education Act, one of the centerpieces of President Lyndon Johnson's Great Society. Once it takes full effect, the statute will require states that receive ESEA subsidies annually to test third to eighth grade students in reading and mathematics. By 2014 the states must bring all of their students up to the "proficient" level on those tests. In the meantime the states must demonstrate "adequate yearly progress" (AYP) toward the goal of 100 percent proficiency—including progress toward eliminating achievement disparities between ethnic subgroups. Schools that receive subsidies under the ESEA Title I program for disadvantaged children and that repeatedly fall short of their AYP targets are subject to an escalating series of corrective measures: allowing their students to transfer to other public schools after two years, providing supplementary services such as private tutoring after three years, and possibly becoming subject to mandatory restructuring thereafter.

NCLB's success will depend on whether it is possible to produce excellent educational performance through centralization. Its advocates are in a self-contradictory position. They recognize that the educational policies of the last four decades, a period of almost uninterrupted centralization, have failed, but their remedy for that failure is yet more centralization. While invoking the principles of an "ownership society" on issues such as Social Security reform, they are pursuing almost the exact opposite model in schools. In a period of growing social mobility and individual autonomy, they are promoting a top-down, Great Society model of reform—transferring power from individual parents, teachers, and principals to distant bureaucracies such as state education agencies.

Ironically, the Bush administration has made a key exception to its "ownership society" precisely in the area of social policy that by its very nature is *least* susceptible to centralization. Education is inherently personal and inherently value laden. The key relationships in schools are those between individual teachers and individual students: If the teachers are not committed and highly motivated, no centralized rule books or formulas are going to inspire peak performance from their students. To use social science jargon, schools are "loosely coupled systems"; therefore, decrees from centralized administrators have little power to boost school performance but enormous power to impede progress. Indeed, before the mid-20th century such administrators were either nonexistent or mostly irrelevant; key decisions were made at the level of the individual school by principals and teachers.

Moreover, schooling inescapably involves judgments about truth and virtue, about what kind of person a youngster should aspire to be. In an increasingly pluralistic society, Americans are inevitably going to disagree with each other about those judgments. Which historical figures should children be encouraged to revere as heroes? What should they be taught about ancient belief systems such as Christianity and Islam—and about modern ideologies such as feminism and environmentalism? Should "traditional values" such as piety, chastity, and asceticism be celebrated, ridiculed, or simply ignored? Americans in the 21st century have no more chance of reaching consensus on those questions than of agreeing on what church (if any) we should all attend. That is why we keep the state out of controlling churches, just as we keep it out of other value-forming institutions such as publishing and journalism. The more we entrust such decisions to centralized state agencies, the more conflicts we foment—conflicts that in a truly free society would be unnecessary. As legal scholar Stephen Arons observed in 1997: "One civic group after another attempts to impose its vision of good education, and all join in a struggle over the one true morality to be adopted by the public schools. The outcomes of the conflicts over curriculum, texts, tests, and teachers seem less and less like constructive compromises that knit communities together; more and more they resemble blood feuds, ideological wars, episodes of selfishness wrapped in the rhetoric of rectitude."

Zero-sum "culture wars" for control of coercive state monopolies thus make enemies of people who could otherwise be friends. Perhaps in some bygone era each local public school reflected a local consensus. But in today's ultra-mobile society, in which communities are less and less defined by geography, the only way to keep the culture wars from engulfing the schools is a comprehensive strategy of parental choice. The key to rescuing our children from the bureaucratized government schools is radical decentralization: tuition tax credits, tax deductions, and vouchers. Unfortunately, NCLB is taking us in precisely the opposite direction.

Granted, NCLB does not explicitly call for national curricula. The statute mandates standards for testing, not for curricula, and it leaves the specific content and design of the tests up to the states. But in the long run the tests will, at least to some degree, drive the curricula, and that will loom even larger if NCLB is extended to high school programs as well as to elementary-level reading and math. The statute is already promoting centralization within each state, to the detriment of pluralism and local control. It could become a force for national centralization as well if future administrations should exercise to its full potential their power to deny federal funding to states whose testing programs are deemed inadequate.

So far, the Bush administration has been cautious in exercising that power. During last year's presidential election campaign, the administration wanted to avoid headlines about conflicts with state education agencies; it tried to perpetuate as best it could the congenial atmosphere of the bipartisan signing ceremony when NCLB became law in January 2002. Nevertheless, the states are restive. Many are complaining that NCLB is excessively intrusive; dozens of state legislatures have passed resolutions criticizing the statute. Such complaints are not necessarily unjustified. Any statute as long and complicated as NCLB inevitably requires that state and local school officials spend thousands of manhours filling out federal forms and complying with procedural requirements from Washington—even if that red tape produces little or nothing in the way of genuine academic improvement. It would be not at all surprising if NCLB turned out to be both meddlesome and impotent, as have many previous federal programs.

The Bush administration, and future administrations, will now face a dilemma. The NCLB statute virtually guarantees massive evasion of its own intent: It orders the state education agencies to do things that many of them don't want to do, such as institute detailed, rigorous testing programs that enable the public to distinguish successful from unsuccessful schools, and it gives those agencies broad discretion about just how to do those things. The U.S. Department of Education has little role in creating content standards and assessments under NCLB; it only decides whether to approve those created by the states. But as the states devise various tactics for evading both the letter and the spirit of the law, lawmakers will be forced either to let them get away with those tactics or to continuously amend NCLB's statutory text (already about 1,100 pages long) and associated regulations in order to keep up with the states' ever more inventive evasions.

If policymakers choose the former course, NCLB might as well not exist; it will just be one more drain on taxpayers, like scores of previous education programs, and one more source of special-interest group subsidy—in this case to the testing companies. But if Washington policymakers instead choose to amend the statute, they will end up making it steadily more detailed, prescriptive, and topheavy. Washington's education officials will more and more resemble Soviet central planners trying to improve economic performance by micromanaging decisions from Moscow. Unlike Soviet bureaucrats, however, the federal government lacks a captive labor force; the more centralized the system becomes, the more likely those teachers and potential teachers with the greatest creativity and leadership ability will be to seek careers elsewhere rather than accept being mere pawns of the federal government. As a strategy for promoting "excellence," centralization will be inherently self-defeating.

Thus, NCLB is a reform strategy at war with itself: It can work only if federal officials ride tight herd on their state counterparts, overriding them whenever they sacrifice reform to special-interest pressures. The authors of NCLB have already said that they will do no such thing, rightly invoking principles such as states' rights and the absence of a constitutional warrant for federal control of local schools. But if they were serious about those principles, they would never have enacted NCLB to begin with. On the other hand, if they decide to use NCLB as a tool to muscle through fundamental reforms against the will of the entrenched special interests, they will find that they have to discard whatever remains of their constitutional scruples. They or their successors may even conclude that that is the best possible outcome: If the Constitution and the principles it embodies stand in the way of urgently needed reforms, then the devil take the Constitution. Many previous would-be reformers have made that judgment, from the advocates of centralized economic planning who created the short-lived National Recovery Administration in the 1930s to the Supreme Court in its 1972 ban (also shortlived) on all forms of capital punishment.

Future historians, then, may look back on NCLB as simply one more phase in the gradual building of a national ministry of education—a ministry explicitly responsible not only for testing but for curriculum content and even for the administration of schools. Parents with complaints about their children's textbooks or teachers would have to take those complaints, not to their local school board, but to Washington. That scenario may seem far-fetched: There is no clear evidence that the proponents of NCLB consciously intend to create a national curriculum or a national, European-style ministry of education. But few members of Congress who voted for the 1965 Elementary and Secondary Education Act, which was only a few dozen pages long, consciously intended to start down a path leading to ever more detailed federal controls and culminating in the 1,100-page NCLB. Once Washington sets up such regulatory and spending machines, they tend to acquire a life and logic of their own. Moreover, one should consider that it took only seven years from the congressional elections of 1994 for many of that year's "Republican revolutionaries" to reverse course and vote for the most centralizing education bill in American history. It seems not at all implausible that Congress may be willing to enact even more sweeping centralization within the next decade—especially if an increasingly comfortable Republican majority grows ever more accustomed to bloating the Department of Education's budget with "pork-barrel" earmarks for its political allies.

Setting aside its difficulties from the standpoint of constitutionalism and the rule of law, would such hypercentralization actually bring genuine reform? Optimists might suggest that it could bring us back to the educational standards of 1901, when the College Entrance Examination Board published a list of specific literary classics that it recommended that every would-be college freshman should have read before matriculating. The firm, exacting standards of those educators stand in striking contrast to the curricular relativism of the late 20th century, with its faddish lessons in popular culture. If education means requiring a youngster to learn things that he is unlikely to learn if left unsupervised, then perhaps centralized coercion is a good thing.

What that argument ignores is the crucial fact that in America, unlike much of Europe and Asia, curricular relativism and fragmentation have grown hand in hand with the growth of centralized power over education policy in both Washington and the state capitals. The people who control the key institutions in this country's government school establishment—the teachers' unions, the teacher-training institutions, the state education agencies, the career staff of the federal education colossus—are not Victorian-style elitists seeking to mold the masses according to lofty standards of classical learning. Quite the opposite. In today's America, the masses are more elitist (in the desirable sense of demanding serious academic standards) than is the educational establishment with its focus on "self-esteem." When given a free hand, American working-class parents make sounder educational choices than the establishment tries to dictate to them. Consider, for example, the nearly total absence of destructive fads such as bilingual education in private schools, even when those schools have large minority enrollments.

Judging from the experience of the last four decades, NCLB may end up giving us the worst possible scenario: unconstitutional consolidation in Washington of power over the schools, with that power being used to further mediocrity rather than excellence. Experience shows that centralized government agencies are especially prone to capture by ideological factions that want to shield children from unwelcome facts and opinions. In a 2001 study for the Cato Institute, Sheldon Richman cited the case of the proposed national history standards developed in the early 1990s by the National Center for History in the Schools at the University of California at Los Angeles under a grant from the U.S. Department of Education and the National Endowment for the Humanities. According to Richman, those draft standards "set off a firestorm of controversy led by Lynne V. Cheney, who had chaired the NEH when the National Center was commissioned to write the standards. . . . Cheney condemned the standards as an exercise that put Western-bashing political correctness ahead of good history. She feared that an 'official knowledge' would be adopted, 'with the result that much that is significant in our past will begin to disappear from our schools.' The irony is that, until the standards were released, she favored in principle the government's adoption of an 'official knowledge.'"

Richman rightly concluded that "we do not face a choice between government standards for education and no standards at all, no more than we face a choice between government standards for computers and no standards at all." Those who call for educational statism in the name of "standards" seem blind to the vital distinction between standards set by private institutions and standards set by government. . . .

Some observers hope that the statute can be fixed by further amendments, but experience with most other large federal programs, from health care subsidies to the tax code, suggests the opposite. With the passage of time, such programs tend to become even more complicated, internally contradictory, and captive to various lobbies with their own inconsistent objectives.

Before NCLB, several states imposed accountability systems on schools with statewide testing, reporting, and (supposedly) clear consequences for failure. Frederick Hess found that over time those state systems have tended to drift from "tough" to "soft," with standards and penalties being relaxed as interest groups mobilize against them. As summarized by Martin West and Paul Peterson of Harvard University's Program on Education Policy and Governance, the findings of Hess and other researchers suggest that

> keeping intact the necessary political will over the long run is likely to be highly problematic. . . . If authentic accountability is to be established, presidents, governors, and mayors, backed by a well-organized business community, need to remain committed to the effort. Yet such leaders, with their numerous responsibilities, are easily distracted. Fighting wars, preventing terrorism, maintaining economic growth, balancing budgets, and many other issues, too unpredictable to anticipate, can easily shift educational accountability to the back burner. When that happens, well-organized, narrow interests gain the upper hand. All in all, there is every reason to believe that tough, coercive accountability will gradually evolve into something softer, nicer, more acceptable to those directly affected.

Conclusion and Recommendations

NCLB reflects an ideological strain that is novel for Republican presidents: utopianism. As did the older, left-wing forms of utopianism, the Bush administration emphasizes collective action rather than individual responsibility: NCLB implicitly treats students not as individuals but as passive commodities mass-produced by state programs. In its plans for extending NCLB to the high school level, the Bush administration has yet to signal that it will even try to revive the parental choice provisions that were part of its original proposal in early 2001—and that it utterly failed to defend against the implacable statists among Capitol Hill Democrats. As individuals who respond to incentives, both parents and students are for the most part curiously absent from NCLB; its focus, like that of nearly all federal education programs for the last four decades, is on administrative units such as schools and school districts.

Utopianism usually ends up transforming rhetoric more than reality. In the real world, the chance that not one child in America will fall short of academic "proficiency" within a decade is the same as the chance that not one child will be a juvenile delinquent: zero. By 2014, if not before, NCLB will be seen to have failed, just as the centralized education programs enacted from the 1960s through the 1990s have failed. But like those programs, NCLB may be so deeply entrenched by then that it will be difficult to repeal. In any case, it will have absorbed time, money, and energy that could otherwise have been spent on more promising measures. Like the so-called reform measures of the 1980s and 1990s, NCLB has not destroyed the chances of genuine, radical reforms in America's profoundly dysfunctional school system, but it has almost certainly postponed them.

It will always be true that some of America's tens of thousands of schools are excellent and some mediocre (or worse). Rather than continue to use centralized government decrees (both state and federal) to turn mediocre institutions into excellent ones, as they have been trying but failing to do for the last several decades, the state and federal governments should empower individual families to "vote with their feet" by transferring to the schools of their own choice. That strategy would bring three advantages that are absent from the monopolistic command-and-control model embodied in NCLB. First, it would allow parents to rescue their children from dysfunctional schools immediately rather than continue to wait for the public school establishment's endless tinkerings with the status quo to produce the glorious results that have long been promised but never arrive. Second, it would allow families to pick schools that are compatible with their own philosophical and religious beliefs instead of locking them into poisonous, zero-sum conflicts to determine which groups will win the power to impose their beliefs on other groups within the coercive, one-size-fits-all government schools.

Third, a reform model based on free markets rather than state monopolies would unleash the dynamic force of competition. When schools know that they cannot take their customers for granted, they face a whole new incentive structure: They have to concentrate on producing solid results rather than on paper compliance with top-down regulations. Nothing concentrates the mind as effectively as the threat of having to go out of business. Real, ongoing accountability to customers who are free at any moment to take their children (and dollars) elsewhere is qualitatively different from imitation accountability to centralized government structures that can almost always be coaxed or pressured into keeping the money flowing to schools that are manifestly failing. The latter model, as practiced by so-called reform strategies such as NCLB, simply adds one more layer of bureaucracy to a system that is far too bureaucratized already. As education researchers John Chubb and Terry Moe observed 15 years ago in a now-classic study for the Brookings Institution, parental choice is a "revolutionary reform" rather than a "system-preserving" one: "The whole point of a thoroughgoing system of choice is to free the schools from these disabling constraints by sweeping away the old institutions and replacing them with new ones."

The key locus for such revolutionary reforms is the states. Under the Constitution it is the states that have legal responsibility for education. Even after decades of unconstitutional federal education programs, more than 90 percent of government financing for elementary and secondary schools still comes from state and local taxes. Education is thus one of the most promising areas for taking advantage of the flexibility and diversity that the nation's Founders gave us: Let some states try tuition tax credits or tax deductions, let others try vouchers, and let all learn from each other's experience.

This process has of course begun with the parental choice programs already enacted in Wisconsin, Ohio, Florida, and elsewhere. In education as in other areas, the 18th-century principles built into the country's federalist design are better adapted to the challenges of the fast-moving, down-sizing, open-ended 21st century than are the static, top-heavy, homogeneous structures left over from the mid-20th century.

POSTSCRIPT

Should Local Schools Have National Standards?

Born out of our revolutionary heritage of mistrusting distant centralized government, many important elements of governance were either reserved for state and local governments or, as contained in the Bill of Rights, explicitly denied to the central government (those proscriptions were eventually extended to include all government levels and entities with the addition of the Fourteenth Amendment to the Constitution). The historical primacy of state and local governments in matters related to education was underscored by the U.S. Supreme Court in its 1954 decision in *Brown v. Board of Education* with the following statement: "Education is perhaps the most important function of state and local governments." That strong tradition of state and local rights to control education creates a political challenge for those who believe that children and their schooling would be better served by a more centralized approach. The following statement by Margaret Spellings, U.S. Secretary of Education, exemplifies the caution that politicians manifest when they approach this issue:

> Education is primarily a State and local responsibility in the United States. It is States and communities, as well as public and private organizations of all kinds, that establish schools and colleges, develop curricula, and determine requirements for enrollment and graduation. The structure of education finance in America reflects this predominant State and local role. Of an estimated $909 billion being spent nationwide on education at all levels for school year 2004–2005, about 90 percent comes from State, local, and private sources. That means the Federal contribution to national education expenditures is about 10 percent. . . . (2006)

(It is interesting to note that federal expenditures for education were in the 7 percent range only a couple of decades back.) It is through the allocation and administration of those federal dollars that the federal government gains the ability to become involved with education. If states wish to receive federal funding, they must agree with the provisions attached to the allocations. In effect it is a contractual arrangement.

When discussing national curricular and assessment standards for education, most proponents are astute enough to emphasize that national standards do not necessarily need to be federal government standards. They suggest that national curricular standards could emerge from national groups representing certain content areas such as the National Council for Social Studies, the National Council of Teachers of English, the National Science

Teachers Association, and so on. National assessment standards could be based on national tests and evaluations such as the National Assessment of Educational Progress (NAEP) or approaches developed by testing organizations or textbook publishers. Although such nonfederal government approaches are possible, it is difficult to imagine that states would voluntarily give up their rights to determine curricular and assessment standards. Including "voluntary" national standards in federal funding legislation such as NCLB would be very complex in terms of political overtones and might even be viewed by the courts as a coercive act by the federal government.

Detailed information regarding national standards can be found in publications from various national education organizations including the groups noted above, as well as the National Council of Teachers of Mathematics, the Center for Civic Education, and the International Society for Technology in Education.

Contributors to This Volume

EDITOR

JOHN WOOD, Ph.D., teaches political science at Rose State College. He has a master's degree in political science and a doctorate in environmental policy and conflict from Oklahoma State University in January 2007. Wood is the Rose State faculty senate president and was awarded the Oklahoma Political Science Professor of the year for two-year colleges in 2007 by the Oklahoma Political Science Association. He is additionally the faculty advisor for the Rose State's Vocal Oklahomans in Civic Engagement (VOICE) and the Oklahoma Intercollegiate Legislature (OIL). Wood represents Guthrie, Oklahoma City Council, Ward I. He also serves on the Guthrie Streets Committee and Guthrie Transportation Authority, and cofounded First Capitol Neighborhood Solutions.

The former U.S. Marine and Gulf War vet lives in Guthrie, Oklahoma, with his wife Bonnie.

AUTHORS

PATRICK BASHAM is founding director of the Democracy Institute and an adjunct scholar with Cato's Center for Representative Government.

MARC F. BERNSTEIN is superintendent of the Bellmore-Merrick Central High School District in North Merrick, New York.

BRADY CENTER TO PREVENT GUN VIOLENCE is an organization that works to reform the gun industry by enacting and enforcing sensible regulations to reduce gun violence, including regulations governing the gun industry.

BRUCE CAIN is a professor of political science at UC Berkley. He has commented on elections, the recall, presidential politics, census data, and economic stimulus plans. He was a national consultant to the Los Angeles Times from 1986–1989 and has been a political commentator for numerous radio and television stations in Los Angeles and the Bay Area. Cain has been on *Newshour* and National Public Radio.

CALIFORNIA BUSINESS ROUNDTABLE is a non-profit, nonpartisan organization composed of chief executive officers of leading California businesses. Since 1976, the Roundtable has provided essential leadership on high-priority public policy issues.

CALIFORNIA CHAMBER OF COMMERCE has worked as an advocate for private-sector employers giving them a voice in state politics and providing a full range of California-specific products and services.

ROBERT CORDY is associate justice of the Massachusetts Supreme Judicial Court. He received a J.D. from Harvard Law School in 1974. Prior to being appointed to the bench, he was a partner at the law firm of McDermott, Will & Emery.

THOMAS J. DILORENZO is a professor of economics at Loyola University in Maryland. He has authored several books, including *The Real Lincoln: A New Look at Abraham Lincoln, His Agenda, and an Unnecessary War* and *How Capitalism Saved America: The Untold History of Our Country, from the Pilgrims to the Present.*

RICHARD DOERFLINGER is deputy director of the secretariat for Pro-Life Activities at the U.S. Conference of Catholic Bishops in Washington, D.C. He is also Adjunct Fellow in Bioethics and Public Policy at the National Catholic Bioethics Center in Boston. Speaking on behalf of the Catholic Bishops, he has prepared policy statements and given congressional testimony on abortion, euthanasia, human embryo research, and other bioethical issues.

DRUG WATCH INTERNATIONAL is a volunteer nonprofit drug information network and advocacy organization that promotes the creation of healthy drug-free cultures in the world and opposes the legalization of drugs. The organization upholds a comprehensive approach to drug issues involving prevention, education, intervention/treatment, and law enforcement/interdiction.

CHESTER E. FINN JR. is president of the Thomas B. Fordham Foundation and is a senior fellow at the Manhattan Institute. He served as assistant U.S. secretary of education from 1985 to 1988.

LOIS G. FORER was an author, a retired Philadelphia judge and a lifelong advocate for the young, the elderly and the poor.

STEVEN GINSBERG is a staff writer for the *Washington Post*.

ROB GURWITT is a staff correspondent for *Governing* magazine.

JOHN HANLEY is a graduate student in political science at the University of California, Berkeley. His research interests include American politics, elections, and public opinion. John's dissertation project looks at legislative investigations of governmental and non-governmental institutions.

TIMOTHY HOWELL is associate professor of psychiatry and director of the geropsychiatry program at UW Health—a health and medical network affiliated with the University of Wisconsin. He is active in both teaching and clinical care.

LIAM JULIAN is a research fellow at the Hoover Institution, Stanford University, and managing editor of *Policy Review*, Hoover's Washington, D.C.–based bimonthly journal of essays, social criticism, and reviews on politics, government, and foreign and domestic policy. Before working at *Policy Review*, Julian was associate writer and editor at the Thomas B. Fordham Institute.

THAD KOUSSER is associate professor of political science at the University of California–Berkley. He has authored, coauthored, or edited the books *Term Limits and the Dismantling of State Legislative Professionalism* (Cambridge, 2005), *Adapting to Term Limits: Recent Experiences and New Directions* (PPIC, 2004), *The New Political Geography of California* (Berkeley Public Policy Press, 2008), and *The Logic of American Politics,* 4th edition (Congressional Quarterly Press, 2009).

LOS ANGELES COUNTY DEMOCRATIC CENTRAL COMMITTEE (LACDP) is the official governing body of the Democratic Party in the County of Los Angeles. LACDP works in cooperation with the State and National Democratic Committees. LACDP is the largest local Democratic Party entity in the United States, representing over 2.2 million registered Democrats and a population larger than that in 42 states, in the 88 cities and the unincorporated areas of Los Angeles County.

JAMES MADISON was an American politician and political philosopher who served as the fourth President of the United States (1809–1817) and is considered one of the Founding Fathers of the United States.

MARGARET MARSHALL is chief justice of the Massachusetts Supreme Judicial Court. A native of South Africa, she graduated from Witwatersrand University in Johannesburg in 1966 and later received a J.D. from Yale Law School. Before her appointment to the Supreme Judicial Court, she was vice president and general counsel of Harvard University. She was appointed as an associate justice of the Supreme Judicial Court in November 1996 and named chief justice in September 1999.

MATT MILLER is a senior fellow at the Center for American Progress and the author of *The Two Percent Solution: Fixing America's Problems in Ways Liberals and Conservatives Can Love* (2003) and *The Tyranny of Dead Ideas (2009).*

DEAN MURPHY was the *New York Times* bureau chief in San Francisco.

NATIONAL RIFLE ASSOCIATION is an American nonpartisan, nonprofit organization which is a staunch supporter of the Second Amendment of the United States Bill of Rights and the promotion of firearm ownership rights as well as marksmanship, firearm safety, and the protection of hunting and self-defense in the United States.

SANDRA DAY O'CONNOR was an associate justice of the U.S. Supreme Court. She worked in various legal capacities both in the United States and in Germany until she was appointed to the Arizona State Senate in 1969. She served as a state senator for four years and served in the Arizona judiciary for six years before she was nominated to the Supreme Court by President Ronald Reagan in 1981.

PHILIP J. PALIN is a senior fellow with the National Institute for Strategic Preparedness. He is coauthor of the *Catastrophe Preparation and Prevention* series published by McGraw-Hill Higher Education.

MICHAEL J. PETRILLI is Vice President for National Programs and Policy at the Thomas B. Fordham Institute, where he oversees the Institute's research projects and publications, including *The Education Gadfly.* He is also research fellow at Stanford University's Hoover Institution, executive editor of *Education Next,* and contributor to Fordham's *Flypaper* blog.

GERALD PRANTE is a senior economist at the Tax Foundation. While at the Tax Foundation, Gerald has done work on issues at both the federal and local levels with a special emphasis in data analysis, including microsimulation models and local geographic data. On issues, he specializes in the federal income tax at the federal level, specifically in the area of distributional analysis. His work has been featured in the *New York Times*, *Atlantic Monthly*, the *Economist, Wall Street Journal, Washington Post, USA Today*, and the *New York Post*, among others. He has appeared on C-SPAN's *Washington Journal* program, as well as CNBC and numerous radio programs.

DAVID RISLEY is an Assistant United States Attorney in the Central District of Illinois, where he serves as the Lead Organized Crime Drug Enforcement Task Force Attorney over that district's 46 counties.

JOHN ROBERTS is the current chief justice of the U.S. Supreme Court. He received an A.B. from Harvard College in 1976 and a J.D. from Harvard Law School in 1979. He served as a law clerk for former U.S. Supreme Court Chief Justice William H. Rehnquist during the 1980 term, and in various other legal capacities until his appointment to the U.S. Court of Appeals for the District of Columbia Circuit in 2003. President George W. Bush nominated him as chief justice in 2005.

DAVID SOUTER is an associate justice of the U.S. Supreme Court and a former judge for the U.S. Court of Appeals for the First Circuit in Boston, Massachusetts. He was nominated by President George Bush to the Supreme Court in 1990.

JOHN PAUL STEVENS is an associate justice of the U.S. Supreme Court. He worked in law firms in Chicago, Illinois, for 20 years before being nominated by President Richard Nixon to the U.S. Court of Appeals in 1970. He served in that capacity until he was nominated to the Supreme Court by President Gerald Ford in 1975.

CLARENCE THOMAS is an associate justice of the U.S. Supreme Court. A former judge on the U.S. Court of Appeals for the District of Columbia, he was nominated by President George Bush to the Supreme Court in 1991. He received his J.D. from the Yale University School of Law in 1974.

U.S. NORTHERN COMMAND (USNORTHCOM) was established October 1, 2002, to provide command and control of Department of Defense (DOD) homeland defense efforts and to coordinate defense support of civil authorities.

LAWRENCE A. UZZELL is president of the International Religious Freedom Watch, which is a Christian organization committed to protecting religious believers of all faiths from persecution by their own governments.

DAVID T. WATTS is a practicing physician, a poet, a radio commentator, and an author. His most recent book is *Bedside Manners: One Doctor's Reflections on the Oddly Intimate Encounters Between Patient and Healer* (Three Rivers Press, 2006).

JOE WILLIAMS is a nonresident senior fellow with Education Sector and author of *Cheating Our Kids: How Politics and Greed Ruin Education* (2005).

ROBERT YATES was a politician and judge, well known for his Anti-Federalist stances.

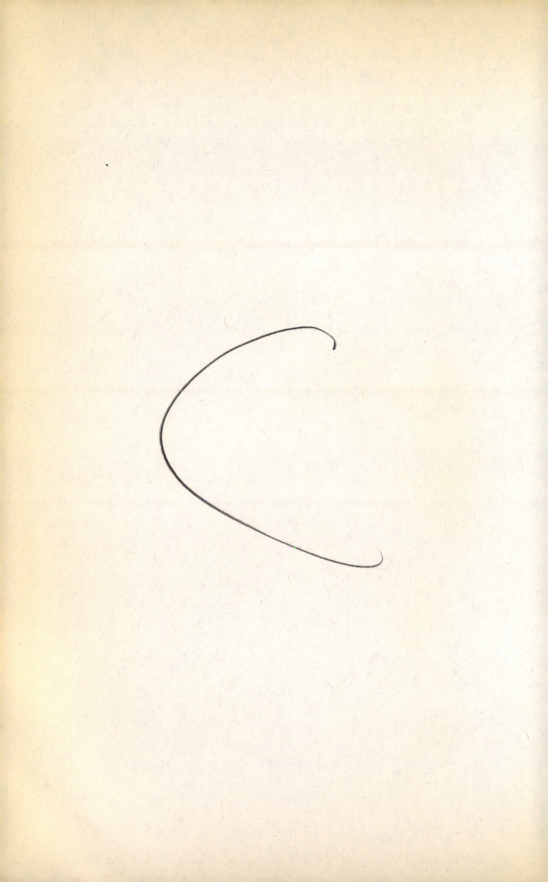